DATE DUE

~~JA 7 '97~~			
~~JE 24 '97~~			
NO 20 '97			
~~DE 19 '97~~			
~~MY 13 '98~~			
~~MAY 28 1998~~			
~~MY 5 '99~~			
~~DE 18 '02~~			
~~JE 9 '04~~			
DE 1 '04			

DEMCO 38-296

Transit Villages
in the 21st Century

Transit Villages
in the 21st Century

MICHAEL BERNICK

ROBERT CERVERO

McGraw-Hill

New York   San Francisco   Washington, D.C.   Auckland
Bogotá   Caracas   Lisbon   London   Madrid   Mexico City
Milan   Montreal   New Delhi   San Juan   Singapore
Sydney   Tokyo   Toronto

ublication Data

ury / Michael S. Bernick, Robert
Burke Cervero.
     p.   cm.
   Includes bibliographical references.
   ISBN 0-07-005475-4 (hardcover)
    1. City planning—United States. 2. Local transit—United States.
3. Local transit stations—United States. 4. Community development,
Urban—United States. I. Cervero, Robert. II. Title.
HT167.B48   1996
388.4'0973—dc20   96-34617
                                     CIP

McGraw-Hill

A Division of The McGraw·Hill Companies

1 2 3 4 5 6 7 8 9 0   9 0 1 0 9 8 7 6

ISBN 0-07-005475-4

The sponsoring editor for this book was Wendy Lochner,
the editing supervisor was Penny Linskey, and the production supervisor
was Pamela Pelton. Interior design and composition by North Market Street Graphics.

McGraw-Hill books are available at special quantity discounts to use as premiums and sales promotions,
or for use in corporate training programs. For more information, please write to the Director of Special
Sales, McGraw-Hill, 11 West 19th Street, New York, NY 10011. Or contact your local bookstore.

This book is printed on acid-free paper.

To Donna and Sophia

Contents

Preface

Mass transit's falling fortunes—eroding ridership, ballooning deficits, second-class image—
are often explained as unavoidable consequences of the automobile's ever-growing popularity. While true to a degree, we believe another factor, often overlooked, is that America's
cityscape has increasingly turned its back on new mass transportation investments. Too
many recently built light rail, heavy rail, and commuter rail systems in the United States feature stations enveloped by parking lots, vacant parcels, open fields, warehousing, and
marginal activities. This stands in marked contrast to the colorful streetcar suburbs that
sprung up along trolley lines around a century ago, or to much of urban Europe where
apartments, shops, cinemas, and offices continue to cluster around rail transit stops.

Why have our cities and mass transit systems grown so much out of synch? Can this dis-
cordance be reversed? We believe it can, given the will and a strong dose of public-private
partnership. In this book, we propose the *transit village* as an organizing principle for creating places—built environments, social environments, and economic environments—that
embrace and evolve around mass transit systems. Resurrecting mass transit as an integral
form of transportation in urban America calls for, we believe, the emergence of viable,
functional, and attractive transit villages. It is to the challenge of creating such places that
this book has been written.

Much of the credit for articulating the meaning of transit villages and conducting the
research that led to the writing of this book goes to Peter Hall. As Director of the Institute of Urban and Regional Development at the University of California, Berkeley, Peter
encouraged us to set up a research forum devoted to studying the link between mass transit and urban development. In 1991, the National Transit Access Center (NTRAC) was
formed at UC Berkeley. After Peter left Berkeley for London in 1992, we assumed the roles
of co-directors of the Center. At NTRAC, Cervero has led research focused on the market potential and ridership impacts of transit-oriented development, as well as evaluative
studies of installing paratransit and electric mini-cars as means of accessing rail stations.
Bernick's work has been most concerned with evaluating legal and planning approaches
toward stimulating transit-oriented development.

While we worked closely in writing this manuscript, the division of labor more or less
fell according to our respective interests. The book's introduction and conclusion, chapters

1, 14, and 15, were co-authored. The justification for transit villages—chapters 3 through 6—and international cases, chapters 11 through 13, were authored by Cervero. Bernick was the principal author on the history of transit villages in the U.S., chapter 2, and of case summaries on transit village initiatives in the U.S., chapters 7 through 10.

Peter Hall deserves our thanks not only for founding NTRAC, but also for his unwaivering encouragement and critique of our work. We are also indebted to Melvin Webber, until recently the Director of the University of California Transportation Center, who over the years has generously supported NTRAC's work and long been a source of ideas and insights on linking transit with the city. Other academic colleagues at Berkeley who have helped us think more systematically and critically about the transit-land use nexus include Peter Bosselmann, John Landis, Dan Solomon, Alan Jacobs, and Elizabeth Deakin. More than thirty graduate students from the Department of City and Regional Planning at UC Berkeley have worked on NTRAC research since its inception, and many have gone on to work in the urban transit field. We particularly thank Val Menotti, a 1995 graduate of the Department, who provided not only solid research assistance, but set up and continues to maintain an NTRAC list-service on the Internet devoted to stimulating dialogue on the transit village topic. Barbara Hadenfeldt and Miho Rahm have been the able administrators of NTRAC, since the start, and David van Arnum has cheerfully handled the word processing duties for much of our writing.

Throughout the United States, individuals in and out of transit agencies are working to make the transit village concept a reality. A number have generously given us their time and shaped our thinking about implementing transit villages: Nick Patsaouras, John Dyer, Jim Amis, Michael Francis, John Given, and Mark Futterman in Los Angeles; Jack Lambert, Nancy Bragado, and Bill Lieberman in San Diego; Alvin McNeal, Robert Klute, and Callum Murray in Washington, D.C.; Tony Hiss, Bob Yaro, and Howard Permut in New York; Larry Miller in Seattle; and Ed Thomas and Effie Stallsmith of the Federal Transit Administration. Abroad, our thanks goes to: Per-Olof Wikström, Magnus Carle, Åke Boalt, and Stig Svallhammar of Stockholm; Katsutoshi Ohta, Keiro Hattori, and Masahara Fukuyana in Tokyo; Bruno Wildermuth, Pannir Ramaza, and Anthony Chin in Singapore; and Jeff Kenworthy, from Murdoch University in Australia, who took some of the photos used for Stockholm. Credit also goes to Jane Sterzinger for some of the fine maps she prepared for us.

We are fortunate to have loving and understanding families who endured our absences while away conducting field work as well as while at home holed up in our studies, pounding out this manuscript. If it was not for them—Sophia, Christopher, and Alexandria, and Donna, William, Sonia, and Elena Christine—this work would have never been completed.

Robert Cervero and Michael Bernick

PART ONE

Transit Villages: Retrospective and Prospective

America's transit village movement is in many ways a reaction to the perceived declining quality of urban and suburban living. Traffic jams, faceless sprawl, and disconnected land uses are among the many reasons more Americans are looking for new and different paragons of suburbia. Failed public housing and inner-city entitlement programs are among the reasons that different approaches to urban revitalization are sought.

Part One of this book presents the transit village as a paradigm for creating attractive and sustainable communities, both in the city and the suburbs, where rail transit systems are or will be in place. The most important physical elements of the transit village—civic plazas near train entrances, pleasant walking environs, diversity in housing, compactness—are identified as are the purposes and hopes of the transit village movement.

Part One also reminds us that the transit village model is not new, and in fact, it was successfully put into practice a good century ago in a number of U.S. cities. There are important historical lessons in this field that we must not lose sight of as we consider, plan, and build transit villages of tomorrow.

Transit Villages and the Contemporary Metropolis

The Bay Area Rapid Transit (BART) train is distinctive in its futuristic design, featuring shiny, sleek rail cars, spacious interiors, and a metallic blue logo. The design represents a time (in the late 1960s) when Bay Area residents saw in technology and high-speed rail the solution to traffic gridlock.

The 71-mi BART system, which opened in September 1972, spans three Bay Area counties—San Francisco, Alameda, and Contra Costa. At the time, proponents hoped that BART would replace the automobile as the preferred means of travel. It has not, though mainly for reasons that have nothing to do with BART, like declining real gasoline prices. Still, by early 1994, BART's ridership had grown to over 255,000 passengers per weekday, and the system carried most East Bay residents commuting to jobs in downtown San Francisco. Despite cost overruns and unfortunate incidents, like a fire in the Transbay tube, BART today enjoys widespread public support. In the late 1980s, Bay Area residents voted overwhelmingly to increase local sales taxes to fund a $2.1 billion BART extension to the far ends of the East Bay and down the Peninsula to the San Francisco International Airport.

As the BART train travels through Contra Costa, it passes a series of post-World War II suburbs: Orinda, Moraga, Lafayette, Walnut Creek, Concord. Here, BART is enveloped in a sprawling landscape—single-family homes and duplexes, one- to two-story commercial buildings, and lots of hillside open space. The notable exception, however, is what until recently was the next to last station on the line, Pleasant Hill.

At Pleasant Hill, one disembarks to find the beginnings of an entirely new type of suburban community: one with a mix of clustered housing, mid-rise offices, small shops, a hotel, and a regional entertainment complex, all huddled around the transit station, and with a street configuration and landscaping that encourage people to walk to and from the station.

Housing, the primary land use in the area, lies slightly beyond the station core. Park Regency, a 892-unit complex of three- and four-story French-Regency style buildings, stands across the BART parking lot to the north. To the station's east is the 510-unit Treat Commons, featuring one- and two-bedroom garden-style apartments and the 360-unit Bay Landing. In all, over 1600 residential units built in the past 5 years lie within a 3- to 5-min walk of the Pleasant Hill station.

Office and commercial development are located even closer to the station. PacTel Corporate Plaza, housing the regional administrative offices of the telecommunications giant, is less than 100 yd from the station entrance, and next to it is the pastels-and-glass Embassy Suites convention hotel. Other Fortune-500 companies with offices that dot the station area include Levi Strauss, Chevron, General Electric, Citibank.

At the station core, there are currently 11 acres of BART surface parking. Much of this asphalted space is in the process of being converted to an entertainment-retail complex, with a movie theater, bookstore, and a variety of small shops and restaurants. To the developers, this is a very sensible business decision. They expect to draw heavily from the foot traffic generated by the transit station, as well as from nearby residents and workers.

The Pleasant Hill station area seeks to offer an alternative to the low-density, auto-oriented suburban development that characterizes virtually all of Contra Costa. It is a radical departure from business as usual in the suburbs. It is a transit-oriented development or, what local planners and local elected officials have taken to calling, a "transit village."

Twenty miles from Pleasant Hill in a long-depressed part of East Oakland, a second transit village is beginning to take form around the Fruitvale BART station. For 20 years, the Fruitvale station area has been in a state of neglect and disrepair, surrounded by surface parking lots, dilapidated buildings, and vacant lots. Nearby East 14th Street, a vibrant commercial corridor in the 1950s and early 1960s, today hosts mostly marginal businesses: two discount shoe stores, a tacqueria, a discount furniture store, and a few repair shops. Many storefronts are empty. Few people stroll the street.

Although several economic development plans were drawn up to turn East 14th Street around, the street and surrounding neighborhood continued to falter during the 1980s. In 1991, a grass-roots community group, the Spanish Speaking Unity Council, put forward a new vision for revitalizing the area, revolving around the neighborhood BART station as the catalyst. A transit village site plan has recently been formulated for a quarter-mile radius around the station. The plan calls for a mix of housing (market and below-market senior housing), a Hispanic-themed retail complex and cultural center, a public plaza, childcare facilities, a health-care facility, and a police substation—laced together by an attractive integrated pathway system that ties the community to the train station.

Today, Fruitvale's transit village has already broken ground. Federal grants and private contributions have gone into financing some of the key public elements: the civic plaza, the health-care facility, a new bus transfer facility, and senior housing. Upfront public improvements, backers hope, will lure a wave of private investors attracted by not only the neighborhood amenities but also by the area's superior access to BART. By mid-1995, the first private retail tenants were being courted: A private developer for the open-air mercado came on board, as did a private partner for building market-rate housing.

Transit villages are not just a Bay Area fad. Throughout the nation, new transit-oriented communities are taking form: along the Washington Metrorail system in suburban Virginia and Maryland; in the vicinity of downtown and suburban light rail stations in Portland and San Diego; near half-century-old commuter rail stations on the New York Metro-North line heading into Connecticut; and even in the heartland of the automobile, southern California, near stations planned along the 400-mi Los Angeles County Metro-

rail network. Recent symposiums devoted to the transit village concept held in Los Angeles, New York, Oakland, and San Diego have brought together developers, planners, politicians, and community activists, all hoping to find common ground. New rail lines and extensions under design in St. Louis, San Juan, and Sacramento are guided not only by engineering criteria but also by a growing public desire to transform station areas, in built-up neighborhoods and greenfields alike, into new transit-based communities.

As we head into a new millennium, the transit village movement represents a paradigm of community building that departs sharply from the standard design practices of the postwar era. Whether with time it proves to be a passing fad or a bold, new approach to how we design our cities and neighborhoods will largely depend, we believe, on the kinds of policy responses, public-private initiatives, and political leadership that emerge over the next decade or so. It is in the spirit of informing the debate and helping to illuminate our understanding of the transit village concept that this volume has been written.

1.1 THE TRANSIT VILLAGE

The transit village brings together ideas from the disciplines of urban design, transportation, and market economics. It is partly about creating a built form that encourages people to ride transit more often. However, equally important, it embraces goals related to neighborhood cohesion, social diversity, conservation, public safety, and community revitalization.

At its core, the transit village is a compact, mixed-use community, centered around the transit station that, by design, invites residents, workers, and shoppers to drive their cars less and ride mass transit more. The transit village extends roughly a quarter mile from a transit station, a distance that can be covered in about 5 min by foot. The centerpiece of the transit village is the transit station itself and the civic and public spaces that surround it. The transit station is what connects village residents and workers to the rest of the region, providing convenient and ready access to downtown, major activity centers like a sports stadium, and other popular destinations. The surrounding public spaces or open grounds serve the important function of being a community gathering spot, a site for special events, and a place for celebrations—a modern-day version of the Greek agora.

In recent years, the terms *neotraditional development* and *new urbanism* have gained currency to describe the designs of places that are compact, "quaint," and conducive to walking. New urbanists, such as Miami-based Andres Duany and Elizabeth Plater-Zybeck and California-based Peter Calthorpe, borrow many of the successful elements from traditional American towns like Princeton, New Jersey, and Annapolis, Maryland. Among the hallmarks of neotraditional designs are a commercial core within walking distance of a majority of residents, a well-connected gridiron street network, narrow roads with curbside parking (to buffer pedestrians), back-lot alleys, mixed land uses, and varying styles and densities of housing. Thus, transit villages share many of the attributes of traditional communities, though their unique and distinguishing feature is that the train station and its immediate surroundings function as the focal point of a community.

It is important to emphasize that transit villages are not just physical entities. There are important social and economic dimensions behind the transit village movement. Socially, the hope is that transit villages will bring people from many walks of life into daily face-to-face contact. Today's auto-oriented suburbs have isolated people by age, class, and race—the young from the old, the rich from the poor, whites from blacks. Many upper-class suburbanites are confined to their cars and security-controlled, walled-in subdivisions. By creating an attractive built environment, complete with a civic core and prominent transit node, people are more likely to feel a sense of belonging and an attachment to the community.

Transit villages must also be economically viable and financially self-sustaining. Creating attractive urban environments that have good transit access to the rest of the region should, by definition, produce economic benefits. Foremost, the advantages of being near rail in a quality urban setting should be translated into higher property values and commercial rents. To the degree that governments can recapture some of these economic benefits, such as through property tax proceeds or special benefit assessments, then transit villages can become economically self-supporting. Transit villages can also spin off secondary economic benefits such as providing opportunities for joint development (e.g., building a retail store adjacent to the transit station and generating lease revenues for a transit agency), station-area concessions (e.g., fruit stalls at farmer's markets), and community-based services (e.g., operating jitney connections between a neighborhood and the transit stop). Transit villages can also serve as a catalyst to economic and community redevelopment. Recently, the Federal Transit Administration (FTA) and Department of Housing and Urban Development (HUD) joined forces to create a Livable Communities program that aims to economically empower struggling inner-city neighborhoods across the United States by making them eligible for special grants and tax credits. Assistance has gone to siting child-care centers, building police substations, and improving access to rail stops in Cleveland, St. Louis, Baltimore, and Oakland. The hope is that by creating better quality neighborhoods in areas with superior transit services, private investors will return to these areas, putting them on a road to financial recovery.

1.2 THE HALLMARKS OF A TRANSIT VILLAGE

In many ways, transit villages are about increasing choices—opening up more options in how to travel, where to live and work, places to go, and how to spend one's free time. Most Americans have only one or two reasonable alternatives to driving—taking a bus that comes by every half an hour or catching a taxi for a goodly sum. Mass transit is impractical to many because waits are too long, and for those living in cities with rail systems, driving their cars to remote parking lots and then transferring modes are too much of a hassle.

Transit villages present the possibility of a more seamless form of mass transportation travel by bringing the community closer to the transit node itself. The train station is the village's gateway. By physically and symbolically linking surrounding neighborhoods to the station, transit becomes a respectable means of traveling outside of the village. Transit villages widen our mobility options.

Transit villages also offer alternative living and working environments that combine the suburban values and lifestyle preferences for open space, human-scale buildings, and a sense of security with the more traditionally urban values of walking to neighborhood shops, meeting people on the street, and being in a culturally diverse setting. In older urban districts, the transit village offers an opportunity to revitalize decaying neighborhoods through the transit station's role in stimulating economic activity and enhancing public safety. This is a break from earlier approaches to inner-city revitalization, owing to its village scale (in contrast to high-rise public housing), mixes of residences by incomes and tenancy, and codevelopment of new residential and commercial projects. The inner-city transit village builds on the value that the train station brings to both office and retail activity in the form of increased walk-on traffic. It also builds on the value added from creating a neighborhood where there is a 24 h per day presence of homeowners and a centrally located police substation.

Each of the elements—enhanced mobility, environmental quality, pedestrian friendliness, alternative suburban living and working environments, neighborhood revitalization, public safety, and public celebration—is vital to long-term success of a transit village. The importance of each element is amplified in the pages that follow.

Elements of the Transit Village

Enhanced mobility and environment

Pedestrian friendliness

Alternative suburban living and working environments

Neighborhood revitalization

Public safety

Public celebration

1. *Enhanced mobility and environment:* The primary transportation benefit of congregating housing, jobs, shops, and other activities around transit stations, of course, is that transit ridership is likely to increase as a consequence. Replacing auto trips with train rides can help relieve traffic congestion along corridors served by rail. One important spinoff benefit is improved air quality, especially to the extent that park-and-ride trips are converted to walk-and-ride or bike-and-ride. Currently, over 80 percent of suburban Bay Area residents who ride BART reach stations by private automobile. For a 5-mi journey, the typical distance of a BART park-and-ride trip, around 85 percent of hydrocarbon emissions are due

to cold starts (inefficient cold engines during the first few minutes of driving) and hot evaporative soaks. The potential of transit village development to reduce tailpipe emissions is particularly important in states like California where all cities with rail systems currently exceed federal and state clean air standards for ground-level ozone and carbon monoxide.

2. *Pedestrian friendliness:* By definition, transit villages should be inviting places to walk in. Mixes of land uses, with some housing built above ground-floor shops, can encourage walking, as can the narrow tree-lined streets, wide sidewalks, and an absence of large surface parking lots and long building setbacks. The transit village's pedestrian orientation can be contrasted with the auto-dependent, insular designs of large-scale suburban office centers and residential subdivisions of the past three decades, epitomized by *edge cities* like Tysons Corner outside of Washington, DC, and Bishop Ranch east of Oakland. Gone are the large surface parking lots and six-lane streets. Gone also are the apartments perched on top of parking podiums, with few connections to the street, and inward-focused campus-style office parks. In their place are mid-rise office structures with parking tucked below, housing of all kinds in neighborhoods with moderate blended densities, outdoor eateries, and shops that directly front onto the street.

Take the emerging transit community of Rosslyn, across the Potomac from Washington, DC, and the first Metrorail station when heading into Arlington County as an example. Rosslyn was a boomtown in the 1960s and early 1970s, when a patchwork of 30 or so mid- to high-rise commercial structures and federal office buildings quickly went up. Following design standards of the time, the built environment that emerged features widely spaced buildings, wide boulevards, narrow and sometimes disconnected sidewalks, and streetscapes of blank walls. In recent years, Arlington County has sought to reconfigure the Rosslyn area into a more pedestrian-friendly and transit-oriented area. Starting with the Commonwealth Building in 1994, office structures are being retrofitted to incorporate street-level retail shops, and the street network is being modified (e.g., rerouting, traffic calming, midblock crossings) to encourage walking. A three-block area around the station is being transformed into Central Place, featuring a well-lit, active transit station, a nicely landscaped public plaza, street art, and a continuous pathway network that ties the station to nearby bus lines and taxicab stands.

3. *Alternative suburban living and working environments:* The transit village offers the opportunity to live in the suburbs without being entirely dependent on the automobile and with the rich variety of activities and services usually associated with cities. It poses no threat, however, to the kind of low-density living cherished by millions of Americans. In fact, transit villages should relieve pressures to intensify existing suburban neighborhoods, enabling them to maintain their cultural hegemony and low-density qualities. As metropolitan areas continue to grow and development pressures mount, transit villages provide a kind of safety valve: They produce additional housing that minimizes impacts on local

and regional roads, does not contribute to sprawl, and enables existing neighborhoods to remain intact.

As an alternative suburban community, the transit village vision calls for a mix of housing suited to a range of incomes and lifestyle preferences: condominiums, duplexes, apartments, and single-family detached units. At the emerging transit village of Rio Vista West in San Diego, several three-story structures with 240 units surround the light rail station. As one leaves the station, densities taper to condominiums and then to single-family homes. This "wedding cake" pattern of densities also characterizes the Residences at Grosvenor transit village being designed in Montgomery County, outside Washington, DC. The first two phases of the Residences at Grosvenor are on tracts of land that are farthest from the Metrorail station and will feature four-story apartments and for-sale condominiums as well as a community center and swimming pool. In later phases, parcels closer to the station will house two eight-story mixed-use buildings and a mid-rise residential tower adjacent to the station with 28,000 ft^2 of ground-floor, neighborhood-serving retail space.

The diversity of housing in transit villages can mean a much-needed increase in the stock of affordable housing. Many U.S. cities, particularly on both coasts, suffer from a shortage of affordable housing, which forces many young families and first-time homebuyers to reside on the exurban fringes. Working parents often spend more time getting to and from work than with their families. Transit villages could do a lot to provide more live-travel options for young families as well as retirees, empty nesters, and others wanting to economize on housing and transportation expenses.

Since we have characterized the transit village as an alternative suburban community, a word should be said about the term *community* itself. For the most part, Americans find the emotive ties of community in the myriad voluntary associations, churches, charities, and neighborhood groups they belong to rather than in nation or place. This is to be expected in a pluralist society of some 250 million people. It is increasingly so in an era of fast-pace living and in a landscape of faceless sprawl. However, there is a sense in which a place can be a community: where the residents see themselves as part of a cooperative enterprise, pursuing similar ideals and common cause, be it neighborhood safety, historical preservation, traffic calming, or whatever. An attachment to place has spawned thousands of grassroots neighborhood associations across the United States in recent times. A transit village, whose village scale and makeup promote social interaction and indeed entice people to get to know each other, is consonant with the notion of "community as place."

4. *Neighborhood revitalization:* The transit village offers a fresh, new approach to stimulating economic growth in inner-city neighborhoods served by rail. It invites private investment by creating the conditions for financial gain—from the foot traffic of the commuters regularly heading to stations, from the value added of siting commercial buildings near viable transit nodes, and from the benefits of a well-planned urban milieu. In this sense, the transit village breaks ranks with earlier antipoverty approaches. Mid-20th-century American liberalism viewed declining inner-city areas as opportunities for massive urban renewal

under the stewardship and control of the public sector. Wide swaths of established neighborhoods were bulldozed and replaced by public housing high-rises, owned and operated by government. Social service agencies replaced local businesses as major employers, and programs created by the Great Society and urban renewal bureaucracies became the major source of jobs.

At the time urban America's welfare state was being assembled, more perceptive analysts recognized the inherent limitations of these approaches in transforming depressed neighborhoods or in breaking the cycle of poverty. Vast public housing tracts were overwhelmed by the sheer numbers of low-income, unemployed persons. Social service agencies grew into bureaucratic empires, most concerned with their own expansion and unresponsive to either market forces or neighborhood needs. Many residents grew increasingly dependent on the government largesse, and some withdrew from gainful employment altogether.

The transit village stands in marked contrast to this big government approach in its village scale, its entrepreneurial orientation, and its respect for the skills and abilities of residents. In Oakland's Fruitvale neighborhood, for example, redevelopment has been limited to a quarter-mile ring around the station. The emerging transit village is being designed for households from different incomes and backgrounds, not just the poor. Public seed monies seek to leverage private investment. The residents of Fruitvale are not passive observers, but rather are directly participating in village development and business ownership. Some have recently started a mobility enterprise that provides neighborhood van services and reverse-commute runs to suburban job centers, with local residents in charge of operating, dispatching, maintaining, and servicing the vehicles. This is grass-roots empowerment, not top-down entitlement.

Of course, there remains an important role for government leadership in bringing about successful transit villages. Although many inner-city neighborhoods, like Fruitvale, enjoy good regional accessibility by virtue of their rail stops, too many lack decent housing, job opportunities, good schools, and neighborhood security. Combining transit village planning with aggressive programs to improve the social and physical infrastructure of such neighborhoods can provide a formula for progressive change. In this sense, transit villages must be part of a larger effort of *community rebuilding*. Drawing on the strengths of both the private and the public sectors, transit villages will ultimately depend on forging effective partnerships for bringing about positive changes. An important asset will be their social diversity. As places that bring people of different ages, incomes, and walks of life into daily contact and that encourage social interaction, transit villages can be important catalysts to community rebuilding.

5. *Public safety:* No issue is more important to attracting people to transit villages than public safety. Residents, in particular, must regard the transit village, with its many activities and offerings, as a secure and safe place in which to live. Residents themselves are the most valuable asset in this regard. They become the eyes of the community 24 h a day. Many dis-

tricts surrounding transit stations are perceived as unsafe places in part because they are often vacated after 6 P.M. and on weekends. Vast parking lots, vacant lots, and unoccupied buildings can be breeding grounds for random acts of violence. A transit village populated by residents, workers, and shopkeepers is a place where there is a continual security presence. Building a police substation, a common feature in many transit village plans, can further enhance public security and safety.

6. *Public celebration:* A public plaza that leads into the village's station entrance provides a natural spot for community gathering—a place for celebrations, parades, performances, and protests. The square can be chameleonlike. In the mornings, it might be converted to a colorful farmer's market, populated by flower stalls, fruit kiosks, and gazebos. On weekends, concerts might be held there. What is important is that the transit station, functioning as the window to the rest of the region, is physically tied to and associated with the village's major gathering place. Such milieus are common at rail transit stations throughout Europe. Residents are drawn to transit nodes by the attractiveness and vibrancy of the surrounding public areas. Concessionaires, street artists, and vendors are drawn by the heavy walk-on transit traffic.

   This book adopts a case study approach in illustrating these key elements of a transit village, using examples of emerging transit villages in the United States and more established transit villages from abroad—notably Stockholm, Singapore, and Tokyo. Although the particulars of designing and building a transit village are important, it is also important to recognize the connections of the transit village to the larger metropolis. A single transit village in a sea of sprawling, auto-oriented development will yield few transportation, environmental, or social benefits over the long run. However, a collection of functionally related transit villages can form the building blocks of a successful and sustainable transit metropolis.

1.3   THE TRANSIT METROPOLIS

The great transit metropolises of the world—metropolitan Stockholm, Singapore, and Tokyo, among others—owe much of their success to the communities that have blossomed around rail nodes. In these places, rail transit and urban development have become codependent.

   In Scandinavia's two largest metropolises, Stockholm and Copenhagen, dozens of compact, mixed-use satellite communities are interconnected by regional rail systems. All are built on a scale that encourages pedestrian circulation. Most rail stops focus on town centers with a public square and an outdoor marketplace. The accent on livability is showcased by pedestrian amenities—park benches, newspaper kiosks, bus shelters, sidewalk cafes, open-air markets, flower stands, and arcades designed to protect pedestrians from the elements. In Vällingby, one of Stockholm's rail-served satellites, the rail station shares space with a supermarket, where returning commuters can do their daily shopping on the way home. The station is adjacent to a car-free village square lined with more shops and service establishments, including several day-care centers. More than 50 percent of Vällingby's employed residents commute by transit despite the fact that Sweden has one of the highest per capita car ownership rates in Europe.

The transit villages that form the transit metropolis need not, and perhaps should not, be of the same design and character. Some are apt to be employment centers. Others will be known as cultural and entertainment destinations. Many will contain housing, but even here diversity will prevail. Some will be master planned, whereas others will evolve more organically. While some will have a dominant land use, others will feature a kaleidoscope of urban activities. What matters most is that the collectivity of transit villages adds up meaningfully to form a functional and sustainable transit metropolis. By this we do not mean one where transit replaces the automobile or even captures the majority of trips. Rather, the transit metropolis represents a built form where transit becomes a far more respectable alternative to traveling than currently is the case in most U.S. cities, in addition to being a regional structure that helps to nurture and support individual transit-oriented communities. Ultimately, it will be the social and economic interactions that take place both within and between transit villages, within the structure of a transit metropolis, that we believe will place urban America on a more sustainable path.

This idea of a transit metropolis borrows from the visions of early city planners like Sir Ebenezer Howard in England and Frederick Law Olmstead and Edward Bellamy in America, who advanced the idea of building pedestrian-oriented "garden cities." Howard's vision was to build self-sufficient satellite communities of around 30,000 inhabitants that would orbit London, separated by protected greenbelts and connected by intermunicipal railways. Some vestiges of transit villages survive in the former "streetcar suburbs" of turn-of-the-century America, such as Shaker Heights in Cleveland, Chestnut Hill in Boston, Riverside near Chicago, Roland Park in Baltimore, and Country Club Plaza in Kansas City. Streetcar suburbs depended on pedestrian access to transit to reach downtown jobs and neighborhood centers because many were built prior to the invention of the automobile. America's early rail-served neighborhoods featured a range of housing from large estates to small cottages, had distinctive gridiron street patterns, and focused on prominent civic areas near rail stops to instill a sense of community. In order to attract residents to these distant suburbs, early transit villages were designed as safe, secure, and attractive places, notably with the placement of the train depot and public space in the heart of the community and the use of restrictive covenants and other development standards to control the physical environment.

As a vision of urban development, the notion of a transit metropolis cannot be ignored if for no other reason than billions of dollars are today being invested in rail transit throughout the United States. In nearly every major metropolitan region of America, rail transit systems are being built, revived, or expanded. Nearly all major heavy rail systems—in Washington, DC, Atlanta, New York, Baltimore, Chicago, and the San Francisco Bay

Area—are being augmented by miles of new track, in projects ranging from $250 million to over $2 billion per system. Light rail lines in San Jose, Portland, San Diego, and Sacramento built during the 1980s are today being extended into what a decade or so ago were largely exurban areas and farmland. New light rail systems have recently opened in Denver and St. Louis and have broken ground in Dallas.

This rail renaissance reflects a growing recognition of the limits of automobility in America. Although the private car remains Americans' overwhelming choice of travel, opinion polls show that more urbanites than ever want other travel options and view rail as an attractive alternative. Many seem willing to support rail at the ballot box and with their pocketbooks, voting to increase taxes to pay for new rail lines. During the 1980s and early 1990s, for example, California voters rejected most new tax measures. However, in each of its major metropolitan areas—Los Angeles, San Diego, Santa Clara County, Sacramento, and the San Francisco Bay Area—voters approved tax increases to fund new urban rail systems and extensions.

1.4 IMPLEMENTING THE TRANSIT VILLAGE VISION

The current rail renaissance provides opportunity for the new mobility and new lifestyle of the transit village, but implementation will be a formidable challenge. For to think about transit villages is to think about the process of influencing land form in contemporary urban America, a process fraught with financial, political, and logistical obstacles. In this process, the transit village concept and even the transit village design are only first steps. Architecture magazines and journals are filled with ideas for innovative approaches to community design, 90 percent of which never get off the ground. The work of the "new urbanists," for example, has created great excitement among planners, environmentalists, and academics, but it is only slowly being translated into built forms.

Among transit village plans, the majority have ended up on the shelves of transit agencies and local governments. Westlake-MacArthur Park in Los Angeles, Atlantic Center in New York, and Howard Station in Chicago are just a few of the neighborhoods for which transit village schemes were formulated but never put into practice. Government inertia, neighborhood opposition to any densification, difficulties in assembling land, and conservative lending practices have all conspired to block the implementation of transit village proposals.

Still, a number of transit village plans are today making progress toward implementation, all of which share certain common traits: local government participation in financing; a proactive redevelopment authority; a market-realistic site plan; neighborhood support; and a political champion, often a local elected official who shepherds the plan along every step of the way. America's emerging transit villages indicate the possibilities, but also the considerable efforts of individuals, companies, and public offices, that are needed to advance beyond the conceptual design stage.

Implementation is one of the central themes of our examination of America's flowering transit village movement. Much of our attention goes to parts of the country that have made the most headway in putting theory to practice, notably the San Francisco Bay Area, the Washington, DC region, southern California, and the greater New York metropolitan area. Before this examination, though, we need to say more about the social, economic, and political underpinnings of the contemporary transit village movement and specifically something about its predecessor, the rail transit-based communities that arose in America nearly a century ago.

America's Early Transit Villages

Before looking at the emerging transit villages of today, it is worth going back in time, back to the late 19th century and early 20th century when rail transit networks sprouted throughout America's cities and suburbs. These networks, first the commuter railroads and later the electric interurbans, greatly expanded the geographic boundaries of America's cities, which historically stretched just a few miles in each direction since walking and horse-carts were the principal means of conveyance. With streetcar lines and interurban railroads came a new type of metropolis, one with limbs that stretched well into the countryside and one that gave rise to new possibilities for mobility, home ownership, and community.

The railroad and streetcar suburbs that took root a century ago were some distance away from the industry, commerce, and culture of great American cities, though they were conveniently linked to urban centers by regular and reliable rail services. America's railroad suburbs set out new patterns not only of travel but also of community settlement, housing production, and neighborhood design. Though forgotten for much of the 20th century, America's legacy of railroad suburbs has been "rediscovered" in recent decades. Urban historians, social commentators, and reform-minded architects are finding in these early transit villages values lost in the contemporary 20th century American community.

In this chapter, the evolution of railroad suburbs in four areas of the country is chronicled: the commuter railroads that linked New York City to its northern suburbs; the giant Pacific Electric streetcar network that laced the greater Los Angeles region; its counterpart to the north, the Key System in the eastern half of the San Francisco Bay Area; and the consciously community-shaping Shaker Heights line in Cleveland. Additionally, lessons that might be relevant to today's transit village movement are highlighted.

2.1 NEW YORK CITY, 1898

It is New York City about a century ago. Grand Central Station is the destination of 118,000 daily commuters who reach the city each day via the Hudson River, Harlem River Valley, and Long Island Sound commuter railroads. These three commuter lines have given rise to an entirely new breed of community—fairly affluent places surrounded by countryside where those with the means can own their own stand-alone home.

In just a short time, the new railroads have channeled population expansion beyond the five boroughs of New York, giving birth to townships with names like Scarsdale, New Rochelle, Rye, Mount Vernon, and Bronxville. Foremost, New York's outer suburbs have become residential havens of businessmen and well-paid professionals who value owning a large home and are willing to commute an hour or so each day to reach their well-paying jobs.[1] They offer a refreshing alternative to crowded city life. Lots are large and surrounded by greenery. Parks are plenty. While home mostly to upper-middle and upper-class households, the new suburbs are culturally diverse, like their urban counterparts, including a substantial (a third or so of the population) laboring class that provides gardening, domestic, and other services.

Near Scarsdale's train station is a town center comprised mainly of shops that serve the local population. Laborers who do not reside on the estates of employers live in modest boardinghouses and small cottages near the station. Farther out are spacious homes on landscaped grounds of a quarter acre or more. Despite the large lots, people are close enough to regularly socialize on the street, and one can walk to and from most points in the village. The community has a distinct edge, beyond which is the countryside.

Downtown New York is where breadwinners head for work each day, and it is also a popular destination for entertainment and culture. The suburb's wealth draws from the city's industry. Yet, the city is also rewarded: Residents of the railroad suburbs help support the city's concert halls, clubs, restaurants, museums, and department stores.

Kenneth T. Jackson, a student of America's suburbs, has described New York's railroad suburbs, linked to Manhattan, as "beads on a string." Each suburban community was in many ways self-contained and self-sufficient. Except for going to work and an occasional excursion to the bright lights of the city, the railroad suburbs of New York provided their residents with enough basic shopping, recreation offerings, and services to keep people near their homes and, as a result, instill a sense of community. A natural limit to the spread of houses was the walking distance to the railroad station. Only the very wealthy who could afford a horse and driver were able to live in open country. Scarsdale, 20 mi from midtown Manhattan, was smaller than 2 mi^2 in 1890.[2]

Jackson finds in New York's railroad suburbs a model of affluence, architectural integrity, and the fine equilibrium between urbanity and rural values, writing:

> The railroad suburbs, although small in size and number, stood as a model for success. In the nineteenth century the image of suburbia as an affluent community of railroad commuters was set, and the image remained under the interstate suburbs developed in the 1960s. Such suburbs reached their apex around 1920, when Grand Central Terminal alone was handling more than 680 commuter trains per week, when Pennsylvania Station was even larger, and when every large city took special pride in the affluence and distinction of its railroad suburbs.[3]

In 1979, the Smithsonian Institution's National Museum of Design sponsored an exhibition on "America's suburbs," prepared by architect Robert A. M. Stern. In his work,

Stern singled out the railroad suburbs for their compact, walkable design that facilitated social interaction as well as for their architectural charm and integrity. The suburb, Stern reminds us, represents a state of mind based on imagery and symbolism. The gently curving roads, the tended lawns, and the houses with pitched roofs, shuttered windows, and colonial or otherwise elaborated doorways all speak of a community which values the traditions of family, pride of ownership, and rural-semirural life.[4]

□ □ □

Westchester County, north of New York City, is the home to several railroad suburbs that arose in the late 19th century: Mount Vernon, White Plains, Scarsdale, and Bronxville. The British first settled the county of Westchester in 1683, and for the next 100 years the area remained largely agricultural. As New York emerged as a global center, Westchester County became one of the city's chief suppliers of agricultural produce. By the 1840s, when the first railroads were built, the county was a thriving agricultural center with close economic ties to the great industrial metropolis to the south.[5]

The railroads strengthened these ties and hastened the county's transformation from a collection of agricultural hamlets to a constellation of industrial towns and commuter suburbs.[6] The population of Westchester County grew by 75 percent between 1850 and 1860, enough to support multiple train runs each day. Towns that dotted the rail lines evolved into the county's chief economic centers. Yonkers, situated at the southern end of the county and along the Hudson River Railroad, grew from a settlement of some 2500 inhabitants in 1846 to one with a population of nearly 20,000 in 1880, making it the largest city in the county. New towns proliferated along the rail lines, as real estate developers began acquiring inexpensive farmland for building rail-oriented communities.[7] Many real estate ventures were financed by industrialists and oil magnates who, with the infancy of financial markets and security exchanges, saw land acquisition as a safe and promising way to invest their considerable wealth.

When the railroad arrived at Scarsdale in the mid-19th century, the town was no more than a brief stop on the Harlem line en route to White Plains. The 1860 census showed that 70 percent of Scarsdale's adult population worked as farmers and farm laborers, with its professional population consisting of seven merchants, two brokers, a lawyer, a clergyman, and a physician. By 1915, the number of farms in Scarsdale had fallen from 35 to 12, the population had grown from several hundred to several thousand, and more than 60 percent of the village's households could be classified as upper-middle-class, headed largely by professionals who commuted daily to their jobs in New York City.[8]

With the arrival of railroads, Scarsdale's farmland was quickly subdivided and transformed into residential neighborhoods. The first residential subdivision was built in 1891 by the Arthur Suburban Home Company on what before was a 150-acre farm. The company laid out new streets, drove in stakes marking the lot boundaries, and advertised for home-dwellers of the new Arthur Manor neighborhood by extolling the beauty of its location, the covenants against business uses, and the ease of commutation to New York City.

The Arthur Manor project was soon followed by other subdivisions, varying in lot sizes and housing costs, but located in reasonably close proximity to either the central Scarsdale railroad station or the Hartsdale station in northern Scarsdale. In 1902, the most exclusive of the developments to date, the Heathcote subdivision, opened and became Scarsdale's showcase neighborhood, with new homes beginning at $7500 (compared to $1500 at Arthur Manor). Heathcote attracted the attention of *County Life in America* magazine, which described it as combining "the seclusion of country life" with the advantages of being 30 min from the hustle and bustle of the city.

While residential neighborhoods were close to the railroad stations, parcels immediately adjacent to the rail station developed into Scarsdale's commercial center. In the early 1900s, the station was replaced with a structure bearing "an elegance far out of keeping with its prospective revenues,"[9] and Depot Place was built, a small town center with the O'Farrell drugstore, Flagge & Hooley grocery, Luikert meat market, plumbing firm of Curran & Curran, and real estate offices of Angell & Company. These businesses were joined by the Scarsdale National Bank and Trust Company and a motion picture theater. As shown in Photo 2.1, the commercial buildings were constructed in a plaster-and-timber English Tudor style to emphasize the village scale, design, and setting. Vestiges of these designs remain today in old town Scarsdale.

Bronxville is another Westchester railroad town that blossomed in the late 1800s. As with Scarsdale, the village was masterminded and shaped mainly by a single entrepreneur. At the time, William Van Duzer Lawrence, a wealthy chemical manufacturer, bought 100 acres near the Bronxville train station, turning it into Lawrence Park. Adjacent to the station, the Hotel Gramatan and a complex of stores, offices, eateries, and a penny arcade were erected. Also sited near the station were multifamily apartments, terrace houses, and group homes built in country village style. Farther out, but still within easy distance of the station, single-family homes went up, closely spaced along winding, hilly roads. What decades later would become standard community planning doctrine in the designs of celebrated new towns like Radburn, New Jersey, and the garden cities of England, like Hemel Hempstead, the commercial core and tapered population densities were already prominent features of New York's railroad suburbs at the turn of the century.

In a commentary on the physical makeup of Westchester County's rail-oriented communities, one of the great minds of urban planning, Lewis Mumford, noted in *The City in History*:

> These suburbs, strung along a railroad line, were discontinuous and properly spaced; and without the aid of legislation they were limited in population as well as area; for the biggest rarely held as many as ten thousand people, and under five thousand was more usual. ... The size and scale of the suburb, that of a neighborhood unit, was not entirely the result of its open planning, which favored low densities. Being served by a

Photo 2.1 The Scarsdale Business District in 1925, Opposite the Commuter Rail Station. Automobiles have entered the scene, allowing people to live farther from the train station, but the station area remains one of a concentration of businesses and residences in walking distance of each other and the station.

railroad line, with station stops from three to five miles apart, there was a natural limit to the spread of any particular community. Houses had to be situated 'within easy walking distance of the railroad station,' as the advertising prospectus would point out.[10]

Scarsdale, Bronxville, and other turn-of-the-century railroad towns in Westchester County were indeed the precursors, both in design and character, of today's transit village movement.

2.2 LOS ANGELES, 1910

In Los Angeles, circa 1910, the Pacific Electric Railway crisscrosses what at the time are largely orange groves and virgin land, spanning 1164 directional mi of track. The interurban railway links downtown

Los Angeles to San Bernardino and Riverside Counties, 30 to 40 mi inland to the east, Orange County, 40 mi to the south, as well as to the mostly farmlands of the San Fernando and San Gabriel Valleys. Moreover, the various corners of the region are linked to each other: San Bernardino to Riverside, Hollywood to the San Fernando Valley, Huntington Beach to Compton.

Southern California's vast railroad system is not propelled by steam, as in many east coast cities, but rather by electricity. By the turn of the century, electric streetcar systems had sprouted throughout the United States, and by 1910, the Pacific Electric Railway is the largest system in the nation and, in fact, in the world.

In just a little over 30 years, southern California grew from a collection of sleepy farm towns to one of the great transit metropolises of all time. Electric streetcars were introduced in downtown Los Angeles in 1887. In 1895, the Los Angeles and Pasadena Railway built the first interurban rail line from downtown Los Angeles to Pasadena, followed in 1896 by a 15-mi line to Santa Monica, at the time an isolated resort and retirement community by the ocean.[11]

It took a visionary with a huge bankroll to move southern California's rail system to full realization. In 1901, Henry Huntington bought and assumed the presidency of the Pacific Electric Railway Company. Under Huntington's helm, railway construction accelerated: Lines were extended to Long Beach in 1902 (at a staggering rate of 7800 ft of rail set each day), and in quick succession, rail arrived in Orange County, down the coast in Redondo Beach, and in the budding seaside towns of Huntington Beach, Newport Beach, and Balboa. Southern California's streetcar lines also began to penetrate the inland empire, reaching the farming communities of Upland, Fontana, and Redlands, as well as the resort town of Arrowhead Hot Springs. Ridership on the Pacific Electric steadily increased through the 1910s and 1920s: 68.3 million passengers in 1919, 84.5 million passengers in 1920, and over 100 million passengers in 1924. At its height, the Pacific Electric Railway blanketed southern California, serving some 50 communities with 1164 directional mi of track and 270 trains a day. The Big Red Car became a familiar part of southern California life.

The Pacific Electric Railway system was financed totally in private. Huntington's personal fortune was the main source of capital, and he invested millions of dollars. Huntington believed he could increase his fortune by coupling streetcar expansion with real estate investment—namely, purchasing inexpensive land on the metropolitan fringe and increasing its value through the provision of rail transit services. At the time, Huntington-owned real estate companies purchased enormous tracts of undeveloped land in areas that would later be linked to the downtown core and other parts of the region by the Pacific Electric Railway. Huntington acquired land near Alhambra and San Marino, and at the same time, he extended lines to these cities. His real estate holdings soon stretched into Glendale, Seal Beach, Huntington Beach, Olinda, and the San Fernando Valley, as well as downtown Los Angeles.

But financial considerations alone cannot explain Huntington's investment. When Huntington assumed the Pacific Electric presidency, he was already worth more than $40 million—the value of stock in Southern Pacific that Huntington inherited from the estate of his uncle, Collis Huntington. There was no compelling financial reason for Huntington to risk his fortune in speculative transit and real estate ventures. For Henry Huntington, the desire to build and shape a great metropolis was what primarily motivated him. In transit, Huntington saw a chance to break the bonds of the traditional city, enabling development to disperse widely and into numerous communities, but still linked to the urban core. In 1905, Huntington told a newspaper reporter, "I am a foresighted man, and I believe Los Angeles is destined to become the most important city in this country if not in the world. It can extend in any direction as far as you like." It is to his credit that Huntington recognized the value of extending rail lines in advance of demand. He was a patient man, willing to put up much of his wealth for what he strongly believed would not only produce big profits but also leave an indelible mark on the form and character of greater Los Angeles. Remarked Huntington, "It would never do for an electric line to wait until demand for it came. It must anticipate the growth of communities and be there when the homebuilders arrive—or they are very likely not to arrive at all, but go to some section already provided with arteries of traffic."[12]

Huntington's prophecies proved accurate. The Pacific Electric Railway defined southern California's cityscape, forming the radial spines that channeled growth throughout the first half of the 20th century. During the 1910s and 1920s, small rail-served towns like San Bernardino, Long Beach, Monrovia, and Santa Monica exploded in population. Long Beach had slightly more than 2000 residents when the Red Cars connected it to downtown Los Angeles in July 1902. Within 8 years, Long Beach's population exceeded 17,000, and by 1920, it eclipsed 55,000. Newport Beach, 38 mi from downtown Los Angeles, was a village of fewer than 1000 residents when the Red Cars arrived in 1906; 4 years later, its population had quadrupled. Of the 18 southern California cities boasting populations of more than 1000 residents in the 1910 census, only 2 were located away from a Pacific Electric line.[13]

The Los Angeles region multiplied in size during the first decades of the 20th century, forming a continuously developed land mass larger than any in recorded history. In 1890, Los Angeles County's population was 101,000. By 1910, it had increased fivefold to 504,000, and by 1920, it was just under a million. By 1930, county population had leaped to over 2.2 million. During this period, the county's growth rate—population approximately doubling every decade—far exceeded that of any jurisdiction in the country.

One of the most distinguishing features of Los Angeles's growth was its housing composition. Housing was not concentrated in three-story walk-ups and tenements near the downtown commercial core, as in eastern cities. Instead, southern Californians, rich and poor alike, took up residence primarily in single-family dwellings. A multicentered metropolis had taken form, with over 50 different communities linked together and tied to the Red Car system.

Robert Fishman, an urban historian, finds southern California's streetcar-shaped form "a remarkable balance of urban and rural environments." The rail system, remarks Fishman, has resulted in "a collection of villages, devoid of the slums and overcrowding of the past, offering to almost everyone a suburban home on its own land."[14] San Bernardino, Redondo Beach, the city of Orange, and Pasadena were four of the first Pacific Electric transit villages. All of these communities existed prior to the Pacific Electric, though it took the Red Cars to transform them into urban centers in their own right.

Pasadena, first settled by a group of farmers from Indiana in 1873, quickly prospered as a center for citrus agriculture and ranching, and within a few years, merchants and professionals began to take up residence. By the early 1880s, less than 10 years after its founding, stately homes were constructed along many of the town's principal streets, and a commercial district blossomed along Colorado Street.[15]

It took relatively little time, however, for real estate development to supplant agriculture as Pasadena's fastest growing industry. Between 1886 and 1888, the city's population grew threefold and real estate prices skyrocketed. A lot that sold for $2000 in 1881 was subdivided 6 years later and sold for $120,000.[16] Although the bubble of this initial boom quickly burst, it established a pattern that held true for decades to come in southern California: explosive growth and rampant real estate speculation in the wake of Americans migrating westward in search of a warm climate, new frontiers, and the good life.

Pasadena's rapid expansion prompted an immediate need for improved transportation, both within and outside of town. In response, a system of privately owned rail lines was built through franchise with the municipal government. These services, beginning with horsedrawn trolleys in 1886 and upgraded to electric streetcars in the 1890s, provided comfortable, affordable, and convenient links between the town's central business district and its residential neighborhoods, radiating outward to nearby settlements such as Altadena, Linda Vista, and Lamanda Park. Southern California's first "interurban" trolley line, the Pasadena & Los Angeles Electric Railway Company, began service in 1895, providing frequent passenger service between Pasadena and the central business district of Los Angeles.

The Red Cars solidified Pasadena's position as an important subcenter in the vast expanses of southern California. As shown in Photo 2.2, commercial uses congregated in the city's core, creating a vibrant urban center that attracted people from around the region. New residential enclaves sprung up immediately adjacent to the commercial core, radiating outward to the edge of orchards, farmland, and undeveloped hillsides. Pasadena's central business district featured tightly packed buildings of two to four stories that hugged the main thoroughfares, while the flanking residential districts were almost exclusively comprised of single-family Victorians and brownstone homes built on large lots and set back from the tree-lined streets.

The distinction between living in Pasadena and residing within a much larger southern California region sharpened with the inauguration of interurban rail service. Pasadena could maintain a small-town atmosphere, but still be less than a half hour away from downtown Los Angeles and an hour or so from the Pacific Ocean or the desert spas of the

Photo 2.2   Pasadena, Colorado Street Looking West, 1910. By 1910, the Colorado Street business district had become a bustling center of activity. Local streetcars provided service to outlying neighborhoods, linking with the interurban service to downtown Los Angeles and communities throughout southern California.

inland empire (Photo 2.3). To many residents, living in Pasadena meant living in the mobility epicenter of southern California.

While southern California is today known for its crisscrossing freeway network, the fact is that rail transit defined the axes along which most commercial development has occurred this century. To a large degree, freeways followed the same paths laid out by the Red Car lines. The auto-freeway era also led to the filling in of the mostly undeveloped wedges unserved by the old streetcar and interurban rail lines. Overall, southern California's multicentered settlement pattern of today—anchored by prominent urban centers like Pasadena, San Bernardino, Santa Ana, and Long Beach—owes much to the considerable investments in electric trolley lines of yesteryear.

2.3   SAN FRANCISCO-OAKLAND, 1910

Five hundred miles up the California coast, an extensive interurban rail system is also taking shape in the early years of the 20th century. This network—incorporated as the San Francisco, Oakland & San Jose

Photo 2.3 Pasadena, Pacific Electric Billboard, 1930. The increasing traffic congestion in Los Angeles has become one of the rail system's main selling points.

Railway but soon commonly known as the Key System—spans 245 directional mi of track laid throughout the East Bay. By 1912, the Key System connects the East Bay to San Francisco and ridership exceeds 100 million passengers annually.

Like the Pacific Electric, the Key System was privately financed in its entirety. The principal venture capitalist was a wealthy entrepreneur, Francis Marion "Borax" Smith. In 1872, Smith, 26 years of age and working as a woodcutter, discovered a major deposit of borax, used as a cleanser, in the hills of Nevada. From this find, Smith proceeded to build the Pacific Coast Borax Company and a personal fortune.

In 1881, Smith settled in Oakland, one of three small East Bay cities located across the Bay from teeming San Francisco. (From the 1890 census, Oakland and these other two cities, Berkeley and Alameda, claimed 65,000 residents, compared to nearly 300,000 residents in San Francisco.) Smith gradually saw an opportunity to urbanize the East Bay by linking it to San Francisco with reliable and convenient interurban rail service. In the 1880s, the only service to San Francisco was the irregular and slow Southern Pacific trains.

Intercity rail service came to the East Bay in 1891 and quickly gained popularity. A few years later, Smith started purchasing these streetcar lines and set out to extend new lines to 13,000 acres of mostly virgin land in the Oakland and Berkeley hills that he had purchased through his Realty Syndicate Company. On October 26, 1903, the East Bay rail network was connected to San Francisco through a first-of-its-kind train-to-ferry water crossing (Photo 2.4). This connection opened the floodgates to East Bay development on a mass scale.

The transbay rail network was an immediate success, attracting thousands of daily riders wanting to shave an hour or more commuting time to San Francisco. The Southern Pacific trains required 68 min to go from Berkeley to San Francisco. In contrast, the Key System trains made this run in 36 min, and at 20-min intervals. In 1915, the Key System's civil engineer, E. M. Boggs, wrote of the first years of the transbay service:

> Minerva-like it sprang into existence full grown and it was an instant success. From the first day it transported the thousands who had awaited its advent with impatience and who welcomed the smooth, swift and quiet electric trains of the Key System . . . The contrast between the old and the new types of services was most striking. The trains of the Southern Pacific were drawn by steam locomotives whose noise and smoke emitted . . . were highly objectionable . . . The electric trains were free from smoke and cinders and practically noiseless.[17]

As in Los Angeles, streetcar lines had a lasting imprint on the East Bay's physical form. The main commercial corridor in Berkeley, home of the University of California, sprang up alongside the streetcar tracks (Photo 2.5). The network between Oakland and Berkeley was especially dense, with a Key System line being no more than 1000 ft away from the

Photo 2.4 Key System Train Operating on the Berkeley Pier, Site of the Ferry Transfer, 1903. The train-ferry connection meant San Francisco workers could live in the wooded hills of the East Bay and get to work and back home in under an hour.

Photo 2.5   University Avenue, Berkeley, 1905. The Key System first connects Berkeley and San Francisco in 1903, and over the next years, East Bay development clusters at Key System stations.

core parts of these cities (Figure 2.1). Between 1913 and 1922, over 80 percent of all building permits issued in Oakland were for projects within three blocks of a Key System line.[18]

Entire townships owe their existence to the Key System, most notably Piedmont (Photo 2.6). As late as 1903, Piedmont, in the Oakland hills, counted only a few homes. Shortly after the Key System reached Piedmont in 1904, residential construction began in earnest. By 1915, Piedmont's population grew to 2375, and by 1930, it exceeded 9000. And between 1913 and 1920, over 92 percent of residential building permits issued in Piedmont were for homes built within three blocks of a trolley line.[19]

2.4   SHAKER HEIGHTS, 1920

Shaker Heights, located some 6 mi east of downtown Cleveland, is the brainchild of two enterprising brothers, Oris and Mantis Van Sweringen. Through speculative real estate purchases, subdivision, and the extension of a new streetcar line to serve those subdivisions, the Van Sweringen brothers transformed the former religious colony of Shaker Heights into one of America's premier planned residential communities, centered around a streetcar line.

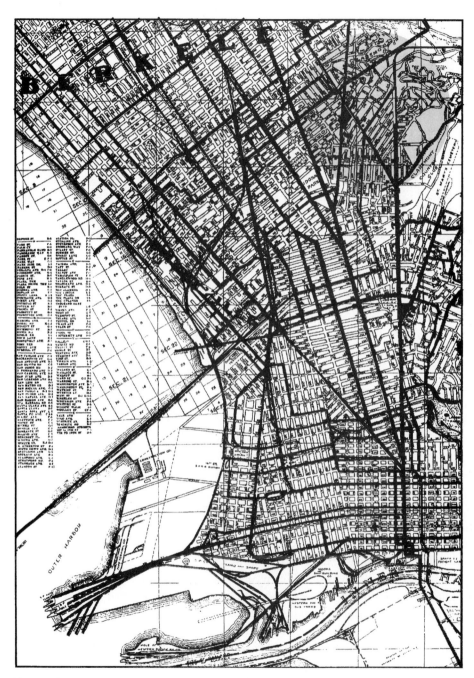

Figure 2.1 Dense Network of Key System Lines in Oakland and Berkeley, 1924.

Photo 2.6 Piedmont Station, 1910. Piedmont is vacant land when the Key System arrives in 1905, but by 1915, the population of this streetcar suburb is over 2000.

Shaker Heights was founded in 1822 by a group from the United Society of Believers in Christ's Second Appearing, commonly known as the Shakers. Following the Civil War, the Shaker colony lost followers, and by 1889, the 27 remaining members sold their 1366-acre site for $316,000 to the Shaker Heights Land Company. By this time, Cleveland was becoming an important industrial center. In 1900, its population stood at 381,000, up from 44,000 in 1860. With a rapidly growing middle class, market conditions were ripe for creating a stable and comfortable suburban settlement removed from the unpleasantness of heavy industries. In 1890, a local real estate entrepreneur, Patrick Calhoun, purchased and subdivided land on Cedar Hill. Soon thereafter, Calhoun built a streetcar line to climb the hill and serve the subdivision. The resulting community of Euclid Heights featured imposing estates situated on meandering streets, with the streetcar line running up the median of the broad Euclid Heights Boulevard.

Not to be outdone, the Van Sweringen brothers purchased land in nearby Cleveland Heights and in 1906 constructed the Shaker Lakes line, a branch of the Euclid Heights line, to serve Cleveland Heights. Also in 1906, the Van Sweringens acquired from the Shaker Heights Land Company all remaining acreage of the original Shaker colony. To duplicate their success in Cleveland Heights, the Van Sweringens reached an agreement with the Cleveland Railway Company (the city's new, consolidated streetcar company) to build a spur line into the heart of Shaker Heights village. As part of the deal and as a precondition to receiving franchise permits, the Van Sweringens agreed to pay for all construction costs and to provide a monthly subsidy to cover any operating losses. The new streetcar line began operating in December 1913.

With streetcar service in place, the Van Sweringens turned their attention to the design and development of the Shaker Heights community, at the time the largest planned residential development in the country under single ownership. They hired the F. A. Pease Engineering Company to prepare a comprehensive plan for the community that specified street layouts, property subdivisions, zoning controls, and design standards. Shaker Heights was platted to maximize use of the streetcar, and land-use controls were introduced to ensure high-quality building design and construction. Two broad east-west boulevards traversed Shaker Heights and provided a wide median for the streetcar tracks. The remaining streets discouraged through traffic by intersecting with the transit rights of way only every third of a mile. This also allowed for faster streetcar running times by minimizing the number of required transit stops.

Zoning controls and deed restrictions were introduced to ensure that the "exclusive residential character [of the village] is preserved from incursion by commerce." Furthermore, design standards and one of the first design review processes anywhere were instituted to ensure that "each house should be distinct in design and detail from every other house," though only traditional designs were allowed and the size and placement of homes on their parcels were strictly controlled. The codes went so far as to stipulate suitable color schemes for exterior house paint and to control the material used for leading in glasswork.

Apartment complexes and commercial properties were sited at Shaker Square, the confluence of the two streetcar line boulevards. In 1929, the village commons at Shaker Square was completed: a series of low-rise Georgian-style commercial buildings in the form of an octagon, with an interior green space through which the Shaker Rapid Transit ran (Photo 2.7).

From Shaker Square, the community's primary transportation corridors—Shaker Boulevard and South Moreland—branched out into residential enclaves of the community, where stately homes faced green lawns and tree-lined streets. The rapid transit service placed most residents within several blocks of a convenient, reliable, and safe transit connection to downtown Cleveland. By 1930, the population of Shaker Heights had reached nearly 17,800, making it one of Cleveland's largest suburbs at the time.[20]

2.5 TRANSIT VILLAGES: YESTERDAY AND TODAY

The streetcar suburbs of Shaker Heights, Pasadena, and the East Bay and the railroad suburbs of New York all were soon overshadowed by a new kind of suburb in the 1920s, one devoted almost exclusively to automobile access. In each case, the explosive growth in automobile ownership and usage in the 1920s and 1930s served to transform suburbia into

Photo 2.7   Shaker Heights, 1930. The construction of Shaker Square in the 1920s created a town center for Shaker Heights, with Georgian-style commercial buildings encircling a central green space and the rail station. The Shaker Rapid's tracks run in the foreground.

a sprawling landscape where the vast majority of houses were no longer within a 5-min walk of a rail stop. Streetcar suburbs soon gave way to freeway suburbs and exurbs.

In southern California, as early as 1924, the intermixing of automobiles and streetcars on the same city streets often created traffic tie-ups. Two proposals were put forward to solve the traffic mess. The transit proposal called for a series of elevated rail lines and subway tunnels, converging in a downtown terminal, which would grade-separate the Red Cars from automobile traffic. The automobile proposal called for moving full-throttle on new highway investments—a dense network of north-south and east-west boulevards capable of handling three lanes of traffic in each direction.

In 1926, the two proposals were put to the public for a vote, and the automobile-highway alternative won hands down. Funds for highway construction were approved by the electorate while the ballot initiative to fund a new central rail and trolley station was soundly defeated. With this single turn of events, the stage was set for southern California to embark on a path of road expansion that remains unparalleled today. By the 1930s, Los Angeles road-builders had laid more miles of asphalt per capita than any American city. This provided only ephemeral relief, however. Congestion continued to worsen as growth in automobiles outstripped road construction. A 1937 Automobile Club study showed that the time required to reach popular southern California destinations had increased each year over the prior decade. As a remedy, a gargantuan network of grade-separated expressways was proposed to allow southern Californians to travel effortlessly from anywhere to everywhere within the region in the comforts of their own automobiles.[21]

The Los Angeles freeway system was steadily expanded over the postwar era, reaching 500 directional mi in the late 1960s. The massive roadway network, combined with subsidized federal (FHA and VHA) home mortgage loans, prompted hundreds of thousands of southern Californians to flock to the suburbs of the San Fernando Valley, Orange County, and the inland empire of San Bernardino and Riverside Counties in search of the coveted prize: a new detached single-family home. With a cityscape that fanned out in all directions and with older commercial districts built along the Red Car lines beginning to lose customers to large shopping centers, the Red Car's days were clearly numbered. Pasadena gradually transformed from a streetcar suburb to an auto suburb. Patronage on the Pacific Electric system plummeted following World War II, and in 1958, southern California's remaining streetcar link was closed.

Southern California's years without rail services proved to be short-lived. In the 1980s, the Los Angeles region began planning and constructing a 400-mi network of subway, light rail, and commuter rail services, including a line from Pasadena to Los Angeles. Tens of billions of public dollars have been spent or pledged to more or less re-create the privately financed rail network that existed some 70 years earlier. In 1993, the city of Pasadena commissioned several studies and sponsored design charettes to explore the possibility of attracting moderate-density housing and retailers to its new rail stations, particularly the downtown Del Mar station. After a half century of following the path of highway-led development, the city of Pasadena has today opted to redirect future growth to its rail nodes and reestablish a downtown zone focused on rail transit.

In contrast, Shaker Heights has maintained its rail nexus and also its high-quality stock of housing since World War II. When the Shaker Rapid line suffered ridership losses and financial difficulties following World War II, the city of Shaker Heights stepped in to take over the operation. City leaders, supported by prominent citizens and business merchants, saw in the Shaker Rapid not only a valuable transit service but also a distinctive and important historical feature of their suburb. In 1975, the Greater Cleveland Regional Transit Authority assumed operations of the Shaker Rapids. A new station was built, and soon thereafter the system was upgraded to a light rail service. "Taking the Rapid" continues to be a popular form of travel in the eastern suburbs of Cleveland today.

Scarsdale also managed to maintain its rail connection and its village atmosphere. With the construction of express parkways in the 1920s through Westchester County, including the Bronx River Parkway and the Hutchinson River Parkway, Scarsdale was poised to follow an expansion path similar to many other American suburbs. Like most suburbs, growth in Scarsdale during the 1940s and 1950s was fueled by the automobile. Yet, because of an unwaivering local commitment to historical preservation and maintaining a small town atmosphere, along with the draw of New York City itself as a major destination, rail services did not end, as in Los Angeles, with the onslaught of the automobile. Today, Scarsdale remains unabashedly a commuter rail town that is more dispersed than before, but still dependent on the rail link as both a vital transportation service and organizing principle for village development.

In closing, America's railroad suburbs offered advantages that could be fully appreciated only after they had disappeared. With its evenly spaced station stops, reliance on foot access to train stations, and surrounding greenbelts, the railroad suburb was pretty much hemmed in and prevented from spilling into the countryside. This gave it a defined edge and instilled in its residents a sense of place. The natural greenbelts, often still under cultivation as market gardens, became absolutely essential in preserving the streetcar suburbs by delineating village boundaries and creating a visual openness. "Whatever one might say of the social disadvantages," Lewis Mumford wrote, "this was in many ways an idyllic physical environment. But it lasted less than a generation."[22]

With the dawning of a new century before us, a number of communities in metropolitan areas that were the foci of this chapter—Los Angeles, San Francisco-Oakland, New York, and Cleveland—have once again embraced the idea of a transit village. The lessons of history are as important as ever as we look ahead. As to the challenges of this enterprise, we turn to Parts Two and Three of this book.

NOTES

1. Kenneth Jackson, *Crabgrass Frontier: The Suburbanization of the United States* (New York: Oxford University Press, 1985), p. 95.
2. Ibid., pp. 94–102.
3. Ibid., p. 102.
4. Robert A. M. Stern, *The Anglo American Suburb* (London: Architectural Design, 1981). Writing in 1979, at a time of periodic concern about the enormous inner-city wastelands like the South Bronx, Stern even posits the railroad suburb as a model for redevelopment. America needs to reject the traditional urban high-rise designs in lower income communities, Stern argues. It needs to raze the high-density inner-city housing and replace it with a railroad suburb design: moderate-density, widespread home ownership, residences within walking distance of convenient public transportation to speed around the region.
5. Susan Swanson and Elizabeth Green Fuller, *Westchester County: A Pictorial History* (Norfolk, VA: Donning Co., 1982), pp. 11–13.

6. The Hudson River Railroad reaches Peekskill in 1849, with trains running daily to New York, as indicated in this announcement in a Westchester newspaper:

New York to Peekskill—42 miles in 59 minutes. The Road is now fully tested, and found to be in prime running order; and daily the iron horse whirs to and fro along the track between these points, and causing the valleys to re-echo with his shrill whistle for miles along his path. The cars to be placed upon this Road, are of the most superb finish and comfort, and the engines are of unsurpassed speed and power; and everything in connection with it tends to render it superior in fitness and facility of travel to any road in the country, and we doubt not the patronage of the Road will be immense.

"Hufeland Scrapbooks," courtesy of the Westchester County Historical Society. Ibid., p. 71.

7. Ibid., p. 53.

8. Carol A. O'Connor, *A Sort of Utopia: Scarsdale 1891–1981* (Albany: State University of New York Press, 1983).

9. Harry Hansen, *Scarsdale: From Colonial Manor to Modern Community* (New York: Harper & Brothers, 1954), p. 2.

10. Lewis Mumford, *The City in History: Its Origins, Its Transformations, and Its Prospects* (New York: Harcourt, Brace & World, 1961), p. 504.

11. Spencer Crump, *Ride the Big Red Cars* (Los Angeles: Crest Publications, 1962).

12. Ibid., p. 44.

13. Robert Fogelson, *The Fragmented Metropolis: 1850–1930* (Cambridge, MA: Harvard University Press, 1967).

14. Robert Fishman, *Bourgeois Utopias: The Rise and Fall of Suburbia* (New York: Basic Books, 1987), pp. 155–156.

15. Charles Seims, *Trolley Days in Pasadena* (San Marino, CA: Golden West Books, 1982), p. 15.

16. Ibid., p. 24.

17. Harre Demoro, *The Key Route* (Glendale, CA: Interurban Press, 1985), p. 20.

18. Dallas Walker Smythe, *An Economic History of Local and Interurban Transportation in the East Bay Cities* (PhD Thesis in Economics, University of California, Berkeley, May 1939).

19. Maria Lombardo and Tom Wieczorek, Historical Overview of the Key Route Transit System (unpublished paper, University of California, Berkeley, 1993).

20. James Toman, *The Shaker Heights Rapid Transit* (Glendale, CA: Interurban Press, 1990).

21. Fishman, op. cit., p. 58.

22. Mumford, op. cit., p. 504.

PART TWO

The Case for Transit Villages

Transit villages have been criticized by some commentators as "boutique" planning and design—nice to look at, but not terribly important. Such critiques fall into a larger argument that the connections between transportation and land use are today too weak to matter. Skeptics contend that because urban areas in the United States are already so accessible, settlement patterns are so well-established, and people are more concerned with quality of schools and security when choosing neighborhoods in which to live than proximity to workplaces, transportation plays an ever-decreasing role in locational decisions.

We disagree. Creating attractive and functional communities that are physically linked to transit stations throughout a region can produce important societal benefits. In this light, Part Two of the book aims to make a case for America's budding transit village movement.

Chapter 3 argues that transit villages deserve serious attention because they can contribute to the attainment of important public policy objectives, such as improving air quality, relieving traffic congestion, and rejuvenating inner-city neighborhoods. The chapter examines social, political, and economic factors that have been behind the rise and fall of America's transit industry over the past 100 years. The recent renaissance in rail transit in the United States is investigated in terms of the opportunities and liabilities presented for transit village development.

Chapters 4 and 5 describe the physical and design characteristics of transit villages and their implications for mobility and sustainability. Three dimensions of transit villages—density, diversity, and design—are related to travel characteristics of residents, workers, and shoppers. The results of various empirical studies, including our own, that shed light on these relationships are presented. In view of the many pressing public policy issues discussed in Chapter 3, Chapters 4 and 5 aim to demonstrate that transit villages hold considerable promise for luring Americans out of their cars and into trains and buses.

Chapter 6 probes whether transit villages yield private-sector benefits as well. The chapter demonstrates that there is a small but rapidly emerging niche market for transit village living, working, and shopping. This is reflected by higher rents, higher occupancy levels, and more rapid space absorption for buildings in well-planned neighborhoods that are near rail stops. Our work suggests, moreover, that increasing numbers of Americans are seeking homes in attractive neighborhoods near transit stations in order to economize on travel, to ease their commutes, and sometimes to reduce or eliminate the need to own a second or third car.

The case for transit villages rests on demonstrating that numerous stakeholders—public authorities and other safekeepers of the public interest, as well as individuals and private interests—have something to gain from seeing more transit villages take form. How to build a united front among vested interests and move toward implementation are addressed in Parts Three and Four of the book.

┌─────────┐
│ **3** │
└─────────┘

Transit Villages and Public Policy

3.1 SETTING A POLICY CONTEXT

Over the past century, America's transit industry has been on a roller-coaster ride. From modest beginnings around the turn of the century when motorized transport was still in its infancy, to the heights of World War II when the average American rode transit 166 times annually (versus just 32 times today), to the depths of the early 1970s when U.S. transit ridership fell to a 70-year low, to today's rail renaissance, America's transit industry has had its ups and downs. Historically, episodic events and national upheavals, like the Great Depression, World War II, and the oil embargoes of the 1970s, have exerted powerful influences on transit ridership. More insidious but just as influential, however, have been the growing popularity and, what some environmentalists charge, the growing underpricing of transit's chief competitor, the private automobile. And as transportation has come to be viewed under a wider lens, not only in terms of mobility but with respect to issues like air quality, energy conservation, and social justice as well, the attention and political support given to transit have ebbed and flowed.

This chapter sets a policy context for evaluating the prospects for transit villages in the United States, framed around a retrospective look at how the transit industry itself has evolved, and an examination of contemporary policy issues and themes tied to urban mass transit. It closes with a discussion of the renaissance in rail construction over the past decade, trends in ridership and performance, and the implications of expanding rail transit services on the transit village movement.

3.2 RISE AND FALL OF STREETCAR AMERICA

The history of urbanization in the early part of the 20th century is very much the history of electric streetcar development. As discussed in Chapter 2, the extension of electric streetcar lines to suburbia around the turn of the century led to mass decentralization and the emergence of streetcar suburbs outside of New York, Los Angeles, and many other cities. Prior to this, America's urban centers were very dense, with factories, shops, and households tightly packed together. Most Americans had to live and work nearby because the only way to get around was by foot, bicycle, or horsecar. The compact settlement patterns of the day reflected the need to minimize travel. Pre-1900 cities were also extremely polluted, overcrowded, and regarded by most social commentators of the time as oppressive environs. Soon after the nation's first electric trolley line opened in Richmond, Virginia, in 1887, streetcars were heralded by many as a long-awaited savior, allowing middle-class Americans to flee decaying central cities for the suburbs. The tripling of average travel speeds (to over 15 mi/h) relative to horsedrawn carts brought a large band of open space into commuting range, fueling the suburbanization of residences and eventually shops, stores, and factories.

By 1900, 2107 mi of electric trolley track was in place in American cities. This number jumped to more than 15,500 mi by 1916.[1] Streetcar expansion mirrored the country's explosive growth in urban population, propelled by the industrial revolution and mass in-migration. By 1920, the total population of U.S. cities with 10,000 or more inhabitants reached 45 million, one-half the national total and more than four times what it had been four decades earlier. As the nation emerged victorious from the World War I and headed into the Roaring '20s, transit had become a prominent fixture in most American cities. Over 15 billion transit trips were made in 1920 compared to 600 million in 1880. One study estimated that as much as a quarter of the U.S. population resided at the time in urban or suburban areas whose settlement patterns were shaped by the electric streetcar.[2] Trolley lines not only defined the radial spines of large east-coast and west-coast metropolises, giving them a distinct, star-shaped settlement pattern, but also for the first time allowed for the physical separation of home and work—that is, with streetcars came the rhythmic cycle of daily commuting.

As discussed in Chapter 2, real estate syndicates built most of America's early electric streetcar lines. Trolleys and real estate projects were often bundled together. Transit itself was usually a loss leader that allowed huge windfall profits from land sales. Many rail lines were overextended in pursuit of speculative profits, leaving streetcar operators with huge debt loads and unprofitable services. Frequently, public utilities companies acquired streetcar systems from real estate syndicates in the 1910s and 1920s, seeking to monopolize the market for electricity sales. These electric traction companies, however, were often forced by local authorities to extend lines to sparsely populated areas that could not support transit and to charge low fares, often a nickel. Many were unable to withstand the economic pressures brought on by the Great Depression and antitrust rulings that forced public utilities to divest themselves of streetcar holdings. From 1929 to 1934, streetcar operations folded in some 250 U.S. cities.[3]

A conspiracy theory is often advanced in explaining transit's falling fortunes. This theory contends that automobile manufacturers and petroleum companies formed holding companies (e.g., National City Lines, owned by General Motors and Firestone, Inc.) in the 1920s and 1930s which proceeded to buy financially strapped trolley systems, remove trackage from streetbeds, and replace services with motorized buses, mainly in the interest of eliminating competition and promoting gasoline-propelled transportation. While there might be some degree of truth to this theory, many economists contend that Detroit's automobile manufacturers were simply responding to market demand for private automobile travel brought on by America's rising affluence and lifestyle preferences for single-family home living.[4]

Historian Robert Fishman suggests that both forces, monopolistic motives by corporate America and the middle class's utopian lifestyle preferences, had a hand in transit's decline during the first half of this century. In tracing Los Angeles's evolution, Fishman observes that: "To open the region for suburban development, the city created the world's largest mass transit system. When in the 1920s that system appeared to threaten the viability of the single family house, it was ruthlessly sacrificed and a massive automobile system put in its place."[5] Fishman contends that the compact growth wrought by streetcar investments became increasingly perceived by Los Angelenos as a threat to the utopian ideal of single-family home living. While in 1910 no one dared advertise a home that wasn't within an easy walk of a train depot, by the 1920s no one dared offer one that didn't have a garage and easy road access.

With competition from the automobile, transit ridership in the United States began to fall after the late 1920s, with the exception of a surge during World War II (due to wartime rationing of fuel and tires and a shift from domestic to military production). Over time, Americans were also changing their pattern of transit usage, relying on it mainly for commute trips and less for everyday needs such as shopping, recreation, and weekend outings (using their cars instead for these purposes). The resulting peaks in transit ridership dealt a severe blow to transit's profitability. Transit cars, and the increasingly expensive labor needed to run them, were fully used during commute hours only; the rest of the week they remained underutilized and unprofitable.

Following World War II, transit ridership tumbled throughout the United States, even more precipitously than before the war. From a peak of nearly 24 billion riders in 1945, ridership plummeted to 11 billion 10 years later. The shift to a domestic economy and pent-up consumer demand after years of rationing lead to a postwar boom in the sale of automobiles and single-family homes. Federally subsidized mortgages, cheap land in the suburbs, and Congress's passage of the 1956 interstate highway program, the most expensive public works project ever, had largely sealed the fate of mass transit. By the late 1950s and early 1960s, America's transit industry, which was still largely privately owned and operated, was on the verge of collapse. Transit was caught in a vicious cycle of plummeting ridership, which induced service cuts, chased more riders away, and forced even deeper cuts.

3.3   GOVERNMENT'S RESURRECTION OF MASS TRANSIT

At the insistence of big-city mayors who were too cash-strapped to buy failing transit companies and who feared absolute pandemonium if their transit services ceased, Washington had little choice but to enter the picture in the 1960s. In 1961, the Kennedy administration provided a modest amount of capital support for transit fleet expansion and modernization. However, it was the passage of the Urban Mass Transportation Act of 1964 under the Johnson administration that provided the first-ever sustained source of capital assistance. This landmark legislation would disburse $3.3 billion in federal grants over 10 years to help municipalities purchase transit systems, replace aging fleets, and build and equip new rapid transit systems. In 1950, only 28 percent of mass transit services in the United States were provided by publicly owned and operated firms; by 1970, this figure jumped to 70 percent.

During this period of an expanding federal role in mass transit, a grass-roots environmental movement was beginning to surface that called for a reappraisal of America's auto-oriented transportation system and its attendant social and environmental costs. San Francisco's freeway revolt of 1959 saw the city's board of supervisors withdraw support for new freeway construction because freeways would require excessive "demolition of homes, destruction of residential areas, and the forced uprooting and relocation of individuals, families, and businesses."[6] Similar revolts soon followed in Boston, Toronto, and a dozen or so other North American cities.

By the early 1970s, urban riots had called national attention to the plight of the urban poor, the OPEC oil embargo exposed America's vulnerability to foreign control of petroleum supplies, and defining events like Earth Day had brought environmental concerns to the forefront of the national policy agenda. Republicans and Democrats alike rallied behind transit. In fact, to the surprise of many, the Nixon administration proved to be one of transit's staunchest advocates, spearheading the passage of the Urban Mass Transportation Assistance Act of 1970, which provided $10 billion over 12 years for new system construction. Even the American Road Builder Association backed this legislation and Secretary of Transportation John A. Volpe, formerly a highway builder, gave his blessing. Alan Altshuler credits transit's popularity at the time to the fact that transit proved to be a policy for all perspectives on urban problems:

> Though its direct constituency was relatively small, its ideological appeal proved to be extremely broad. Whether one's concern was the economic vitality of cities, protecting the environment, stopping highways, energy conservation, assisting the elderly and handicapped and poor, or simply getting other people off the road so as to be able to drive faster, transit was a policy that could be embraced. This is not to say that transit was an effective way of serving all these objectives, simply that it was widely believed to be so . . . Thus the Nixon administration, while striving to distance itself from the big city, pro-black, welfare state image of the Johnson administration in domestic affairs, felt comfortable promoting sharp increases in mass transit spending . . . Transit turned out, in short, to be an ideal centerpiece for urban policy of a conservative administration.[7]

By 1970, transit's annual operating deficit had reached the $300 million mark, a sizable sum considering that the industry had been largely self-sufficient just 4 years earlier. Many local treasuries were beginning to feel the weight of this new financial burden, so for pro-transit interests, the creation of a federal transit operating assistance program was the next logical step. A confluence of events led to Washington's eventual capitulation to subsidize local transit operations. The Arab oil embargo of 1973–1974, the Watergate scandal and Nixon's subsequent resignation, New York City's financial crisis, and growing signs of defeat in Vietnam provided a context where newly inaugurated President Gerald Ford needed to mount new domestic programs that demonstrated his administration's leadership in difficult times. Barely a week after Ford's confirmation, a delegation of 14 big-city mayors met with the president and, after hard-fought negotiations, won his support for transit operating aid, culminating in the passage of a 1974 act that provided $11.8 billion in both transit capital and operating assistance through 1980. Throughout the remainder of the 1970s, the transit industry found a receptive and supportive political climate in Washington.

As the '70s came to a close, federal dollars seemed to be providing very little in the way of tangible dividends, however. Though operating assistance had almost doubled from $3.45 billion to $6.32 billion between 1975 and 1980, ridership (ignoring transfers) was moving at a snail's pace, increasing just 13 percent—from 5.65 billion to 6.36 billion—during the same period. Most of the aid, research showed, was dissipated by inflation, rising wage levels, and diminishing productivity.[8] Between 1960 and 1980, transit operating expenses per seat mile went up 55 percent in constant (inflation-adjusted) dollars; higher wages accounted for three-quarters of this increase, and higher factor prices (e.g., fuel) and lower productivity accounted for much of the remainder.[9] As critics of transit subsidies had feared, operating assistance was not spurring ridership increases, but instead was insulating local operators from escalating costs and productivity declines.

The Reagan administration was elected partly on a mandate to slash federal spending and divest Washington's involvement in local affairs. Mass transit support was one of the first federal programs earmarked for elimination. Federal operating aid decreased by 25 percent during the 1980s, totaling just over $3 billion in 1990. However, state and local governments made up most of the difference, increasing their support from $2.6 billion in 1980 to $8.3 billion in 1990. Shifting more of transit's financial responsibility to the local and state levels, however, along with other Reagan initiatives like promoting competition through private-sector contracting, failed to produce big changes. Although nationwide transit ridership increased modestly in the 1980s, from 8.5 billion passengers in 1980 to 8.8 billion in 1990, transit's market share of commute trips fell from 6.2 percent in 1980 to 5.1 percent in 1990.[10] By comparison, vehicle miles of urban automobile travel increased 43 percent during the 1980s, and the share of commute trips by solo drivers rose from 64.4 percent to 73.2 percent.[11]

There are at least three key reasons why transit has lost ground in recent times to the private automobile. One is spatial. Decentralized growth, especially the rapid exodus of jobs to the suburbs in the 1980s, has diluted transit's ridership base. Environments with trip origins and destinations thinly spread in all directions are environments where few people patronize transit. In 1990, less than 2 percent of all commute trips that began and ended in a U.S. suburb were by mass transit. In greater Detroit, San Antonio, Austin, Memphis, and El Paso, transit carried less than 0.5 percent of suburban residents heading to suburban jobs. Second, transit has increasingly found itself at an economic disadvantage. Between 1980 and 1990, the average cost per mile of driving a car fell by 45 percent; this was because of lower gasoline prices (down 35 percent in real terms) and higher fleet-average fuel efficiency (up 19 percent). Over the same period, however, average transit fares in the United States kept up with inflation, in large part because of federal withdrawal of operating support. Lastly, powerful demographic shifts have increased automobile ownership and driving. Foremost has been the movement of baby-boomers into midlife, a time when their disposable incomes and amount of travel are usually at their highest. Additionally, transit has lost market share due to the rapid growth in working women (from 32 percent of the work force in 1960 to 45 percent in 1990). Women tend to rely more than men on cars because they make more linked trips, such as between work, a child-care center, a grocery store, and home, trips for which there are few viable options to the private automobile.

Despite these trends, transit has enjoyed a resurgence of popularity in the 1990s. This is partly because of two landmark pieces of federal legislation: the 1990 Clean Air Act Amendments (CAAA) and the 1991 Intermodal Surface Transportation Efficiency Act (ISTEA). The CAAA promotes improved transit services as 1 of 16 transportation control measures for metropolitan areas that are in violation of national clean air standards.[12] And by promoting more balanced, multimodal transportation programs and by emphasizing integrated land use and transportation planning as well as attention to the social, economic, and environmental (SEE) impacts of investment decisions, ISTEA has provided a newly found legitimacy for mass transit. ISTEA's set-aside of $6 billion in Congestion Management and Air Quality (CMAQ) funds has further promoted transit improvements in large cities that violate clean air standards. Overall, ISTEA authorizes unprecedented levels of funding support for transit, giving states and localities the ability to spend upward of half of the bill's 7-year $151 billion authorization on transit, though to date most flexible funds have gone to highways and not to transit.[13]

3.4 CONTEMPORARY POLICY CONCERNS AND MASS TRANSIT

Continuing financial and political support for mass transit is rooted in many of the pressing urban policy dilemmas we face in the United States. Although the detractors of mass transit, especially those of rail systems, are many and vocal, they are often outnumbered (and sometimes "outshouted") by transit's supporters. Reasons for backing transit vary widely, but draw largely upon growing concerns over the sustainability—environmentally, economically, and socially—of a highly automobile-dependent society. This section reviews some of the escalating policy concerns that are behind the continuing support of mass transit in the United States.

3.4.1 Traffic Congestion

Rapid increases in automobile travel coupled with limited road expansion have brought unprecedented levels of traffic congestion in recent years, especially in the suburbs. During the 1980s and for the 39 largest U.S. metropolises, the number of lane-miles of expressways and major arterials combined increased just 13.7 percent, but vehicle miles driven rose 31.4 percent.[14] Community opposition, environmental concerns, building moratoria, and funding shortages all contributed to the slowdown in new highway construction, while suburbanization, rising incomes, and increases in working women helped fuel automobile travel. With the growth in auto trips outpacing the growth in road capacity, traffic delays rose sharply, by 57 percent from 1985 to 1988 according to one estimate.[15] Public opinion polls in cities like San Francisco, Houston, Phoenix, and Washington, DC, confirmed these studies, citing traffic congestion as the number one local problem during the mid-1980s to early 1990s, eclipsed only by problems of unemployment and crime in more recent years.

Today, some of the worst traffic congestion anywhere is in America's suburbs. With trip origins and destinations thinly spread in all directions, commuting patterns have become increasingly complex and random, similar to "thousands of pick-up sticks dropped on the floor—trips flow from everywhere to everywhere."[16] Suburban gridlock is partly a result of the mismatch between the geometry of traditional highway networks (hub-and-spoke) and the geography of commuting (increasingly lateral and cross-county in direction). Outlying freeway corridors designed for moderate volumes of suburbanites heading to the central city have been swamped as a consequence.

The social costs of traffic congestion are difficult to measure, though they can be significant, including wasted time and energy, added pollution, increased accidents, a reduction in economic productivity, and a growing perception that the overall quality of life is slipping. Some estimates place the social costs of highway congestion in the United States at $73 billion per year, or 2 percent of the GNP.[17] A study by the Texas Transportation Institute estimates that congestion costs each driver $375 annually (in 1990 dollars) in extra fuel and maintenance expenses.[18] What is particularly annoying about traffic congestion today is its unpredictability. Knowing when and where one might get stuck in traffic is increasingly a guessing game.

Transit is one of many possible alternatives to road expansion for staving off traffic congestion. Because of budgetary constraints and environmental opposition, the days of inner-city superfreeways are rapidly coming to an end. Los Angeles's recently opened Century Freeway, a 17-mi stretch that cost $3 billion and displaced 3700 households, has been dubbed "the last urban freeway."[19] Over time, highway departments have learned that you cannot build your way out of congestion. New roads usually provide only ephemeral relief. All too often, new capacity unleashes new demand, what transportation planners call *induced demand*. Opening new freeway lanes generally results in people switching routes or modes (e.g., from buses to cars) to take advantage of better flowing traffic. In a short time, the road is filled to capacity again. Anthony Downs has called this the "law of peak-hour expressway congestion."[20] He and others maintain that managing traffic demand—shifting traffic by time, mode, and space—deserves at least equal attention in the war on traffic congestion as supply-side initiatives, such as road expansion. Good quality transit services can induce modal shifts, and concentrated development around transit nodes can induce spatial shifts in travel. In this sense, one could argue, transit village development is a form of transportation demand management.

3.4.2 Air Quality

There is probably no other issue today that is driving transportation policy making as much as concerns over air quality. Photochemical smog remains a serious problem in more than 100 U.S. cities, with the worst conditions in California and industrial areas of the northeast. At extreme levels, smog can impair visibility, damage crops, dirty buildings, and most troubling, threaten human health. In response to the Clean Air Act Amendments of 1990, many "nonattainment" areas in violation of national clean air standards, most notably greater Los Angeles (which exceeded clean air standards 183 days in 1992), have introduced far-reaching programs that require large companies to substantially reduce single-occupant automobile trips made by their workers. Mandatory trip reduction requirements, like southern California's Regulation XV, have forced large companies to subsidize vanpools, provide transit vouchers, and incur other costs in hopes of reducing solo commuting.[21] Regulatory requirements have also been imposed on the automobile industry. Most contentious is California's Zero Emissions Vehicle (ZEV) requirement that stipulates 10 percent of all new motor vehicles sold in the state must be nonpolluting (e.g., battery operated) by the year 2003.

In America, air pollution is largely a product of an auto-dependent society. Around 40 percent of manmade hydrocarbon and nitrogen oxide emissions, two of the chief precursors to the formation of photochemical smog, and two-thirds of carbon monoxide emissions come from the tailpipes of cars. From a health standpoint, some research suggests that the most serious damage comes from small particulate matter (PM-10), a byproduct of vehicle attrition (e.g., wear of tires) and road dust.[22] Nationwide, the damage costs attributable to auto-related air pollution have been placed at around $10 billion annually.[23] Despite much cleaner automobiles (1993 cars emitted 80 percent less pollution than the typical 1970 model) and trip reduction mandates, air quality in many urban areas has improved little, and in some places it has deteriorated. This is because these measures have largely been swamped by the growth in vehicle population and miles driven, especially in slow-moving traffic.

The value of transit in reducing air pollution has long been a source of contention. Some have argued that half-empty diesel buses and the construction emissions from building lightly used rail systems have hurt air quality in many cities. This has not deterred Washington from actively promoting transit as a palliative to air pollution in clean air legislation and the 1991 surface transportation act (ISTEA). Nor has it quieted the American Public Transit Association (APTA) from touting the air quality virtues of transit when testifying before Congress, such as the contention that over the past three decades transit riders have prevented the emissions of 1.6 million tons of hydrocarbons and 10 million tons of carbon monoxide into urban air basins.[24]

3.4.3 Other Environmental Concerns

Automobiles are also major contributors to the production of greenhouse gases. Some scientists predict that increased levels of greenhouse gases, such as carbon dioxide and methane, in the earth's atmosphere will eventually induce changes in precipitation, ocean currents, and seasonal weather patterns and cause crop damage, rising sea levels, and possibly the extinction of plant and animal species.[25] Currently, automobiles and trucks are the two largest sources of carbon dioxide emissions in the United States, responsible for 20 percent of the total emissions.

Environmentalists often attribute other costs to the automobile and the spread-out cities it has helped create. Roadways and parking lots consume over 30 percent of developed land in most U.S. cities and as much as 70 percent of downtown surface areas. In 1988, the United States averaged 82 ft of roadway per capita compared to about half this amount in western Europe.[26] Other external costs that have been associated with automobile dependence include premature loss of open space and wetlands (from auto-induced sprawl), oil spill damage to the environment, water pollution from drainage of automobile fluids and road salt, and scarring the landscape from scrapping vehicles and tires.[27] Additionally, noise from roaring engines, screeching tires, blaring horns, and road construction is increasingly objectionable to many city dwellers. Although sound walls help attenuate noise pollution (at the expense of visual obstructions), depressed property values near busy highways remind us that no road can be made totally soundproof. One estimate puts the noise damage to residential properties from car and trucks at about $9 billion (in 1989 dollars) per year.[28]

3.4.4 Energy Conservation

Although the horrors of hour-long queues at gasoline stations have become a distant memory for most Americans, we remain a society highly dependent on imported oil and finite supplies of fossil fuels. Currently, transportation accounts for around three-quarters of the petroleum used in the United States, and about two-thirds of this amount is burned by motor vehicles. Since 1975, transportation demands for oil have exceeded domestic production, making the nation dependent on foreign sources for imports (40 percent of consumption in 1993) and therefore vulnerable to disruptions in flows.[29]

Although automobiles are far more fuel efficient today than ever before, as in the case of air quality, these gains have been offset by ever-increasing traffic volumes and lengthening trips. In the United States, annual energy consumption in the transportation sector increased 2.6 percent per year between 1983 and 1989. In their book, *Cities and Automobile Dependence,* Peter Newman and Jeff Kenworthy have estimated that sprawling, heavily auto-oriented cities like Houston and Phoenix average around five times as much fuel consumption per capita as comparably sized and equally affluent, but much more compact, European capitals like Stockholm and Copenhagen.

Transit villages could conserve energy in two ways. One, more compact development, in theory, should shorten trip lengths. And two, conversion of some motorized trips to mass transit should cut down on per capita consumption. In 1989, the average commute trip by private automobile consumed 7246 BTUs per passenger mile, whereas commuters on rail transit consumed 1790 BTUs per passenger mile.[30] Moreover, in addition to moving more people with less energy, rail transit normally uses nonpetroleum energy sources for electrical power generation, thereby reducing the nation's dependence on foreign imports. Critics claim, however, that when the energy expenditures of constructing rail systems are counted, rail investments are net energy losers. One study estimated that, because of the high energy outlays in building the transbay tube, San Francisco's BART uses 3.6 percent more energy annually than would an exclusive busway along the Bay Bridge.[31] Clearly, unless trains attract large numbers of former motorists, the energy conservation benefits of new subways will be highly suspect.

3.4.5 Social Equity

Perhaps the most pernicious and troubling effects of an increasingly auto-dependent society are the social injustices that result from physically and socially isolating significant segments of society. Those who are too poor, disabled, young, or old to own or drive a car are effectively left out of many of society's offerings. For the inner-city poor, this means isolation from job opportunities. For older Americans, it can mean loneliness and inadequate attention to medical needs. While America might be able to reengineer the car and better manage traffic flows to solve air pollution, energy, and congestion problems, nothing can be done to the car or road system to reduce the social isolation and inequalities in access to jobs, clinics, and shops that many people experience.

In his book, *New Visions for Metropolitan America,* Anthony Downs blames low-density and class-segregated growth, made possible by the automobile, for creating deep divisions in American society by physically and socioeconomically isolating blacks, Hispanics, and recent immigrants.[32] He warns that unless there is a collective wake-up call to bring about significant social change, all Americans will eventually suffer the social costs of continuing to isolate a significant segment of society in inner-city ghettos, in the form of rising crime, drug abuse, births out of wedlock, fatherless households, and gang warfare. Douglas Massey and Nancy Denton have equated the systematic segregation of African Americans to *American Apartheid,* the title of their recent book, concluding that isolated ghetto conditions stimulate the antisocial behavior that middle-class Americans deplore.[33]

Sociologists have labeled the effects of physical isolation on the economic well-being of the inner-city poor as the *spatial mismatch problem.* This view holds that inner-city joblessness and intergenerational poverty are rooted in the physical separation of the urban poor, and in particular young black males, from the expanding job opportunities in the suburbs. Today, two out of every three jobs in large metropolitan areas are being created in the suburbs. A study of commuting in Philadelphia, Chicago, and Los Angeles found that unequal accessibility to jobs explained nearly half of the difference in employment rates between black and white teenagers.[34] Besides poor transit alternatives, the study suggested black youths lacked information about jobs farther away and were not inclined to seek jobs in "unfamiliar areas."

Mark Alan Hughes of Princeton University has suggested three policy strategies for mitigating the spatial mismatch problem.[35] One would be to bring more jobs and private capital to inner-cities through various incentives, such as corporate tax breaks and property tax abatements. Another would be to open up the suburban housing market to inner-city (largely minority) residents by targeting apartment construction in these areas and by eliminating frictions to residential mobility, like housing discrimination, exclusionary (large-lot) zoning, and "racial steering" (wherein real estate brokers limit neighborhoods where minorities are shown available housing). Hughes and others hold the most promise, at least in the near term, to the third option: improving "reverse-commute" transit connections from central cities to suburban job sites. Following the McCone Commission report in the wake of the Watts (Los Angeles) riots of 1965, federally funded reverse-commute bus services were initiated in 14 cities between 1966 and 1970. Most services were community based, operated by neighborhood churches and advocacy groups. Studies found high attrition rates among participants.[36] Only 18 percent of the several hundred original participants of a nonprofit van program that ferried Washington, DC, residents to jobs in Fairfax County, Virginia, were with the program 1 year later. Critics charged that these "poverty transportation programs" overestimated the willingness of inner-city poor to endure lengthy commutes to unfamiliar (and sometimes uncomfortable) territories for low-paying, dead-end service jobs. On closer inspection, however, it was found that the reason many quit riding vans was that once they had enough income, people bought their own cars and began commuting to work, just as most Americans, and sometimes to different and better jobs. Some became entrepreneurial, forming reverse-commute carpools for other inner-city residents for a modest fee. Thus, while these programs might not have been successful from a mass transportation ridership standpoint, in terms of their ultimate goals of helping poor people land jobs, they appear to have had a moderate degree of success.

More recently, public transportation authorities have gotten into the business of running reverse-commute services in greater Philadelphia, Los Angeles, Milwaukee, St. Louis, and other U.S. cities. The Southeastern Pennsylvania Transportation Authority's (SEPTA) 200 series bus routes, for instance, directly connect inner-city neighborhoods to office and industrial parks in suburban Montgomery County. In most rail-served inner-city neighborhoods, small SEPTA vans shuttle residents to the closest train station during the day, providing access to employment, educational, and cultural destinations throughout the region.

Perhaps the most encouraging initiative in recent times to rejuvenate poor transit-served neighborhoods and make them more accessible is FTA's Livable Communities program. Many Livable Communities demonstration projects emphasize economic revitalization and land-use initiatives that bring people back to urban centers and strengthen community-based transportation services. The fusion of transit-oriented development and community rebuilding can be found in such projects as Baltimore's Reistertown Metro Station enhancement that will site a large child-care center on an underutilized parking lot; construction of new housing, retail shops, and pedestrian walkways near the 35th Street Station on Chicago's Green Line; and the rehabilitation of the Windemere Station in East Cleveland to incorporate a Head Start educational facility.

3.4.6 Quality of Life

Perhaps the least articulated but most deeply felt gut-level reason why many Americans support mass transit is the growing and unsettling feeling that something is seriously amiss in suburbia. After decades of fleeing to the suburbs to get away from problems of the central city, many now feel that the city's problems have also migrated to the suburbs, and as a consequence, their suburban quality of life is rapidly eroding. In large part, a perceived declining quality of life is a catchall for the collective costs of a heavily auto-dependent society as already defined (e.g., congestion, pollution, and faceless sprawl).

In a sign of the times, a *Newsweek* cover story in May 1995 carried the banner "Bye-Bye Suburban Dream: 15 Ways to Fix the Suburbs," posing the question: How can we bring civility back to suburban life? Many of the "fixes" were culled from the manifesto of a growing city design movement called The New Urbanism and involve such actions as narrowing the width of streets, mixing housing types, and improving mass transit services. The Bank of America, California's mightiest financial institution, recently joined several environmental groups in releasing a report, *Beyond Sprawl: New Patterns of Growth to Fit the New California,* that passionately calls for an end to scattershot, unplanned development.[37] Since the Bank of America helped finance and indeed profited from sprawling postwar patterns of growth, this about-face appeal caught the attention of many. Though short on concrete suggestions, the report encourages infill over speculative, leapfrog development and calls for forging new political alliances between local officials, business leaders, developers, and environmentalists to support orderly growth. Ken Orski notes that: "Without the bank's name on it, the report likely would have passed largely unnoticed, dismissed as just another conservationist manifesto. But, because of Bank of America's pre-eminent position in the mortgage field and its close ties to developers and the home building industry, its ringing condemnation of current development patterns cannot be easily ignored."[38]

3.5   THE REBIRTH OF RAIL IN THE UNITED STATES

Partly in response to concerns over traffic congestion, air quality, energy dependence, and social inequities, a number of U.S. cities have sought to bolster mass transit in recent times by building new rail systems or extending existing ones. Rightly or wrongly, America is in the midst of a rail renaissance.

3.5.1   Light Rail Transit

Light rail transit (LRT) is essentially a modern-day version of turn-of-the-century electric streetcars. Light rail's growing popularity can be attributed, in part, to the fact that it adapts nicely to existing cityscapes. Among its advantages are: light rail is relatively quiet, thus environmentally less obtrusive; it is electrically propelled, thus less dependent than buses on the availability of petrochemical fuels; it can operate effectively along available railroad rights of way and street medians and is thus far cheaper, less disruptive, and easier to build than heavy rail; and it can be developed incrementally, a few miles at a time, eliminating the need for the long lead times associated with heavy rail construction. LRT's lack of exhaust fumes and its comparatively slow speeds make it particularly compatible with pedestrian settings like downtown malls. G. B. Arrington, head of planning for Portland, Oregon's Tri-Met transit agency, has touted the following virtues of his city's MAX light rail system:

> Light rail operates at the surface and offers visibility. Store fronts become billboards for passengers. Light rail penetrates the community and is not separated from it like heavy rail, which is down in a hole or up in the air. Light rail is part of the urban experience—an amenity, a signature for the area. You can put light rail right into the middle of the action. At Pioneer Place you walk across the platform into the front door. It's the most convenient way to arrive. At Portland's Saturday Market, a weekly street fair attended by thousands, the festival literally surrounds the train; it's part of the experience; it's the way to get there.[39]

Though it sometimes operates in mixed-traffic settings, LRT is also considered safer than heavy rail because electricity comes from an overhead wire instead of a middle third rail. There is thus no need to fence in the track, not only saving costs but also allowing LRT cars to mix with traffic on city streets.

While early proponents of LRT contended that it would be cheaper to build and operate than heavy rail, some constructions costs for light rail systems with grade-separated tracks have proven to be comparable, most notably the $36.6 million per route mile spent on Los Angeles's Blue Line. Still, in an era of escalating construction costs, LRT generally offers the promise of affordable rail technology to many aspiring cities that could not muster sufficient resources to build full-fledged heavy rail systems. Medium-sized cities with fairly low densities, like Sacramento, have managed to build LRT for as low as $10 million per route mile; in Sacramento's case, costs were slashed by sharing a freight railroad right of way, building no-frills side-platform stations, and relying predominantly on single-track services.

Currently, 20 U.S. and Canadian cities have light rail lines (excluding tourist trolleys and downtown circulators in Dallas, Detroit, Fort Worth, Galveston, and Seattle)[40] (Table 3.1). Of these 20, 7 LRT cities are in the process of constructing new extensions, and 18 of the 20 (Calgary and Philadelphia being the only exceptions) are either designing or planning extensions. In addition, at least 12 cities currently without light rail are in some state of planning or designing new systems. All together, 32 mostly medium-sized cities across the United States and Canada either now have or are planning light rail lines, with new possibilities continually surfacing.

Until the late 1970s, there were around 190 track mi of LRT in the United States and Canada (Figure 3.1). Edmonton's 1978 opening of a 4.5-mi northeast line marked the first introduction of a modern-day version of a streetcar line in over 40 years. Edmonton was sooned followed by its sister city, Calgary, which opened a 7.7-mi south line in 1981, followed by a northeast extension and the opening of a northwest line to the University of Calgary campus in time for the 1988 Winter Olympics. The LRT renaissance gained momentum in the mid- to late-1980s with Buffalo, Portland, Sacramento, San Jose, and Pittsburgh opening lines in quick succession. By this time, the transit industry grew more comfortable with light rail technology, as favorable construction and operating experiences began to accumulate from the early North American projects. In 1990, Los Angeles completed the 22.2-mi Blue Line to Long Beach, increasing North America's inventory of LRT trackage to 331 mi. With new systems having opened in Baltimore, St. Louis, Denver, and Memphis in the 1990s, by 1995 North America's LRT trackage reached almost 400 guideway mi, more than double what it was 20 years earlier (though less than 10 percent of the total streetcar and interurban track miles that had existed some 80 years earlier).

From Table 3.1, several U.S. cities stand out as pursuing ambitious LRT development programs. Dallas plans to open some 20 mi of LRT lines connecting several employment centers to downtown by 1997, with another 26 mi in various stages of design and planning. Portland plans to open 17.5 mi of LRT track on its west side by 1998, and is designing and planning 25 more mi into next century, including a line that would run from Vancouver, Washington, southward to Oregon City via downtown Portland. By 1998, Los Angeles plans to expand its LRT system by another 34 mi (including the extension of the Blue Line from Union Station to Pasadena), the third phase of what could eventually be one of the largest rail transit programs anywhere. Scheduled to open toward the end of the 1990s are several other projects in final engineering or early construction: Chicago's Central Area

TABLE 3.1

U.S. and Canadian Light Rail Systems by Status, Dates, and Route Miles, as of 1995

In Operation

Pre-1970	Post-1970	Extensions	In Design — New Cities
Toronto: 65.8 mi	Edmonton (1978): 8.5 mi	San Jose: 12.4 mi	Northern New Jersey: 28.8 mi
Philadelphia: 33.1 mi	Calgary (1981, 1986): 18.2 mi	St. Louis: 10.9 mi	Salt Lake City: 17.0 mi
Boston: 25.9 mi	San Diego (1981, 1992): 38.6 mi	Denver: 8.7 mi	San Juan: 11.8 mi
San Francisco: 23.1 mi	Buffalo (1985): 6.2 mi	Baltimore: 7.3 mi	Chicago: 9.9 mi
Cleveland: 10.1 mi	Portland (1986): 15.1 mi	Portland: 6.0 mi	Dallas: 2.5 mi
New Orleans: 8.5 mi	Sacramento (1987): 18.2 mi	San Diego: 5.7 mi	New York City: 2.2 mi
Newark: 4.3 mi	San Jose (1987): 21.0 mi	San Francisco: 2.0 mi	
	Pittsburgh (1988): 19.4 mi		
	Los Angeles (1990): 22.2 mi		
	Baltimore (1992): 22.5 mi		
	St. Louis (1993): 18.0 mi		
	Denver (1994): 5.3 mi		
	Memphis (1995): 2.2 mi		

Under Construction

New Cities	Extensions	In Planning — New Cities
Dallas: 20.2 mi	Los Angeles: 33.6 mi	Seattle: 67.8 mi
	Portland: 11.5 mi	Dallas: 23.9 mi
	San Diego: 7.1 mi	Detroit: 14.0 mi
	San Francisco: 5.1 mi	Columbus: 11.6 mi
	Cleveland: 2.5 mi	Kansas City: 11.0 mi
	Toronto: 2.3 mi	Norfolk: 10.0 mi
	Sacramento: 2.3 mi	

Extensions

St. Louis: 65.4 mi
San Francisco: 30.0 mi
Portland: 25.0 mi
San Jose: 17.5 mi
San Diego: 16.1 mi
New Orleans: 12.1 mi
Sacramento: 11.3 mi
Toronto: 6.4 mi
Pittsburgh: 5.2 mi
Memphis: 4.4 mi
Edmonton: 4.0 mi
Cleveland: 3.0 mi
Boston: 2.1 mi
Buffalo: 0.1 mi

Source: American Public Transit Association, *Transit Fixed Guideway Inventory*, April 10, 1995.

Line Miles

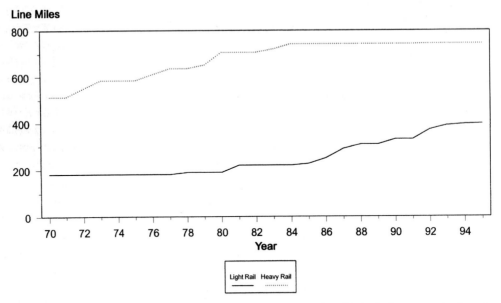

Figure 3.1 Light and Heavy Rail Route Miles in the United States and Canada, 1970–1995. (Source: American Public Transit Association, *Transit Fixed Guideway Inventory*, April 10, 1995.)

Circulator, the Hudson River Waterfront line, Toronto's Spadina line, and system extensions in Baltimore, San Francisco, Sacramento, San Diego, and Cleveland. If all goes according to schedule, St. Louis hopes to have 94.3 mi of LRT in place sometime over the next 15 years, which would earn it top honors for the largest LRT network in North America. If all LRT proposals listed in Table 3.1 get built, there would be some 950 mi of LRT in U.S. and Canada, more than double what existed in 1995 and eclipsing the rail mileage of heavy rail systems (Figure 3.2).

3.5.2 Commuter Rail Transit

Commuter rail services typically link outlying towns and suburban communities to a region's downtown. They are characterized by heavy equipment (e.g., locomotives that pull passenger coaches), wide station spacing, and high maximum speeds that compete with cars on suburban freeways, though slow in acceleration and deceleration. Services tend to be of a high quality, with every passenger normally getting a comfortable seat and ample leg room. Routes are typically 25 to 50 mi long and lead to a stub-end downtown terminal.[41] Because they are used by professional suburbanites to reach core-area jobs, commuter rail ridership tends to be highly concentrated in the peak.

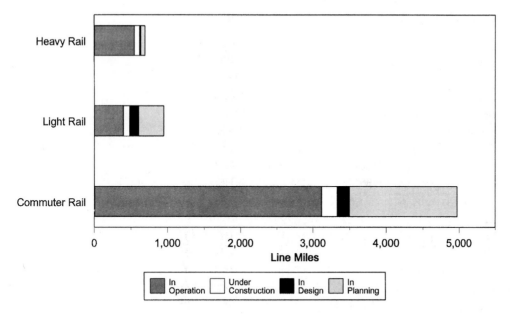

Figure 3.2 Status of Rail Systems in the United States and Canada, as of 1995. (Source: American Public Transit Association, *Transit Fixed Guideway Inventory,* April 10, 1995.)

Currently, 10 U.S. and Canadian cities have commuter rail systems, totaling nearly 2,500 route mi. Two (Los Angeles and Vancouver) are currently building extensions, and seven others are either planning or designing extensions. And at least eight cities currently without commuter rail are at various stages of planning or designing new systems. In all, 18 U.S. cities either have commuter rail services or hope to have them within the next decade. This would raise total U.S. and Canadian commuter rail trackage to nearly 5000 mi, more than five times as long as LRT and seven times as long as heavy rail (Figure 3.2).

Southern California is poised to build one of the most expansive commuter rail networks anywhere. In 1992, Metrolink began operating 75 trains each weekday on five routes radiating from downtown Los Angeles's Union Station to as far as Santa Clarita and Moorepark in the northwest and San Bernardino and Riverside in the east, distances of some 60 mi. The system was expanded to 10 lines totaling nearly 400 mi in 1995 (Table 3.2). To the south in San Diego County, new services have begun between Oceanside and downtown San Diego, a distance of 43 mi. Atlanta also hopes to join the ranks of commuter rail cities by the turn of the century, having recently completed a feasibility study of operating over 500 mi of track along 12 operating freight lines that radiate from the city deep into Gwinett and other exurban counties.

TABLE 3.2

U.S. and Canadian Commuter Rail Systems by Status, Dates, and Route Miles, as of 1995

In Operation

Pre-1970	Post-1970
New York	Los Angeles: 334.2 mi
Long Island RR: 319.1 mi	Baltimore: 187.0 mi
Metro North RR: 267.0 mi	Washington, DC/
Northern New Jersey: 471.3 mi	Northern Virginia: 80.9 mi
Chicago	Miami-Ft. Lauderdale:
Metra: 429.6 mi	66.4 mi
Northern Illinois: 75.8 mi	
Boston: 284.0 mi	
Toronto: 223.0 mi	
Philadelphia: 219.8 mi	
San Francisco: 76.8 mi	
Montreal: 56.6 mi	

In Design

Extensions	New Cities
Boston: 87.1 mi	Dallas: 24.0 mi
Chicago: 40.0 mi	
Baltimore: 13.5 mi	
Miami-Ft. Lauderdale: 2.0 mi	
San Francisco: 1.5 mi	
Northern New Jersey: 0.2 mi	

Under Construction

Extensions	New Cities
Los Angeles: 52.1 mi	San Diego: 43.0 mi
Boston: 52.0 mi	Dallas: 10.0 mi
Vancouver: 40.4 mi	
Northern New Jersey: 12.0 mi	

In Planning

Extensions	New Cities
Chicago: 183.2 mi	Atlanta: 535.3 mi
New York (Metro North): 117.0 mi	Cleveland: 149.0 mi
Los Angeles: 107.8 mi	Seattle: 81.0 mi
Philadelphia: 74.4 mi	Hartford: 38.8 mi
Northern New Jersey: 63.2 mi	St. Louis: 35.0 mi
Boston: 29.5 mi	San Diego: 26.0 mi
Miami-Ft. Lauderdale: 8.0 mi	Denver: 24.0 mi
	Dallas: 3.0 mi

Source: American Public Transit Association, *Transit Fixed Guideway Inventory*, April 10, 1995.

3.5.3   Rapid Rail Transit

Sometimes called heavy rail or metros, rapid rail transit services are high-speed, high-performance systems within urbanized areas that connect neighborhoods and major activity centers (e.g., sports stadia, airports) to downtowns. In the city core, rapid rail lines almost always operate below ground, whereas outside of downtowns they are typically elevated or at grade. Stations tend to be about a mile or so apart, except in downtowns where they might be three or four blocks away. Heavy rail systems are electrically propelled, usually from a third rail, and each car has its own motor. Since contact with the third rail (usually 600 V) can be fatal, rapid rail stations usually have high platforms, and at-grade tracks are fenced.

Boston, New York City, and Philadelphia pioneered rapid rail services, laying subway lines in the early 1900s (Table 3.3). Chicago did likewise during the 1940s, followed by the opening of new systems in the 1950s and 1960s in Toronto, Cleveland, Montreal, and Philadelphia (the extension of the Lindenwold Line from downtown to southern New Jersey). The first of the recent generation of automated rapid rail systems was San Francisco's BART, which opened its 71-mi system in 1972. Four years later, the nation's capital joined the ranks of heavy rail cities; Washington Metrorail is now nearing its ultimate planned size of 103 mi and eight lines. Metrorail has been the most expensive of all heavy rail systems, with total construction costs so far having eclipsed $7 billion. Atlanta's MARTA system opened in 1979, followed by Baltimore's northwest line to Owings Mills in 1983, Miami's northwest-southwest line in 1984, and Vancouver's skytrain in 1986.

Presently, the only U.S. city embarking on a major heavy rail expansion program is the nation's second largest, Los Angeles. Los Angeles hopes to reclaim its one-time standing as a great rail city, though the $6–10 billion Metrorail project, currently the costliest public works program in the United States, is mired in controversy. Critics contend that building rail in a city that epitomizes America's "love affair with the automobile" is a public boondoggle in the making of mammoth proportions. In a freeway-dominated metropolis like greater Los Angeles, rail detractors believe that Metrorail is "too little, too late" to have much impact. The new 4.4-mi Red Line cost approximately $1.5 billion; another $4.3 billion is to be spent on 6 mi of treacherous tunneling through the Hollywood hills and eventually into the vast expanse of the San Fernando Valley. Proponents counter that decades from now, when fossil fuels are nearing depletion and congestion levels become unbearable, future generations of Los Angelenos will ultimately praise city leaders for resurrecting rail services in the Southland, just as New Yorkers today benefit from the rail investments by their ancestors a century ago.

In contrast to light rail and commuter rail systems, rapid rail transit is entering a slowdown rather than an expansion phase, mainly for fiscal reasons. Of the 14 U.S. and Canadian systems in place today, 9 are in construction, design, or planning extensions, but there are no cities without heavy rail now seriously contemplating this form of rail. If everything on the drawing board and under construction eventually gets built, the existing 783 mi of

TABLE 3.3

U.S. and Canadian Heavy Rail Systems by Status, Dates, and Route Miles, as of 1995

In Operation		In Design	
Pre-1970	Post-1970	Extensions	New Cities
New York: 256.3 mi	San Francisco (1972): 71.0 mi	Los Angeles: 8.8 mi	None
Chicago: 105.6 mi	Washington (1976): 82.2 mi	Washington: 6.5 mi	
Toronto: 35.3 mi	Atlanta (1979): 39.5 mi	Atlanta: 1.8 mi	
Boston: 37.9 mi	Baltimore (1983): 14.0 mi	Miami: 1.4 mi	
Montreal: 30.0 mi	Miami (1984): 21.1 mi	New York: 0.4 mi	
Philadelphia: 52.8 mi	Vancouver (1986): 16.0 mi		
Cleveland: 19.1 mi	Los Angeles (1992): 3.0 mi		

Under Construction		In Planning	
Extensions	New Cities	Extensions	New Cities
San Francisco: 22.7 mi	None	Los Angeles: 21.0 mi	None
Chicago: 18.8 mi		San Francisco: 12.4 mi	
Los Angeles: 13.0 mi		Atlanta: 10.8 mi	
Washington: 8.0 mi		Cleveland: 9.7 mi	
Atlanta: 7.0 mi		Washington: 2.9 mi	
Baltimore: 1.5 mi			

Source: American Public Transit Association, *Transit Fixed Guideway Inventory*, April 10, 1995.

heavy rail services will increase to 931 mi, a rise of just 19 percent. This compares to a projected 166 percent increase in LRT mileage and a 65 percent increase in commuter rail mileage for projects in the pipeline. Overall, the greatest prospect for building transit villages around new rail stations lies with LRT and commuter rail services. Of course, converting existing neighborhoods into transit villages around existing stations holds promise for all forms of rail systems.

3.5.4 Urban Rail Stations

The enormous possibilities of station-area redevelopment are suggested by simple tabulations of existing rail station counts across the United States. Today, most stations are in older metropolitan areas with long-established rail networks (Figure 3.3). In fact, 37 percent of the 2445 U.S. urban rail stations that existed in 1993 were within the greater New York region, comprised mainly of heavy rail (New York City Transit Authority) and commuter rail (Long Island Railroad and Metro North Railroad) stations. Nationwide, the most stations were on commuter lines (1079 in all, typically side-platform stations surrounded by large park-and-ride lots), followed by heavy rail (979 subway and elevated stations), and then light rail (387 stations, most with modest boarding platforms). For new station-area development, however, the greatest opportunities in terms of sheer numbers lie with light rail. Among U.S. rail systems built between 1980 and 1995, LRT accounted

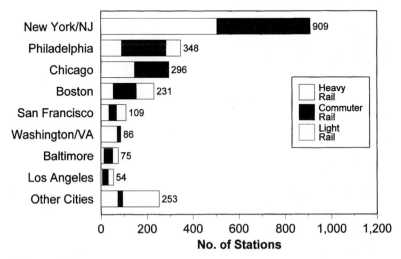

Figure 3.3 U.S. Metropolitan Areas with the Largest Number of Rail Transit Stations, 1993. (Source: American Public Transit Association, *Transit Fixed Guideway Inventory,* Washington, DC, April 10, 1995.)

for the lion's share of new rail stations—161 compared to 97 new commuter rail stations and 38 new heavy rail stations. San Diego Trolley takes top honors among new light rail systems for numbers of stations—in all, 35 in 1995.

3.6   TRANSIT RIDERSHIP AND PERFORMANCE TRENDS

The many hoped-for benefits of mass transit—congestion relief, cleaner air, fuel conservation—only accrue, of course, if people switch from driving cars to riding trains and buses. Despite the billions of dollars invested in rail projects throughout the United States over the past decade and the billions more in the pipeline, overall ridership growth has been anemic. In fact, all but 4 of the 50 largest U.S. metropolitan areas—Houston, Orlando, Dallas-Ft. Worth, and San Diego—saw transit's market share of commute trips slip during the 1980s.

3.6.1   U.S. Rail Transit Ridership Trends

Nationwide, total passenger trips by all modes of transit fell from 8.71 billion in 1984 to 7.43 billion 10 years later in 1993 (Figure 3.4).[42] Most of this decline, however, consisted of lost bus patronage. Over this same period, heavy rail ridership remained fairly constant (at over 2 billion passenger trips annually), whereas the number of light rail and commuter rail trips increased by 22.8 percent and 20.3 percent, respectively. Additional rail passengers do not necessarily translate into new transit patrons, however. Although precise numbers are not available, experiences show that a significant share of new rail riders formerly traveled by bus or shared rides.[43]

Of course, a major reason light rail and commuter rail passenger volumes have grown rapidly is that service levels have likewise grown rapidly; for instance, vehicle revenue miles of service increased by 65 percent on light rail systems and by 30 percent on commuter rail systems during 1984–1993.[44] Adjusting ridership counts for vehicle miles of service, Figure 3.5 shows that the "passenger productivity" of all modes declined from 1984 to 1993. The sharpest fall-off in passenger trips per vehicle mile was for bus transit (from 4.10 in 1984 to 2.99 in 1993) and light rail (from 9.37 in 1984 to 6.97 in 1993) services. Despite these declines, Figure 3.5 shows that among all transit modes light rail systems are still the most intensely utilized and carried more than twice as many passengers per vehicle mile as bus systems and nearly three-quarters as many as heavy rail systems in 1993. It is partly because of higher average loads, coupled with potential construction cost savings, that light rail has gained such recent popularity. Heavy rail, however, still ranks well above all modes in passenger throughput. The highest hourly volume ever recorded over a single track is the 65,340 passengers carried on the NYCTA's Queens-53rd Street tunnel in 1991.

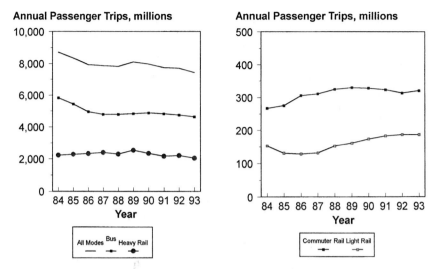

Figure 3.4 Trends in U.S. Transit Ridership by Mode, 1984–1993. (Source: American Public Transit Association, *1994–1995 Transit Fact Book,* Washington, DC, 1995.)

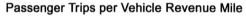

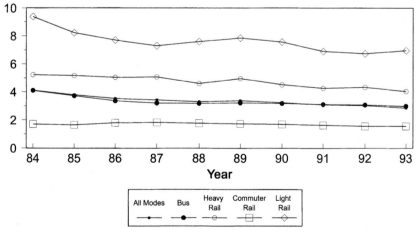

Figure 3.5 Trends in Transit Trips per Vehicle Mile by Mode, 1984–1993. (Source: American Public Transit Association, *1994–1995 Transit Fact Book,* Washington, DC, 1995.)

A danger of looking only at aggregate national statistics is that they ignore the vital role that transit plays in particular metropolitan areas and corridors. Granted, transit carried only 5.1 percent of all U.S. work trips in 1990 (down from 6.2 percent in 1980); however, in New York City and several other urban centers, rail transit is absolutely indispensable in moving massive volumes of people around and avoiding gridlock. Table 3.4 shows that over half of those working in New York City in 1990 arrived to work by mass transit.[45] Over a third of those working in Washington, DC, and San Francisco, moreover, com-

TABLE 3.4

Top 20 U.S. Cities in Terms of Percentage of Workers Commuting by Mass Transit, 1990

City	Percentage Commuting by Mass Transit	Types of Mass Transit Services
1. New York, NY	53.4	HR, CR, LR, B, O
2. Hoboken, NJ	51.0	HR, CR, B, O
3. Jersey City, NJ	36.7	HR, CR, B, O
4. Washington, DC	36.6	HR, CR, B
5. San Francisco, CA	33.5	HR, CR, LR, B, O
6. Boston, MA	31.5	HR, CR, LR, B, O
7. Chicago, IL	29.7	HR, CR, B
8. Philadelphia, PA	28.7	HR, CR, LR, B, O
9. Atlantic City, NJ	26.2	B, O
10. Arlington, VA	25.4	HR, CR, B
11. Newark, NJ	24.6	HR, CR, LR, B, O
12. Cambridge, MA	23.5	HR, CR, B
13. Pittsburgh, PA	22.2	LR, B, O
14. Baltimore, MD	22.0	HR, CR, LR, B
15. Evanston, IL	20.9	HR, CR, B
16. Atlanta, GA	20.0	HR, B
17. White Plains, NY	19.1	CR, B
18. Camden, NJ	18.1	HR, CR, B
19. Oakland, CA	17.9	HR, B, O
20. Hartford, CT	17.1	CR, B

Key: HR = Heavy Rail; CR = Commuter Rail; LR = Light Rail; B = Bus (motor and trolley); O = Other, including ferry and legal general-public paratransit services.

Sources: American Public Transit Association, *1994–1995 Transit Fact Book,* Washington, DC, 1995; U.S. Bureau of the Census, *1990 Census, Journey to Work Characteristics of Workers in Metropolitan Areas,* Washington, DC, 1993.

muted on trains and buses. Quite simply, there is no way that the extraordinarily high concentrations of jobs in Manhattan, San Francisco's financial district, or the nation's capital could be accommodated without rail connections. With over 50,000 jobs per square mile in the downtown cores of these cities, high-capacity rail transit is absolutely essential in sustaining high employment densities and the associated agglomeration benefits (e.g., the innovations and profitable business deals that come from easy, face-to-face contact; the ability to quickly access specialized knowledge and to subcontract out work; the ease of comparison shopping; and the advantages of having cultural attractions, specialty shops, theaters, and special events close by). Vukan Vuchic of the University of Pennsylvania, one of the few academic defenders of U.S. rail investments, argues that large rail-served cities like New York and Philadelphia produce significant national benefits by functioning as centers of finance, commerce, trade, fashions, culture, and innovations.[46] It is noted that 19 of the 20 U.S. cities in Table 3.4, ranked in order of shares of workers who commute by transit, are served by some form of rail transit services, the only exception being Atlantic City (the only U.S. city where private jitneys predominate, mainly serving casino workers and tourists 24 h a day along the 3-mi boardwalk stretch).

The sheer dominance of the New York metropolitan area in the national transit arena is further underscored by Figure 3.6. In 1993, nearly 3 out of 10 transit trips occurred in the greater New York region (including northeastern New Jersey). For heavy and commuter rail trips, the share in the New York region was closer to 6 out of 10. Greater Chicago also comprised a significant share of the nationwide commuter rail trip total (20 percent) while metropolitan Washington and Boston made up respectable shares of heavy rail journeys (about 9 percent each). America's three largest light rail systems—San Francisco, Philadelphia, and Boston, all older systems—accounted for 55 percent of light rail trips in 1993 (versus 45 percent of track mileage). Top ridership honors for new light rail systems go to the San Diego Trolley, which carried 16.5 million passengers in 1993, 9 percent of the national light rail total.

It has been on commuter rail systems, however, that recent gains in ridership have been most impressive. South Florida's Tri-Rail service along the busy corridor connecting Miami, Fort Lauderdale, and West Palm Beach saw daily ridership climb from 2500 passengers when it first opened in 1989 to over 12,000 daily patrons in 1994. The Virginia Railway Express (VRE) ties Washington, DC's Union Station to the exurban counties of Prince William and Fauquier in northern Virginia. In the first full month of service in mid-1992, VRE averaged 3700 daily passengers; 2 years later, daily counts exceeded 10,000. Other commuter rail systems enjoying ridership gains exceeding 5 percent annually during the first half of the 1990s are the Metrolink in Los Angeles, the Connecticut DOT's New Haven service, and Maryland's MARC system.

The success of these commuter rail services confirms what demographers have been telling us for some time: Population is growing the fastest in once-rural counties, beyond the outer edges of metropolitan areas. Between 1980 and 1990, the 20 fastest growing counties in the United States were all situated beyond traditional suburbs in the exurban

Metropolitan Area

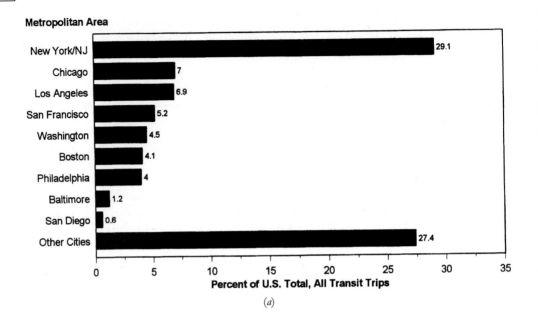

(a)

Metropolitan Area

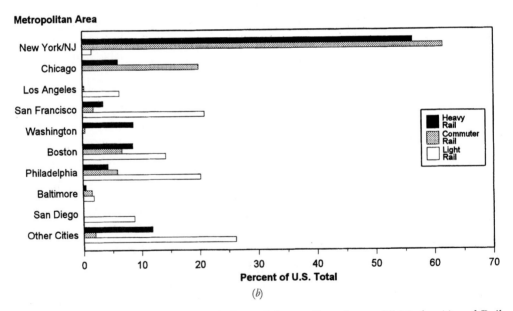

(b)

Figure 3.6 Share of Transit Trips in Large Metropolitan Areas, All Modes (*a*) and Rail Modes Only (*b*), 1993. (Source: American Public Transit Association, *1994–1995 Transit Fact Book,* Washington, DC, 1995.)

zone between cities and countryside.[47] Many who moved to these places were fleeing the suburbs, much as earlier generations of suburbanites fled the city, generally in search of more affordable housing and a better place to raise their children.

3.6.2 Ridership Hopes and Disappointments

Ten to twenty years ago, transit planners were fairly optimistic about the prospects of rail. In the Alternatives Analyses and Environmental Impact Statements (AA/EIS) prepared for many projects, transit ridership was expected to outpace regional population growth in most cities that proposed rail projects. In a retrospective study of new-generation U.S. rail projects, Don Pickrell, an economist with the Transportation Systems Center in Cambridge, Massachusetts, found that in eight of nine cases the actual number of weekday passengers was less than half of that predicted by project planners.[48] The most egregious forecast error was for Miami's 21-mi Metrorail system, which was expected to carry 239,900 weekday passengers several years after opening, six times higher than the actual 35,400 daily passengers recorded. Pickrell found that assumptions on demographic variables (e.g., average household size), transit service levels, and automobile costs accounted for less than half of the forecast error, inferring that estimates were massaged to favor rail over less glamorous busway options.

The Pickrell report sparked a firestorm of controversy over the motivations, ethics, and methods of rail ridership forecasts. Other studies of U.S. rail investment decisions found that ridership forecasts were biased upward to appease political backers and advocate "high-tech" transportation.[49] In an analysis of forecasts used to justify a proposed $2.9 billion, 93-mi LRT system for Dallas, John Kain of Harvard University claims the city's transit authority purposely tried to deceive the public by concealing facts and misrepresenting forecasts.[50] A referendum to let the transit district issue revenue bonds was badly defeated by voters in 1988 regardless. Over the years, Kain has been relentless in his criticism of U.S. rail projects, attributing these investments to a host of rationales that have nothing to do with economics and everything to do with politics: civic boosterism; political monument building; a "make no small plans" mentality, in deference to Daniel Burnham's plea to all city planners; a belief that, like being home to a professional baseball and football team, all "great cities" must have a subway system; the prospect of job creation through federally funded capital grants; the self-interests of downtown merchants bent on stemming the tide of retail losses to suburban malls; and what Kain calls the "Lionel train complex"—"a major part of the appeal of rail transit is a childish fascination with electric trains" (an argument that sounds similar to "the only difference in men and boys is the price of their toys").[51] Kain and others suggest that a frequent reason taxpayers vote for sales tax referenda in support of rail transit is the naive belief that the "other guy" will now start riding transit, freeing up more road space so they can drive their cars unobstructed.

Perhaps overriding all explanations for rail transit's relatively poor performance over the past decade is the continuing underpricing of the private automobile. Studies show roadway users in the United States pay only around 60 percent of the costs of roadway construction, maintenance, administration, and law enforcement through fuel taxes and user fees.[52] The remaining 40 percent (amounting to $30.7 billion in 1990) is subsidized through general government revenues (often hidden in the budgets for police departments to patrol highways, ambulance services to respond to roadside emergencies, and municipal utility expenditures for lighting highways).[53] Adding the social costs of externalities not borne directly by motorists, such as air pollution and highway accidents, brings the estimated annual subsidies given to America's highway users to anywhere between $300 billion on the low end and $780 billion on the high end.[54] Of course, the long-run consequence of underpricing is spread-out, auto-oriented development. In a distorted marketplace where most American commuters don't pay for the full cost of highway services or externalities like air pollution, it is perhaps no great surprise that many voice a preference for low-density living and vote with their feet and commute with their wheels.

Many economists argue that the best way to correct this mispricing is not to subsidize transit as a countervailing measure, but rather to attack the problem directly through proper road pricing, such as higher gasoline taxes, congestion fees, increased bridge tolls, and mandatory parking charges. Higher motoring costs mean that, over time, Americans would move closer to jobs and transit stops to economize on travel. As a result, there would be little need for proactive public initiatives like designing transit-oriented communities or planning for balanced growth. However, then again, true market pricing of automobile travel might be even more unattainable than building transit villages in a pluralistic, democratic society such as ours. So far, the only places with even a cursory form of road pricing are either ruled by heavy-handed centralized planning doctrine (the city-state of Singapore) or are sparsely populated, culturally homogeneous countries (Norway).[55] Martin Wachs, as chairman of a Transportation Research Board Committee on Congestion Pricing, concluded that except for "professors of transportation economics and planning—who hardly constitute a potent political force—I can think of few interest groups that would willingly and vigorously fight for the concept."[56] In the absence of true market-rate pricing of the automobile, we would argue that public initiatives that increase the attractiveness of other modes of travel, including transit village development, are among the next best things.

3.6.3 Cost Performance

As much as early forecasts were off on future rail ridership, they were just as off on the eventual capital and operating costs of new rail systems. In his review of 10 U.S. rail projects, Pickrell found capital and operating costs were underestimated in every case.[57] The biggest offender was Washington's Metrorail—actual construction costs exceeded forecasts by 83 percent. A separate study of light rail investments in Buffalo and San Jose found that cost estimates tended to be biased downward to meet the cost-efficiency standards set by federal and state funding authorities.[58]

Rail advocates have attacked the critiques of Pickrell and others not only on methodological grounds,[59] but also on the very presumption that rail projects alone have been guilty of gross miscalculations. For instance, the final price tag for the 42,500-mi interstate highway system was over three times higher than original forecasts, even after adjusting for inflation. In 1990, California's voters approved a gas tax increase in large part to provide $3.5 billion in additional funds to pay for increases in the cost of highway projects approved in 1988. Rail proponents also argue that transit's long-term benefits far exceed short-term capital expenditures. In reaction to the Pickrell report, Hank Dittmar, executive director of the Surface Transportation Policy Project in Washington, DC, remarks: "Rail is a long-term investment, and evaluating it at three years or even five years of age is like judging a human infant at that age—it's mostly potential."[60] And not all LRT ridership forecasts have been so self-serving. St. Louis's recently opened 18-mi MetroLink from east of the Mississippi to Lambert International Airport was averaging 40,000 riders per weekday 2 years after its 1993 opening, more than twice what was forecasted, and even higher than the year 2010 forecast of 35,000 daily riders. Much of MetroLink's success stems from the smart routing of the system, connecting downtown to a sports stadium, universities, medical centers, recreational hubs, and the airport, land uses that generate traffic throughout the day and week.

For older U.S. rail systems, capital outlays also rose rapidly during the 1980s, mainly due to upgrading subway and commuter rail systems in New York, Boston, Chicago, and Philadelphia through station modernization and rehabilitating tracks, tunnels, and signaling systems. From 1984 to 1993, some $20 billion was spent on rail modernization in the United States, comprising about 40 percent of all transit capital expenditures during this period (though less than 8 percent of all highway capital expenditures).

From 1984 to 1993, the national operating expense for rail transit services, ignoring capital depreciation and debt payments, rose from $3.29 billion to $6.06 billion, an 84 percent increase in actual dollars, or 46 percent adjusting for inflation. This compares to an increase in vehicle revenue miles of service of 22.8 percent and a 3.7 percent drop in ridership over the same period. From a net productivity standpoint, rail transit services have clearly declined, carrying fewer passengers and operating fewer miles for every dollar expended.

Figure 3.7 shows that in 1993 there was considerable variation in cost performance among rail modes. On a per vehicle revenue mile basis, light rail and commuter rail services were about twice as costly to operate as bus transit (again ignoring capital depreciation). Because light rail services are not geographically as extensive as other transit modes, and thus vehicles do not log as many miles, their operating expenses per vehicle mile are particularly high. On a per passenger basis, however, both light and heavy rail services are relatively economical, around $1.70 to $1.80 per rider, compared to about $2.10 per rider for all modes of transit combined. Still, the difficult financial times are forcing some rail agen-

1993 Operating Expense per

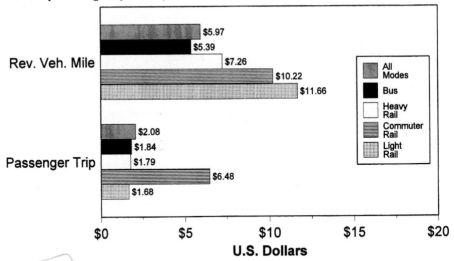

Figure 3.7 Comparison of Cost Performance Among Transit Modes, 1993. (Source: American Public Transit Association, *1994–1995 Transit Fact Book,* Washington, DC, 1995.)

cies to become frugal and cost conscious. With federal transit assistance slated to be curtailed and states facing their own financial problems, cities can no longer count on substantial outside support. In what may be a harbinger of trends to come, the Los Angeles Metropolitan Transportation Authority drastically scaled back its light rail proposal, from 296 to 95 mi. Gone from the plan are eight LRT lines that would have crisscrossed the county, victims of lower than expected sales tax revenues and California voters' rejection of a $1 billion rail bond issue.

Clearly, the costliest transit service on a per passenger basis is commuter rail at $6.48 per trip in 1993. Because commuter rail often serves relatively affluent suburbanites heading to downtown jobs, critics charge that high subsidies used to cover expensive commuter rail services are highly regressive (i.e., taking tax dollars from the general public to help pay for the commuting costs of many well-off suburbanites). The average fare paid by commuter rail passengers in 1993 was $3.09, meaning an average subsidy of $3.39 per commuter rail trip (versus a per trip subsidy of $0.92 for heavy rail and $1.14 for light rail).[61] Of course, one could also argue that the total social cost (e.g., more air pollution and traffic congestion) of commuter rail passengers driving to work instead would be much higher than these subsidies, especially given that commuter rail passengers average very long trips (23.3 mi in 1993). Indeed, an argument often made for subsidizing transit in the first place is to help offset the historical and continuing underpricing of the private automobile. Given the estimated $300 to $780 billion in subsidies granted to motorists each year (depending on whose study you believe), the $15.4 billion in local, state, and federal operating and capital assistance to America's transit industry in 1993 seems paltry by comparison.

3.7 TRANSIT VILLAGES IN THE LARGER SCHEME OF THINGS

It would be easy to infer from recent ridership and performance trends that a black cloud looms over the rail transit industry and any programs connected to it, including transit villages. However, we find comfort in the ancient Chinese proverb that "within every crisis lies an opportunity." A cynical view would hold that nothing can be done to turn around transit's decades of decline. An opportunistic view would hold that transit villages worked quite successfully a century ago and that, despite the ascendancy of the automobile, the growing interest in traditional neighborhoods that are pedestrian friendly and diverse in land uses and housing types holds some promise for the future of America's transit industry in general and transit villages in particular. Moreover, recent success stories like St. Louis's MetroLink and south Florida's Tri-Rail commuter service provide some cause for optimism about rail transit's future. Transit villages, in and of themselves, are clearly no panacea to today's congestion, air quality, or social equity problems, nor are they a cure-all for reversing the falling fortunes of America's transit industry over the postwar era. However, along with other initiatives that remove subsidies to motorists (e.g., mandatory parking charges, higher gasoline taxes) and provide respectable alternatives to driving one's car (e.g., improved pedestrian paths to transit stops, telecommunications advances), transit villages, we believe, would make a positive contribution toward improving social and environmental conditions in our cities and, indeed, attracting more motorists to trains and buses. It could very well prove that the benefits of transit villages have less to do with transportation and more to do with providing more choices on where to live and how to travel, rejuvenating urban neighborhoods, bringing more people into everyday face-to-face contact, and increasing the social and cultural diversity of urban neighborhoods. It is to the matter of demonstrating that transit-oriented development can create positive public and private benefits, and that there is a burgeoning though largely pent-up demand for transit village living, that we now turn in the remaining chapters of Part Two.

NOTES

1. James Flink, *The Automobile Age* (Cambridge, MA: MIT Press, 1988).
2. George Smerk, The Streetcar: Shaper of American Cities, *Traffic Quarterly*, Vol. 21, No. 4, pp. 79–91, 1967.
3. David E. Jones, Jr., *Urban Transit Policy: An Economic and Political History* (Englewood Cliffs, NJ: Prentice-Hall, 1985).

4. John Kain and David Harrison have argued that rising incomes were more strongly associated with rising automobile ownership rates and declining transit ridership during the 1920 to 1970 period, based on a study of trends in 49 U.S. metropolises over this period. See David Harrison and John Kain, *Transportation and the Dynamics of Urban Land Use* (Cambridge, MA: Harvard University, Department of City and Regional Planning, Discussion Paper D78–22, 1978).

5. Robert Fishman, *Bourgeois Utopias: The Rise and Fall of Suburbia* (New York: Basic Books, 1987), p. 157.

6. David Jones, *California's Freeway Era in Historical Perspective* (Berkeley: Institute of Transportation Studies, University of California, 1989), pp. 279–280.

7. Alan Altshuler, *The Urban Transportation System: Politics and Policy Innovation* (Cambridge, MA: MIT Press, 1980), p. 36.

8. See James Sale and Bryan Green, Operating Costs and Performance of American Public Transit Systems, *Journal of the American Planning Association,* Vol. 4, No. 2, pp. 22–27, 1978; Darold Barnum and John Gleason, *Measuring the Influences of Subsidies on Transit Efficiency and Effectiveness* (Washington, DC: Department of Transportation, Urban Mass Transportation Administration, 1979); Robert Cervero, The Anatomy of Transit Operating Deficits, *Urban Law and Policy,* Vol. 6, No. 3, pp. 477–497, 1984.

9. Don H. Pickrell, Rising Subsidies and the Uses of Transit Subsidies in the United States, *Journal of Transport Economics and Policy,* Vol. 19, No. 3, pp. 281–298, 1985.

10. The notable exception was the ridership gains in the west. Phoenix, San Diego, Sacramento, and Denver all recorded increases of over 100 percent in transit commuting between 1970 and 1980, though compared to east coast cities, total numbers of transit riders in these cities were fairly minuscule.

11. Alan Pisarski, *New Perspectives on Commuting* (Washington, DC: U.S. Department of Transportation, Federal Highway Administration, 1992).

12. Section 108(f)(1)(A) of the Clean Air Act Amendments of 1990.

13. In fiscal years 1993 and 1994, $1.08 billion, or around 5 percent of eligible flexible funds, were transferred from highway to transit programs.

14. Federal Highway Administration, *Highway Statistics* (Washington, DC: U.S. Department of Transportation, 1993).

15. Elmer Johnson, *Avoiding the Collision of Cities and Cars: Urban Transportation Policy for the Twenty-First Century* (Chicago: American Academy of Arts and Sciences, 1993).

16. Robert Cervero and Peter Hall, Containing Traffic Congestion in America, *Built Environment,* Vol. 15, No. 3/4, p. 178, 1989.

17. R. Rowand, You Sit, and You Wait, and You Boil, *Automotive News,* p. 25, December 1989.

18. T. Lomax, D. Bullard, and J. Hanks, *The Impact of Declining Mobility in Major Texas and Other U.S. Cities* (Austin: State Department of Highways and Public Transportation, Texas Transportation Institute, Research Report 431–1F, 1989).

19. Dean Hesterman, Joseph DiMento, Dru van Hengel, and Brenda Nordenstam, Impacts of a Consent Decree on "The Lost Urban Freeway": Interstate 105 in Los Angeles County, *Transportation Research,* Vol. 27A, No. 4, pp. 299–313, 1993.

20. Anthony Downs, The Law of Peak-Hour Expressway Congestion, *Traffic Quarterly,* Vol. 16, pp. 393–409, 1962.

21. Because of mounting political pressure, high implementation costs (around $200 per employee per year), and growing resentment of unfunded federal mandates, the Los Angeles area repealed these more stringent employer-based trip reduction requirements in 1995, opting for more voluntary initiatives instead. Studies also showed that these programs were ineffective. A study of southern California's Regulation XV employee trip reduction requirement, for instance, found only a small overall reduction in single-occupant commuting (a 0.4 percent decline in private car miles driven) and no increase in public transit ridership. See Martin Wachs, Learning from Los Angeles: Transport, Urban Form, and Air Quality, *Transportation,* Vol. 20, No. 14, pp. 329–359, 1993.

22. Extended exposure to PM–10, or particulate matter of 10 microns or less, poses risks of chronic respiratory disease because it bypasses the body's natural filtration system more easily than larger particles and can lodge deeply in the lungs.

23. John MacKenzie, Roger Dower, and Donald Chen, *The Going Rate: What It Really Costs to Drive* (New York: World Resources Institute, 1992); Kenneth Small and Camilla Kamzimi, On the Costs of Air Pollution from Motor Vehicles, *Journal of Transport Economics and Policy,* Vol. 29, No. 1, pp. 12–24, 1994.

24. American Public Transit Association, *Public Transportation: The Federal Partnership* (Washington, DC: February 1995).

25. Deborah Gordon, *Steering a New Course: Transportation, Energy, and the Environment* (Washington, DC: Island Press, 1991).

26. Peter Newman and Jeffrey Kenworthy, *Cities and Automobile Dependence: A Sourcebook* (Brookfield, VT: Gower, 1989).

27. For discussions on these environmental costs, see MacKenzie et al., op. cit.; Douglass B. Lee, Jr., Full Cost Pricing of Highways, paper presented at the annual meeting of the Transportation Research Board, January, 1995, Washington, DC; Mark E. Hanson, Automobile Subsidies and Land Use, *Journal of the American Planning Association,* Vol. 58, No. 1, pp. 60–71, 1992.

28. MacKenzie et al., op. cit., p. 21.

29. Bureau of Transportation Statistics, *Transportation Statistics: Annual Report* (Washington, DC: U.S. Department of Transportation, 1994).

30. Gordon, op. cit., p. 33. British thermal units (BTUs) are standardized measures of energy-use intensity.

31. Charles Lave, Rail Rapid Transit and Energy: The Adverse Effects. *Transportation Research Record,* Vol. 648, pp. 14–30, 1977.

32. Anthony Downs, *New Visions for Metropolitan America* (Washington, DC: The Brookings Institution and Lincoln Institute of Land Policy, 1994).

33. Douglas Massey and Nancy Denton, *American Apartheid: Segregation and the Making of the Underclass* (Cambridge, MA: Harvard University Press, 1993).

34. Keith R. Ihlanfeldt and David L. Sjoquist, The Impact of Job Decentralization on the Economic Welfare of Central City Blacks, *Journal of Urban Economics,* Vol. 26, pp. 110–130, 1989.

35. Mark Alan Hughes, Moving up and Moving out: Confusing Ends and Means About Ghetto Dispersal, *Urban Studies,* Vol. 24, pp. 503–517, 1987.

36. Sandra Rosenbloom, *Reverse Commute Transportation: Emerging Provider Roles* (Washington, DC: U.S. Department of Transportation, Federal Transit Administration, 1992).

37. Bank of America, California Resources Agency, and Greenbelt Alliance, *Beyond Sprawl: New Patterns of Growth to Fit the New California* (San Francisco: January 1995).

38. C. Kenneth Orski, Urban Sprawl Revisited, *Innovation Briefs,* Vol. 6, No. 3, p. 1, 1995.

39. G. B. Arrington, Jr., *Portland's Light Rail: A Shared Vision for Transportation & Land Use* (Portland: Tri-Met, May 1992), p. 19.

40. The St. Charles trolley line in New Orleans (6.6 mi in length) is both historic and a functioning daily mass transit system, and is thus included in the total.

41. Alan Black, *Urban Mass Transportation Planning* (New York: McGraw-Hill, 1995).

42. All ridership data are expressed in unlinked passenger trips (i.e., for each trip segment). If someone transfers from a bus to a subway, that is treated as two unlinked trips (or one linked trip). The source of data cited in this section is Federal Transit Administration, *National Transit Summaries and Trends* (Washington, DC: May 1995).

43. When San Francisco's BART commenced transbay services in September 1974, within 6 weeks it was carrying around 25,000 passengers per day. Surveys showed, however, that over half of these passengers previously commuted by bus and 8 percent were previously auto passengers. Only a third had previously traveled as auto drivers. See Melvin Webber, The BART Experience: What Have We Learned? *The Public Interest,* Vol. 12, No. 3, pp. 79–108, 1976.

44. Revenue miles represent the mileage that vehicles accumulate while in revenue service (i.e., when they are carrying fare-paying customers). Remaining out-of-service mileage consists mainly of distances covered in returning vehicles to storage barns, maintenance yards, and for deadheading.

45. Among New York's employed residents, 8 percent commuted by bus and 18.8 percent commuted by rail transit in 1990, by far the highest market shares in the country.

46. Vukan Vuchic, Urban Transit: A Public Asset of National Significance, *Urban Resources,* Vol. 4, No. 1, pp. 3–7, 1987.

47. C. Kenneth Orski, The Flowering of Commuter Rail, *Urban Innovations,* Vol. 5, No. 5, pp. 1–2, 1994.

48. Don H. Pickrell, *Urban Rail Transit Projects: Forecast Versus Actual Ridership and Costs* (Cambridge, MA: Transportation Systems Center, U.S. Department of Transportation, 1989).

49. Martin Wachs, Techniques Versus Advocacy in Forecasting: A Study of Rail Rapid Transit, *Urban Resources,* Vol. 4, No. 1, pp. 13–28, 1986; Robert Johnston, Daniel Sperling, Mark DeLuchi, and Steve Tracy, Politics and Technical Uncertainty in Transportation Investment Analysis, *Transportation Research,* Vol. 21A, No. 6, pp. 459–475, 1987.

50. John Kain, Deception in Dallas: Strategic Misrepresentation in Rail Transit Promotion and Evaluation, *Journal of the American Planning Association,* Vol. 56, No. 2, pp. 184–196, 1990.

51. John Kain, Choosing the Wrong Technology: Or How to Spend Billions and Reduce Transit Use, *Journal of Advanced Transportation,* Vol. 21, No. 3, pp. 197–213, 1988.

52. In contrast, roadway user taxes exceed government roadway expenditures in every European country. The ratio of roadway taxes to expenditures ranges from 5.1:1 in The Netherlands to 1.3:1 in Switzerland, but most European countries collect at least twice as much from roadway user taxes as they spend on highways. See John Pucher, Urban Passenger Transport in the United States and Europe: A Comparative Analysis of Public Policies: Part 1, Travel Behavior, Urban Development, and Automobile Use, *Transport Reviews,* Vol. 15, No. 2, pp. 99–117, 1995.

53. MacKenzie et al., op. cit., pp. 9–10.

54. See MacKenzie et al., op. cit.; Lee, op. cit.; Todd Litman, *Transportation Cost Analysis* (Victoria, British Columbia: Transportation Policy Institute, 1994).

55. Singapore was the first city to introduce congestion pricing when it introduced an Area Licensing Scheme (ALS) in 1975 which required motorists to prepurchase a permit that allowed them to enter downtown and the Orchard Road retail district during peak hours. Presently, this system is being replaced by a fully automated, stored-value, debit-card system that will "debit" a monetary amount when vehicles pass entry points to the downtown and other congested areas. See Chapter 13 for further discussions of road pricing in Singapore. The Norwegian cities of Trondheim, Bergen, and Oslo have introduced similar road charges for entering central areas or crossing bridges, though unlike Singapore, charges are usually levied for all time periods, not just peak travel hours.

56. Martin Wachs, Will Congestion Pricing Ever Be Adopted? *Access,* No. 4, p. 16, 1994.

57. Pickrell, op. cit., 1989.

58. Aurelio Menendez, *Estimating Capital and Operating Costs in Urban Transportation Planning* (Westport, CT: Praeger Publishers, 1993).

59. Rail advocates charge that the Pickrell report looked at cost estimates in the planning phase, not in the engineering phase of the project. Between planning and engineering, costs normally rise because of environmental problems and mitigation, construction

setbacks, and factor price increases. (Pickrell has counterargued that early projections are most relevant since they most directly affected the local decision to proceed with the rail alternative.) Rail supporters also claim that in some cases Pickrell compared "apples and oranges," such as one case of comparing estimated ridership in 1983 with projected ridership in 2000. For a lively debate on the Pickrell report, see *TR News,* Vol. 156, pp. 2–19, 1991, including essays by Don Pickrell, Urban Rail Transit Systems: Are They Fulfilling Their Promise? pp. 3–5; Jesse Simon, Let's Make Forecasts and Actual Comparisons Fair, pp. 6–9; Charles A. Lave, Playing the Rail Transit Forecasting Game, pp. 10–12; and Vukan Vuchic, Recognizing the Value of Rail Transit, pp. 13–19.

60. Hank Dittmar, Is Rail Transit Right for Your Community? Asking the Right Questions, Measuring the Benefits. Paper presented at the Railvolution Conference, Portland, OR, September 17, 1995, City of Portland, Federal Transit Administration, and the Surface Transportation Policy Project.

61. American Public Transit Association, *1994–1995 Transit Fact Book* (Washington, DC: 1995).

4

The Built Environment and the Demand for Transit

Three physical attributes of transit villages are thought to significantly increase transit ridership and thus distinguish them from other urban settings. These are the three dimensions, or 3-Ds, of what we believe make for successful transit villages: Density, Diversity, and Design. By density, we mean having enough residents and workers within a reasonable walking distance of transit stations to generate high ridership. By diversity, we mean a mixture of land uses, housing types, and ways of circulating within the village. And by design, we mean physical features and site layouts that are conducive to walking, biking, and transit riding. This chapter discusses these physical dimensions of transit villages and presents comparative findings from different studies on how these dimensions influence travel behavior. Chapter 5 extends these insights by presenting the results of some of our own work on the effects of transit-oriented development on transit riding, drawing largely from California experiences. Relative to other research in these areas, our work has focused centrally on the connection between transit villagelike development and travel behavior.

Demonstrating that transit-supportive designs and patterns of development do encourage people to ride trains and buses, and to walk and bike more often, is important from a public-sector perspective. If we are to build a sound and compelling rationale for governments and institutions to take transit-oriented planning and development seriously, it is essential that there be some evidence that society at large benefits as a result, especially in the form of more transit riding and, by extension, less automobile dependence. Thus, building a case for future transit village development partly hinges on demonstrating that the physical makeup of neighborhoods that surround transit stations matters. And for transit villages to produce the public benefits that are hoped for, they need to have the kinds of densities, diversity, and design that will draw significant numbers of people out of cars and into trains, buses, and other forms of travel.

4.1   DENSITY AND COMPACTNESS

Implicit in the creation of transit villages is an increase in residential densities above those typically found in American suburbs. It stands to reason that mass transit needs "mass," or density, if people are to ride trains and buses in appreciable numbers. If origins and destinations are thinly spread throughout a region, those with access to a car will drive rather than take mass transit. As noted in Chapter 3, fewer than 2 percent of all Americans making a work trip that began and ended in a suburb took mass transit in 1990. Nearly all of these suburb-to-suburb trips were by private car. Low-density settings are clearly not transit's natural habitat.

Many suburban developments across the United States are built at densities that are intrinsically dysfunctional from a transportation standpoint. Today, for example, most suburban office and commercial projects average floor-area ratios (i.e., building area divided by land area) of 0.2 to 0.3—densities that are too low to support frequent transit services, yet are sufficiently high to produce spot congestion. In the San Francisco Bay Area, a number of cities downzoned land near rail stations during the 1980s in fear of higher densities causing traffic snarls on connecting surface streets. Walnut Creek, an East Bay suburb served by BART, passed a moratorium in 1985 that banned new construction over 10,000 ft^2 on the very grounds that large-scale development would overwhelm streets connecting to BART. The problem with such actions is that they end up pushing growth farther out to the exurban fringes, often in the form of more auto-oriented shopping plazas and office parks, and thus, while perhaps temporarily holding the line on congestion locally, exacerbating transportation and environmental problems for the region as a whole. Banning growth near rail stations and displacing it to the metropolitan fringe only means more vehicle miles of travel and tailpipe emissions.

4.1.1   Effects of Density on Travel

The preponderance of evidence shows that higher densities and compact patterns of development lead to substantially higher rates of transit riding. Three lines of empirical work have been conducted on this question: intercity comparisons, international comparisons, and activity center and corridor studies. The following sections highlight some of the key findings from these studies.

4.1.2   Intercity Comparisons

These studies use comparisons between average density and built-environment characteristics of cities and transit usage, statistically controlling for such factors as differences in incomes and traffic congestion. In reality, however, these studies never do fully control for these other factors, so it is difficult to unambiguously infer exactly the importance of the built environment in shaping travel demand.

In a seminal 1977 study, *Public Transit and Land-Use Policy,* Boris Pushkarev and Jeffrey Zupan, both planners with New York's Regional Plan Association, developed a set of *land-use thresholds* that are necessary to financially justify different types of transit investments, based on intermodal comparisons of transit unit costs and intercity comparisons of transit trip generation rates.[1] They found the key determinants of transit demand to be the size of a downtown (defined by nonresidential floorspace), distance of a site to downtown, and residential densities. To justify the cost of a light rail transit investment, for instance, Pushkarev and Zupan concluded that minimum residential densities of nine dwelling units per acre were needed over a 75-mi^2 service area with the light rail line connected to a downtown that has at least 20 million ft^2 of nonresidential floorspace. Cities like Buffalo and Baltimore generally met these land-use thresholds and, in part because of the Pushkarev and Zupan study, opted to proceed with building light rail transit systems during the 1980s. Notwithstanding some of the limitations of Pushkarev and Zupan's analysis (e.g., data were predominantly from the New York metropolitan area, and the effects of suburban centers on mode of travel were ignored), the work is still frequently cited and has been used often as benchmarks in feasibility studies of proposed rail projects.

In another cross-city comparison of six U.S. metropolises (ranging in size from Springfield, Massachusetts, to the New York region), Wilbur Smith found that transit trips rose most sharply when residential densities increased from around 7 dwelling units to 16 units per acre.[2] In the case of greater New York, for instance, this residential density jump increased average weekday transit trips per person from 0.2 to 0.6. At residential densities of 100 dwelling units per acre, Smith found that each New Yorker was averaging around one mass transit trip per day.

4.1.2.1 Density Effects on LRT and Commute Rail Demand   The classic work by Pushkarev and Zupan that has been cited was recently updated as part of a study on transit and urban form relationships sponsored by the National Research Council, under the Transit Cooperative Research Program (TCRP).[3] This 1995 study concentrated on how densities, downtown employment, and travel distance influence transit ridership for light rail and commuter rail systems, the types of systems that have been the focus of recent U.S. rail investments. Using data from 19 light rail lines (and 261 stations) across 11 U.S. cities, the study showed that ridership increases exponentially with both central business district (CBD) employment and employment density, controlling for a host of other variables, including income. Higher ridership levels also occurred with higher residential densities, especially for those making longer trips. The elasticity between ridership and population density was 0.592—that is, controlling for other factors, every 10 percent increase in population densities surrounding the 261 stations studied was associated with about a 6 percent increase in boardings at LRT stations. This relationship is further

revealed by Figure 4.1. This figure, produced from the TCRP study, shows how daily boardings fall with both increases in population density and distance to CBD for a setting where the downtown has 100,000 workers at a density of 100 workers per acre, and the typical access distance to the light rail station is 1 mi. Assuming a station is 10 mi from the CBD, the experiences across these 19 light rail lines show that a neighborhood with an average of 20 persons per gross acre (e.g., small lots, some duplexes) could be expected to produce 2000 daily boardings, compared to just 900 daily boardings for a neighborhood averaging 5 persons per acre (e.g., ranch estates, quarter-acre lots).

The analysis of commuter rail services was conducted for six cities with 47 commute rail lines and 550 stations.[4] The TCRP study found rail ridership also increased with CBD size and employment density, though not in the same exponential fashion as for light rail.

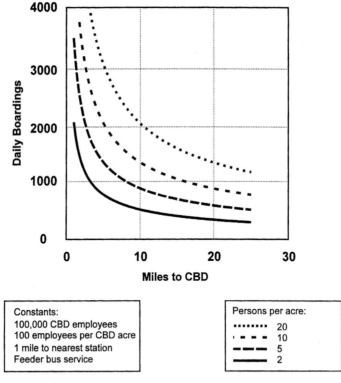

Figure 4.1 Light Rail Station Boardings by Distance to CBD and Residential Density. (Source: Parsons Brinckerhoff Quade & Douglas, Inc., Robert Cervero, Howard/Stein-Hudson Associates, Inc., and Jeffrey Zupan, *Topic 1 Report: Regional Transit Corridors: The Land Use Connection* [Washington, DC: Transportation Research Board, Transit Cooperative Research Program, 1995, p. 28].)

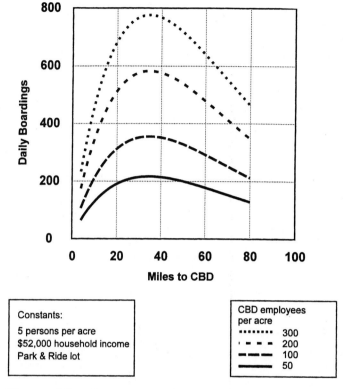

Figure 4.2 Commuter Rail Station Boardings by CBD Distance and Employment Density. (Source: Parsons Brinckerhoff Quade & Douglas, Inc., Robert Cervero, Howard/Stein-Hudson Associates, Inc., and Jeffrey Zupan, *Topic 1 Report: Regional Transit Corridors: The Land Use Connection* [Washington, DC: Transportation Research Board, Transit Cooperative Research Program, 1995, p. 30].)

Figure 4.2 shows that for a commuter rail station 40 mi from the CBD that has a park-and-ride lot and is surrounded by a neighborhood with average annual household incomes of $52,000 and five persons per acre, if the downtown destination has 300 workers per acre, nearly 800 boardings would be produced at this station. If, on the other hand, the downtown destination has just 50 workers per acre, the number falls to approximately 200 boardings.

Merging these demand-side results with cost models, the TCRP study was able to estimate relative cost efficiency, defined in terms of total annual costs divided by annual vehicle miles of service, for different land-use scenarios.[5] Figure 4.3 shows that for a 10-mi LRT line surrounded by denser housing (10 persons per acre), the cost per vehicle mile to a downtown with 100,000 workers (at 300 workers per acre) would be around $7. At the

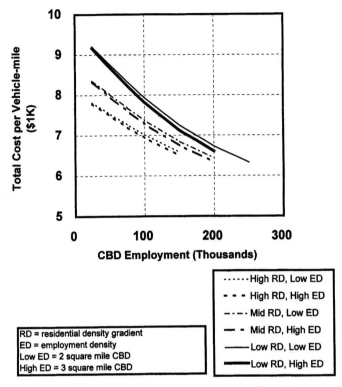

Figure 4.3 Light Rail Cost Efficiency by CBD Employment and Densities. (Source: Parsons Brinckerhoff Quade & Douglas, Inc., Robert Cervero, Howard/Stein-Hudson Associates, Inc., and Jeffrey Zupan, *Topic 1 Report: Regional Transit Corridors: The Land Use Connection* [Washington, DC: Transportation Research Board, Transit Cooperative Research Program, 1995, p. 78].)

other extreme, if the corridor densities were low (3 persons per acre), and employment size and densities were low also (20,000 workers at 100 workers per acre), then cost per vehicle mile would exceed $9. The lower cost efficiency reflects the fact that as ridership levels fall, service frequencies are usually scaled back, resulting in lower resource utilization (and thus higher costs per mile of service).

4.1.2.2 Density Effects on Heavy Rail: The Case of BART We recently developed similar demand models using 1990 ridership and land-use data for the 34 BART stations (shown in Map 4.1).[6] Land-use data were compiled for station-area catchments, defined as a contiguous area that captured 90 percent of all access trips to and egress trips from a

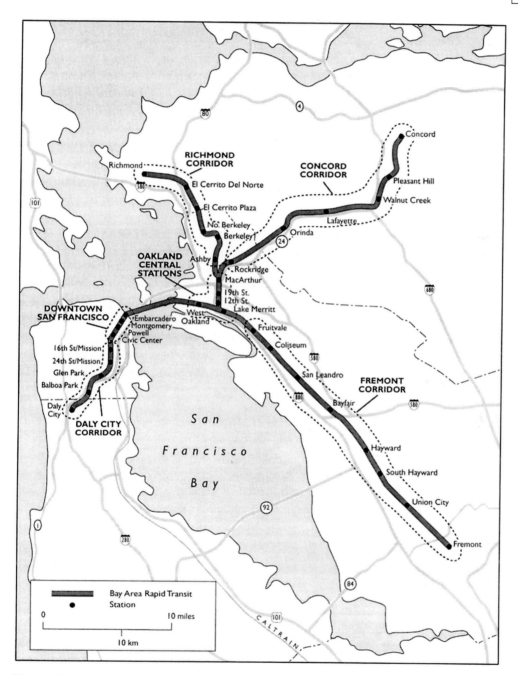

Map 4.1 Bay Area Rapid Transit System (BART), 1995.

BART station. BART's average catchment area is quite large, around 90 mi^2 with a radius of about 7 mi, though there was considerable variation around these averages.

Using statistical models that controlled for factors like levels of feeder bus service and household income in station catchment areas, we found that BART ridership per 1000 population (within the catchment) went up with population and employment densities (within 2 mi of stations).[7] On average, an increase of 10 workers per acre for a radius of 1 to 2 mi of a BART station increased the weekday turnstile counts entering and leaving the station by 6.5 per 1000 catchment population. Additionally, an increase of 1000 inhabitants per square mile added an average of 8 more rail trips per 1000 residents.

The effects of employment densities on ridership per square mile of catchment area were plotted for three different fare scenarios—$1, $2, and $3 fares to downtown San Francisco. BART has distance-based fares, so these scenarios also reflect length of trips and, indirectly, geographic setting (i.e., higher fares tend to be made by suburbanites). The plot in Figure 4.4 clearly reveals that ridership rates rise with employment densities and fall with price. At 150 employees per acre (e.g., downtown San Francisco's Embarcadero station) and a $2 average fare, there are nearly 250 daily turnstile entries and exits per square mile of catchment area; at 20 workers per acre, the rate is only about 150 turnstile counts.

Relationships were even stronger as a function of population densities, as suggested by the relatively steeper slopes for the sensitivity plots shown in Figure 4.5. Again assuming a fare of $2, Figure 4.5 shows that there would be nearly 200 trips per square mile for a station with a catchment zone that averages 4000 residents per square mile; this compares to

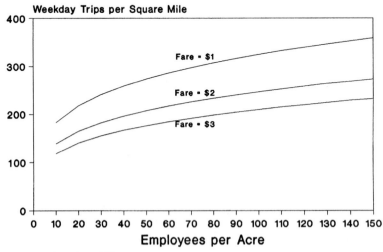

Figure 4.4 BART Weekday Rail Trips per Square Mile of Catchment Zone by Employment Density and Fare to San Francisco's CBD.

just 135 trips per square mile for a catchment zone with 2000 inhabitants per square mile. The most fortuitous scenario would be an average population density of 5000 residents per square mile (around 50 percent higher than the net residential density for the three BART-served counties) and an average fare to downtown San Francisco of $1. This combination could be expected to produce over 300 weekday trips per square mile of catchment area.

4.1.3 International Comparisons

Several notable studies with an international focus have examined the impacts of density on mode choice and such consequences of travel demand as gasoline consumption. The most influential, albeit controversial, is the work by Peter Newman and Jeff Kenworthy from Murdoch University in Perth, Australia.[8] Using international comparisons of U.S., European, and Asian cities, Newman and Kenworthy found that sprawling, auto-oriented U.S. cities like Phoenix and Houston averaged four to five times as much gasoline consumption per capita as comparably sized European cities (e.g., Copenhagen, Frankfurt). Differences in petroleum prices, incomes, and vehicle fuel efficiency explained only about half of these differences. The authors argued that the remaining difference was explained by urban structure: Cities with strong concentrations of central hubs, and accordingly a better developed public transport system, averaged much lower energy use than cities where jobs are scattered. Newman and Kenworthy also found a strong relationship

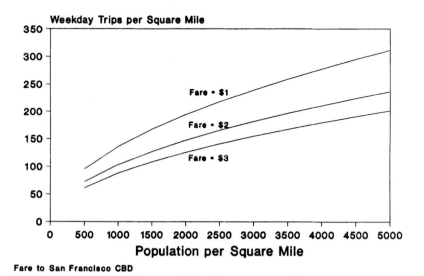

Figure 4.5 BART Weekday Rail Trips per Square Mile of Catchment Zone by Population Density and Fare to San Francisco's CBD.

between density and energy consumption within metropolitan areas. In the case of greater New York, for instance, Manhattanites averaged 90 gal of fuel consumption per capita annually compared to 454 gal per capita in the outer suburbs.[9]

In another study, John Pucher compared transit modal splits among 12 countries of Western Europe and North America (Canada and the United States). On average, European cities were found to be on the order of 50 percent denser with substantially more mixed-use neighborhoods than their American counterparts. Pucher found the percentage of all trips made by the automobile in U.S. cities to be more than double that of the majority of Western European countries, most of which have per capita incomes comparable to those of the United States. Pucher argued that transit's success in Europe can be explained by more supportive urban development patterns and automobile taxation policies rather than by factors like fare subsidies. Although impossible to measure, historical and cultural factors have also played a strong role in transit's relative success in Europe.

4.1.4 Intrametropolitan Comparisons

A final body of research has focused on how transit riding is influenced by densities at the neighborhood, activity center, or corridor level, typically within a single metropolitan area. These studies largely confirm the results of more macrolevel studies. Several studies have shown, for instance, that suburban employment centers and edge cities with above-norm densities typically average 3 to 5 percent more commute trips by mass transit among their work forces.[10] Bellevue, Washington, for instance, an edge city outside of Seattle, east of Lake Washington, has relatively high densities in its core, averaging 5 acres of building area for every acre of developed land. These densities are approximately one-third higher than in the nearby I-90/Eastside office-commercial strip and two-thirds higher than in Redmond, a community 5 mi east of Bellevue that has attracted a number of corporate tenants (e.g., Microsoft, Inc.) and campus-style office developments in recent times. In 1989, Bellevue averaged a 27 percent transit/ridesharing modal split for work trips headed to its center. This was two to three times higher than for the I-90/Riverside corridor and Redmond. Bellevue's success is not attributable to higher densities alone, however. Complementing the core's high-rise profile have been reductions in parking spaces, commercial-rate charges for parking, and good quality bus connections.

One common result from intrametropolitan studies of density's effects on travel demand is that the relationship is stronger at lower ranges of density and weaker at higher levels. Statistically, the relationship follows an exponential decay form—travel demand falls at a decreasing rate as density rises, whether travel is measured as trips per household, share of automobile trips, or gasoline consumption per capita. Using 1990 census data for the Bay Area, we found a strong inverse correlation between "percent commute trips by drive-alone auto" and "net residential densities" for 34 Bay Area subregions, as plotted in Figure 4.6; every doubling of mean residential densities was associated with roughly a 20 to 30 percent decline in the share of commute trips by drive-alone auto.[11] In a more recent study of 28 California communities, John Holtzclaw found that the number of automobiles and vehicle miles traveled (VMT) per household fell by one-quarter as densities doubled and by approximately 8 percent with a doubling of transit service levels.[12] Similar patterns have been found for the greater Seattle area.[13] Moreover, these relationships hold not only within metropolitan areas, but between them as well. For instance, Newman and Kenworthy's plot of gasoline consumption versus urban densities across 30 international cities also followed a decay function.

This remarkable consistency in the relationship between density and travel demand provides a useful policy lesson to the transit village movement: The biggest benefits come from going from very low to moderate densities, say from an average of 4 units per acre to 10 to 15 units per acre—that is, from a setting with quarter-acre estates to one with a mix of small-lot single-family homes and duplexes/triplexes. Increasing densities to mid- and high-rise apartments add relatively smaller benefits in terms of trip reduction. One doesn't need Hong Kong-like densities to sustain mass transit. If super-high densities were required, the term *transit village* itself would be a misnomer. Transit villages suggest places with more moderate residential densities, the kinds of settings sought by most middle-class households and that are in keeping with most Americans' lifestyle preferences.

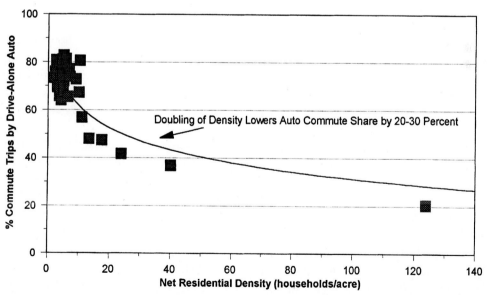

Figure 4.6 Higher Density Areas Average Lower Shares of Auto Commuting in the San Francisco Bay Area. Data are for 34 superdistricts in the nine-county Bay Area. Every doubling of residential density is associated with a 20 to 30 percent decline in drive-alone commuting shares.

4.1.5 Density, Design, and Perception

Today's typical suburban planned unit developments (PUDs) are designed at 5 to 6 dwelling units per residential acre (dua), well below the minimum of 12 dua necessary to support moderate levels of rail transit services.[14] Of course, communities are not designed singularly for the purpose of shaping travel behavior, much less to lure people to mass transit. More important, according to urbanologists Hans Blumenfeld and Jane Jacobs, is to design places at a proper human scale so as to impart a sense of identity and belonging to a place.[15] Hans Blumenfeld, with the assurance that comes from long practice, maintains the "right" residential densities are between 12 and 60 dua. Such a range, he contends, ensures people can easily reach places by foot and have frequent face-to-face contact without being overawed by a monumental scale. Jane Jacobs advocates even higher densities, more in the 50 to 150 dua range, to create a vibrant community and instill an attachment to place.

Many people wrongly equate density with high-rise buildings. The French architect Le Corbusier's Radiant City, the ultimate futuristic high-rise residential city, featured gross densities of only 120 to 150 dua. Since towers were separated by vast expanses of open space, the buildings in Radiant City covered only 12 percent of the ground. Four- to five-story residential buildings can produce average densities above those of Radiant City, in the 140 to 220 dua range.

Built environments are extremely malleable, able to accommodate a variety of spatial organizations and housing types. It is possible to build at 12 dua and still accommodate single-family detached units. Ebenezer Howard's garden cities, forerunners of today's transit village schemes, featured single-family homes built at 12 dua. Row houses (connected single-family homes with zero lot lines) can be developed as high as 6 dua. Mixing building types can nudge average densities up to the level where transit trips outnumber automobile trips. For instance, 50 dua can be achieved by designing a project where half of the units are single-family dwellings at 12 dua, 30 percent are row houses at 36 dua, and 20 percent are mid-rise apartments at 160 dua.

The reality is that most Americans prefer low-density areas with detached buildings not because they like spread-out development per se, but rather because they perceive such settings as safer and less hectic. Residential preference surveys consistently show that upward of 95 percent of Americans prefer single-family to multifamily dwellings.[16] Many associate density with noise, overcrowdedness, urban blight, and stress. Preference for single-family living also reflects the strong North American value placed on home ownership, secured tenancy, and privacy.[17]

Only recently have designers begun to recognize that actual and perceived densities can vary widely. Density is a perceived experience shaped by visual cues, some of which suggest crowdedness (e.g., busy sidewalks) and others that convey spaciousness (e.g., tree-lined streets).[18] James Bergdall and Rick Williams, in a study of three San Francisco streets with similar densities (39–47 dua) lined with buildings of identical height but different architectural details, concluded that facades with greater articulation (e.g., visible roofs, individual bay windows, and recesses) were perceived as lower in density than streets with facades of a uniform appearance.[19]

Architectural critics Lloyd Bookout and James Wentling contend that people will trade off higher densities in return for more amenities and better quality living environments.[20] Ways of making higher density projects acceptable include: extensive landscaping; adding parks, civic spaces, and small consumer services in neighborhoods; varying building heights and materials to break the monotony of structures; detailing rooflines; designing mid-rise buildings on podiums with tuck-under, below-grade parking; and replacing row apartments connected by exterior breezeways with eight-plex buildings (two-story stacked flats with four ground-level patios and second-level decks).

It is the prospect of reducing the perceived densities of transit villages by providing attractive amenities that motivated research on market acceptance of compact transit village development. The findings of this research are presented in Chapter 6, The Market for Transit Villages.

4.2 LAND-USE DIVERSITY

In addition to being compact, transit villages should be diverse in their land-use composition. The separation of land uses is a legacy of Euclidean zoning principles that, when applied in the 1920s, sought to protect residences from nuisances like smokestacks and foul odors. In today's cities where clean, nonpolluting businesses and shops are the norm, the logic of separating and excluding urban activities makes little sense. There are potential efficiencies in mixed land-use environments. By clustering eight neighborhoods around village centers and linking them with a community bus system and bike network, the developers of Columbia, Maryland, were able to achieve annual savings of $810,000 in 1975. From travel surveys, they estimated that households averaged 30 fewer miles driven per month.[21]

The transportation benefits of mixed land uses can be significant but are not always obvious. Settings with a mixture of land uses can encourage people to walk or ride to various destinations instead of driving. Having shops and restaurants connected to a nearby suburban job center with a nicely landscaped pathway likely means more people will walk to these destinations during, say, lunch time. It might also mean some who otherwise would have driven to work now ride transit instead because they don't need a car to be mobile in the midday.

Mixed land uses also promote resource efficiency. One example is shared parking. In a transit village, for instance, theatergoers might use the spaces vacated by office workers in the evenings. Shared parking can shrink the scale of suburban activity centers by as much as 25 percent, which might translate into a 25 percent more pedestrian-friendly environment. Also, less road capacity is necessary if a development is mixed instead of single use. At an executive park with only office space, for instance, most tenants will arrive in the morning and leave in the evening. This means sizing the road infrastructure to handle peak loads. If the same amount of floorspace was instead split between offices, shops, and residences, trips would be more evenly balanced throughout the day and week, reducing the amount of peak road capacity needed. Efficiencies can also be enjoyed by transit operators. Balanced mixed uses often translate into balanced, bidirectional travel flows. This means buses and trains will be more fully utilized along a route. When residences and workplaces are poles apart, the all too frequent spectacle of near-empty transit vehicles in certain directions is inevitable.

Mixed land uses are important beyond inducing people to ride transit or walk. Having shops, restaurants, newsstands, coffeehouses, and open-air markets near neighborhoods and work centers adds variety and vitality to an area. One only has to go to a suburban office park on a weekend to see how devoid of life these places can be. A mixed-use area, on the other hand, has people present throughout the day and week. Because of continuing activity and casual surveillance of many eyes, mixed-use environments feel safer. To seniors and others concerned with safety and alarmed about escalating crime, an attractive mixed-use transit village might be viewed as a safe haven and respite from the frenetic pace of a city. It is for such reasons that urban sociologist Jane Jacobs has argued that an essential feature of any healthy city is "an intricate and close-grained diversity of uses that give each other constant mutual support, both economically and socially."[22]

Some U.S. cities have been particularly active in targeting mixed-use development near transit stations. In Montgomery County, Maryland, a TS-M (Transit Station-Mixed) zoning classification has been established in the vicinity of some Metrorail stations, which allows for a wide range of commercial, service, and residential uses that serve transit users and residents in the area. The purpose of the TS-M zone is to:

(a) promote the optimum use of transit facilities by assuring the orderly development of land in transit station development areas and enhancing access, both vehicular and pedestrian access;

(b) provide for the needs of the workers and residents of transit station development areas;

(c) provide for the incidental shopping needs of transit facility riders at Metrorail stations;

(d) minimize the necessity for automobile transportation by providing, in largely residential transit station areas, the retail commercial uses and professional services that contribute to the self-sufficiency of the community.

Several west coast cities have been particularly active in zoning for mixed-use activities near transit in recent years. Hillsborough, Oregon, has created a mixed-use overlay zone for areas in close proximity to the planned Hillsborough Extension light rail line in the

Portland area. The city of San Diego provides density bonuses for developments that include child-care centers near light rail stops. And Lynwood, Washington, has created a special Mixed Use/Transit-Supportive zone that grants special use permits to any of the following activities that are sited near transit lines: banks, professional buses, retail stores, offices, and child-care centers.

Are there any special mixes of services that are compatible with a transit-oriented community? This partly depends on the parameters of a transit village. At blended densities of around 12 units per acre, a transit village with a one-quarter mile radius can accommodate a residential population of around 3800 (assuming an average of 2.5 persons per household). This range is generally large enough to support most neighborhood commercial uses, like a bakery or deli. Of course, to the degree that other neighborhoods abut a transit village, the retail market shed could easily expand outward. Among the "appropriate" uses proposed by the city of San Jose for a mixed-use infill neighborhood with a strong pedestrian orientation are:

bakeries	*galleries*	*post office*
banks	*grocery stores*	*professional offices*
bookstores	*gift shops*	*public/government uses*
camera stores	*hardware stores*	*radio, TV, video, music stores*
clothing stores	*health clubs*	*restaurants, bars*
collectible shops	*home furnishings*	*schools—private*
day-care centers	*ice cream parlor*	*shoe stores*
delis	*instruction studios*	*small appliance repairs*
drugstores	*laundromats*	*small theater*
dry cleaners	*office supplies*	*specialty foods*
florists	*personal service shops*	*sporting goods*
food vendors	*pet stores*	*tailor*

4.2.1 Mixed Use and Travel at Employment Centers

Two studies have examined how adding retail and other mixed uses at employment centers can shape travel behavior. A 1989 study of 59 large-scale suburban employment centers in the United States found that centers with on-site retail averaged about 8 percent higher rates of midday walk travel and lower rates of drive-alone commuting.[23] A more recent study by Cambridge Systematics explored the connection between the work environment and commute modes among 330 companies in the Los Angeles region that had introduced Transportation Demand Management (TDM) measures (e.g., ridesharing) in response to the Regulation XV trip reduction mandates aimed at improving air quality. The study found that transit captured 6.4 percent of commute trips in "diverse-mix" employment areas versus 2.9 percent of commute trips in "no-mix" areas (with both figures for companies that had introduced TDM measures and various incentives, such as free transit passes).

4.2.2   Mixed Use and Travel Within Neighborhoods

Empirical evidence on the transportation benefits of mixed-use environments outside of large-scale employment centers is only beginning to accumulate. In a comprehensive study of mixed-use sites in Colorado, average trip rates for individual shops in retail plazas and other mixed commercial settings were 2.5 percent below the mean rates published in the Institute of Transportation Engineers's *Trip Generation* manual.[24] The study recommended adjusting trip rates downward by this amount to reflect the higher likelihood of linked walk trips, instead of separate vehicle trips, between establishments in mixed-use settings.

More recent work has examined the implications of retail and other mixed uses in predominantly residential neighborhoods on nonwork travel specifically. In a comparison of shopping trips among residents from four neighborhoods in the San Francisco Bay Area, Susan Handy found those living in two traditional, mixed-use neighborhoods made two to four more walk/bicycle trips per week to neighborhood shops than did those living in nearby areas that were served mainly by automobile-oriented, strip retail development.[25] Residents of mixed-use neighborhoods, however, averaged similar rates of auto travel to regional shopping malls, suggesting that internal walk trips might not have replaced external auto trips but rather have been supplemental. In a recent comparison of work and nonwork travel among residents of six communities in Palm Beach County, Florida, Reid Ewing and his colleagues at Florida International University found that the presence of shopping, recreation, and school facilities within communities can significantly lower vehicle hours traveled (VHT) per capita.[26] A low-density planned suburban community, Wellington, whose residents commuted the farthest and drove the most, also averaged the shortest shopping and recreation trips because various retail shops and services were available within their community.

Another recent study addressed the influence of mixed uses on both work and shop trips in the Seattle-Tacoma region. That work, by Lawrence Frank and Gary Pivo, found that mixed-use neighborhoods were most strongly correlated with walk trips to work, but rather surprisingly they had little influence on mode choice for shop trips.[27] Our own recent study of work trips across 11 large U.S. metropolitan areas similarly found having retail shops near residences can be an inducement toward walking or riding transit to work.[28] Specifically, having retail shops and other nonresidential uses within 300 ft of one's residence lowered the probability of auto commuting in greater Boston, Dallas, Phoenix, Philadelphia, and seven other large metropolitan areas. Having stores between a transit stop and one's residence, for instance, allows transit riders to conveniently shop while en route home in the evening, thus linking work and shop trips in a single tour.[29] This research suggested, in fact, that the presence of retail uses can yield almost as many transportation benefits as higher densities in residential neighborhoods. Based on mode choice models estimated using 1985 travel data from these 11 metropolitan areas, Figure 4.7 plots the probability of walking or bicycling to work for commute distances of 0.125 to 1.5 mi. The graph shows that, for a commute distance of around 1 mi, one out of four work trips was by foot or bicycle if someone lived in a neighborhood with low densities and mixed uses or one with mid- to high-rise apartments but no nearby retail outlets. Of course, the highest transit ridership came from a combination of high densities and mixed land uses. At a 1.5-mi commute distance, there was a 25 percent chance that someone living in a mid- to high-rise neighborhood with surrounding stores walked or biked to work in these 11 metropolitan areas.[30]

4.2.3 Jobs-Housing Balance

Another form of mixed land uses that is engendered in the transit village concept is a balance of jobs and housing. Jobs-housing balance has been touted as a means of shortening commute trips, thus reducing vehicle miles of travel (VMT), freeway traffic, and tailpipe emissions.[31] California's two largest metropolitan areas—greater Los Angeles and the San Francisco Bay Area—sought to set subregional jobs-housing balance targets in the 1980s.

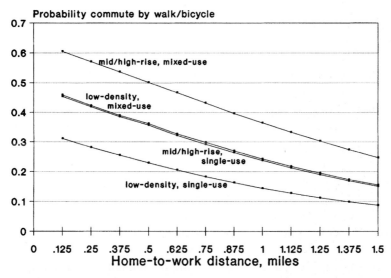

Figure 4.7 Probability of Commuting by Walking or Bicycling for Four Land-Use Scenarios as a Function of Commute Distance.

Genevieve Giuliano, Anthony Downs, and other observers have questioned whether jobs-housing balance will ever be an effective tool for producing transportation and air quality benefits for several reasons: workers in two-earner households usually work in different locations; exclusionary zoning policies limit residential mobility; and factors other than job access, such as quality of schools, exert strong influences on residential location choices.[32]

Peter Gordon and Harry Richardson further argue that jobs-housing balance will have little impact on the fastest growing travel segment, the nonwork trip, which already accounts for three-quarters of all trips in the United States and the majority of trips during the peak hour.[33] Others point out, moreover, that regional balance is a natural evolutionary process brought on by market conditions; over time, jobs and housing colocate so as to maintain an equilibrium in commuting time. For this reason, critics charge that planning initiatives that aim to balance growth (e.g., developing self-contained new towns or transit villages) are unnecessary. Martin Wachs and his colleagues at UCLA recently presented evidence that supports this colocation hypothesis: The average commute distances of 8000 hospital workers in southern California fell from 10.0 mi in 1984 to 9.7 mi in 1990. This and other research are consistent with the Law of Constant Travel Time that maintains transportation technologies and locational decisions adjust to maintain a fairly constant amount of time devoted to commuting, which according to Arnulf Grubler is in the 1 to 1.5 h per day range. He notes that this time budget has remained "close to an anthropological constant" since ancient Rome.

Other data paint a much different portrait of recent commuting trends, however. The National Personal Transportation Survey showed that the average commute length in the United States increased from 9.2 mi in 1983 to 10.6 mi in 1990. Moreover, census data reveal that the average work trip time increased from 1980 to 1990 in 35 of the 39 U.S. metropolitan areas with populations over 1 million. Three of the four areas experiencing the greatest increases in commute durations were California metropolises that have invested in rail transit over the past decade: metropolitan San Diego (19.5 to 22.2 min, +13.8 percent), Los Angeles-Long Beach (23.6 to 26.4 min, +11.9 percent), and Sacramento (19.5 to 21.8 min, +11.8 percent).

Recent research makes an even stronger case for public policies, like transit villages, that encourage balanced jobs and housing growth. In their study of travel in the Puget Sound area, Frank and Pivo found that commute distances and times tended to be shorter for those living in balanced areas. The average distance of work trips ending in balanced census tracts (with jobs-to-housing ratios of 0.8 to 1.2) was 28 percent shorter (6.9 versus 9.6 mi) than the distance of trips ending in unbalanced tracts. A recent study by Reid Ewing, titled "Before We Write off Jobs-Housing Balance . . . ," used 1990 census data to compute the proportion of work trips that remain within over 500 cities and towns in Florida. Ewing found that the share of internal, or within-community, commuting significantly increased with greater balance in the number of local jobs and working residents.

Our own recent work largely substantiates these findings from Seattle and Florida. Using 1990 census data for the 23 largest cities in the San Francisco Bay Area, the average one-way commutes of workers in cities with 50 percent more jobs than housing units were over 3 min longer than the regional average. Cities with high housing prices relative to the earnings of their workforce also tended to have very large shares of their workers living elsewhere. The city of Pleasanton, 35 mi east of San Francisco, experienced the fastest employment growth during the 1980s in the region (365 percent increase), changing from a predominantly bedroom community to a job-surplus city in 1990 (13 percent more jobs than housing units). Paralleling this trend have been rapid increases in commute distances among Pleasanton's work force, from approximately 13 mi in 1987 to 18.8 mi in 1993.

Creating mixed-use, balanced transit villages would clearly be consonant with the objective of reducing distances and drive-alone shares of commute trips. Notwithstanding the harsh criticism leveled at jobs-housing balance as an object of public policy, evidence shows that balanced growth matters.

4.3 TRANSIT-SUPPORTIVE DESIGN

The final element in the triad of supportive physical characteristics of transit villages is urban design itself. Transit villages should encourage walking and transit riding. Since all transit trips involve some degree of walking, it follows that transit-friendly environments must also be pedestrian-friendly.

A common theme of transit-supportive design is to create places that, in addition to being more compact and diverse, have design features (e.g., landscaped sidewalks, parking in the rear, and retail streetwalls) that make walking and transit riding more enjoyable. The aim is to reorient community building away from the planned urban developments (PUDs) of the 1960s and 1970s toward patterns reminiscent of earlier streetcar suburbs and pre-World War II traditional communities.

A 1993 survey across the United States and Canada found 26 examples of completed design guidelines prepared by transit agencies that promoted transit-friendly development. The main purpose of these guidelines has been to influence the project design decisions of developers at the conceptualization as well as the plan review stages. Commonly accepted transit-supportive designs often include the following types of treatments:

- ☐ Continuous and direct physical linkages between major activity centers; siting of buildings and complementary uses to minimize distances to transit stops (Figure 4.8).
- ☐ Streetwalls of ground-floor retail and varied building heights, textures, and facades that enhance the walking experience; siting commercial buildings near the edge of sidewalks.

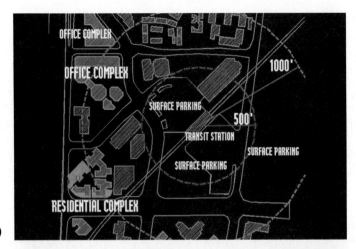

NO

YES

Figure 4.8 Are Land Uses Complementary and Within Walking Distance? Compact versus spread-out development around a transit station.

☐ Integration of major commercial centers with the transit facility, including air rights development (Figure 4.9).

☐ Gridlike street patterns that allow many origins and destinations to be connected by foot; avoiding cul-de-sacs, serpentine streets, and other curvilinear alignments that create circuitous walks and force buses to meander or retrace their paths; direct sight lines to transit stops (Figure 4.10).

☐ Minimizing off-street parking supplies; where land costs are high, tucking parking under buildings or placing it in peripheral structures; in other cases, siting parking at the rear of buildings instead of in front.

NO

Random disposition and orientation of the built forms;

No logical relations between transit infrastructure and buildings

YES

Disposition and orientation of the building according to a main axial system;

Direct link between transit infrastructure and building

Figure 4.9 Do Buildings Fit with and Complement the Transit System? Building detachment versus building integration.

- ☐ Providing such pedestrian amenities as attractive landscaping, continuous and paved sidewalks, street furniture, urban art, screening of parking, building over-hangs and weather protection, and safe street crossings.
- ☐ Convenient siting of transit shelters, benches, and route information.
- ☐ Creating public open spaces and pedestrian plazas that are convenient to transit.

The rationales for these design treatments are obvious. Any one treatment would unlikely be noticed. Collectively, however, they would create a fundamentally different suburban milieu than what the vast majority of Americans are used to. For the most part, these treat-

NO

YES

Figure 4.10 Are Walk Paths Direct and Separated from Parking? Direct versus disconnected sight lines to a transit station.

ments would not add terribly much to the cost of new planned developments. However, one only has to drive around most contemporary suburban subdivisions in the United States to know that these design approaches are more the exception than the rule.

Urban designers often stress the importance of public spaces in creating lively and interesting urban milieus. Having plazas, courtyards, gathering places, and greenery near transit stations, we believe, is vital to the transit village, a subject we address in more detail in Chapter 6. Among the activities taking place in public spaces, Jan Gehl, an urban

Transforming suburban neighborhoods into more pedestrian-friendly, transit-supportive environments might occur over a number of stages. Figure 4.11 shows a typical auto-oriented commercial district with a vast expanse of parking that separates buildings from the main street, numerous driveways and curbcuts, no internal or curbside sidewalks, exposed pathways, and minimal landscaping. Over time, this rather hostile environment for walking and transit riding could be redesigned, modified, and retrofitted so that it is more human in scale, compact, and attractive to pedestrians. In the early stages, less expensive things could be done: installing sidewalks and street lighting, improving pedestrian crossings, and consolidating driveways. The public improvements ideally would be enough to increase property values and spark a renewed interest in the area. This might lead to the intensification of uses, including the addition of housing. Figure 4.12 portrays how the setting might look after such measures as relocating parking, consolidating driveways, integrating walkways, improving the landscape, and filling in the main street with more neighborhood-oriented uses like restaurants and specialty retail shops are accomplished. The final stage of transformation is depicted by Figure 4.13. A light rail line penetrates the neighborhood. Flanking it is a public plaza that ties into a community complex. Courtyards, tree-canopied walkways, and further landscaping improvements enhance the setting. Additional housing densifies the neighborhood even more. The end result is the transformation of an auto-oriented commercial strip into a mixed-use neighborhood more conducive to walking and transit riding.

designer from Copenhagen, has identified three types: necessary activities, optional activities, and social activities.[34] Necessary activities are what you must do, such as walking to school, waiting for the bus, sitting because you are tired, etc. These activities take place at all times and more or less regardless of the quality of physical environment. There is no choice. Gehl maintains that a good neighborhood makes sure that all necessary activities take place in pleasant circumstances.

Optional activities are what you are tempted to do, given the right circumstances. They might include standing about looking at streetlife, sitting for a while to enjoy a place or scenery, having a latte at a sidewalk cafe, and so on. These are things you do when the situation is nice and inviting. Last, social activities involve meeting fellow citizens. This can involve major civic events such as festivals, parades, protests, and ceremonies. Another

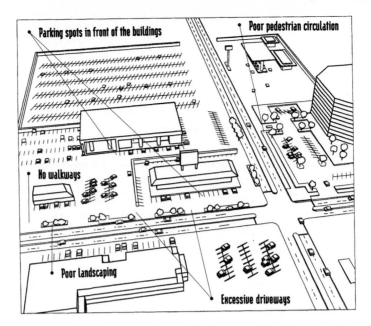

Figure 4.11 Auto-Oriented Commercial District Unfriendly to Pedestrians and Transit Users.

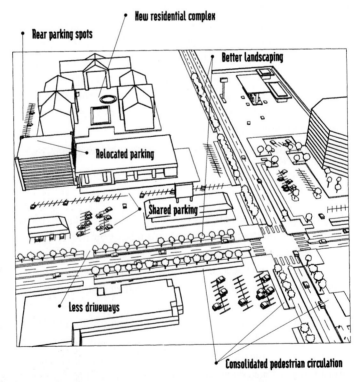

Figure 4.12 Initial Improvements Friendly to Pedestrians and Transit Users.

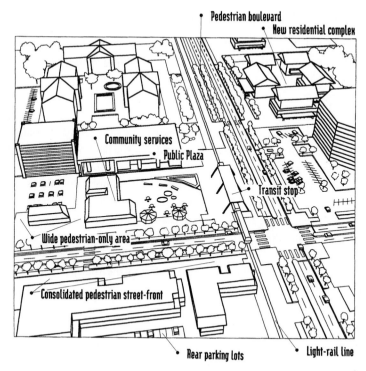

Figure 4.13 Transformation into a Transit-Oriented Neighborhood.

very important category of social activities is the multitude of humble everyday encounters, including passing others on sidewalks, seeing and overhearing people, and taking in the life and atmosphere of the city. Unplanned and unexpected meetings, and the sheer pleasure of serendipity, are what make social encounters so important. Great neighborhoods can accommodate both city celebrations and humble encounters.

Good neighborhoods make sure that this network of meetings of its people can prosper. Gehl has equated planning a neighborhood to planning a party along these simple lines: a feeling of welcome from the moment you arrive; enjoyable spaces and enough room for everyone; good catering—nice locations while eating and having refreshments; entertainment and music; and good places for standing about and sitting. Many of Gehl's prescriptions for neighborhood design have applicability to transit villages. Notably, transit villages must be places that are enjoyable for people to go and interact, whether en route to the train station or simply to take in village life. Having splendid public spaces, we believe, would perhaps do as much to draw people from different walks of life into the community as any single design element.

4.3.1 Transit-Supportive Design and Travel

Presently, our knowledge of how transit-supportive and pedestrian-friendly urban designs shape travel behavior is limited. After reviewing experiences with transit-supportive urban designs in greater Chicago, San Diego, San Francisco, Seattle, and Washington, DC-Baltimore, one study concluded that:

> the evidence on the impacts of transit-supportive site designs is admittedly thin. . . . With the exception of several sites in the Seattle and Washington, D.C. areas, employees at transit-supportive sites were generally as dependent on their cars to get to work as those working in more auto-oriented sites. Quite simply, the effects of micro-features tend to be too "micro" to exert any fundamental influence on travel choices. It is more likely that transit-friendly design elements influence midday travel, such as the incidence of walk trips during lunch hour, than peak-period commuting. Had data for other trips purposes as well as for internal trips within activity centers been available, a more positive light might have been cast on the transportation benefits of transit-supportive designs.[35]

In recent years, a number of studies have sought to gauge the importance of traditional neighborhood designs on travel choices in American cities. None of these studies has successfully isolated the unique effects of transit-supportive design features, as discussed in this section. However, these studies have measured differences in modal splits and rates of walk trips in traditional neighborhoods with transit- and pedestrian-friendly design features as well as land-use diversity and moderate levels of density.[36] Often, impacts are assessed by comparing travel statistics in these traditional neighborhoods with those from more typical auto-oriented subdivisions.

Quite a few of these neighborhood comparisons have been conducted for the San Francisco Bay Area. Using data from smog-check odometer readings, John Holtzclaw found that residents of dense, mixed-use, and pedestrian-friendly San Francisco neighborhoods drove, on average, only one-third as many miles each year as residents of Danville, a low-density, auto-oriented East Bay suburb with comparable incomes.[37] Another study found a dramatic difference in mode choice between auto-oriented suburbs and traditional pre-World War II neighborhoods with moderate to high densities.[38] In 1980, 23 percent of the trips in traditional Bay Area neighborhoods were on foot and 22 percent were by transit. By comparison, suburban residents made only 9 percent of their trips by foot and 3 percent by transit. Other studies have shown similar travel differences between auto-oriented and transit-oriented suburbs, both in the Bay Area and elsewhere.[39]

Many comparative studies to date can be faulted for not adequately controlling for confounding factors, most notably income, that might explain travel differences. Most comparisons have also failed to control for differences in transit service levels and geographic location. In the following chapter, we present our own recent research on this subject that introduces controls for removing the effects of these confounding factors. Chapter 5 aims to further strengthen the case, using our recent research findings, that transit villages can yield important social and public benefits.

NOTES

1. Boris Pushkarev and Jeffrey Zupan, *Public Transit and Land-Use Policy* (Bloomington: Indiana University Press, 1977).
2. Wilbur Smith, Mass Transit for High-Rise, High-Density Living, *Journal of Transportation Engineering,* Vol. 110, No. 6, pp. 521–535, 1984.
3. Parsons Brinckerhoff Quade & Douglas, Inc., Robert Cervero, Howard/Stein-Hudson Associates, and Jeffrey Zupan, *Regional Transit Corridors: The Land Use Connection* (Washington, DC: National Research Council, Transportation Research Board, Transit Cooperative Research Program H-1). Jeffrey Zupan and David Kerr were the principal analysts of the effects of the built environment on national transit ridership. Robert Cervero, Samuel Seskin, Jack Dean, Phil Smelley, Brent Baker, and Susan Serres assisted in the analysis.
4. The six cities were Boston, Chicago, Los Angeles, Philadelphia, San Francisco, and Washington, DC.
5. Cost components included annual operating and capital depreciation, including land acquisition. Many of these costs vary considerably according to operating settings. Average figures were relied upon. In the case of right of way, for instance, costs of $990,000 per track mile were assumed.
6. This analysis was carried out by Robert Cervero and is presented as Appendix B in the report titled *Regional Transit Corridors: The Land Use Connection,* cited in note 3.
7. Multiple regression models were estimated that, when expressing all variables in natural logarithm terms, took the following form:

    Estimated turnstile counts per 1000 population = 4.412 + 0.1351 (employees per acre) − 0.241 (land area) + 0.283 (feeder bus service per 1000 population) + 0.364 (household income).

    This model produced an R^2 of 0.833, with all variables statistically significant at the .01 probability level. Other model versions included variables measuring fares to downtown San Francisco, average household income, land-use mixture levels, and type of station (terminal or not).
8. Peter Newman and Jeffrey Kenworthy, Gasoline Consumption and Cities: A Comparison of U.S. Cities with a Global Survey, *Journal of the American Planning Association,* Vol. 65, No. 2, pp. 161–182, 1991.
9. This work sparked a firestorm of controversy about the methods used in drawing these inferences. Critics charged that Newman and Kenworthy failed to introduce

proper statistical controls that account for variations in fuel consumption, such as differences in the distribution of vehicle sizes across comparison cities. Amsterdam and Copenhagen, for instance, average much higher shares of subcompact and compact vehicles than cities like Houston and Phoenix, thus partly explaining lower fuel consumption per capita in European cities. For a critique of this work, see Peter Gordon and Harry Richardson, Gasoline Consumption and Cities: A Reply, *Journal of the American Planning Association,* Vol. 55, No. 2, pp. 342–345, 1989; José Gomez-Ibanez, A Global View of Automobile Dependence, *Journal of the American Planning Association,* Vol. 57, No. 3, pp. 376–379, 1991.

10. See Robert Cervero, *Suburban Gridlock* (New Brunswick, NJ: Center for Urban Policy Research, 1986); Robert Cervero, *America's Suburban Centers: The Land Use-Transportation Link* (Boston: Unwin Hyman, 1989); Kevin Hopper, *Travel Characteristics of Large-Scale Suburban Activity Centers* (Alexandria, VA: JHK & Associates, NCHRP Project Report 3-38[2], 1989); Cambridge Systematics, *The Effects of Land Use and Travel Demand Strategies on Commuting Behavior* (Washington, DC: U.S. Department of Transportation, Federal Highway Administration, 1994).

11. Data were obtained from the 1990 Census Transportation Planning Package, made available by the Metropolitan Transportation Commission in Oakland.

12. J. Holtzclaw, *Residential Patterns and Transit, Auto Dependence, and Costs* (San Francisco: Resources Defense Council, 1994).

13. Lawrence Frank and Gary Pivo found that higher population densities increased the share of shopping and work trips made by transit and on foot. Their research found that increasing population density from 20 to 40 persons per acre, holding factors like household income constant, would increase bus transit usage in the Puget Sound region from 1.7 percent to around 7 percent of all shopping trips. See L. Frank and G. Pivo, The Impacts of Mixed Use and Density on the Utilization of Three Modes of Travel: The Single Occupant Vehicle, Transit, and Walking, *Transportation Research Record,* Vol. 1466, pp. 44–52, 1994.

14. To support light rail services, Pushkarev and Zupan maintain that a minimum of 12 dua is necessary over a 50-mi^2 area in a region with a central business district with at least 25 million ft^2 of nonresidential floorspace.

15. See H. Blumenfeld, *The Modern Metropolis: Its Origins, Growth, Characteristics, and Planning* (Cambridge, MA: MIT Press, 1968); J. Jacobs, *The Death and Life of Great American Cities* (New York: Vintage Books, 1961).

16. W. Michelson, Most People Don't Want What Architects Want, *Transaction,* Vol. 5, No. 8, pp. 37–43, 1968; L. Bookout, The Future of Higher-Density Housing, *Urban Land,* Vol. 51, No. 9, pp. 14–18, 1992.

17. See N. Foote, J. Agu-Lughod, M. Foley, and L. Winnick, *Housing Choices and Housing Constraints* (New York: McGraw-Hill, 1960); W. Michelson, *Environmental Choice, Human Behavior, and Residential Satisfaction* (New York: Oxford University Press, 1977); C. Cooper-Marchus and W. Sarkissian, *Housing as if People Mattered* (Berkeley: Univer-

sity of California Press, 1986); J. Dillman and D. Dillman, Private Outside Space as a Factor in Housing Acceptability, *Housing and Society,* Vol. 14, No. 1, pp. 20–29, 1987.

18. See A. Rappaport, Toward a Redefinition of Density, *Environment and Behavior,* Vol. 7, No. 2, pp. 25–36, 1975.

19. J. Bergdall and R. Williams, Perception of Density, *Berkeley Planning Journal,* Vol. 5, pp. 15–38, 1990.

20. L. Bookout and J. Wentling, Density by Design. *Urban Land,* Vol. 47, pp. 10–15, 1988.

21. Comptroller General, *Report to Congress: Greater Energy Efficiency Can Be Achieved Through Land Use Management* (Washington, DC: EMD 82–1, December, 1981).

22. Jacobs, op. cit., p. 14.

23. Robert Cervero, *America's Suburban Centers: The Land Use-Transportation Link* (Boston: Unwin Hyman, 1989).

24. Colorado/Wyoming Section Technical Committee, Institute of Transportation Engineers, Trip Generation for Mixed Use Developments, *ITE Journal,* Vol. 57, No. 2, pp. 27–29, 1987.

25. Susan Handy, Regional Versus Local Accessibility: Neo-Traditional Development and Its Implications for Non-Work Travel. *Built Environment,* Vol. 18, No. 4, pp. 253–267, 1992.

26. Reid Ewing, P. Haliyur, and Gregory Page, Getting Around a Traditional City, a Suburban PUD and Everything In-Between, *Transportation Research Record,* Vol. 1466, pp. 53–61, 1994.

27. Frank and Pivo, op. cit.

28. Robert Cervero, Mixed Land Uses and Commuting: Evidence from the American Housing Survey. *Transportation Research* (forthcoming).

29. In transportation planning parlance, a tour is a complete circuit between one's residence and some other destination or destinations. As used in this example, the person is making a work-trip tour since the primary destination is the workplace. Other stops, such as to a cleaners or grocery outlet, are secondary to the purpose of going to work.

30. This analysis was conducted using 1985 commuting data from the American Housing Survey. For the probability plots shown in Figure 4.7, these relationships hold under the following conditions: public transit services are rated as "adequate" (by respondents to the American Housing Survey) and the person lives in a household with two automobiles available.

31. Robert Cervero, Jobs-Housing Balancing and Regional Mobility, *Journal of the American Planning Association,* Vol. 55, No. 2, pp. 136–150, 1989.

32. Genevieve Giuliano, Is Jobs-Housing Balance a Transportation Issue? *Transportation Research Record,* Vol. 1305, pp. 305–312, 1991; Anthony Downs, *Stuck in Traffic: Coping with Peak-Hour Traffic Congestion* (Washington, DC: The Brookings Institution, 1992).

33. Peter Gordon and Harry Richardson, The Commuting Paradox: Evidence from the Top Twenty, *Journal of the American Planning Association,* Vol. 57, No. 4, pp. 416–420, 1991.

34. Jan Gehl, *Giving the City a Human Face, A Challenge for the City* (Perth, Australia: Perth Beyond, 1992).

35. Robert Cervero, *Transit-Supportive Development in the United States: Experiences and Prospects* (Washington, DC: Federal Transit Administration, 1993), p. 122.

36. In some ways, it is more revealing to compare travel characteristics of traditional neighborhoods that are dense, mixed-use, and pedestrian friendly with travel from low-density, auto-oriented neighborhoods. In reality, there is a close correlation between density and the presence of mixed land uses and more pedestrian-oriented development.

37. John Holtzclaw, Manhattanization Versus Sprawl: How Density Impacts Auto Use Comparing Five Bay Area Communities, *Proceedings of the Eleventh International Pedestrian Conference* (Boulder, CO: City of Boulder, 1990), pp. 99–106. In a more recent study, Holtzclaw found similar results. This analysis of 28 California communities showed that the number of automobiles and VMT per household fell by 25 percent as densities doubled and by around 8 percent with a doubling of transit services, again controlling for factors like household income. See John Holtzclaw, *Residential Patterns and Transit, Auto Dependence, and Costs* (San Francisco: Resources Defense Council, 1994).

38. Fehrs and Peers Associates, *Metropolitan Transportation Commission Bay Area Trip Rate Survey Analysis* (Oakland: Metropolitan Transportation Commission, 1992).

39. See Ritachi Kitamura, Pat Mokhtarian, and Lynn Laidet, *A Micro-Analysis of Land Use and Travel in Five Neighborhoods in the San Francisco Bay Area* (Davis: University of California at Davis, California Air Resources Board, 1994); Maryland National Capital Park and Planning Commission, *Transit and Pedestrian Oriented Neighborhoods* (Silver Spring: Maryland National Capital Park and Planning Commission, 1992); White Mountain Survey Company, *City of Portsmouth Traffic/Trip Generation Study* (Ossippee, NH: White Mountain Survey Company, 1990).

5

Transit-Oriented Development and Travel Choices: Lessons from the San Francisco Bay Area

This chapter builds upon the previous one by presenting the results of recent work we've completed that is central to the question of how built environments shape transit riding, using the San Francisco Bay Area as a case context. The San Francisco Bay Area is a particularly appropriate case setting for addressing this question for historical and contextual reasons. As discussed in Chapter 2, in the early part of this century, the Bay Area had one of the most extensive interurban streetcar networks anywhere—the Key System, which served much of the East Bay until the 1950s. Some neighborhoods that evolved around the Key System still retain the character and qualities of a transit village and thus are logical places to begin looking at how transit-supportive built environments shape travel behavior. Additionally, despite rapid rates of postwar suburbanization, as in much of the United States, the Bay Area has retained a relatively strong transit orientation, particularly along major urban corridors, in part because of topographic constraints. In 1990, 10.1 percent of the work trips by Bay Area residents were by mass transit (sixth highest rate nationally) compared to a transit modal split of 4.8 percent for its much larger metropolitan counterpart to the south, the Los Angeles-Orange County-Riverside area (ranked 22nd nationally in transit modal split for work trips).

The first analysis presented in this chapter compares commuting characteristics of Bay Area neighborhoods that are transit-oriented versus automobile-oriented in their designs. The second comparison is a more in-depth look at two rail-served Bay Area neighborhoods: Rockridge, which is arguably the closest thing to a transit village the Bay Area has to offer, versus Lafayette, a post-World War II community dominated by suburban tract housing, spacious community designs, and auto-oriented retail strips and plazas. We then present findings on how rail-oriented housing, office, and retail development in the Bay Area has influenced transit ridership. The effects of proximity to stations as well as characteristics of station-area environments, such as the availability of parking, on ridership rates are explored. We close the chapter by arguing that transit villages are not just "boutique" design concepts, as some detractors have suggested, but rather are purposeful places with the potential to reap significant and lasting transportation and environmental benefits.

5.1 COMMUTING IN TRANSIT- VERSUS AUTO-ORIENTED COMMUNITIES

Most of the Bay Area's neighborhoods that predate World War II show some remnants of once having been served by the Key System streetcar network. Besides being relatively compact, many have finely grained grid streets, neighborhood retail shops, a continuous sidewalk system, and limited off-street parking. Postwar neighborhoods, on the other hand, typically have more of an automobile design orientation characterized by spread-out development, wider and more curvilinear streets, few sidewalks, and a separation of land uses. Comparing travel characteristics of residents from these distinctly different neighborhoods, we believe, offers illustrative insights into the transportation implications of transit villages.

We conducted a matched-pair analysis of seven sets of Bay Area neighborhoods, shown in Map 5.1. The neighborhoods were matched in that they had comparable household incomes, levels of transit services, topography, and geographic locations.[1] They differed, however, in terms of population densities, street systems, and historical patterns of development. Specifically, the transit neighborhood of each pair was:

- ☐ initially built along a streetcar line;
- ☐ primarily gridded (and thus more pedestrian oriented, with over 50 percent of its intersections four-way); and
- ☐ laid out and built up prior to 1945.

The paired auto neighborhood, on the other hand, was:

- ☐ laid out without regard to transit, generally in areas without rail lines, either present or past;
- ☐ primarily a random and curvilinear street pattern (and thus less pedestrian oriented, with over 50 percent of its intersections either three-way T-intersections or cul-de-sacs); and
- ☐ laid out and built up after 1945.

Applying these criteria whittled down the number of candidate neighborhood pairs in the Bay Area from over 400 to just 7.[2] Neighborhoods varied in size from 0.25 to 2.25 mi^2. Map 5.2 illustrates differences in the street configurations of one of the neighborhood pairs, central Palo Alto and Mountain View-Stevenson Park. Central Palo Alto is laid out in a traditional grid, whereas its paired neighborhood, Stevenson Park, has a curvilinear

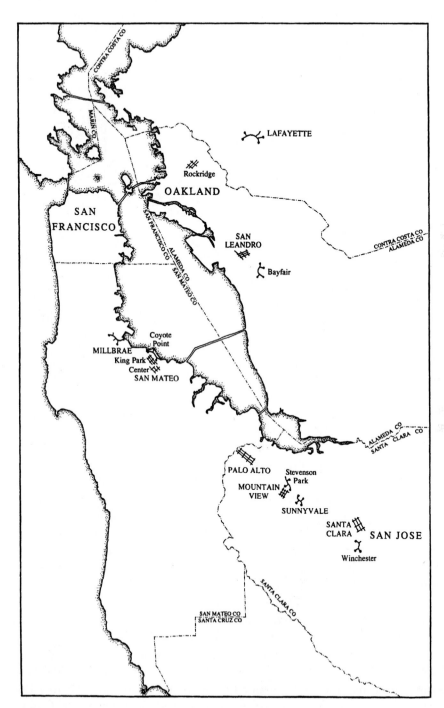

Map 5.1 Location of Paired Neighborhoods in the San Francisco Bay Area.

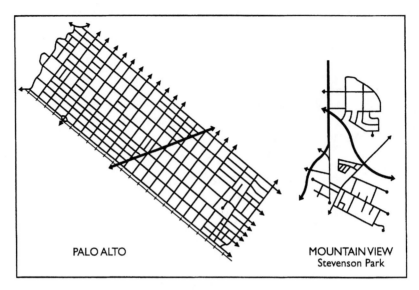

PALO ALTO

MOUNTAIN VIEW
Stevenson Park

Map 5.2 Palo Alto and Mountain View-Stevenson Park Neighborhoods.

road layout, more T-intersections, and more cul-de-sacs. Central Palo Alto also has far more varied land uses. For a pedestrian, central Palo Alto is an easier and more visually exciting area to navigate. In other respects, the two neighborhoods are fairly similar. There is only a 4 percent difference in median incomes between them, both have comparable levels of bus services, and both have a fairly flat topography. In addition, both neighborhoods have a CalTrain (commuter rail) station nearby.

Tables 5.1 and 5.2 summarize characteristics of the paired Bay Area neighborhoods in terms of control and distinguishing criteria. Overall, neighborhoods match closely in terms of median incomes and transit service types, though transit neighborhoods tend to enjoy more intensive bus services (as might be expected since, after all, they are more transit-oriented). Importantly, neighborhoods tend to differ markedly on distinguishing criteria: Transit neighborhoods have 35 to 50 percent more four-way intersections and higher residential densities.

The 1990 modal shares and trip generation rates for work trips made by transit and walk-bicycle for paired communities are shown in Figures 5.1 through 5.4. Pedestrian-bicycle modal shares and trip generation rates were in all cases higher in transit neighborhoods than in auto neighborhoods. Moreover, all transit neighborhoods except central Palo Alto generated more transit trips (Figure 5.1) and had higher shares of commutes by transit than their auto-oriented counterparts (Figure 5.3). Central Palo Alto, however, had three times the share of residents walking or cycling to work as its paired neighborhood. In all, the evidence is fairly persuasive in the Bay Area: Controlling for

TABLE 5.1

Comparison of Bay Area Neighborhoods: Control Factors, 1990–1992

Transit Neighborhood	Auto Neighborhood	Median Household Income			Bus Service in Daily VMT per Acre			Type of Transit Service		Distance Between Centroids (in Miles)
		TN	AN	% Difference	TN	AN	% Difference	TN	AN	
Palo Alto	Mountain View-Stevenson Park	47,500	45,486	4.2	0.27	0.23	11.8	Bus, CR	Bus, CR	3.50
Santa Clara	San Jose-Winchester	32,400	34,826	7.5	0.66	0.58	11.4	Bus, CR	Bus	2.00
San Mateo-Center	San Mateo-Coyote/Point	37,159	38,873	4.6	0.47	0.22	53.3	Bus, CR	Bus	1.00
Oakland-Rockridge	Lafayette	46,512	43,108	7.3	1.43	0.12	91.5	Bus, HR	Bus, HR	6.00
Downtown Mountain View	Sunnyvale-Mary Ave	40,379	40,398	0.1	0.71	0.51	29.3	Bus, CR	Bus	1.75
San Mateo-King Park	Millbrae	32,080	31,829	0.8	0.53	0.65	23.2	Bus, CR	Bus, CR	3.50
San Leandro	Bayfair	30,115	31,282	3.9	0.87	1.00	14.3	Bus, HR	Bus, HR	2.00

Note: TN = Transit Neighborhood; AN = Auto Neighborhood; CR = Commuter Rail; HR = Heavy Rail

Data Source: 1990 United States Census, STF-3A, and data from local transit agencies.

TABLE 5.2

Characteristics of Bay Area Neighborhoods: Differentiation Criteria, 1990–1992

Transit Neighborhood	Auto Neighborhood	% X Intersections			% Cul-de-Sacs			Net Residential Density (Dwelling Units per Acre)		
		TN	AN	% Difference[1]	TN	AN	% Difference[1]	TN	AN	% Difference
Palo Alto	Mountain View-Stevenson Park	62.4	15.5	46.9	2.4	24.2	21.9	6.27	6.25	0.3
Santa Clara	San Jose-Winchester	63.6	28.3	35.3	3.5	18.9	15.4	6.18	4.03	53.3
San Mateo-Center	San Mateo-Coyote/Point	67.0	19.2	47.8	3.2	20.5	17.3	6.91	5.00	38.2
Oakland-Rockridge	Lafayette	44.7	9.6	35.1	10.5	4.0	6.5	5.32	2.12	150.9
Downtown Mountain View	Sunnyvale-Mary Ave	69.8	32.1	37.7	3.2	19.6	16.4	7.08	8.31	17.4
San Mateo-King Park	Millbrae	65.9	29.0	36.9	5.5	19.6	14.1	6.89	5.09	35.4
San Leandro	Bayfair	64.5	26.1	38.4	5.4	10.2	4.8	7.34	5.94	23.6

Note: TN = Transit Neighborhood; AN = Auto Neighborhood

[1] Percentage point difference.

Data Source: 1990 United States Census, STF-3A, and field surveys.

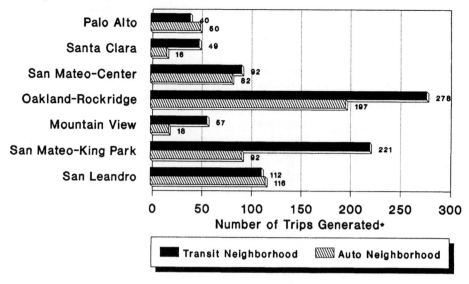

* per 1,000 dwelling units

Figure 5.1 Neighborhood Comparison of Transit Work Trip Generation Rates, 1990.

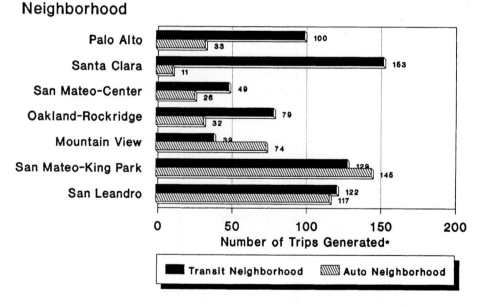

* per 1,000 dwelling units

Figure 5.2 Neighborhood Comparison of Walk-Bicycle Work Trip Generation Rates, 1990.

109

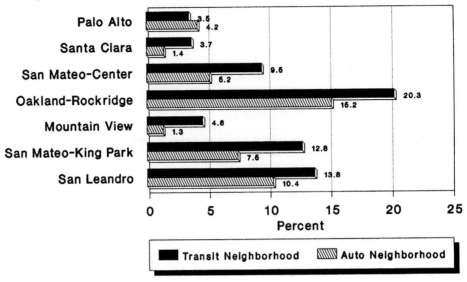

Figure 5.3 Neighborhood Comparison of Transit Modal Splits, 1990 Work Trips.

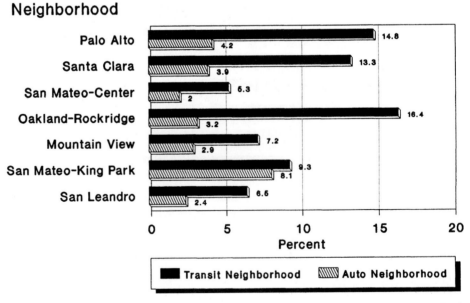

Figure 5.4 Neighborhood Comparison of Walk-Bicycle Modal Splits, 1990 Work Trips.

income and to the extent possible, transit-service levels, transit-oriented neighborhoods were less auto-dependent. Although there was considerable variation among the pairs, on average, the Bay Area's transit-oriented neighborhoods generated around 70 percent more transit trips and 120 percent more pedestrian-bicycle trips than nearby auto-oriented neighborhoods.

While these findings are encouraging, it cannot be said that commuting behavior is fundamentally different in the Bay Area's transit-oriented and auto-oriented neighborhoods. Indeed, in the case of all transit neighborhoods, the drive-alone automobile captured twice as many commute trips as did transit or walking-bicycling. In short, the automobile still reigns supreme in the neighborhoods defined as transit-oriented. It may be that the region's overall form has as great a role, if not greater, in influencing modal choice than the design or layout of particular neighborhoods. That is, the "macro" settlement pattern of regions like the Bay Area may be too auto-dependent for the "micro" urban designs of particular neighborhoods to matter. Islands of transit-oriented development in a sea of freeway-oriented suburbs will do little to change fundamental commuting habits.

Thus, a lesson from this analysis is that, if transit villages are to yield important mobility and environmental benefits, they cannot stand in isolation. Successful transit villages will need to be part of a transit metropolis. This might take the form of linear axes of transit-oriented development, much like pearls on a necklace. Another lesson from any contemporary analysis of how land-use environments shape travel demand is that in America the price signals passed on to motorists and parkers are far, far stronger and thus swamp the influences of physical environments. We must always keep in mind that the evaluations of how built environments, including transit-oriented development, impact travel demand are taking place in a distorted marketplace of cheap automobile travel and a failure to price externalities. It is no surprise that the effects of built environments on travel have been suboptimal in a world of suboptimal pricing. This, we argue, is not so much an indictment of transit villages or any other physical planning initiative as it is an indictment of how we currently price and manage our transportation and land resources. Surely, if fuel costs $4 per gal, as in most of Europe, and all workers have to pay at least $5 per day for parking to cover true costs, then the commuting impacts of transit-oriented development in the Bay Area or elsewhere would no doubt be far greater.

5.2 NONWORK TRAVEL IN TRANSIT- VERSUS AUTO-ORIENTED NEIGHBORHOODS

The previous analysis focused on commuting mainly because only the census provides enough data cases to study travel at the neighborhood level and the census only records work trips. Yet transit-oriented designs and mixed land uses are thought to exert their strongest influence on nonwork trips, in particular, trips for convenience shopping and more discretionary purposes. In a transit village, for instance, one is more apt to walk to a local bakery, perhaps on to a cleaners, and then back home than to drive out of the neighborhood to conduct the same business.

To better understand how transit-oriented development affects nonwork trips, we carried out a similar matched-pair analysis, albeit for just one neighborhood pair: Rockridge and Lafayette. These two neighborhoods in the East Bay made up one of the pairs from the previous analysis, and their regional locations are shown in Map 5.1. Dividing Rockridge and Lafayette are the East Bay hills. To study nonwork travel, in 1994 we gathered survey data from 620 randomly sampled households in the two neighborhoods.[3]

5.2.1   Rockridge Neighborhood

The Rockridge neighborhood of Oakland is a prototypical transit-oriented community. Rockridge lies west of the hills in the older, more urbanized part of the East Bay. Rockridge blossomed around the turn of the century as a major stop on the early Key System streetcar line and today retains many vestiges of a streetcar suburb. It is very compact, with mostly apartments and detached units with small yards and narrow sidelots. And it features a finely grained and integrated mixture of land uses. As shown in Map 5.3, the influence of the early streetcar system is clearly expressed in Rockridge's somewhat rectilinear layout.

At the heart of the neighborhood is a retail district aligned along College Avenue, a street which once accommodated a cross-town streetcar line. Map 5.4 shows the grain of development along the College Avenue district south of the BART station and along residential side streets. Retail shops form an unbroken streetwall that defines the avenue. Few blocks are interrupted by curbcuts, a legacy of Rockridge's streetcar days. Storefronts are scaled to the pedestrian, with shops typically 40 ft or less in width producing four or more shops on a typical block. Building entries open directly onto the sidewalk providing a nearly continuous sequence of showcase windows and shop entries. Many stores have loft apartments or offices above. Parking is accommodated on the street or behind buildings; few parking lots directly face College Avenue.

Like many streetcar suburbs which depended on trolleys for real estate speculation, Rockridge's residential areas feature regularity in lotting patterns and architecture. California bungalows, with porches facing the street and garages tucked behind, dominate residential streets. Small two-, three-, and four-unit residential buildings make up 22 percent of Rockridge's housing stock, and an estimated one-third of detached units have rear-lot accessory units. This mix of housing has created high average densities on many lots that do not disrupt the prevailing scale and grain of the neighborhood.

The entire Rockridge neighborhood is linked by an integrated network of sidewalks and pedestrian paths. Shade trees occupy the planting strip between most sidewalks and streets. In some locations, midblock pedestrian paths allow convenient access to transit lines. Overall, Rockridge is a very pedestrian-friendly neighborhood.

Rockridge

Lafayette

0'   1000'

Map 5.3   Comparison of Street and Block Patterns, Rockridge and Lafayette.

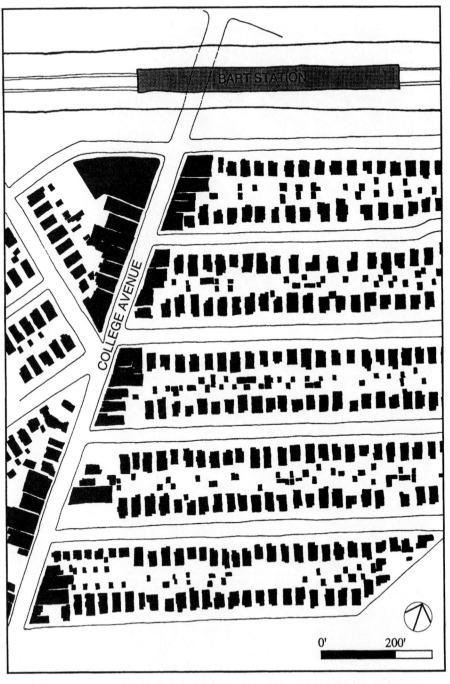

Map 5.4 Building Pattern Around the Rockridge BART Station, 1995.

5.2.2 Lafayette Neighborhood

The community of Lafayette lies west of the East Bay hills and in many ways is Rockridge's polar opposite with almost exclusively large-lot tract housing, curvilinear streets, and an auto-oriented retail strip. Lafayette largely postdates World War II. Prior to this, it was primarily an agricultural and summer home community. The completion of the twin-bore Caldecott Tunnel through the East Bay hills in 1937 greatly improved access to Lafayette and paved the way for new growth beginning in the 1950s.

The scale and configuration of development in Lafayette reflect a strong automobile orientation. As shown in Map 5.3, Lafayette's street network is less regular and more curvilinear than Rockridge's. Streets are also wider. Mount Diablo Boulevard, the community's major thoroughfare, is 75 ft from curb to curb, with four lanes and a median strip over most of its stretch. Sidewalks exist in the commercial core, but are sporadic elsewhere.

The land-use mix in Lafayette is more coarsely grained than in Rockridge, as reflected by the layout of the parcels near Lafayette's BART station (Map 5.5). The retail core transitions to multifamily housing and offices and then to single-family residences. There is little mixing within land-use zones and no mixing vertically within structures. Retail is configured mainly along Mount Diablo Boulevard as stand-alone buildings with off-street parking fronting the boulevard.

As in Rockridge, Lafayette is bisected by State Highway 24, and its elevated BART station lies within the median of the highway. The station is also adjacent to the main retail district, but pedestrian connections are poor due to the elongated block faces and circuitous pathways. Overall, Lafayette's built environment is not particularly inviting to any kind of movement other than that by private automobile.

5.2.3 Similarities and Differences

Table 5.3 summarizes the common and differing characteristics of the two case study neighborhoods. In 1990, both Rockridge and Lafayette averaged fairly high median household incomes, well above the regional average of $41,600. Housing prices and rents were also relatively high in both areas. Both neighborhoods also have a similar age structure and are predominantly white.[4] And, as noted, both communities are on the Concord BART line and have a rail station near their commercial districts. Surface bus services are also similar— AC Transit operates three bus routes in each community, though Rockridge enjoys more frequent services (average peak headways of 2.8 min versus 9.7 min in Lafayette).

In terms of their land-use environments, Table 5.3 reveals how different the two neighborhoods are. Rockridge is far denser and has many more apartments and attached housing units. And as shown in Map 5.3, Rockridge also has a more finely grained urban pattern with around twice as many blocks and intersections within a square mile of its BART station as does Lafayette. The more gridlike, pedestrian-oriented street pattern of Rockridge

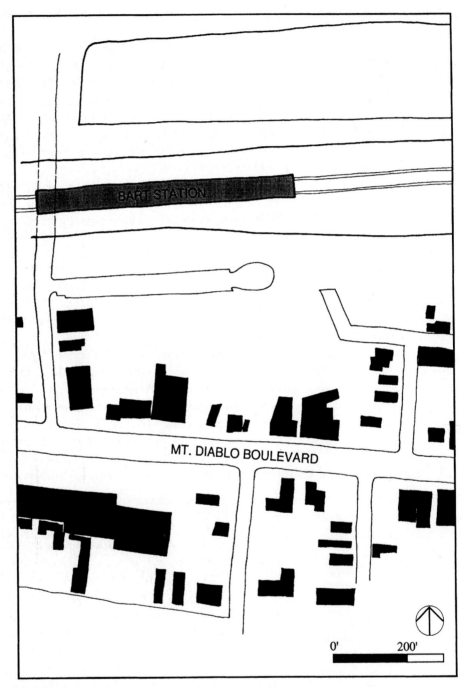

Map 5.5 Building Pattern Around the Lafayette BART Station, 1995.

TABLE 5.3

Comparison of Rockridge and Lafayette Communities, 1990

	Rockridge	Lafayette	Percent Difference
Common Characteristics			
Household and Housing Attributes			
Median household income	$58,770	$61,071	3.9
Persons per household	2.2	2.5	13.6
Median housing value	$322,595	$392,853	21.7
Median monthly rent	$682	$843	23.6
Resident Attributes			
Median age	37.3	39.8	6.7
Percent persons who are white	73.8	88.2	14.4[1]
Percent adults college educated	44.5	40.7	3.8[1]
Transportation Attributes			
BART headways (min, A.M. peak)	3	3	0.0
No. of bus lines serving area	3	3	0.0
Differing Characteristics			
Residential Attributes			
Housing density (units per square mile)	2,194	655	234.9
Percent housing that is single-family detached	63.6	78.4	14.8[1]
BART Station Vicinity[2]			
Blocks per square mile	103	47	119.2
Intersections per square mile	127	64	98.4
T-intersections	37	85	129.7
Four-way intersections	29	8	262.5
Cul-de-sacs	5	31	520.0
Retail District Attributes			
Average block length (ft, major roads)	80	380	375.0
Percent of blocks with curbcuts	100	10	90.0[1]

[1]Percentage data are expressed as percentage point difference.

[2]One square mile area around station.

Sources: 1990 Census of Population and Housing, U.S. Bureau of the Census, and field surveys.

is also reflected by the much higher share of four-way intersections, matched by relatively few T-intersections and cul-de-sacs.

5.2.4 Comparison of Nonwork Trips

For all nonwork trips, including travel for shopping, personal business, recreation, and medical appointments, Figure 5.5 shows Rockridge residents are less auto-dependent. They are about five times as likely to go to a store or other nonwork destination by foot or bicycle as their Lafayette counterparts. This is partly because of the shorter average nonwork trip lengths in Rockridge, 6.8 mi compared with 11.2 mi in Lafayette. Shorter trips

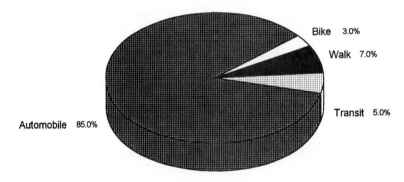

Figure 5.5 Modal Split Comparison for Nonwork Trips, Rockridge Versus Lafayette.

are largely a product of Rockridge's more compact structure. However, even for trips of similar length, Rockridge averaged much higher nonauto shares (Figure 5.6). For nonwork trips of 1 mi or less, for instance, Rockridge residents made 15 percent fewer auto trips and 22 percent more walking trips than Lafayette residents. For trips of 1 to 2 mi, 15 percent were by nonauto means in Rockridge versus just 6 percent in Lafayette.

Among nonwork trip purposes, the largest modal split difference was for shop trips; 19 percent made by Rockridge residents were by a nonauto mode compared to just 2 percent for Lafayette residents. Walking accounted for 13 percent of the shop trips among Rockridge residents; none of the surveyed Lafayette residents walked to shops. In addition, 17 percent of the social-recreational trips by Rockridge residents were by transit, walking, or bicycling compared to just 5 percent for their Lafayette counterparts.

A statistical (logit) model was also developed that predicted the probability of nonauto travel as a function of which of the two neighborhoods respondents live in as well as other control variables.[5] From the model, we were able to plot the likelihood of making a nonwork trip by transit, walking, or some other nondriving mode. Figure 5.7 shows the estimated probabilities according to levels of automobile availability.[6] The figure shows that there is a .35 probability that a Rockridge resident with one car available will make a shopping or other nonwork trip by foot or some other nondriving mode compared to a .17 probability for Lafayette residents. With four cars in a household, the odds of walking, bicycling, or riding transit for a shop trip is less than 1 in 10 in Rockridge and less than 1 in 20 in Lafayette. From these plots, we can infer that relatively compact, mixed-use, transit-oriented neighborhoods average approximately a 10 percent higher share of nonwork trips by foot, bicycle, or transit, controlling for factors like vehicle availability and household income.

In our survey of the two neighborhoods, we also compiled data on how residents reached their respective BART stations. These travel differences were even more striking: 31 percent of the access trips to the Rockridge BART station were by foot compared to only 13 percent of those to the Lafayette station. For both neighborhoods, 94 percent of the walk trips to BART stations were under 1 mi in length. Rockridge's higher incidence of walk access trips clearly reflects its more pedestrian-oriented development pattern. As shown in Maps 5.4 and 5.5, the 1 mi^2 surrounding Rockridge's station is platted at a much finer grain than the 1 mi^2 around Lafayette's station. Rockridge also averaged a 7 percent higher share of bus access trips to BART. In contrast, 81 percent of surveyed Lafayette residents who took BART park-and-rode or kiss-and-rode, compared to just 56 percent of Rockridge residents who commuted by BART.

Overall, the higher incidence of walking and transit riding by residents of Rockridge lends considerable credibility to the transit village concept. A transit-oriented neighborhood seems capable of inducing walk trips as a substitute for automobile travel. Among Rockridge residents, 28 percent of the nonwork trips under 1 mi in length were made by foot and 66 percent were by automobile; among Lafayette residents, just 6 percent were by walking and 81 percent were by car. The Rockridge neighborhood also averaged nearly a 20 percent higher share of walk access trips to its BART station.

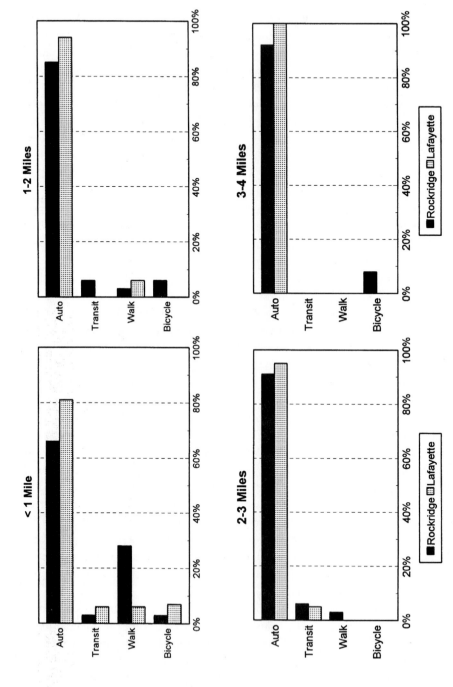

Figure 5.6 Nonwork Trip Modal Split Percentages, Four Distance Categories.

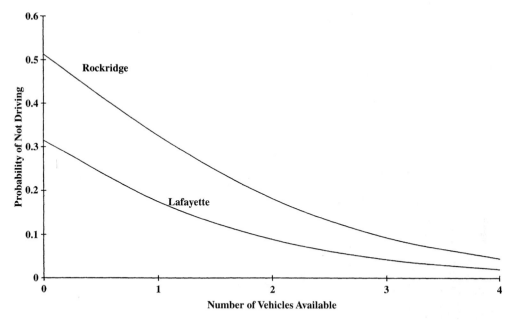

Figure 5.7 Nonwork Trips by Nondriving Modes as a Function of Neighborhood Origin and Vehicle Availability.

5.3 RIDERSHIP AND RAIL-ORIENTED HOUSING

A central premise of transit villages is to concentrate development within a quarter-mile walking distance of rail stations. Richard Untermann, an urban designer from the University of Washington, has examined American's walking behavior as closely as anyone.[7] His research shows that for nonwork and casual trips, most Americans are willing to walk 500 ft, 20 percent will walk 1000 ft, and only 10 percent will walk half a mile. For more crucial trips, such as to work, acceptable walking distances are farther, with nearly half of middle-aged Americans willing to walk up to a quarter of a mile. In short, proximity matters a lot. Placing housing, shops, offices, and other activities near a rail stop is essential if transit villages are to induce high transit ridership.

Over the past several years, we have been studying how large-scale developments such as apartments, office towers, and shopping plazas that are near rail stations influence ridership. In 1992 and 1993, we surveyed the travel characteristics of 885 households across 27 apartment and condominium projects that were within walking distance of one of the following California rail systems: BART, Santa Clara County Light Rail Transit, Peninsula CalTrain, Sacramento Regional Transit, and San Diego Trolley.[8]

While most station-area residents traveled by car, more than 15 percent of the over 2500 surveyed trips were by rail transit. In the case of BART, more than one-quarter of the trips were by rail. Among the 27 surveyed housing projects, rail shares as high as 79 percent and as low as 2 percent were found. The highest rail shares were for work trips. In the case of BART, 32 percent of the commute trips by station-area residents were by rail. This is six times the rail modal split (of 5 percent) for all work trips in the three BART-served counties.

City-by-city comparisons most clearly highlight the ridership benefits of transit-based housing. Table 5.4 compares work-trip modal splits of station-area residents versus city-wide averages for Bay Area cities. On average, those living near rail stations were five times more likely to commute by rail transit as the average worker living in the city, and in some cases as much as seven times as likely.

TABLE 5.4

Comparison of Work-Trip Transit Modal Splits Between Bay Area Station-Area and Citywide Residents

	Work-Trip Transit Modal Splits (%) for:	
City	Station-Area Residents[3]	Citywide[4]
BART[1]:		
Pleasant Hill	46.7	16.0
Fremont	12.9	2.7
Union City	27.5	3.8
Hayward	25.7	4.4
San Leandro	27.7	6.1
Oakland	10.0	6.1
CalTrain[1]:		
San Mateo	26.2	2.8
SCCTA[2]:		
San Jose	7.0	3.6

[1]Statistics presented for urban rail transit trips only.

[2]Statistics presented for all transit modes combined, including both rail and bus transit.

[3]Based on survey results from 1992–1993, aggregated according to city jurisdiction.

[4]1990 statistics.

Sources: Metropolitan Transportation Commission (1993) and 1990 journey-to-work census statistics, STF-3A. All statistics exclude workers who work at home.

TABLE 5.5

Comparison of Current Mode for Work Trip and Usual Mode at Prior Residence

Usual Mode for Prior Residence	Current Usual Mode to Work					
	Drive Car	**Ride Car**	**Rail**	**Bus**	**Walk**	**Other**
Drove Car	82.0%	65.5%	28.8%	23.5%	40.0%	20.0%
Rode Car	2.0	10.3	3.9	5.9	0.0	0.0
Rail	9.3	6.9	42.5	23.5	13.3	0.0
Bus	2.6	10.3	13.7	41.2	20.0	30.0
Walk	3.2	6.9	4.6	5.9	20.0	15.4
Other	0.9	0.0	6.5	0.0	6.7	34.6
Total	100.0%	100.0%	100.0%	100.0%	100.0%	100.0%

Station-area residents were also asked how they commuted at their prior residence, if that residence was in the same metropolitan area. Table 5.5 shows that many residents changed modes of travel once they moved close to rail—around 29 percent who usually drove alone to work at their previous residence now commute by rail. The conversion of these trips to rail represents a real economic benefit, measured in terms of reduced vehicle miles travelled and tailpipe emissions.

5.3.1 Factors Influencing Rail Commuting by Station-Area Residents

The two most important determinants of rail usage among surveyed station-area residents were found to be trip destination and whether parking is free. This is revealed in Figure 5.8 which plots the probability of rail commuting by vehicle availability, parking prices, and destination based on the results of a logit mode choice model.[9] If someone living near a Bay Area rail station owns 1 car, works in San Francisco, and has to pay for parking, there is nearly a 80 percent likelihood that the person will commute via rail transit. If the person can park free in downtown San Francisco, the probability of rail commuting drops to 25 percent. For commutes to secondary urban centers like Oakland and Berkeley where commercial parking rates are typically charged, there is around a 35 percent chance the person will commute by BART. For all other destinations (where often workers park free), on average only 4 percent of the commute trips by station-area residents will be by rail. Clearly, clustering housing around rail stops will do little good if, as during much of the 1980s, job growth occurs mainly along suburban freeway corridors. Both ends of work trips—housing and job sites—must be within reasonable proximity of stations if clustered growth is to pay significant transportation and environmental dividends. In short, more mixed-use transit village development is necessary.

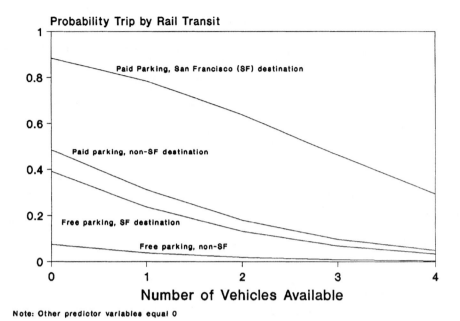

Figure 5.8 Rail Transit Usage as a Function of Parking Charges, Destination, and Vehicle Availability.

5.3.2 Ridership and Proximity: Earlier Work

Outside of California, the main studies of transit ridership by station-area residents have been conducted for rail systems in Washington, DC, Toronto, and Edmonton. These studies have produced particularly useful insights into rail transit's ridership gradient—how quickly ridership falls off with walking distances to stations.

The Washington study, conducted by JHK and Associates in 1987 and 1989, examined ridership rates for multifamily projects with at least 75 units that were between 300 and 3800 ft from a station.[10] The 1987 results are summarized in Table 5.6. Shares of work trips taken by rail ranged from 18 to 63 percent. For The Consulate complex, closest to any station (300 ft from the Van Ness-UDC Metrorail station), 63 percent of the residents commuted via rail. Overall, the share of trips by rail transit declined by about 0.65 percent for every 100-ft increase in distance of a residential site from a Metrorail station portal.

JHK and Associates followed this survey with a similar one in 1989, carried out at 10 different residential sites near five stations. A similarly high transit modal share was found in the 1989 survey, ranging from 30 to 74 percent of commute trips. As found in our research of BART, transit ridership varied considerably depending on trip destination. For instance, in the case of the 507-unit Randolph Towers complex in Arlington, Virginia, which lies 500 ft from the Ballston station portal, 69 percent of the residents commuted

TABLE 5.6

Modal Splits for Residential Developments
Near Metrorail Stations, Washington, DC, Area, 1987

Metrorail Station	Project	Distance to Station	% Rail	% Auto	% Other[1]
Rosslyn	River Place North	1000 ft	45.3	41.5	13.3
	River Place South	1500 ft	40.0	60.0	0.0
	Prospect House	2200 ft	18.2	81.9	0.0
Crystal City	Crystal Square Apts.	500 ft	36.3	48.8	14.9
	Crystal Plaza Apts.	1000 ft	44.0	45.0	11.0
Van Ness-UDC	The Consulate	300 ft	63.0	32.6	4.4
	Connecticut Heights	3800 ft	24.0	56.0	20.0
Silver Spring	Twin Towers	900 ft	36.4	52.3	11.4
	Georgian Towers	1400 ft	34.7	43.1	0.8

[1]Other consists of such forms of access as riding the bus, walking, and bicycling.

via Metrorail. If they worked in Washington, DC, the modal share was 88 percent. Among those working in nearby suburban Fairfax County, 33 percent rode Metrorail; among those working in Montgomery County, Maryland, 20 percent took rail to work.

This study also surveyed people working in offices near Metrorail stations. Two clear patterns emerged: Ridership was much higher at downtown than at suburban sites, and as in the residential survey, ridership fell off steadily as distance from offices to stations increased. As shown in Table 5.7, nearly 50 percent of those working in downtown office buildings within 1000 ft of the Metro Center or Farragut West stations commuted via Metrorail compared to 16 to 19 percent of the workers in buildings at comparable distances from the suburban Crystal City or Silver Spring stations. The researchers found that for downtown offices, transit ridership fell by 0.76 percent for each 100-ft increase in distance from a Metrorail portal, and for offices, 0.74 percent for each 100 ft. This study concluded that proximity matters and stressed that for transit-oriented development to add up to much both the origins and destinations need to be clustered around rail: "Poor transit accessibility at either end of the trip results in poor transit ridership between those pairs."[11]

The other major study of transit ridership by proximity focused on two Canadian systems: the Toronto subway system and the Edmonton light rail system. The studies, conducted by M. Stringham, examined rail modal splits as a function of distance to stations and modes of access for over 2000 people living near two suburban stations in each city.[12] Within a radius of 3000 ft from a station, rail transit captured between 30 and 60 percent of the work and school trips. Stringham estimated the *impact zone* (the area within which people walk to the station in significant numbers) to extend perhaps as far as 4000 ft from a station. As in the Washington, DC, study, the transit modal split of high-density housing

TABLE 5.7

Modal Splits for Office Developments
Near Metrorail Stations, Washington, DC, Area, 1987

Metrorail Station	Project	Distance to Station	% Rail	% Auto	% Other[1]
Metro Center & Farragut West	International Square	200 ft	48.9	42.4	8.8
	NCPC Building	500 ft	46.6	36.5	16.8
	Olmsted Building	700 ft	43.5	45.4	11.4
	McKee Building	900 ft	50.5	32.5	17.0
	Realtor's Building	1200 ft	45.6	28.3	26.1
	Am. Inst. of Architects	2800 ft	27.4	55.9	16.7
Rosslyn	1300 N. 17th Street	800 ft	19.2	80.0	1.5
	AM Building	1000 ft	24.3	73.4	1.6
	Air Force Assoc.	2200 ft	13.3	85.3	1.5
Crystal City	Crystal Mall 1	200 ft	16.3	81.3	2.4
	Crystal Square 2	1000 ft	17.4	77.2	5.5
	2711 Jeff-Davis	2500 ft	5.4	90.2	5.0
Van Ness-UDC	Van Ness Station	100 ft	21.1	72.8	5.2
	Intelsat	300 ft	27.9	68.4	3.8
Silver Spring	Twin Towers	900 ft	36.4	52.3	11.4
	Georgian Towers	1400 ft	34.7	43.1	0.8

[1]Other consists of such forms of access as riding the bus, walking, and bicycling.

was about 30 percent higher than that of low-density projects at an equivalent distance from a station.

Also consistent with the Washington study, Stringham's work found the transit modal split for offices located near suburban rail stations to be considerably lower than that of residences near the stations, perhaps reflecting the availability of plentiful parking at the suburban businesses surveyed. Stringham's work gives particular emphasis to how modes of access vary with distance from a station. He found that well over 90 percent of rail users whose origin and destination was within 1500 ft of a station walked to the station. At a distance of around 3200 ft, bus transit eclipsed walking as the predominant mode of access. At 3700 ft, virtually no residents or workers walked to the station; approximately 15 percent reached the station by car and the remainder arrived by bus.

Figure 5.9 merges the findings of these earlier studies on proximity and ridership. In general, it appears that, all else being equal, ridership potential is highest within about a one-third of a mile to a station, though from the Canadian studies we see that the impact zone can be extended a half mile out or more. It is this prospect of extending walking dis-

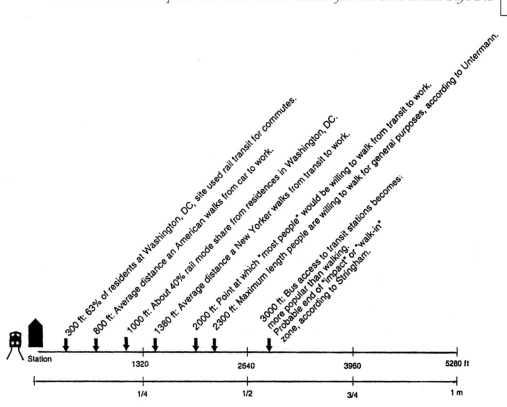

Figure 5.9 Summary of Empirical Evidence on Ridership by Distance.

tances through good quality planning that lends legitimacy to transit village planning. Urban designers like Richard Untermann have shown that acceptable walking distances can be stretched considerably (perhaps as much as doubled) by creating pleasant, interesting urban spaces and corridors. The distaste for walking in unappealing settings is shown in the irony that many Americans will go to great lengths to find a parking spot close to the entrance of a shopping mall, but have no problem walking 1 or 2 mi once inside the mall. Average walking distances are long in large urban centers; 60 percent of the walk trips in downtown Boston are one-quarter mile, and the average walking distance in Manhattan is one-third mile.[13] Clearly, active and varied urban spaces can induce Americans to walk more often and for greater distances.

5.3.3 Ridership and Proximity: Recent Evidence from California

From our 1992–1993 survey of 27 large housing complexes near California rail systems, we also examined how proximity influences ridership rates. As in Washington, DC,

Toronto, and Edmonton, we too found that distance had a significant deterring effect on rail commuting. On average, rail's modal share fell by about 1.1 percent for every 1000-ft increase in walking distance to California's rail stations.

Figure 5.10 was prepared to compare our estimated ridership gradient for the 27 rail-served California housing sites versus those found for Washington Metrorail stations and stations near the Canadian systems. In general, gradients followed the same slope, suggesting the effects of distance are fairly similar; however, due to its lower density, more auto-oriented cities, California's transit shares were consistently below those of the comparison areas. Some of this difference might be explained by the fact that most of the California rail systems studied function mainly as commuter systems and thus have suburban stations with abundant park-and-ride facilities. With more parking lots, larger shares of rail users are likely to be drawn from longer distances. Higher average residential densities, higher primacy (e.g., larger shares of the regional workforce in downtowns), better feeder bus connections, and perhaps even better quality walking environments might also explain why these other cities capture higher shares of rail commuting among

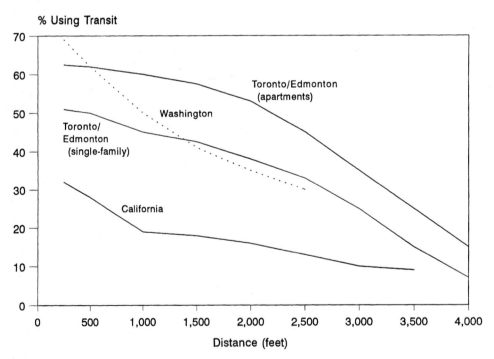

Figure 5.10 Rail Mode Share by Distance to Residential Sites: Comparison of California and Other Systems.

station-area residents.[14] It follows that if transit villages in California and elsewhere had some of these attributes (e.g., more compactness, good bus services, and nicer walking environments), ridership rates might be on a par with those of Toronto, Washington, DC, and Edmonton.

5.4 RIDERSHIP AND OFFICE-RETAIL DEVELOPMENT

5.4.1 Offices and Ridership

In our study of ridership in California, we also examined how proximity of offices influenced demand. We studied 18 rail-served office buildings that were between 50 and 2700 ft from a suburban train station and that housed between 75 and 3000 workers. Commute data were obtained for 1430 trips by office workers. Approximately one out of ten work trips by station-area workers was by rail, considerably above the 1 to 2 percent of rail trips made by the typical suburban workers in these metropolitan areas. In the case of BART, 17 percent of those working near a BART station commuted by rail. This is appreciably above the 1990 average rail commute share of 5 percent for counties served by BART (Alameda, Contra Costa, and San Francisco).

Station-area office workers were more likely to rail commute if they owned relatively few cars, commuted a long distance, had to pay for parking, and lived near rail. For instance, only 3 percent of station-area workers who received free parking commuted by rail, whereas 25 percent of those who faced parking charges opted for rail commuting. Also, among station-area workers, 20 percent of those who lived in a city served by BART commuted by rail compared to 13 percent who did not live in a BART-served city.

We also plotted the rail modal splits against walking distances from offices to stations. Comparing our results with those from Washington, DC, and the two Canadian cities revealed remarkable similarities (Figure 5.11). Within around a quarter-mile radius, there was a moderate degree of elasticity in the relationship—every 10 percent increase in distance from an office to a station was related to an approximate 6 to 8 percent decline in rail modal splits.

Our research also showed that office densities around suburban stations had a positive influence on ridership. For every additional 100 employees per acre, rail ridership rose 2.2 percent on average. Although this relationship does not seem astounding, it carries more significance given that fewer than 1 percent of suburban workers from cities with rail throughout the United States take transit to work. Of course, to the degree office projects are sited near rail stations, it follows that densities will increase. It is the clustering of workplaces and residences near rail stations that has the biggest influence on commuting choices within a quarter-mile radius of stations. As long as office development is geographically close and oriented to rail stations, reasonable shares of workers will commute via transit.

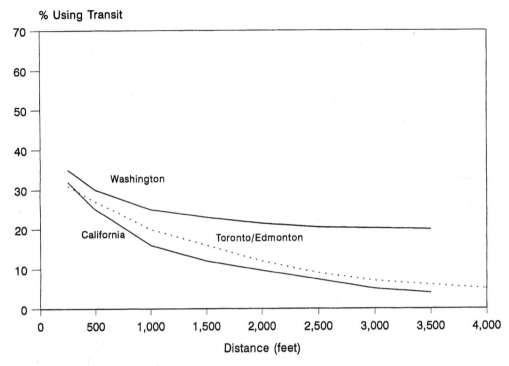

% Using Transit

Figure 5.11 Rail Mode Share by Distance to Office Sites: Comparison of California and Other Systems.

5.4.2 Station-Area Retail and Ridership

Finally, for our ridership study of the BART system, we also surveyed ridership among three large retail complexes near rail stations: one large complex (San Francisco Centre) near BART's busiest station (Powell Street), a large community shopping complex in the East Bay (El Cerrito Plaza), and a regional shopping mall in the East Bay (Bayfair in San Leandro). From interviews of shoppers at each complex, we found a transit modal split of around 15 percent. This is considerably above the fewer than 2 percent of all shop trips in the Bay Area by transit.[15] For the shopping complex in downtown San Francisco, around one in five shoppers arrived by BART, and around one in three arrived by foot.[16] San Francisco Centre is directly connected to the BART and Muni light rail stations by a subway portal. Nearby parking can be quite expensive and hard to find. The combination of parking constraints and physical integration of rail and shopping has no doubt contributed to this high share of nonauto shop trips. The situation at the other two surveyed rail-served shopping centers was much different. Both are surrounded by great expanses of asphalt and free parking. The vast majority of surveyed shoppers in these places drove; in the case of the suburblike El Cerrito Plaza, just 7 percent arrived by BART. Overall, our research suggests that placing retail centers near suburban rail stations will only attract significant numbers of shoppers to rail if some limits are placed on parking supplies and densities are high enough to encourage walking over automobile access.

5.5 TRANSIT VILLAGES: BOUTIQUE PLANNING OR PLACES THAT MATTER?

This chapter shows that density, mixed land uses, and environmental quality matter when it comes to attracting people to transit. Coordinated development is also important. If transit-based housing is to reap significant mobility and environmental benefits, then it must be accompanied by initiatives that attract employment growth to rail stations and that eliminate market distortions such as free parking. Housing clustered around stations does little good if, as in most U.S. rail-served cities, most job growth occurs far removed from rail stations. And having transit-oriented office and commercial development does little good if the vast majority of housing gets built in spacious, planned unit developments and walled-off subdivisions away from rail. In short, for rail transit to compete with the automobile in most U.S. settings, there need to be transit villages—that is, places where housing, jobs, shops, and other uses are near rail. Of course, it is not essential that transit villages be exactly balanced. Some might be predominantly residential communities, whereas others might be more commercially oriented. What is important is that there are enough transit villages, whether balanced or specialized in their land uses, to allow for efficient rail travel. Given that research consistently shows that both the origin and destination ends of trips need to be reasonably close to stations for there to be high levels of rail travel, it follows that, if transit is to capture a significant market share, urban areas need to have a multicentered urban form and axial corridors that resemble "pearls on a necklace." Clearly, for transit villages to succeed, there must be a transit metropolis. Case studies from Stockholm, Singapore, and Tokyo in Part Four of this book underscore this point.

Some observers are fairly skeptical about the prospects of transit-focused development ever doing much good. Anthony Downs, an economist with The Brookings Institution, has argued this point more forcefully than anyone.[17] He and others imply that transit villages are "boutique" design and planning concepts; underneath the physical facade, there are few transportation benefits to be found. Downs argues that the permanence of the existing built environment will prevent dramatic gains in density and that only huge increases in average suburban residential densities would substantially reduce average commute distances and solo commuting. Even under the most generous assumptions, according to Downs, clustered high-density housing near suburban rail stations would be unlikely to reduce vehicle miles traveled (VMT) by more than 2 percent.[18] His conclusion about land-use initiatives that aim to target growth near rail is that the efforts they require are "wholly disproportionate to the severity of the problem, the pain it is causing, and the benefits of ending it."[19]

Our own calculations lend some support to Downs's criticism. Table 5.8 shows that only 8.9 percent of the residents from the three BART-served counties lived within a half mile of a BART station in 1990, ranging from 4.5 percent in Contra Costa County to 12.3 percent in San Francisco. Based on 1990 journey-to-work statistics, only 17.8 percent of these station-area residents commuted by rail transit. Multiplying these percentages indicates that fewer than 2 percent of 1990 commute trips within the three BART-served counties were by station-area rail users. Doubling the number of station-area rail users would have a pretty small impact on current commuting and environmental conditions in the Bay Area.

The problem with these calculations and this critique in general is that it is accepting of current settlement patterns and pricing arrangements. Putting more suburban jobs in office towers near rail instead of sprawling business parks would no doubt make these numbers more impressive. So would dramatically raising the price of fuel and parking. We accept that the benefits of any singular measure, such as transit-based housing, are likely to be minimal. However, transit villages are not about singular measures. They aim to tap the synergy of orienting the future growth of both ends of the commute trip—homes and workplaces—to rail, in addition to retail shops, restaurants, entertainment centers, and other urban uses. They also rely on removing current distortions in our pricing system that create cheap automobile travel by failing to charge motorists for externalities (e.g., time losses from congestion, air pollution, etc.). Land-use initiatives, like transit-supportive development, by themselves are clearly no panacea to today's congestion, air quality, and social equity problems. However, neither are road expansions, tollways, or a host of transportation demand management (TDM) measures like ridesharing promotion or flex-time; individually, any of these actions exert a marginal influence on regional traffic and envi-

TABLE 5.8

**Estimated Share of 1990 Commute Trips
by Station-Area Residents of the Three BART-Served Counties**

	% of County Population Within 0.5 Mi of BART Station (1990)	% Work Trips by BART Among Workers Living Within 0.5 Mi of BART Station (1990)	Estimated % Total Commutes by Station-Area Resident Commuters (1990)
Alameda County	9.8	17.3	1.7
Contra Costa County	4.5	11.3	0.5
San Francisco City/County	12.3	25.5	3.1
Three-County Total	8.9	17.8	1.6

Source: U.S. Census, Summary Tape File 3–A.

ronmental conditions. Does this mean we should abandon road expansions or TDM any more than we should abandon transit-supportive development? We don't think so.

We do believe that the experiences abroad examined in Part Four show what is achievable under a more transit-oriented built form, both at the community and regional levels. In Stockholm, a modern city with an average household income on a par with many American cities and with a high vehicle ownership rate (by European standards), transit's market shares are far higher than that calculated by Downs. In 1990, rail accounted for 42 percent of the commute trips beginning and ending in Stockholm County. In some rail-served new towns, 38 percent of the residents and 53 percent of the workers commuted by rail transit. Urban development patterns alone did not produce these results, however. Parking and motoring are expensive in all Swedish cities, and nearly all apartments are publicly subsidized. Similar stories can be told for Singapore and greater Tokyo. Experiences abroad tell us that it would be rash judgment to write off transit villages as "boutique" concepts or "small potatoes." Simply put, we know from both the United States and other countries that transit-oriented development matters when bundled together with other supportive policies.

NOTES

1. To be matched into pairs, the auto and transit neighborhoods needed to have median household incomes within 10 percent of each other and be no more than 4 mi apart. One of the pairs violated this second criterion; however, the neighborhoods matched up so well in all other respects (and given the shortage of matched pairs) that they were retained for the analysis.

2. The seven matched pairs that met selection criteria were: Palo Alto (central)/Stevenson Park (Mountain View); Santa Clara/San Jose-Winchester; San Mateo Center/San Mateo-Coyote Point; Rockridge/Lafayette; Mountain View (central)/Sunnyvale-Mary Avenue; San Mateo-King Park/Millbrae; and San Leandro (central)/Bayfair.

3. For a complete discussion of this research and data collection approach, see Robert Cervero and Carolyn Radisch, *Travel Choices in Pedestrian Versus Automobile Oriented Neighborhoods* (Berkeley: Institute of Urban and Regional Development, University of California, Working Paper 644, 1995). In all, 4000 questionnaires (with prepaid return address envelopes) soliciting data on nonwork travel were sent to households in the two neighborhoods in the spring of 1994, a period of good weather, and 620 were returned for a response rate of 15.5 percent. Mailing labels for the two neighborhoods were obtained from a direct-mail marketing company. The "occupant lists" were based on information compiled from the U.S. Postal Service and included all households, not just homeowners. The questionnaire itself was streamlined in hopes of increasing response rates. This meant compiling data for a single person in the household who responded to the survey, normally an employed adult. Second, nonwork travel data were collected for up to three "main" trips that the respondent made

the previous day; it was up to the respondent to decide what was a "main" trip for nonwork purposes.

4. Rockridge has a much higher share of African-Americans (16.3 percent) relative to Lafayette (under 1 percent). Rockridge also has a higher share of single households (33.7 percent versus 18.6 percent) and accordingly a smaller average household size. This is partly due to Rockridge's population of students who attend the nearby University of California at Berkeley, which also results in a high share of college-educated adults.

5. The statistical analysis involved the estimation of a binomial logit model. The model estimated the probability of making a nonauto nonwork trip as a function of neighborhood of residence, household size, vehicle availability, and household income. The estimated model fitted the sample data (of 990 nonwork trips) quite well, correctly predicting the mode choice of 88.6 percent of the surveyed trips.

6. The figure plots the results under the assumptions that household size equals 2.6 persons (mean value for the two neighborhoods) and annual household income equals $50,000 (near the mean value).

7. Richard Untermann, *Accommodating the Pedestrian: Adapting Towns and Neighborhoods for Walking and Bicycling* (New York: Van Nostrand Reinhold, 1984).

8. Five of the twenty-seven surveyed complexes were condominiums, two were mixed condo-apartments, and the remaining sites were exclusively rental apartments. Sites were between 360 and 3100 ft from a rail station, with the majority lying closer than a quarter mile away. Projects contained between 76 and 892 units. Among the 885 households surveyed in 1992 and 1993, detailed trip records were compiled for 2560 trips. Surveyed households had the following mean characteristics: 1.89 persons, 1.73 vehicles, and $34,000 annual incomes. For details on this study, see Robert Cervero, *Ridership Impacts of Transit-Focused Development in California* (Berkeley: Institute of Urban and Regional Development, Monograph 45, 1993).

9. Ibid., pp. 178–179.

10. JHK and Associates, *Development-Related Ridership Survey I* (Washington, DC: Washington Metropolitan Area Transit Authority, 1987); *Development-Related Ridership Survey II* (Washington, DC: Washington Metropolitan Area Transit Authority, 1989).

11. JHK and Associates, 1989, p. 1.

12. M. Stringham, Travel Behavior Associated with Land Uses Adjacent to Rapid Transit Stations, *ITE Journal,* Vol. 52, No. 4, pp. 18–22, 1982.

13. John Fruin, Designing for Pedestrians, *Public Transportation in the United States,* G. Gray and L. Hoel, eds. (Englewood Cliffs, NJ: Prentice-Hall, 1992), pp. 188–204.

14. From a statistical analysis we were able to show that, besides proximity, residential density indeed had a significant positive influence on transit modal splits among California's station-area residents. See Cervero, op. cit.

15. Bay Area Travel Survey (BATS), 1990–1991, Metropolitan Transportation Commission, Oakland, data tape.

16. San Francisco Centre draws much walk-on shopping traffic from office buildings, hotels, and residences in the downtown area.
17. Anthony Downs, *Stuck in Traffic: Coping with Peak-Hour Traffic Congestion* (Washington, DC: The Brookings Institution, 1992).
18. If, for example, 10 percent of the suburban population lived within walking distance of a transit stop and 20 percent worked in locations along transit routes, only 0.02 (0.10×0.20) might be rail users.
19. Downs, op. cit., p. 94.

6

The Market for Transit Villages

For transit villages to gain ascendency into the 21st century, there must be a demonstrated market for them. Beyond a general desire to live or work in settings with good transit access, there must also be a "niche" market for transit villages, namely, a segment of the population who wants to live in a more built-up, mixed-use, transit-served setting, whether for reasons of more social contact, to become less car dependent, or to economize on housing.

Markets are not created in a vacuum. Importantly, there must be a receptive institutional and legal environment from which to sustain them. Banks, for instance, must be willing to provide loans to real estate developers who want to build a transit village. Local governments must follow with zoning that allows higher densities and fewer parking spaces than is perhaps the norm in the suburbs. And real estate developers themselves must be convinced that, in a day and age when the automobile and single-family living are so pervasive, there are enough customers willing to live in relatively compact, transit-oriented neighborhoods to generate a reasonable profit. In short, even if there appears to be a burgeoning market demand for living and working in transit villages, stakeholders must be sufficiently convinced that this demand is real and sustainable if they are to risk private capital in bringing the transit village idea to fruition.

This chapter investigates the market dimensions of transit-oriented development in the United States—past, current, and future. Initially, opportunities and barriers to transit village development are discussed. The market potential for large-scale transit village development is then assessed using visual simulation techniques. Next, the market demand for transit-based housing in California is profiled in terms of tenant composition and ridership levels. If there is a pent-up demand for transit-oriented development, this should be reflected by higher rents and healthy market conditions. The degree to which this is so is examined for transit-based housing projects in California as well as office-commercial real estate markets in some of the largest U.S. rail cities. Recent evidence from a 20-year evaluation of the land-use impacts of the BART system is also examined in an effort to further refine our understanding of the market dynamics of transit-oriented development.

6.1 OPPORTUNITIES AND BARRIERS TO TRANSIT VILLAGES

6.1.1 Market Opportunities

Several trends, or opportunities, are working in favor of transit village development in the United States. One opportunity has been demographic growth in population groups that are prime candidates for transit-oriented living: young households, retirees, childless couples, and in-migrants from foreign countries. In the San Francisco Bay Area, for instance, the share of population in the 25 to 34 and 65 and over age groups increased from 23.5 percent in 1980 to 30.8 percent in 1990. These households tend to be small and, for financial and convenience reasons, require less space and are more inclined to live in attached housing units. In greater Los Angeles, 30 percent of the households in 1990 contained no children; in the inner suburbs, two-thirds of the households were childless. In addition, immigration added over 2 million to the population of the Los Angeles-Anaheim Metropolitan Statistical Area (MSA) and nearly 600,000 to the San Francisco-Oakland MSA during the 1980s.[1] Because many new arrivals to the United States migrate to urban centers and seek affordable housing, more compact communities near rail stops might appeal to some.

A second trend that is supportive of transit villages is the growing willingness of transit agencies and local governments to leverage private investments near rail stations. Specifically, the ability of governments to assemble land (e.g., through eminent domain, condemnation, or redevelopment takings) and thus help write down costs is attractive to many developers. For many transit agencies, surface parking lots surrounding stations are their biggest development asset. Parking lots represent large tracts of preassembled, cleared land that are relatively cheap to build upon. Converting park-and-ride lots to housing constitutes de facto land banking. One of the reasons so much urban growth has clustered around rail stations in cities like Toronto and Stockholm is that local governments were able to acquire land over and beyond what was necessary to build rail stations, allowing them to lease or sell supplemental land to real estate developers. In the case of Toronto, local government acquired some 20 extra blocks along the Yonge Street corridor in the 1950s and 1960s. This meant they could control what kind of development occurred through leases and land sales in addition to recapturing some of the value added by the rail investment. The high-rise profile along Toronto's Yonge Street corridor is a visual testament to the value of controlling land to leverage private real estate development. But in the United States, eminent domain laws prohibit excess land acquisitions. Reusing park-and-ride lots achieves similar results to land banking, however. Such was the case at the Ballston station in Arlington, Virginia, when its status changed from a terminal to an intermediate station following the extension of Metrorail's Orange Line to Vienna, Virginia. The relocation of park-and-ride spaces and a bus transfer facility to the new terminal freed up land, helping to trigger a massive redevelopment of the Ballston station area, including the construction of a 28-story office-residential-retail complex above the station.

A third opportunity for transit village development is today's receptive policy and legislative environment for coordinating transit and land-use decisions. Recent federal initiatives such as the 1991 national surface transportation act (ISTEA), 1990 Clean Air Act amendments (CAAA), and Empowerment Zone/Enterprise Communities (EZ/EC) programs provide funding sources and a legislative context for promoting transit-oriented development. ISTEA explicitly calls for closer coordination of transportation projects and urban development. Clean air laws encourage land-use initiatives that promote transit and other travel options as a possible transportation control measure (TCM) for nonattainment areas (where pollution concentrations exceed clean air standards). The EZ/EC program promotes such neighborhood transportation strategies as mobility enterprises (e.g., small neighborhood businesses that run special shuttles to jobs in the metropolitan fringes) and neighborhood intermodal travel centers (e.g., train stops that serve as staging points for buses, jitneys, reverse-commute buses). At the state level, "concurrency" laws in Florida, Washington, Oregon, New Jersey, and Georgia stipulate that communities cannot accept new developments unless there are sufficient road infrastructure and transportation services to accommodate the growth; jurisdictions that violate concurrency laws stand to lose state aid. The state of Maryland has enacted an Adequate Public Facilities Ordinance that requires developers to provide proffers, such as road expansions or financial support for transit shuttles, if their projects threaten to deteriorate local transportation conditions. Collectively, these initiatives encourage transit-oriented development—in part, by penalizing developers who build projects that will generate substantial increases in automobile traffic, and in part, by promoting coordinated transportation and land-use development, something which transit villages would receive high marks for.

6.1.2 Barriers to Transit Villages

Working against transit village development loom two significant barriers. The first is fiscal: factors that detract from the financial feasibility of transit-oriented projects, such as questionable market viability and lack of conventional financing. The second is political: land-use policies and not-in-my-backyard (NIMBY) forces that impede multifamily housing development more generally.

Americans' preference for low-density living is firmly rooted. A recent survey by the Building Industry Association of Northern California found that 82 percent of surveyed households preferred a single-family home over all housing types.[2] It is a fundamental rule, according to one northern California developer, that "as density goes up, the general interest from the consumer goes down."[3] In part because of the questionable marketability of denser housing, coupled with the softness of today's real estate markets and the fallout from the savings and loan crisis of the late 1980s, banks are understandably hesitant to provide permanent financing for largely untested products like transit-based housing. The higher construction costs, development fees, and risks associated with higher density housing are also major financial obstacles. As multiunit buildings become taller, costs for design, construction, and liability insurance increase commensurately. Beyond 40 dwelling units per acre (dua), podium or decked parking structures become necessary. Once construction goes above four stories, the more expensive steel-frame construction, elevators, and lobby areas drive unit costs skyward. While in theory denser housing near rail stops should produce less traffic than if the same number of units were built as single-family homes, in practice denser projects pay relatively higher impact fees. A series of recent lawsuits holding condominium builders liable for faulty construction as late as 10 years after project completion has also frightened some California developers away from the high-density housing market.

A pair of -isms—localism and NIMBYism—stand as the biggest political hurdles to transit village development. In California, Proposition 13 (the 1978 initiative that reduced local governments' capacity to generate revenues through property taxes) is often blamed for prompting communities to be more competitive than cooperative. Some jurisdictions keep high-density housing out through fiscal zoning—"zoning in" high tax-yielding land uses, like office parks, and "zoning out" service-demanding activities, notably apartments (that burden already overburdened schools and city services). To many, transit-based housing carries with it the specter of more crowded schools and congestion, the stigma of low-income projects, and the prospect of tarnishing the character of an established neighborhood, thus lowering property values. NIMBY reactions against apartment proposals have lead to restrictive land-use policies and building moratoria in several neighborhoods surrounding BART stations that were prime for more intensive redevelopment, including Rockridge, North Berkeley, Walnut Creek, and the Mission District in San Francisco. In Hunt Valley, Maryland, a major employment hub north of Baltimore that recently received light rail transit services, NIMBY pressures resulted in the rezoning of prime land that was proposed for some 1500 housing units to a rural-conservation designation, despite the presence of light rail and an imbalance of more than three jobs for every available housing unit in the area.

6.2 PROBING THE MARKET FOR TRANSIT VILLAGES THROUGH SIMULATIONS

Presently, the entire transit village movement is caught in a catch-22: There are few examples in part because of questionable market feasibility, and the market potential of transit villages is questionable because there are few examples. In the absence of any truly good U.S. examples of modern-day transit villages, we were recently involved in a study that attempted to simulate them using computer-generated images.[4] The main objective was to gauge the degree to which people might be willing to accept higher density transit-oriented neighborhoods in exchange for more amenities like open space and small retail plazas. Four village scenarios with varying blended housing densities (12, 24, 36, and 48 dua) were created. As densities increased, so did the amount and quality of neighborhood amenities.

These densities span the minimum necessary to sustain rail transit services (12 dua) as well as the upper boundary (48 dua) of what can be built without going to more expensive steel-framed structures with elevators, lobby space, and structured parking.[5] In sum, it is the prospect of designing attractive transit villages with plentiful amenities that reduce perceived densities that motivated this study. The views of one of the Bay Area's largest housing developers are cause for optimism:

> The market is beginning to put more value on the community than on the house itself. Developers need to do a better job of creating and selling community features—various recreational amenities, a pleasant ambiance (one perhaps harking back to traditional villages), pedestrian-friendly streets, and human building scales.[6]

6.2.1 Visual Simulation and Residential Satisfaction

Past studies on residential satisfaction underscore Americans' preference for ownership of detached single-family homes.[7] In one study, the attitudes of residents from several planned U.S. communities (such as Reston, Virginia, and Irvine, California) were surveyed.[8] Most residents preferred low-density neighborhoods, although only the highest density (above 12 dua) ones were strongly disliked. Residents of these planned communities reacted similarly to townhouses and single-family homes, except at higher densities. Studies also show that seniors and singles are usually most accepting of higher density living.[9]

Not all attitudinal surveys of high-density settings have elicited negative responses. Visual preference surveys (VPS), wherein residents rate between 160 and 240 slides, have been used to build community consensus on urban design. As part of an infill plan for a New Jersey town, residents gave a negative rating to a recently approved multifamily project built according to local zoning requirements, but gave highly positive ratings for several images of higher density urban townhouses clustered around courtyards.[10] VPSs of several thousand people across the United States reveal a repeated preference for traditional communities over sprawling suburban planned urban development (PUD) living.

Little work has been conducted to date on the attitudes of Americans to varying density in simulated neighborhoods, and no work, to our knowledge, has focused explicitly on visually simulating transit villages.[11] While revealed market behavior is always the best way to measure demand, in the absence of true transit villages, we believe that simulations are the next best thing.

6.2.2 Research Design and Methods

In order to elicit viewer responses to transit villages with varying density and amenity mixes, four different hypothetical neighborhood scenarios were simulated. For each neighborhood, nine colored photoslide images simulated a walk from a house in the middle of the transit village to a rail station three blocks away. Over 170 residents from the San Francisco Bay Area were recruited to view the images and rate the neighborhoods.

To test the hypothesis that people will accept higher densities in return for more amenities in a transit village setting, our study was designed so that densities and amenity levels were the only factors that varied across the four simulated neighborhoods. Other factors, such as architectural style, building colors and newness, the amount of sunlight, and street widths, remained constant. Without introducing such controls, we would not have been able to distinguish the influences of amenities like open space from the effects of building designs and other intervening factors on peoples' attitudes and preferences.

Decisions about many details of the simulated environments had to be made, including architectural style, articulation of facades, colors and textures of materials, orientation of entrances and windows, and the landscape design of private spaces. We decided to render building facades in a contemporary style. Other styles could have been chosen, such as postmodern designs. The important decision was not the style per se, but rather maintaining a consistent style that would appear plausible at four very different density levels.

6.2.3 Simulating Transit Villages

The four simulated neighborhoods had densities of 12, 24, 36, and 48 dua, again spanning the minimum necessary to support rail transit (12 dua) as well as the upper boundary (48 dua) of what can be built without going to four stories and incurring the costs of expensive steel-framed structures, elevators, lobby space, and structured parking. The South Hayward station on the Bay Area Rapid Transit (BART) system was selected as the site for modeling hypothetical transit villages. Each simulated neighborhood was designed according to the layout of blocks and streets in the vicinity of this station. The South Hayward station typifies many suburban rail stops: It is surrounded by a large parking lot and vacant land, with single-family homes and a few apartments off in the distance. It thus has an important prerequisite for creating a transit village: vacant, buildable land nearby, including a park-and-ride lot. BART is presently working with local governments to convert surface parking lots into mixed residential-retail projects at the El Cerrito del Norte and Pleasant Hill stations, and there have been discussions of doing likewise one day at South Hayward.

Images of the four simulated neighborhoods were generated using three-dimensional modeling and animation techniques.[12] The simulated 12-dua neighborhood consisted of two-story, free-standing, single-family homes on 2250-ft^2 plots. The next lowest density neighborhood, 24 dua, consisted of two-story, attached, single-family row houses constructed above individual garages, with 18-ft frontages (1260 ft^2 land area per unit). The 12- and 24-dua neighborhoods had no park, only a convenience store near the rail station and a fairly modest public square facing the station. Figure 6.1 shows the nine images created for the lowest density neighborhood. Figure 6.2 shows four of the images for the 24-dua neighborhood.[13]

Figure 6.1 Nine Images of Simulated Neighborhood with 12 Dwelling Units per Acre.

Figure 6.2   Four Images of Simulated Neighborhood with 24 Dwelling Units per Acre.

The row-house design with individual garages was again used for the 36-dua neighborhood, but the frontage was reduced to 16 ft (864 ft^2 per unit). The highest density neighborhood, at 48 dua, was designed as a six-unit, three-story condominium (550 ft^2 land area per unit). Parking extended under a podium into the rear yard. To compensate for higher densities, the 36- and 48-dua neighborhoods had more amenities such as a neighborhood park (at the end of the residential street), a neighborhood retail plaza with a bakery and outdoor café, and a more extensively landscaped public square facing the rail station, with additional commercial space and outdoor seating. Figure 6.3 shows four images for the 36-dua neighborhood, and Figure 6.4 shows all nine images for the highest density neighborhood.[14]

6.2.4   Field Presentations and Survey Responses

Over 170 Bay Area residents viewed the slides of simulated transit villages at eight different venues during the spring of 1994.[15] Newspaper ads, telephone contacts, and passer-by solicitations were used to recruit individuals 18 years of age and over. Participants were screened to ensure that the sample was demographically representative of the Bay Area adult population. Before viewing the slides, respondents were told to imagine themselves visiting the transit village for the purpose of possibly purchasing a home (i.e., we focused on attitudes toward owner-occupied units in transit villages). They were informed that houses in the neighborhood were of identical size (1100 ft^2), with two bedrooms, one and

Figure 6.3   Four Images of Simulated Neighborhood with 36 Dwelling Units per Acre.

a half baths, and a one-car garage. In order to remove the influence of geographic location on how neighborhoods were rated, participants were to consider that the neighborhood lies in a part of the San Francisco Bay Area similar to where they presently live and near a rail station like BART.[16]

Participants viewed each neighborhood slide sequence twice and then responded to a series of questions that asked them to rate and evaluate the neighborhood. Simulated neighborhoods were shown in different random orders at each venue to remove any biasing influences of sequencing.[17] Viewing the slides and answering questions took about 45 min, and participants received $20 for their time.[18]

6.2.5   Overall Ratings and Rankings of Neighborhoods

After viewing the slides for each simulated neighborhood, participants were asked to rate each on a −3 to +3 scale in terms of "overall desirability," with −3 representing highly undesirable, +3 representing highly desirable, and 0 signifying indifference. While none of the simulated transit villages were viewed as overwhelmingly the most desirable, the lowest density village received the highest average rating: 0.24. The average ratings for the others were: 24 dua, −0.45; 36 dua, 0.03; and 48 dua, −0.1. Thus, the least desired transit village had the second lowest density (and few amenities). It was preferred, on average, even less than the neighborhood with twice the density (48 dua).[19]

Figure 6.4 Nine Images of Simulated Neighborhood with 48 Dwelling Units per Acre.

Figure 6.5 summarizes rankings by the percentage of respondents who liked each neighborhood the most and each the least. Fifty-eight percent of the respondents liked the lowest density neighborhood the most. However, far more respondents liked the transit village designed at 36 dua with nicer public amenities than the village designed at 24 dua with fewer amenities. Notably, people preferred tightly spaced two-and-a-half-story row houses with modest backyards located near a public park and small retail plaza to similar row houses with larger rear yards and more street frontage, but with no neighborhood park and fewer local services. Overall, a moderately dense neighborhood without a large park (24 dua) or a very dense neighborhood with a park (48 dua) was disliked by many. The neighborhood that fell in between these two in terms of density and park features (i.e., the one with 36 dua) provoked less of a strong reaction. It was generally liked more and disliked less than the other two neighborhoods.[20]

Overall, these findings confirm the central hypothesis of this study: People are willing to accept higher densities in transit-oriented neighborhoods as long as various amenities, perhaps most importantly a neighborhood park, are provided. As expected, peoples' preferences of neighborhoods fell as densities increased. That is, among the two simulated neighborhoods without a park, they generally preferred the lowest density one (12 dua), and among the two neighborhoods with a park, the lowest density one (36 dua) was also liked the most. The finding that amenities can compensate for densities that are 50 percent higher (36 versus 24 dua) in a transit village setting confirms our belief of a wide gulf between perceived and actual densities.[21]

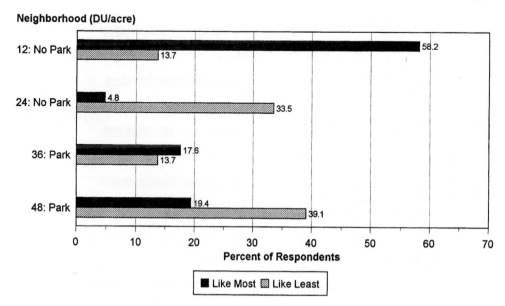

Figure 6.5 Attitudes of Respondents to Neighborhoods.

6.2.6 Ratings of Neighborhood Amenities

Among the neighborhood features shown, having a rail station close by was consistently liked the most (Figure 6.6). The second most liked feature of the denser transit villages was the open space; this was the neighborhood attribute that differed the most visually between the two lower and two higher density neighborhoods. Without a neighborhood park, the two lower density transit villages were rated poorly on open space features. The addition of more services in the two higher density neighborhoods—specifically, a bakery and outdoor cafe in the retail plaza, and more commercial stalls and outdoor seating in the public square near the station—was well received by the respondents. People were fairly indifferent or slightly negative toward community services in the 12- and 24-dua neighborhoods. With regard to building architecture, respondents were fairly neutral toward the 12-dua neighborhood and disliked the three higher density ones. Some were likely responding more to perceived density than to building design. Based on open-ended survey responses, some participants mentioned they did not like the architectural designs of the buildings shown. We might have been able to elicit more positive responses to higher density neighborhoods if the architecture and perhaps quality of buildings "improved" as density rose; however, this would have confounded the research design because building architecture would have no longer been a constant control variable.

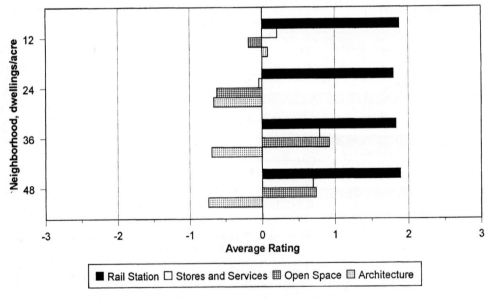

Figure 6.6 Average Rating of Features of Simulated Neighborhoods.

6.2.7   Ratings by Respondent Characteristics

Cross-tabulating neighborhood ratings by characteristics of respondents provided insights into which demographic groups are potential markets for transit village living. Respondents who were most receptive to higher density transit-oriented neighborhoods were young adults with moderate incomes who currently reside in apartment complexes.[22] Half of the respondents who were between 18 and 28 years of age, for instance, gave the 48 dua neighborhood an overall rating of +2 or +3; fewer than a third of the respondents from other age groups rated the neighborhood this high. Those who currently commute to work by transit were also slightly more accepting of denser neighborhoods.

6.2.8   Summary of Transit Village Simulation Work

This simulation study provides some encouragement for the prospects of creating transit villages in large metropolises like the San Francisco Bay Area. The general public seems willing to accept residential densities necessary to sustain rail transit services in return for public parks, in-neighborhood shops, and easy access to rail stops. Notably, row houses with narrow front lots and modest backyards that are near a neighborhood park and retail plaza are preferred to row houses with bigger backyards and more frontage, but with no nearby park and fewer local services.

Being near stores and services was particularly important to those who reacted positively to the denser simulated neighborhoods. Having a central park increased the average ratings of the densest neighborhoods, and not having a park slightly lowered the ratings of the less dense ones. While large open space was clearly perceived as a positive amenity, its ability to compensate for density seemed to hold only up to a certain density threshold, around 36 dua.

Visual simulations provide a new approach for assessing the market potential of different built forms, like transit villages. The use of tightly controlled simulations allowed us to test and confirm the hypothesis that people are willing to trade off higher densities for more neighborhood amenities, up to a limit. The somewhat contradictory findings of this research with those of other marketing studies on attitudes toward higher residential densities might very well be attributable to differences in research methods. Traditionally, housing marketing studies rely on verbal descriptions and written inquiries. Visual images, we believe, provide a much richer context for probing the market potential for transit village development, not only because they are concrete and graphic, but also because they allow for a much wider array of choices to be conveyed. Notes James Constantine: "... it should not be surprising that surveys of consumers' visual preferences often contradict conventional marketing studies. By gauging people's preferences for various types of architecture, streetscapes, commercial centers, and even landscaping, visual surveys can become the basis for creating a more successful image for new development."[23]

6.3   RESIDENT PROFILES OF TRANSIT-BASED HOUSING IN CALIFORNIA

Of course, the limitation of visual simulations, however attractive or fanciful they might be, is that they are nonetheless make-believe. After showing our transit village simulations to a group of leading housing developers in the San Francisco Bay Area, although many in the audience were intrigued by the research itself, there was still a healthy dose of skepticism about the market potential for transit villages. Most developers mentioned they are not inclined to invest in transit-oriented projects until a clear consumer demand can be demonstrated and some financial track record is established.

Modern-day transit villages are only beginning to take form in the United States, but there is plenty of established transit-based housing from which one can begin to infer market profiles. Although we suspect that the market demand for planned communities around transit stations will be somewhat different than that of stand-alone housing projects near rail, looking at the tenant makeup of transit-based housing nonetheless provides insights into the kinds of households that will most likely populate transit villages. In some settings, transit-based housing could very well be the building blocks for future full-blown transit villages.

In general, one would expect the tenants of transit-based housing to be very similar to those living in apartments and higher density housing elsewhere: single people; young couples without children; empty nesters and retirees seeking smaller, simpler, and easier to maintain residences and perhaps wanting to cash in on their accumulated housing equity. That is, households living in higher density housing near transit stops are probably fairly small and at the beginning and later stages of their life cycles. Two other factors, however, are thought to distinguish apartment dwellers and condominium owners near rail stations. First, the high level of regional accessibility afforded by living close to rail, we believe, results in lower than average household vehicle ownership rates. Second, we suspect that residents of transit-based housing tend to work in locations that are well served by rail, namely downtown and other regional employment centers. The *residential sorting hypothesis* maintains that people gravitate to areas which have comparative accessibility advantages to places of employment.[24] In the case of contemporary rail systems with radial configurations, downtown job sites are best served, suggesting if the residential sorting hypothesis is correct that significant shares of station-area residents are downtown office workers.

6.3.1   Data Sources and Methods

To test these hypotheses, residents living in 11 recently built apartment and condominium projects near suburban BART stations were surveyed in 1993.[25] Surveyed housing projects had at least 75 dwelling units and were within a half mile of one of five suburban East Bay stations: Pleasant Hill, Bayfair, South Hayward, Union City, or Fremont (see Map 4.1 in Chapter 4 for a map of the BART system). Self-administered questionnaires were mailed to tenants in all units of the 11 surveyed housing projects. Questionnaires elicited information on family size, number of vehicles, and annual income as well as such occupant characteristics as age, occupation, workplace location, and typical commuting mode.[26]

The hypothesis tests involved comparing the characteristics of households and individuals living in multiunit complexes within a half mile of BART stations to characteristics of their neighbors living in the same census tract but beyond a half mile distance (and in most instances, living in lower density settings). The one-half mile threshold represents the maximum distance that research shows most Americans are willing to walk as part of a commute trip.[27] For the suburban areas studied, most census tracts were 3 to 5 mi in diameter, meaning that most of the "control" populations lived well beyond acceptable walking distance of stations. In drawing comparisons, statistics for households at each surveyed site were netted from 1990 census statistics for the surrounding census tract. This allowed characteristics of households living in large complexes near suburban rail stations to be contrasted to all other households in the vicinity, with vicinity defined by the size of census tracts.

6.3.2 Comparison of Household Characteristics

As expected, households living in apartments and condominiums near BART stations tended to be much smaller than the typical household in the surrounding census tract. The average transit-based household had 1.66 members compared to an average for the surrounding census tracts of 2.39 (Table 6.1). Over 90 percent of the transit-based house-

TABLE 6.1

Matched-Pair Comparisons of Household and Occupant Characteristics of Transit-Based Housing and Surrounding Census Tracts, San Francisco Bay Area, 1993

	Transit-Based Housing		Surrounding Census Tract			
	Mean	Standard Deviation	Mean	Standard Deviation	Matched-Pair *t* Statistic	Probability
Household Characteristics						
Persons/household	1.66	0.81	2.39	1.37	1.90	.091
Number of vehicles available	1.26	0.68	1.61	1.11	1.56	.165
Occupant Characteristic						
Age (17+ years)	36.3	14.7	42.1	17.7	1.38	.196

Note: The Surrounding Census Tract consists of the census tract that encompasses the housing project, with the estimated population for the transit-based housing projects netted from census tract data. The matched-pair *t* statistic is based on paired differences in mean values between transit-based housing and housing in the surrounding census tract, adjusted for the standard deviation in mean differences. The probability is the likelihood of getting a nonzero paired difference from the sample if there is no difference in the population.

holds had just one or two occupants compared to 58 percent of the households in sur-rounding tracts.[28] Fewer than 8 percent of the transit-based households had children.

Consistent with expectations, transit-based projects averaged fewer vehicles per house-hold, 1.26 versus 1.61 for surrounding tracts. Over 70 percent of the surveyed households near BART had one or no vehicles compared to 49 percent of the remaining households in the same census tracts. Vehicle ownership levels were lower for rail-based housing projects partly because these projects averaged fewer occupants.[29]

Fewer vehicles translate directly into less surface parking, thus freeing up land near sta-tions for more productive uses. Lower auto ownership rates also promote both market-rate and affordable housing. Studies show that second car ownership costs about $3000 per year. Those able to give up a second car as a result of living near a transit node can save $250 a month, money that could be put toward housing.[30]

6.3.3 Comparison of Occupant Characteristics

Table 6.1 also compares the average age of adult occupants of the surveyed projects ver-sus the surrounding census tracts.[31] Rail-based housing projects average younger adult occupants than surrounding neighborhoods. Figure 6.7 shows there were particularly higher shares of adults in the 25- to 34-year age group than in the control households. Coupled with the finding that most rail-based households have no children, it appears

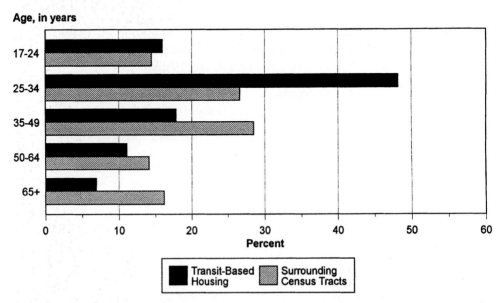

Figure 6.7 Age Distributions: Residents of Transit-Based Housing Versus Surround-ing Census Tracts.

most occupants are in the beginning stages of their adult life cycle and are probably saving to buy a home one day as they filter up the housing market.

From the surveys, whites and Asian-Americans were represented proportionally more in rail-based housing than in surrounding census tracts: 64 percent of the adult occupants were white and 19.6 percent were Asian-Americans in the surveyed housing projects versus 56.3 percent and 15.6 percent, respectively, in the control areas. Six of the eleven surveyed housing projects were more diverse ethnically and racially than their surrounding census tracts.

Figure 6.8 reveals that the East Bay's rail-based housing attracts significant numbers of managerial, professional, clerical, and accounting workers, that is, office occupations that tend to congregate in locations, like downtowns, well served by transit. These white-collar occupations account for nearly 75 percent of all rail-based respondents compared to around 50 percent of employed residents in the surrounding tracts. Relatively few tenants of transit-based housing work in sales, services, and other occupations (including manufacturing, labor, and crafts).

Because of the high share of respondents who work in professional fields, the annual incomes of rail-based households tend to be relatively high (Figure 6.9). Among the 11 rail-based housing projects surveyed, the largest share of households was earning in excess of $60,000 annually. Nearly 60 percent of the surveyed rail-based households had annual incomes above $40,000 compared to 30 percent of the control households.

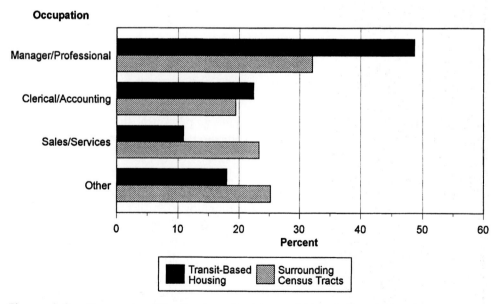

Figure 6.8 Occupation Distributions: Residents of Transit-Based Housing Versus Surrounding Census Tracts.

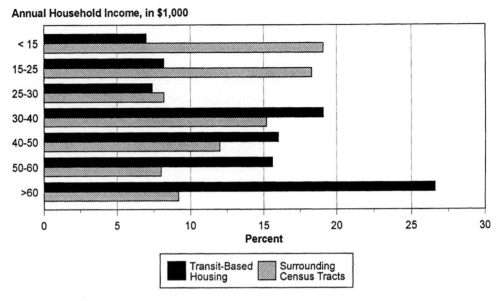

Figure 6.9   Household Income Distribution: Comparison of Transit-Based Housing Versus Surrounding Census Tracts.

6.3.4   Workplace and Commuting Characteristics of Rail-Based Tenants

What most distinguishes residents of housing near rail stations is their tendency to work downtown and in other locations well served by transit. Table 6.2 suggests a high degree of residential sorting for the three geographic submarkets of rail-based housing projects that were surveyed. In the case of the five surveyed apartment and condominium complexes near the Hayward and San Leandro BART stations, 43 percent of the employed residents work in downtown San Francisco or Oakland compared to just 13 percent of the employed residents in the surrounding census tracts.[32] And an estimated one-half of the employed residents of the 1800 apartment units near the Pleasant Hill BART station work in downtown San Francisco or Oakland compared to 10 percent for the control area. Some degree of residential sorting is also evident for those commuting to smaller urban centers, such as Albany-Berkeley-Emeryville just north of Oakland, although the pattern is not as strong.

These findings on residential sorting are consistent with those of Richard Voith in his study of residential location choice as a function of employment accessibility in greater Philadelphia.[33] Voith found regional census tracts with commuter rail services averaged 12 percent more of their residents working in downtown Philadelphia than did surrounding census tracts. Like BART, Philadelphia's rail system radially connects suburban communities to the central business district.

TABLE 6.2

Comparison of Workplace Locations: Percent of Residents in Rail-Based Housing Working in Different Bay Area Workplaces, Compared to Residents of Surrounding Census Tracts

Destination	Fremont-Union City		Hayward-San Leandro		Pleasant Hill	
	Rail-Based Housing	Surrounding Area[1]	Rail-Based Housing	Surrounding Area[2]	Rail-Based Housing	Surrounding Area[3]
San Francisco	14.3	3.7	17.9	4.2	37.9	5.9
Oakland	8.3	2.8	25.3	8.9	12.1	4.1
Albany-Berkeley-Emeryville	3.0	0.2	3.2	1.3	4.8	1.4
San Jose	6.8	9.1	1.1	1.4	2.4	0.8
Pleasant Hill-Walnut Creek	0.8	0.3	2.1	0.1	15.3	11.0
Remainder	66.8	83.9	50.4	84.1	27.5	76.8
Total	100.0	100.0	100.0	100.0	100.0	100.0

[1]Superdistrict 16 of the Metropolitan Transportation Commission (MTC).
[2]Superdistrict 17 of the MTC.
[3]Superdistrict 21 of the MTC.

6.3.5   Rail-Based Markets in Summary

In summary, those living in rail-based housing in the Bay Area's eastern suburbs tend to be young professionals, singles, and childless couples, typically with one car per household. Many hold good paying white-collar jobs. Many also work in locations well served by rail and commute by rail far more often than the average worker. Some developers are starting to realize that a number of downtown workers, many of whom are young professionals earning good wages, are attracted to rail-based housing and represent an untapped market niche. Projects with nice amenities and which cater to the tastes of young professionals seem to appeal to many childless households seeking condominiums and apartments near rail. One example is the Park Regency apartment complex near the Pleasant Hill BART station, an upmarket project complete with a pool, spa-sauna, and recreational building, which has a waiting list to move in. Three-quarters of Park Regency's occupants are in the 18 to 34 year age group, and more than 50 percent earn over $40,000 annually. Another high-amenity project is Del Norte Place near the El Cerrito del Norte BART station; its marketing brochures highlight the project's fireplaces, bay views, ground-floor retail, and proximity to BART. In an interview with *The New York Times,* the project's developer acknowledged that he aggressively put in a bid to the El Cerrito redevelopment authority to build on the site because he believed living near rail stations would become increasingly attractive as regional traffic congestion worsens.[34] (Both the Park Regency and Del Norte Place projects are discussed in more detail in Chapter 7.)

Although the results presented in this section are limited to multiunit projects near suburban BART stations, we believe they are fairly generalizable. They were taken from a larger study that profiled households and occupants of 16 transit-based projects near four other California rail systems—Santa Clara light rail, Sacramento light rail, San Diego light rail, and CalTrain commuter rail (mainly serving San Mateo County)—in addition to the 11 BART-oriented projects.[35] Tenants of these other rail-based projects had sociodemographic, workplace, and commuting characteristics that were very similar to those of the 11 projects examined in this section.

It is worth nothing that those living in transit-based housing in the San Francisco Bay Area were similar in characteristics to those who were most receptive to living in denser simulated transit villages, most notably younger households who place a higher premium on neighborhood amenities. Together, these findings point clearly in the direction of there being a significant, largely untapped niche market of transit village inhabitants.

6.3.6 Policy Inferences

Several clear public policy inferences can be drawn from these research findings. Because rail-based households own relatively few cars and frequently patronize transit (as shown in Chapter 5), zoning standards should be relaxed to allow just one off-street parking space per unit at transit-based complexes instead of the two spaces normally enforced in the suburbs. This would lower construction costs by an estimated $12,000 per unit in the Bay Area (the typical cost of a tuck-under, podium parking space), allow for more compact development, and by shrinking surface parking lots, create a more pedestrian-friendly environment. Tenants with more than one car might be given the option of leasing a second space. Another novel idea, suggested by John Holtzclaw and others, would have banks grant those living in rail-based condominiums an "efficient location" loan for home purchases.[36] If rail-based housing lowers transportation costs (mainly in the form of only having to own one car), then these savings might be subtracted from principal, interest, taxes, and insurance expenses when calculating mortgage qualifications. This acknowledges that lower transportation costs free up more money for housing consumption. Such loan adjustments could further attract prospective homebuyers to transit village locations.

6.4 RAIL-BASED HOUSING AND RENT PREMIUMS

If rail-based housing projects are becoming increasingly desirable addresses, this should generally be reflected in rent levels. There is a substantial literature in America on the influence of rail transit systems on land values. Studies of rail systems in Philadelphia, Washington, DC, Miami, and the San Francisco Bay Area have been mixed in their conclusions on transit's capitalization effects (i.e., its ability to increase land values and produce a rent premium). A 1981 study of Washington's Metrorail concluded that townhouses within 1000 ft of the Pentagon City station sold for $12,300 more than comparable units far from Metro service.[37] A more recent study of residential properties near the 14.5-mi Lindenwold Line in Philadelphia concluded that access to rail created an average housing value premium of 6.4 percent.[38] Using 1990 sales transaction data, John Landis and others found for every meter a home is closer to the nearest BART station in Alameda and Contra Costa Counties its sales price increases in the range of $1.96 to $2.29, all else being equal.[39] Proximity to highways, on the other hand, had a depressing effect on home prices.

Other studies have found rail transit systems to exert far weaker impacts. A recent study of residential values near the Miami Metrorail system concluded that proximity to rail stations induced little or no relative increase in housing values.[40] Additionally, some have found a disamenity effect with being too close to BART; property values immediately adjacent to BART were depressed due to such nuisances as noise and fumes from increased automobile traffic.[41] Collectively, these studies suggest the capitalization effects of rail investments to be highly localized and not easily generalizable.

None of these previous studies focused on multiunit residential projects, the type of housing that would be common in transit villages. In particular, no studies could be found that measured a monthly premium for rental units close to transit; virtually all work done to date on capitalization effects of rail transit has measured impacts on single-family housing values.

In this section, we compared rents at large residential projects near East Bay BART stations with those of similar projects in the general vicinity that are beyond walking distance of BART. As shown in Map 6.1, three geographic submarkets with substantial housing within a quarter-mile radius of BART (as well as a sufficient number of control units) were identified: Concord-Pleasant Hill-Walnut Creek, Albany-El Cerrito-Richmond, and Union City-Fremont. For each submarket, multifamily (rental) apartments with over 75 units built since 1985 near BART stations were identified. Information on 1994 rents and physical characteristics of the units were obtained directly from real estate brokers who were most familiar with each submarket and who were willing to release proprietary rental information.[42] Rent comparisons were then made between projects near BART and similar projects not near BART, stratified by type of unit (i.e., one bedroom, one bath; two bedrooms, two baths). Thus, matched-pair comparisons were used to approximate rent premiums, with geographic location, age of buildings (post-1985), and type of units functioning as control variables. While amenity levels (e.g., swimming pool, fireplaces, etc.) were not directly controlled for, cases were chosen to ensure reasonably similar levels of amenities. The following number of apartment complexes were studied for each submarket: Concord-Pleasant Hill-Walnut Creek, four near BART and twenty away from BART; Albany-El Cerrito-Richmond, one near BART and three away from BART; and Union City-Fremont, two near BART and six away from BART. The matched-pair analysis is fol-

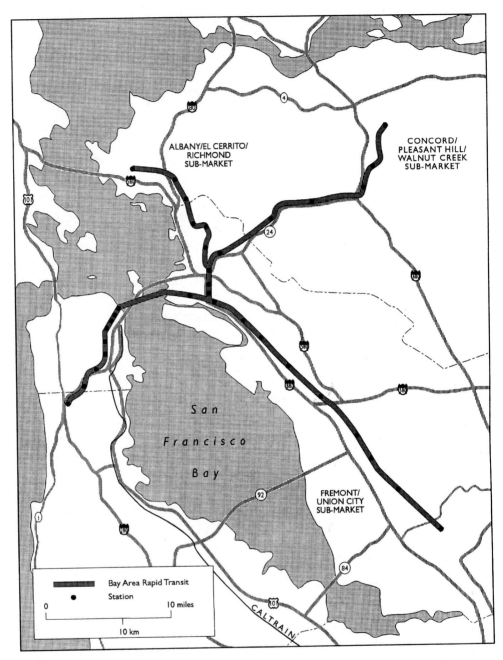

Map 6.1 Three Geographic Submarkets Studied in the San Francisco Bay Area.

lowed by a hedonic price model, estimated for the Concord-Pleasant Hill-Walnut Creek submarket, that statistically controls for factors other than BART proximity in estimating rent premiums.

6.4.1 Matched-Pair Comparisons

Figure 6.10 shows that on a square footage basis there was a modest rent premium associated with being near BART, for both one- and two-bedroom units, for two of the submarkets: Concord-Pleasant Hill-Walnut Creek and Union City-Fremont. Rents in 1994 square foot for one-bedroom units near the Pleasant Hill station were $1.20 per square foot compared to an average of $1.09 for similar projects (in terms of size, age, and amenities) that were in the same geographic submarket but away from BART. Two-bedroom units near the Pleasant Hill station leased for around $1.09 per square foot compared to around $0.94 per square foot for comparable units away from BART. Similar differentials were found in the Union City-Fremont submarket. Differences were negligible for the Albany-El Cerrito-Richmond submarket, however. Overall, these findings translate into approximately a 10 to 15 percent rent premium associated with being near BART for two of the submarkets, with no impact on the third submarket.

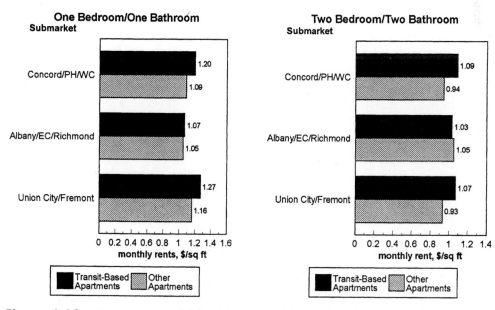

Figure 6.10 Comparison of Monthly Rents: Transit-Based Housing Versus Other Nearby Apartments, One- and Two-Bedroom Submarkets, 1994.

6.4.2 Model Estimates of Rent Premiums

Matched-pair comparisons try to control for confounding factors mechanically. They presume that observations, in our case housing projects, have been matched so that they are virtually identical on all counts except the variable of interest—proximity to rail transit. The use of comps (i.e., simple comparisons) for subjectively valuing housing attributes is standard practice in the real estate industry; however, rarely is it possible to match up units to control for all factors that affect value.

Using multiple regression analysis, hedonic price models attempt to do what matched-pair comparisons are unable to: statistically control for a large number of attributes of the "housing bundle," allowing the unique effects of each attribute (including proximity to rail) to be partialed out.[43] A hedonic price model was estimated for projects in the Concord-Pleasant Hill-Walnut Creek submarket.[44] In estimating a hedonic price model, each type of unit (e.g., one bedroom, one bathroom) was treated as an observation; because most projects had two or three different types of units, multiple observations were generated for most projects. In all, 60 cases of distinct rental products in the Concord-Pleasant Hill-Walnut Creek submarket were available for the analysis.

From the estimated hedonic price model, a rent premium of $34 per month was associated with being very close to BART. That is, units within a quarter mile of the Pleasant Hill BART station rented for around $34 more per month than otherwise comparable units farther away from BART. More bathrooms, bedrooms, and amenities like playgrounds and weight rooms likewise increased monthly rents.[45] Surprisingly, units in more compact projects rented for more than comparable units in lower density ones. Project density, it should be noted, reflects units per acre within a complex as opposed to the density of the surrounding neighborhood. The rental premium associated with compact projects could reflect the benefits of tenants being closer to pools, playgrounds, and other amenities as well as living in a communal setting. The rail-based projects used in this analysis were comparatively dense, suggesting some interaction between these two factors—closeness to stations and project density. The finding that both proximity to transit and project compactness get capitalized into higher rents bodes well for the future of transit-oriented development in the Bay Area and potentially elsewhere.[46]

6.5 RENT PREMIUMS FOR COMMERCIAL DEVELOPMENT

Research on proximity of commercial-retail and office projects to rail transit stations provides further evidence of the value of transit-oriented development and, hence, its potential market demand. Real estate market trends were recently compared between office-commercial development near suburban rail transit stations and nearby freeway-oriented development in the Washington, DC, and Atlanta metropolitan areas. Both regions built new-generation, heavy-rail transit systems during the 1970s. Trends in office and commercial rents, absorption rates, and other real estate market indicators were examined for the 1978–1989 period for three station areas on Washington's Metrorail system—Ballston, Bethesda, and Silver Spring—and two stations on Atlanta's MARTA rail system—Arts Center and Lenox. Maps 6.2 and 6.3 show the locations of the case study station areas in relation to both rail systems. Trends were then compared to nearby commercial centers served by freeways but without rail services.[47] The neighborhoods near rail transit versus those near freeways were matched so that they were similar with respect to

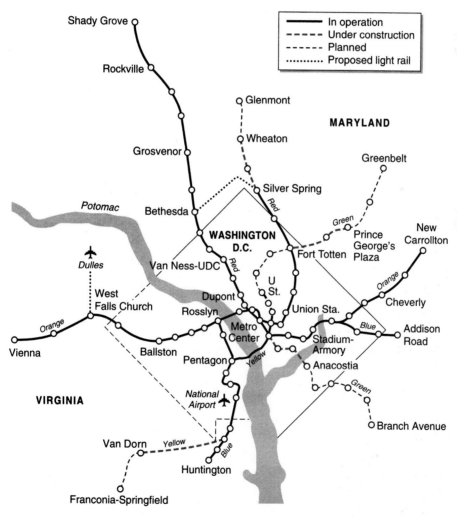

Map 6.2 Washington, DC, Metrorail System: Ballston, Bethesda, and Silver Spring Stations.

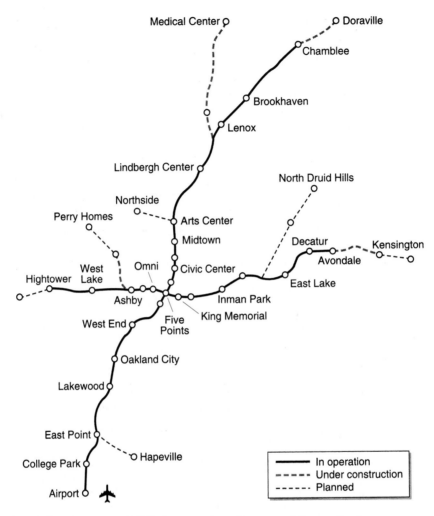

Map 6.3 Atlanta MARTA System: Arts Center and Lenox Stations.

(and thereby controlling for) the following factors: type and mix of land uses prior to the provision of rail services, type and quality of office and commercial spaces, number and type of jobs at the site, and setting along radial corridors from downtown.[48]

The comparisons revealed, in most cases, a modest rent premium for commercial-office properties near rail. Take the case of Ballston on Metrorail's Orange Line versus the edge city of Tysons Corner, which lies some 6 mi southwest of Ballston. When Metrorail services began to Ballston in 1979, the neighborhood was in a state of decline, consisting of low to moderate income tract housing, a small commercial strip, and some incompatible land uses (e.g., car repair shops near apartments). Since then, the area has blossomed into one of Arlington County's "new downtowns," surrounded by mid-rise commercial towers, condominiums, and apartments. Directly above the Metrorail station is the Ballston Metro Center, a 28-story tower with Class A office space, 200 hotel rooms, 284 condominium units, and lower level retail space. (See Chapter 8 for further details on the Ballston station.) Two decades ago, Tysons Corner was a county crossroads with a general store and a few scattered farms and homes. Today, Tysons Corner boasts over 60,000 predominantly white-collar workers, some 15 million ft² of office space, convention hotels, and several regional fashion malls. Although the scale of Tysons Corner is many times greater than that of Ballston, the two are still regarded as primary competitors for new development. During the early 1980s, Tysons Corner enjoyed a rent premium over the Ballston area. However, in 1985 the median rent for new office and commercial-retail space in Ballston surpassed that of Tysons Corner. By the late 1980s, Ballston averaged an annual office rent premium of over $3 per square foot.

Similar patterns were found between properties in rail-served Bethesda, Maryland, and the nearby freeway-oriented Rock Springs Park in Maryland, as well as between MARTA's Lenox and Arts Center station areas and the matched pairs of nearby freeway-oriented development. These rail-served developments commanded more than $2 per square foot in annual office rent premiums over their nearest suburban competitors served by freeways. We attributed most of this premium to the fact that the rail-served areas were more compact, had more mixed land uses, and enjoyed more pleasant walking environments. Rail station areas typically had three to four times as much retail space as the freeway-oriented developments; retail space typically leases for twice as much as office space. Mixed-use projects also tend to average more leasable space because on-site tenants require less parking (partly because of the availability of rail services), and mixed-use projects make shared parking possible. A reflection of the fact that rail-oriented, mixed-use projects command rent premiums is the favorable treatment they often receive in securing permanent financing. Real estate lenders now assign credit in the loan evaluations for mixed-use, rail-oriented projects that are jointly developed by the public and private sectors because of the proven ability of these projects to generate top rents over long periods.

The matched-pair comparisons found that rail-served commercial-office developments also leased up more rapidly. From 1980 to 1989, the inventory of leased office space near MARTA's Arts Center station increased by 10 percent per year. By contrast, office growth along the Northwest Interstate-75 freeway corridor, a collection of campus-style business parks some 2 mi to the west, was fairly sluggish over the same period, increasing by only about 1 percent per year.

Overall, the comparative analysis of rail-oriented versus freeway-oriented development further supports the notion that mixed-use transit villages can be profitable business ventures. The evidence from greater Washington, DC, and Atlanta is that the market for well-planned, rail-served commercial-office development is to be healthy. Combined with the findings of rent premiums for apartments near rail stations, the findings of similar premiums and well-functioning real estate markets for commercial rail-served development bode favorably for the market potential of future transit villages.

6.6   FURTHER EVIDENCE ON MARKET POTENTIAL: THE BART @ 20 STUDY

The recently completed 20-year update of the original BART Impact Study provides useful insights into the longer term impacts of modern-day rail investments on urban development patterns in general and the market demand for sites near transit stops in particular. When BART was first conceived in the early 1950s, planners hoped a modern-era rail system would guide future population and employment growth in the region. By providing one of the largest incremental additions to regional accessibility in the post-World War II era, BART was expected to strengthen the Bay Area's urban centers while guiding suburban growth along radial corridors, leading to a star-shaped, multicentered metropolitan form. The entire BART project was premised on the basis that it would eventually lead to mini-communities mushrooming around suburban rail stations.[49] A 1956 planning document, *Regional Rapid Transit,* contained the first regional land-use plan ever prepared for the Bay Area. The plan called for the Bay Area to become a "subcentered metropolis"—"something between the tightly nucleated clusters which form the typical metropolitan areas of the East Coast and the vast low-density sprawl of the West Coast's Los Angeles."[50] Leonard Merewitz maintains that a tacit reason for building BART was to differentiate the region from its freeway-oriented sibling to the south, Los Angeles.[51] Proponents felt that BART would help catapult San Francisco into the position of "Manhattan of the West." A 1962 alternatives analysis report often and ominously referred to the likely consequences of not building BART: "The outward thrust of our urban area is characterized by scatter and dispersion of land development activities throughout the peripheries . . . [and] this uncoordinated process of land development imposes added costs on the home owner which could be avoided if land development were orderly and compact."[52]

    In view of these expectations, the original BART Impact Studies placed a strong emphasis on gauging the land-use impacts of BART. These studies, carried out in the mid-1970s only a few years after the 1973 opening of the 72-mi BART system, concluded that BART had a modest, though not inconsequential, influence on land uses and urban development in the Bay Area, both directly by improving accessibility and indirectly by inducing various policies supportive of compact development, such as incentive zoning and redevelopment financing. BART did not create new growth, but rather acted to redistribute growth that would have taken place even without a rail investment. The initial study also found that BART's primary land-use impacts occurred at the local rather than regional level. BART, for instance, was credited with focusing much of San Francisco's downtown office construction south of Market Street and rejuvenating inner-city Oakland.[53] BART, however, was only part of the reason. A redevelopment authority was formed at the same time BART was built to encourage development in the south of Market (SoMa) area. New zoning significantly increased allowable floor area ratios within 700 ft of stations and provided density bonuses for buildings adjacent to downtown stations. A $15-million beautification program, complete with new street furniture and landscaping and funded through tax increment financing, helped lure new development to the Market Street corridor. In downtown Oakland and at the Lake Merritt station, significant public efforts to assemble land and site new public buildings around BART stations were critical to redeveloping these areas. Without these public initiatives, far less development would have occurred.

Outside of downtown, the original study found BART's land-use influences to be fairly modest, save for several East Bay station areas. Local opposition to growth, downzoning, and the siting of stations in freeway medians suppressed development outside of downtown. BART largely failed to attract high-density housing around stations. Melvin Webber, in a widely read critique of BART published in *Public Interest,* argued that BART's poor land-use performance outside of downtowns was mainly because it was only marginally faster than buses and was markedly slower than its chief competitor, the private automobile.[54] He and others argued that fixed guideway rail was the wrong technology for the Bay Area given the rapid growth in automobile ownership, home ownership, and freeway building that took place during the postwar period. Noted sociologist Homer Hoyt observed over a half a century ago that urban form is largely a product of the dominant transportation technology during a city's prevailing period of growth.[55] The Bay Area grew most rapidly during the 1950s and 1960s, a period of massive freeway construction and the automobile's ascendency. BART, critics charged, was too little, too late.

6.6.1 Employment Growth Near BART

The 20-year update of the BART Impact Study reveals that in recent times BART has functioned as a magnet for employment growth.[56] Data on regional employment growth from the U.S. Department of Commerce's *County Business Patterns* were disaggregated at the zip code level for the 1981–1990 period. Shift-share analysis was used to measure employment growth differential between the 35 zip codes with BART stations and the remaining 117 zip codes without BART stations in the three BART-served counties (Alameda, Contra Costa, and San Francisco). The BART zip codes gained 139,400 jobs from 1981 to 1990, growing by 30.3 percent and accounting for 57.1 percent of the employment growth in the three counties. Employment in the non-BART zip codes increased by 110,300, or 19 percent. Almost all of the BART-related employment growth, however, occurred in downtown San Francisco; jobs in the East Bay's zip codes, by comparison, increased just 1.1 percent. Among employment sectors, finance-insurance-real estate (FIRE) experienced the greatest absolute job growth and the fastest job growth rate (+108.2 percent) in the BART zip codes, followed by nonbusiness services (+52.9 percent) and business services (+46.2 percent).

Using data from the 1990 Census Transportation Planning Package (CTPP) for the San Francisco Bay Area, the study further examined employment differentials by occupation. Over the 1981–1990 period, businesses near BART were found to have hired relatively high shares of executive, professional, and technical workers (consistent with the finding that BART's primary locational influence was in the FIRE and consumer services sectors). Along the Fremont-Richmond BART corridors, census tracts with BART stations were found to consistently average around 15 to 20 percentage points more of professional and technical workers than do businesses in census tracts in the parallel Interstate-80 and Interstate-880 corridors.

Overall, job growth has been consistently higher around BART stations than elsewhere in the region, though this is mainly attributable to gains in downtown San Francisco. As shown in Figure 6.11, nearly 28 million ft^2 of office floorspace was built within a quarter

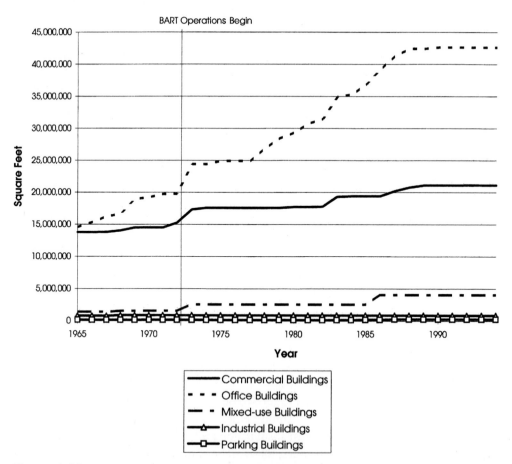

Figure 6.11   Plot of Changes in Nonresidential Building Areas Near Downtown San Francisco BART Stations.

mile of the four downtown San Francisco BART stations—Embarcadero, Montgomery, Powell, and Civic Center—during the 1973 to 1993 period.[59] More than twice as much office space was added to the quarter-mile rings around these four stations than was added to the rings around the 30 remaining BART stations that are outside of downtown San Francisco. In the East Bay, job growth has generally been faster away from BART, with much of it having concentrated along the Interstate-680 corridor (where numerous campus-style office parks were opened in the 1980s). In the context of both national and regional trends toward office decentralization, these findings suggest that BART has helped slow the exodus of jobs from downtown San Francisco. This inference is supported by a 1980–1990 comparison of the downtown share of regional employment in the Bay Area versus California's other megametropolis, greater Los Angeles, which had no urban heavy rail system in 1990. From 1980 to 1990, the share of regional jobs in San Francisco's core fell from 17.4 percent to 16.3 percent, a 1.1 percentage point drop. Over the same period, the share of Southern California jobs fell from 7.6 percent to 5.7 percent, a 1.9 percentage point decline.[58] However, since Los Angeles's percentage base was much lower, the relative loss of regional employment in downtown Los Angeles has been much more substantial. To the degree that maintaining a dominant, primary commercial and employment center has increased economic productivity in the region (e.g., accruing from agglomeration economies), BART has produced real, though immeasurable, economic benefits.

6.6.2 Urban Densities

BART's presence is spatially correlated with population and employment densities. In 1990, over 85 percent of Bay Area census tracts with population densities above 7.5 persons per acre contained a BART station or some segment of a BART line. Map 6.4 shows that BART's alignment was also highly correlated with 1990 employment densities. Over the past half century, the Bay Area has transformed from a predominantly single-centered metropolis to one with multiple, hierarchical centers, many strongly oriented to BART. Although measuring BART's precise role in bringing about this built form is difficult, on the basis of employment growth differentials we believe its role has been significant.

6.6.3 Matched-Pair Comparison of Land-Use Changes

The BART @ 20 study also examined whether land around BART stations densified more since the system's 1973 opening than did properties near freeway interchanges. Since BART stations are access points to the regional rail system and interchanges are the access points to the regional freeway system, this analysis allowed land-use changes around BART to be compared to those of its chief competitor, nearby freeways. At a minimum, we would expect relatively more apartment and condominium construction and denser office-commercial development near BART because rail, in theory, depends on concentrations of nearby urban activities to attract riders.

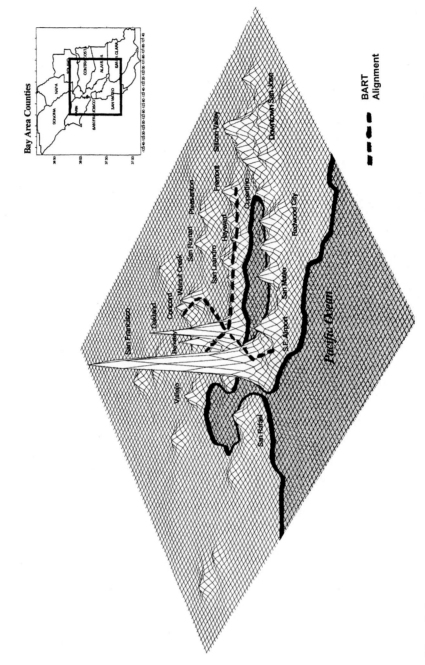

Map 6.4   Bay Area Employment Densities Correlated Closely with BART Alignment in 1990.

A matched-pair analysis was conducted for parts of the Fremont and Richmond corridors since suitable freeway pairs were only available for this stretch. (Most of the other BART corridors either serve built-up downtown areas or lie in the median of a freeway, thus complicating station versus interchange comparisons.) The chief matching criteria were that the station and freeway interchange be within 1 to 2.5 mi of each other and be connected by the same arterial roadway. Invoking these criteria produced nine suitable pairs, five on the Fremont line (San Leandro, Hayward, South Hayward, Union City, and Fremont stations and their nearby I-880 interchanges) and four on the Richmond line (Ashby, Berkeley, North Berkeley, and Richmond stations and their closest I-80 interchanges).

Figure 6.12 reveals that BART stations have attracted far more multifamily housing since BART's 1973 opening than their freeway counterparts. The inventory of commercial-office-industrial floorspace increased only slightly faster around stations (Figure 6.13). In absolute terms, BART stations gained 403,000 ft^2 more of single-family space, 1.58 million ft^2 more of multifamily housing, and 553,000 ft^2 more of nonresidential inventory from 1973 to 1993 than their freeway counterparts.

The Fremont station, the terminus of the Fremont Line, is one of the best examples of moderately dense transit-based housing built after BART. Its nearby development also stands in contrast to the exclusively single-family housing around the nearest freeway interchange, Mowry Avenue-I-88. Map 6.5 shows that considerable land-use changes

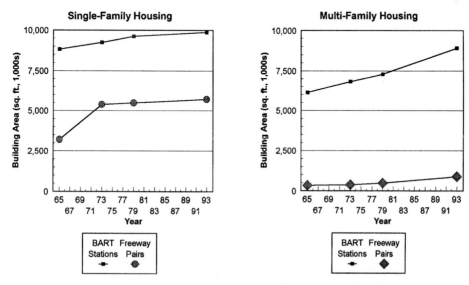

Figure 6.12 Trends in Residential Building Area: BART Stations Versus Freeway Pairs, 1965–1993.

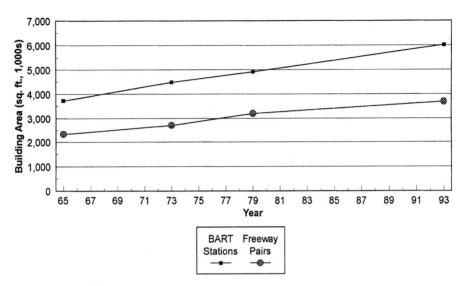

Figure 6.13 Trends in Nonresidential Building Area: BART Stations Versus Freeway Pairs, 1965–1993.

occurred within a half-mile ring of the Fremont station since 1965, including over 150,000 ft^2 of retail shops, over 400,000 ft^2 of office space, and over 800 condominium and apartment units. The most prominent housing addition was the three-story, 392-unit Mission Wells apartment complex, located approximately one-quarter mile from the station. To encourage a transit-oriented project, the city of Fremont zoned the Mission Wells site for 30 dwelling units per acre in the first phase and 50 units per acre in the second. It also reduced parking standards from 2.0 to 1.65 spaces per unit. These initiatives appear to be paying off financially. Mission Wells's average rent per square foot is around 12 percent higher than that of comparable apartment projects in Fremont that are of similar age and have a similar amenity package, reflecting the rent premium associated with being close to rail. In addition, 17 percent of Mission Wells's employed tenants commute by BART compared to just 2.4 percent of all Fremont employed residents in 1990.

6.6.4 Contrasting Development Profiles: Concord Versus Richmond Corridors

Outside of downtown San Francisco, where the lion's share of employment and commercial-office growth in proximity to BART has taken place, BART's development impacts have been spotty and uneven. To a large degree, the aggressiveness of local officials in leveraging private investments through incentives like tax abatements and land write-downs has determined whether much development has occurred outside of downtown San Fran-

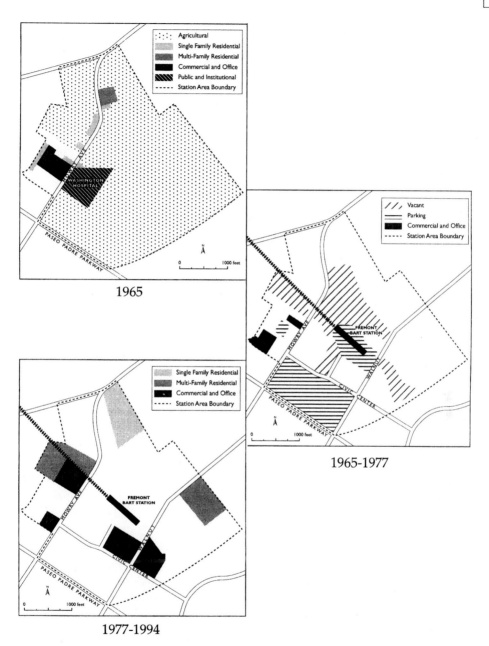

Map 6.5 Land-Use Changes Around the Fremont Station, 1965–1994.

cisco. However, 20 years of experience with BART clearly shows that no amount of development incentives can overcome a weak local real estate market. Not-in-my-backyard (NIMBY) resistance can be an equally powerful barrier to station-area development. The next two sections review the contrasting development experiences of two East Bay BART corridors that underscore these points.

6.6.4.1 Concord Corridor

The Concord Line has received among the least and the most commercial-office development within a half-mile ring of stations. In the affluent communities of Rockridge, Orinda, and Lafayette, stiff neighborhood opposition to proposed apartment and commercial development near rail, followed by building moratoria and downzoning, all but eliminated any possibility of large-scale development along the inner Concord Line. In contrast, the prodevelopment attitude of local officials, coupled with community acquiescence, has produced fairly dense suburban centers at the three outermost stations—Walnut Creek, Pleasant Hill, and Concord. The fact that the three innermost stations lie in a freeway median whereas the three outermost stations do not might have also had some bearing on land-use outcomes.

Walnut Creek has emerged as one of the Bay Area's premier edge cities. Nearly 4 million ft^2 of modern, class-A office space has been built within a half-mile ring of the station since BART opened, more than any nondowntown station (Figure 6.14). While this development would have occurred in the suburbs without BART, it more than likely would have been freeway-oriented, in the form of executive parks and stand-alone structures. Walnut Creek's office boom leveled off in the late 1980s, partly due to a community backlash against escalating traffic congestion (which led to the passage of a growth moratorium in the mid-1980s) as well as an oversupply of local office inventory.

As discussed earlier and in the next chapter, the Pleasant Hill BART station area is one of the best examples of suburban transit-oriented development in the United States. Between 1988 and 1993, over 1600 housing units and 1.5 million ft^2 of prime office space was built within a quarter mile of the Pleasant Hill station. This development occurred despite the fact that during BART's first 20 years, the Pleasant Hill station was surrounded by BART's largest parking lot (3245 spaces) and was located in an unincorporated part of Contra Costa County, which in many situations might have suppressed land development. Although average densities of nearby apartments are around 30 to 45 dwelling units per gross acre, very high by suburban standards, as already noted, these apartments nonetheless cater to a fairly upscale market, with most featuring swimming pools, spas, and other types of recreational facilities. Half of the occupants in the Park Regency complex (892 units at 70 units per acre) earn over $40,000 annually, well above the regional average. An estimated one-half of employed residents living near the Pleasant Hill station work in downtown San Francisco or Oakland compared to a citywide average of just 10 percent. Many take BART to work; our surveys show 36 to 55 percent commute via BART compared to 16 percent of all Pleasant Hill employed residents. And as noted earlier, the strong demand for apartments has also produced a rent premium—two-bedroom, two-

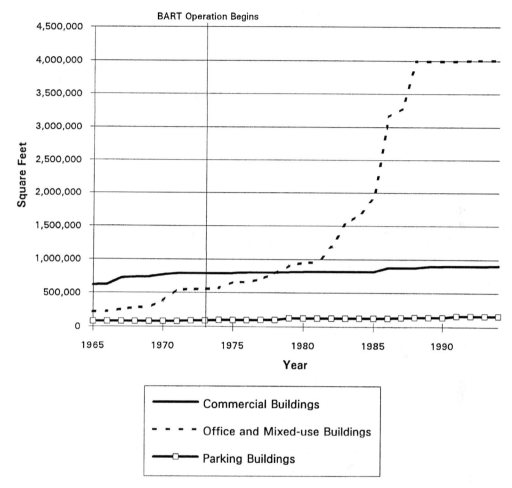

Figure 6.14 Plot of Changes in Nonresidential Building Area: The Walnut Creek BART Station, 1965–1993.

bathroom apartments near the station leased for around $1.09 per square foot in 1994 compared to around $0.94 per square foot for comparable units (in terms of size, age, and amenities) within the city that are distant from BART.

Relative to the Walnut Creek and Pleasant Hill stations, the Concord station was a late bloomer in attracting office development. Commercial-office floorspace remained fairly constant at around one-half million ft^2 until 1985; over the next 3 years, inventory increased fourfold. As in Pleasant Hill, the local redevelopment agency spearheaded much of the station-area development in Concord by helping with land assemblage and financing complementary public infrastructure improvements.

6.6.4.2 Richmond Corridor Among all suburban East Bay BART corridors, the Richmond Line has witnessed the fewest land-use changes. The one notable exception is the El Cerrito del Norte station, which in the past few years has attracted a large mixed apartment-retail project and several large retailers nearby. Elsewhere, the real estate market has been stagnant. Community opposition to apartment proposals has blocked development around the Ashby and North Berkeley stations. Interestingly, the largest inventory of dense housing, offices, and retail-commercial floorspace to come on line along this corridor has been in Emeryville, one of the few East Bay shoreline cities without a BART station.

The greatest disappointment along the Richmond corridor has been at the Richmond station itself. When BART arrived, city officials had high hopes it would trigger a building boom because of the area's intermodal facilities and large inventory of vacant land. But other than the addition of a large public office building and a few small apartment complexes, little has changed around the Richmond station over the past 20 years despite efforts by the city's redevelopment authority to entice new investment through various incentive programs. A depressed local economy, urban blight, and increased crime have suppressed development. Richmond's experiences underscore the fact that opening a rail station, in and of itself, will not stimulate major land-use changes unless there are reasonably favorable local market conditions.

6.6.5 BART's Land-Use Impacts in Summary

The findings of the original BART Impact Study have not been altered much by the passage of two decades. BART's impacts have been highly localized and uneven. BART has allowed downtown San Francisco to continue to grow and maintain its primacy in the urban hierarchy. BART has also played a role in the emergence of a multicentered metropolitan form, as was called for in the original 1956 plan. Today, Walnut Creek boasts a moderately dense concentration of offices, Pleasant Hill features 1800 apartment and condominium units within a quarter-mile ring of the station, and Fremont has a mix of transit-oriented developments. Around most other stations, few significant land-use changes have occurred, often for market reasons, though in some instances because of neighborhood opposition.

Among all BART corridors, downtown San Francisco captured the lion's share of office growth, accounting for over three-quarters of all office construction within a half mile of all BART stations since 1973. Thus, BART clearly helped accomplish the original objective of maintaining downtown San Francisco's preeminence as the region's employment and commercial hub. However, outside of downtown San Francisco, Oakland, and several suburban stations, most employment and office growth over the past two decades have turned their backs on BART, oriented toward freeway corridors instead.

Perhaps the biggest difference in station-area land uses since the original BART Impact Studies has been the addition of a considerable amount of multifamily housing within a quarter-mile ring of BART stations. Much of this is attributable to aggressive actions on the part of local redevelopment authorities to entice housing development by underwriting infrastructure investments, assisting with land assemblage, and in several instances, becoming equity partners in building transit-based housing. Some local officials hope these transit-based housing projects are the building blocks of eventual full-blown, mixed-use transit villages. Many people residing in apartments near BART consciously sought out housing near transit to economize on commuting. And as shown, many apartments near rail are also commanding rent premiums. Transit-based housing, however, will only draw commuters to trains if there is continued growth in transit-based employment. Clearly, mixed-use and balanced transit village development would ensure that, for many, both ends of the commute trip—home and work—are conveniently located near transit stops.

The essential role of local government in promoting station-area development is clearly underscored by BART's experiences. BART has created opportunities for attracting new development and reinvigorating stagnant areas that some communities have successfully capitalized upon. However, the mere presence of BART has been unable to turn around flat or declining local real estate markets, such as around the Richmond station. The presence of BART is clearly not a sufficient condition to significant land development around stations; however, under the right circumstances, it has proven to be an important contributor. Thus, consistent with other research findings, concerted efforts to capitalize upon the availability of rail transit services through supportive public programs, whether it be assisting with land assemblage or actually spearheading the development of a transit village, can lead to meaningful land-use changes around transit stations.

6.7 STIMULATING THE MARKET FOR TRANSIT VILLAGES

The research presented in this chapter consistently points to a potentially large market for transit village living, shopping, and working. For the most part, however, this market remains largely latent, or pent-up. Stated preference surveys of simulated transit village environments reveal some willingness to trade off higher density living in return for neighborhood amenities such as parks and local shops. In the San Francisco Bay Area, surveys reveal that the residents of emerging transit-based housing tend to be young professionals living alone or with another young professional and earning middle-income salaries. Many work downtown or in other locations well served by transit and commute frequently by rail. It appears that many consciously select residences near rail stops to ease their commutes, confirming the residential sorting hypothesis. Most transit-based households also have just one automobile available. Overall, transit-based housing in the Bay Area suburbs attracts a fairly upscale market of renters.

Because rail-based households own relatively few cars and frequently patronize transit, zoning standards should be relaxed to allow just one parking space per residential unit at complexes near rail stations. In the suburbs, two parking spaces per unit are the norm.[59]

Lowering this to one for multiunit complexes near rail stops would substantially lower construction costs and, by reducing the land consumed by parking, create more compact and pedestrian-oriented development. The idea of granting those living in transit villages more leniency in qualifying for home mortgage loans (in light of the need to own fewer cars, thus freeing more income for housing) would likewise make transit-oriented living all the more attractive. And because residents of transit-based housing have consistently been shown to far more readily commute by rail transit, developers of such projects might be rewarded through such measures as credits against impact fee payments, tax abatements, or more expeditious public review of development proposals and processing of building permits. Such financial incentives might reflect the reduced impact that the development has on local road conditions and the societal and environmental benefits associated with developments whose tenants are frequent transit riders. The expectation would be that developers receiving these rewards would pass on at least part of the financial benefits to their prospective tenants and lessees.

Our studies also show that multiunit complexes near rail stations in the East Bay tend to command higher rents, all else being equal. This is consistent with theory and suggests that, barring zoning restrictions or other barriers, more housing will be built near Bay Area rail stops in coming years as developers seek to capitalize on the opportunity to make profits. Likewise, experiences in the Washington, DC, Atlanta, and San Francisco-Oakland region indicate that suburban commercial property owners typically receive financial benefits from being close to rail services. In theory, the existence of a rent premium suggests that value-capture mechanisms (e.g., forming benefit assessment districts) could be used to help finance rail systems, though this is very difficult to implement in practice. Indirectly, of course, property taxes should increase in line with higher real estate values, although not all properties are reassessed following the opening of rail services. Some countries, such as Korea, Taiwan, and Colombia, have relied upon betterment taxes to cover the costs of public infrastructure, mainly roadways, typically involving the apportionment of the cost for a road among landowners whose properties abut the facility. In the United States, benefit assessment financing, wherein all property owners within a defined district are assessed a fee to help defray the cost of infrastructure, was proposed for financing upward of 15 percent of Los Angeles's Metrorail system; however, special assessments were never levied because of legal challenges and political inertia.

Overall, it is encouraging that some housing projects near rail stations are leasing quickly, commanding rent premiums, and attracting residents who patronize transit. It is also encouraging that there is today a receptive policy environment for transit-oriented development. Still, given some of the lingering doubts over the marketability of higher density housing and today's conservative lending practices, some degree of risk sharing between the public and private sectors will likely be necessary if transit villages are ever to proliferate. The public sector can help absorb risks through such actions as writing down the costs of land assemblage, covering the costs of supportive infrastructure, and providing loan guarantees in the event of a market downturn. Relaxing zoning standards to allow fewer parking spaces, high densities, and more mixed land uses near rail stations would also help, as would tax abatements and credits against impact fees. Governments might also consider fast-tracking transit-oriented projects that are compatible with a transit village plan (i.e., expediting the review and approval of development permits). Clearly, public-private partnerships are vital to the success of future transit villages. Together, a burgeoning market demand, public-private cooperation and risk sharing, and a receptive public policy environment would prove a powerful combination in taking the transit village movement from idea to implementation.

NOTES

1. Andrew Speare, *Changes in Urban Growth Patterns 1980–90* (Cambridge, MA: Lincoln Institute of Land Policy, 1993).
2. Building Industry Association of Northern California, *Survey of Housing Preferences for Northern California* (San Francisco: Building Industry Association of Northern California, 1993).
3. Lloyd Bookout, The Future of Higher-Density Housing, *Urban Land,* Vol. 51, No. 9, pp. 14–18, 1992.
4. Robert Cervero and Peter Bosselmann, *An Evaluation of the Market Potential for Transit-Oriented Development Using Visual Simulation Technique* (Berkeley: Institute of Urban and Regional Development, University of California, Monograph 47, 1994).
5. The minimum thresholds established for justifying fixed-rail transit were set in the following publication: Boris Pushkarev and Jeffrey Zupan, *Public Transportation and Land Use* (Bloomington: Indiana University Press, 1977).
6. Bookout, op. cit., p. 16.
7. N. Foote, J. Agu-Lughod, M. Foley, and L. Winnick, *Housing Choices and Housing Constraints* (New York: McGraw-Hill, 1960); M. Baldassare, *Residential Crowding in Urban America* (Berkeley: University of California Press, 1979); J. Shaw, *Transit-Based Housing and Residential Satisfaction* (Berkeley: University of California, Department of City and Regional Planning, doctoral dissertation, 1994).
8. J. Lansing, R. Marans, and R. Zehner, *Residential Location and Urban Mobility* (Ann Arbor: Survey Research Center, Institute for Social Research, University of Michigan, 1970).
9. W. Michelson, *Environmental Choice, Human Behavior, and Residential Satisfaction* (New York: Oxford University Press, 1977).
10. J. Constantine, Design by Democracy, *Land Development,* Vol. 17, Spring-Summer, pp. 11–15, 1992.
11. Two recent studies by graduate students in the city planning department at the University of California, Berkeley, used overlays of slides to create photomontages that simulated housing development near northern California rail stations: Jodi Ketelsen-Johansson, *Perception of Housing Densities That Are Transit-Supportive and Maintain the*

Appeal of Single Family Home Ownership (Berkeley: University of California, master's thesis, 1994); and Shaw, op. cit. Ketelsen-Johansson's work presented front- and rear-lot images of homes in neighborhoods varying from 10 to 36 dua. She found suburbanites disliked higher densities even after neighborhood amenities such as lakes and hillside landscapes were added. Shaw showed Bay Area and Sacramento residents photomontage images of neighborhoods close to both rail stations and freeway interchanges. Housing near transit was generally preferred to housing near freeways; however, the densest housing was preferred near highways instead of rail stops. While these simulations confirmed what others have found, namely that Americans prefer lower density neighborhoods, the overlaying of separate images of dense housing projects and suburban rail stations failed to portray attractive or realistic appearing neighborhoods. Also, these two studies were not able to control for the influences of other factors that likely influenced responses, such as architectural style or illumination of the scene. Moreover, both projects used static slide presentations, showing single images of a street leading to a transit stop, as opposed to dynamically "walking" respondents through a simulated environment. The research summarized in this section sought to overcome some of these shortcomings.

12. The model was designed like a kit of parts with exchangeable components depicting factors that varied (e.g., density, amenity levels) and permanent components depicting factors that remained constant (e.g., street widths, the presence of a BART station). The computer-generated kit of parts was created from digitized drawings. Each image was photorealistically rendered with trees, facade and surface texture, colors, people, and cars. The light sources were set consistently for each image, producing realistic shadows and shaded surfaces. The angle of views was also set consistently at 60 percent. Images were stored in digital files and transferred in full color to photoslides via a film recorder.

13. A weakness of simulation media is the "artificial" quality of the rendered views. State-of-the-art computer-generated renderings have a "stark" appearance, partly because objects in the view appear to be brand new and partly because of the artificial light quality and reflectivity of surfaces and colors.

14. The number of people and parked cars in each viewscape increased with density, though not exactly proportionally (to reflect the likelihood that denser transit villages would encourage more walking and lower automobile dependence).

15. Field presentations took place in the Bay Area cities of San Francisco, Berkeley, Hayward, El Cerrito, Dublin, Walnut Creek, and Ashland. These venues represent different levels of urbanization in the region. Most participants were drawn from residences in the immediate areas.

16. This means each person would rate the four neighborhoods for the same assumed location, thus removing the influence of location on ratings.

17. We suspected ratings might be higher for the initial sequence because of the novelty factor. Ratings might tend to fall for latter sequences because some respondents

might begin to tire from viewing many images. Random ordering of sequences reduced the likelihood of such biases.

18. Participants were fairly representative of the Bay Area population at large. From the survey, the mean respondent age was 38 years compared to 41 years for residents 18 years and above for Alameda, Contra Costa, and San Francisco Counties combined. (These are the three Bay Area counties in which field presentations were held, where most of the participants lived, and that are served by BART.) Around 60 percent of the respondents were single, either living alone, with other singles, or raising children by themselves. This share is slightly above the 53 percent of adults from the three BART-served counties who were single in 1990 (from the 1990 census). Twenty percent of the respondents lived in households with children compared to 28 percent of the adults from the three counties. Forty percent lived in single-family homes versus 46 percent of the households in the three BART counties.

19. Matched-pair comparisons were used to test whether differences in overall desirability ratings were statistically significant. Taking differences in ratings for neighborhood pairs for each respondent effectively removed the influence of all factors other than the variable of interest, desirability rating. Based on t-statistics, ratings were significantly different for all neighborhood pairs at the .05 probability level except for two: 12 versus 36 dua and 36 versus 48 dua. Thus, while respondents preferred living in a 12- versus a 36-dua neighborhood, mean ratings were not significantly different. Nor were they between the two highest density neighborhoods. The paired difference in ratings of the 24-dua versus 36-dua neighborhoods was 0.460, yielding a t-statistic of 4.40 with a probability of .000.

20. After respondents initially ranked neighborhoods (having viewed all of them in sequence), they were told specifically what distinguished the neighborhoods. They were then asked to rank the neighborhoods again one last time. The intent of the second ranking was to ferret out how perceptions might have changed once participants were informed about how the neighborhoods differed. Overall, the second rankings were very similar to the first. Information improved the rankings of the two highest density neighborhoods slightly and lowered those of the two low-density ones just a bit.

21. Responses were also tabulated by levels of respondent "attentiveness." In the questionnaire, respondents were asked to rank order the four neighborhoods in terms of density. Those who correctly identified the relative densities of all four neighborhoods were considered the "most attentive" and those who got at least two of the relative neighborhood density rankings correct were considered "reasonably attentive." In general, respondents seemed to be more sensitive to density as their level of attentiveness increased. Overall, however, neighborhoods were similarly evaluated regardless of levels of attentiveness.

22. The correlations between age and overall desirability for each neighborhood (with significance levels in parentheses) were: 12 dua, −.150 (.046); 24 dua, −.154 (.055); 36

dua, −.098 (.223); and 48 dua, −.080 (.321). The negative association between age and rating fell as the density of a neighborhood increased.

23. Constantine, op. cit., p. 1.

24. See Richard Voith, Transportation, Sorting, and House Values, *American Real Estate and Urban Economics Association Journal,* Vol. 19, No. 2, pp. 117–137, 1991.

25. See Robert Cervero, *Ridership Impacts of Transit-Focused Development in California* (Berkeley: Institute of Urban and Regional Development, University of California, Monograph 45, 1993).

26. Occupant data were collected only for those 16 years of age and above. In comparing demographic profiles of station-area residents with those of surrounding areas, comparisons are only drawn for the 16 and above age cohort. By attaching endorsement letters from property managers to questionnaires and through repeat mailings to nonrespondents, a reasonably good response rate of 22.5 percent was obtained. This yielded fairly complete data records for 885 station-area households.

27. Richard Untermann, *Accommodating the Pedestrian: Adapting Towns and Neighborhoods for Walking and Bicycling* (New York: Van Nostrand Reinhold, 1984).

28. Matched-pair *t*-tests are also shown in Table 6.1; however, from a statistical standpoint, these results must be interpreted with caution because of the small sample size of matched pairs.

29. We might expect vehicle ownership levels to be proportionally even lower (relative to household size) in transit-based households because the availability of rail services should, in theory, reduce the need for owning a car. This, however, was not the case. Transit-based projects averaged 0.78 vehicles per capita compared to 0.71 for households in the surrounding census tracts. This mainly reflected the higher share of household members who were of driving age in transit-based projects than in the typical suburban household.

30. Patrick Hare and Caroline Honig, Using Trip Reduction and Growth Management to Provide Affordable Housing, *Transportation Research Record,* Vol. 1321, pp. 129–131, 1992.

31. Average age for the control areas (i.e., the surrounding census tracts) has been netted of individuals under 17 years of age for comparison purposes.

32. The data source used for studying the workplace locations of employed residents for census tracts surrounding rail-based housing was the 1990 Bay Area Travel Survey (BATS), provided by the Metropolitan Transportation Commission. For background on BATS, see S. Rodenborn and C. Purvis, 1990 Bay Area Travel Surveys: Data Collection and Data Analysis (Paper presented at the 70th Annual Meeting of the Transportation Research Board, Washington, DC, 1991).

33. Voith, op. cit.

34. J. McCloud, High-Density Housing Near San Francisco: Builder Betting Proximity to Commute Line. *The New York Times,* Vol. 141, Section 1, July 5, 1992, p. 23.

35. For the findings of these other California rail systems, see R. Cervero and V. Menotti, *Market Profiles of Rail-Based Housing Projects in California* (Berkeley: Institute of Urban and Regional Development, University of California, Working Paper 622, 1994).

36. John Holtzclaw, *Residential Patterns and Transit, Auto Dependence, and Costs* (San Francisco: Resources Defense Council, 1994).

37. Committee on Banking, Finance and Urban Affairs, *Metrorail Impacts of Washington, D.C. Land Value* (Washington, DC: House of Representatives, U.S. Congress, 1981).

38. R. Voith, Changing Capitalization of CBD-Oriented Transportation Systems: Evidence from Philadelphia, 1970–1988, *Journal of Urban Economics,* Vol. 33, pp. 361–376, 1993.

39. J. Landis, S. Guhathakurta, and M. Zhang, *Capitalization of Transportation Investments into Single-Family Home Prices* (Berkeley: Institute of Urban and Regional Development, University of California, Working Paper 619, 1994).

40. D. Gatzlaff and M. Smith, The Impact of the Miami Metrorail on the Value of Residences Near Station Locations, *Land Economics,* Vol. 69, No. 1, pp. 54–66, 1993.

41. D. Dornbush, ed., BART-Induced Changes in Property Values and Rents, *Land Use and Urban Development Projects, Phase I, BART Impact Study* (Berkeley: Metropolitan Transportation Commission, 1975); R. Burkhardt, *Summary of Research: Joint Development Study* (New York: Administration and Managerial Research Association, 1976).

42. Data for the Concord-Pleasant Hill-Walnut Creek submarket were obtained from Keyser Marston Associates, Inc. Data for the Union City-Fremont and Albany-El Cerrito-Richmond submarkets were obtained from Oewel Properties, Ltd., as well as from field surveys and interviews with property managers.

43. S. Rosen, Hedonic Prices and Implicit Markets: Product Differentiation in Pure Competition, *Journal of Political Economics,* Vol. 82, pp. 34–55, 1974.

44. Unfortunately, data for all three submarkets could not be consolidated since variables differed across data sets (each obtained from different proprietary sources).

45. Freeway proximity did not enter as a significant predictor of rents largely because there was little variation among cases. Since all units were in the same geographic area, all were of a fairly similar distance to Interstate 680, the area's major freeway. In general, levels of highway and freeway accessibility were similar among cases. The only appreciable difference in regional accessibility was in terms of proximity to BART.

46. The dependent variable was monthly rent in dollars. The resulting coefficients indicate the imputed value tenants place on each housing attribute based on their willingness to pay. The following coefficients, or dollar values, associated with each attribute were estimated (with probabilities in parentheses): BART station within one-quarter mile (1 = yes, 0 = no), 34.1 (.133); size of unit (ft^2), 0.43 (.000); number of bedrooms, 29.49 (.141); number of bathrooms, 42.04 (.011); playground on site (1 = yes, 0 = no), 30.46 (.097); weight room on site (1 = yes, 0 = no), 66.54 (.000); project density (units/acre), 0.40 (.174); project age (in years, from 1991), −10.97 (.000); project in

Concord (1 = yes, 0 = no), −129.84 (.000); proportion of total units in project of a specific unit type, −44.55 (.124); laundry room on site (1 = yes, 0 = no), −21.22 (.175). The R-squared statistic of fit was 0.919 based on 60 data observations. Thus, in addition to distance from BART, several other factors had significant depressing effects on rents. Rents fell with building age. A Concord location lowered rents considerably, partly reflecting the city's more peripheral location within the region. Also, the presence of a laundry room was associated with lower rents. This could reflect the tendency of higher rent units to contain their own washer and dryer as opposed to a central facility. In addition, being the dominant housing type in a complex with multiple types of units lowered rents.

47. For further details on this study, see R. Cervero and J. Landis, Assessing the Impacts of Urban Rail Transit on Local Real Estate Markets Using Quasi-Experimental Comparisons, *Transportation Research,* Vol. 27A, pp. 13–22, 1993; R. Cervero, J. Landis, and P. Hall, *Transit Joint Development in the United States: A Review of Recent Experiences and an Assessment of Future Potential* (Berkeley: Institute of Urban and Regional Development, University of California, Monograph 42).

48. By introducing statistical controls, this analysis applies the methods of quasi-experimental comparisons. Under this approach, various measures of commercial-office market performance are compared between selected transit station areas and otherwise comparable "control" areas. To the extent that the station areas and non-station control areas are truly similar, then any observed differences in office rental rates, vacancy rates, absorption rates, or densities may be attributable, at least in part, to the presence of rail transit. This approach is referred to as quasi-experimental in that it is similar in design to actual controlled experiments conducted in fields such as medicine and biology. However, the inability to control fully for all differences between the comparison groups means that the approach is not a true controlled experiment in the scientific sense, but rather a quasi-controlled comparison.

49. R. Johnston and S. Tracy, Suburban Resistance to Density Near Transit Stations in the San Francisco Bay Area, *The Social Constraints on Energy-Policy Implementation,* N. Neiman and B. Burt, eds. (Lexington, MA: Heath and Company, 1983).

50. Parsons, Brinckerhoff, Hall, and MacDonald, *Regional Rapid Transit: A Report to the San Francisco Bay Area Rapid Transit Commission* (New York: Parsons, Brinckerhoff, Hall, and MacDonald, 1956), p. 10.

51. Leonard Merewitz, Public Transportation: Wish Fulfillment and Reality in the San Francisco Bay Area, *The American Economic Review,* Vol. 62, No. 2, pp. 78–86, 1972.

52. Parsons, Brinckerhoff, Tudor, and Bechtel, *The Composite Report: Bay Area Rapid Transit* (New York: Parsons, Brinckerhoff, Tudor, and Bechtel, 1962), p. 83.

53. M. Dyett, D. Dornbusch, M. Fajans, C. Falcke, V. Gussman, and J. Merchant, *Land Use and Urban Development Impacts of BART: Final Report* (San Francisco: John Blayney Associates/David M. Dornbusch & Co., Inc., 1979).

54. Melvin Webber, The BART Experience: What Have We Learned? *Public Interest,* Vol. 12, No. 3, pp. 79–108, 1976.

55. Homer Hoyt, *The Structure of Growth of Regional Neighborhoods in American Cities* (Washington, DC: U.S. Government Printing Office, 1939).

56. For further background on this work, see Robert Cervero, *BART @ 20: Land Use and Development Impacts* (Berkeley: Institute of Urban and Regional Development, University of California, Monograph 49, 1995).

57. The charts produced in this section represent vintage models that track the accumulation of total square footage of residential and nonresidential development within a quarter-mile ring of BART stations and half-mile ring of other stations. This was done by maintaining a running account of the square footage added to each station area each year based on the recorded year of construction. The primary data inputs were the TRW-REDI data base which provides on-line digitized property tax records (square footage, lot area, year of construction) for privately owned parcels within local taxing jurisdictions. For further details, see Robert Cervero, ibid.

58. Sources: Robert Cervero, *Subcentering and Commuting: Evidence from the San Francisco Bay Area, 1980–1990* (Berkeley: Institute of Urban and Regional Development, University of California, Working Paper 668, 1996); Peter Gordon and Harry Richardson, Beyond Polycentricity: The Dispersed Metropolis, Los Angeles, 1970–1990, *Journal of the American Planning Association,* Vol. 62, No. 3, pp. 289–295, 1996. Data for Southern California are for Los Angeles, Orange, San Bernardino, Riverside, and Ventura Counties.

59. For an in-depth discussion of suburban zoning standards for parking, see R. Willson, Suburban Parking Requirements: A Tacit Policy for Automobile Use and Sprawl, *Journal of the American Planning Association,* Vol. 61, No. 1, pp. 29–42, 1995.

PART THREE

Transit Villages in America

The transit village movement takes on different shapes and forms in different parts of the country. Each metropolitan area's experience is unique and tells a different story about the challenges of transit village building in contemporary urban America. In the San Francisco Bay Area, transit villages are part of a larger effort to create "new urban" communities led by a cadre of visionary architects, entrepreneurial transit agencies, and civic leaders. At the southern end of state, transit village proponents face an uphill struggle in implanting a massive rail network in a land whose very icon is the freeway. In Los Angeles and San Diego, rail advocates see in transit villages an opportunity for creating a built form that can sustain a multibillion dollar investment even in the heartland of the automobile.

Across the continent, transit proponents face a different set of challenges. Around the nation's capital, a postedge city phenomenon is underway, a backlash to the poorly planned, traffic-snarled suburban megacenters that popped up throughout metropolitan Washington in the 1980s. Part of the postedge city growth is taking place on the exurban fringe; however, a good part is also occurring around a handful of mature inner-suburban Metrorail stations. A proactive government apparatus has brought about impressive changes to several rail station areas in recent years. And in the greatest rail metropolis in the nation, New York, attention has focused largely on restoring some of the traditional commuter railroad towns to their former luster. A number of plans call for building mixed-income housing on parking lots, targeted at city workers longing for a village lifestyle within a reasonable commute. Implanting transit villages in already built-up districts, however, is proving to be no small feat.

7

San Francisco Bay Area: Transit's New Urbanism

Emerging Transit Villages in the San Francisco Bay Area

Pleasant Hill

Fruitvale

Hayward

El Cerrito del Norte

Mountain View

Pleasant Hill, Fruitvale, Hayward, El Cerrito del Norte: All are rail stations in the San Francisco Bay Area that are the foci of emerging transit villages. The Bay Area is arguably the epicenter of America's budding transit village movement, with a constituency of public officials, developers, and planners, along with several of the most visible "new urbanist" architects and designers united in the cause of creating a new type of community and built form.

Bay Area rail stations, especially Pleasant Hill, are worth examining as they shed light on the obstacles to transit village development (e.g., downturns in the local real estate market, physical impediments to street reconfigurations, neighborhood opposition to higher densities) as well as the prerequisites to implementation: a market-oriented specific plan; public-private partnerships among redevelopment agencies, transit officials, and developers; and a dedicated local elected official who constantly pushes the project forward.

Several of the transit villages planned for the Bay Area's suburbs are the inspirations of new urbanist architects, such as the transit-oriented master plan for the Hayward station by Dan Solomon and Mountain View's recently completed Crossroads community designed by Peter Calthorpe. Others, like El Cerrito del Norte and Pleasant Hill, also bear the influence of new urbanist ideas. Most visionary designs have been tempered or compromised by the sober realities of local market constraints, tax needs of local governments, and community politics. At the same time, these station areas still retain new urbanist features that make them alternative suburban communities and some of the first transit-based new urbanist communities actually being built in the United States.

The Fruitvale station area is the one emerging inner-city transit village in the Bay Area. Its design by Ernesto Vasquez incorporates such new urbanist elements as village scale, mixes of uses, pedestrian orientations, active streetscapes, and a public plaza, as well as the economic development-public safety elements that give life to the urban transit village.

7.1 RAIL TRANSIT AND STATION-AREA DEVELOPMENT IN THE BAY AREA

The San Francisco Bay Area is blessed with three large-scale intrametropolitan rail systems: the heavy rail BART spanning San Francisco, Alameda, and Contra Costa Counties; a new light rail system traversing Santa Clara County; and the CalTrain commuter rail line running from downtown San Jose to San Francisco along the San Mateo County peninsula on the west side of the Bay. BART is the most traveled (as well as the most extensive) system—it presently carries 250,000 passenger trips per weekday compared to fewer than 30,000 passenger trips per weekday each for CalTrain and for Santa Clara light rail—and thus has been the focus of transit village efforts.

An axial perspective of the BART system is shown in Map 7.1. As discussed in the previous chapter, when first envisioned in the early 1950s, BART was to go around the Bay, connecting the far southern reaches of the region (below San Jose) to San Francisco, Marin, and Sonoma Counties.[1] In the early 1960s, San Mateo, Santa Clara, and Marin Counties opted not to join the BART district being formed, thus precluding the chance to encircle the Bay with a single rail system. BART services began in 1973, connecting San Francisco to Oakland and the suburbs of the East Bay. Over the ensuing years, much of BART's ridership has come from long-haul commuting.

All along, system planners expected that suburban BART stations would naturally become magnets for new development centers.[2] Disappointment set in when over time most station areas either remained unchanged or took on the low-density settlement patterns that characterize much of the East Bay. It became apparent that BART, in and of itself, was unable to incite new growth or turn around flat or declining local real estate markets. A more proactive government stance on station-area development was clearly needed. It was only in the late 1980s, through the joint efforts of local governments, private developers, and BART itself, that new transit-oriented communities began to emerge around several East Bay stations.

Today, Pleasant Hill is the most advanced of the suburban transit villages in the Bay Area, but others are following in the wake: BART's Hayward and El Cerrito del Norte stations, Almaden Lake on the Santa Clara light rail system, and Mountain View on the CalTrain commuter line. Transit village schemes proposed for Hayward, El Cerrito del Norte, and Mountain View mainly involve redeveloping areas in decline, whereas the Almaden Lakes proposal calls for intensifying a largely undeveloped part of Santa Clara County.

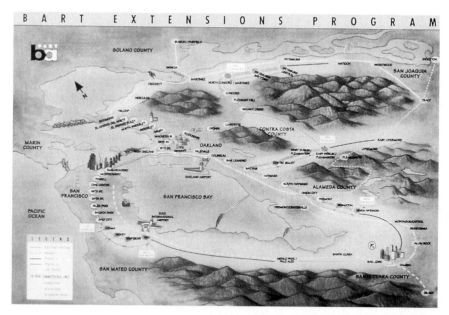

Map 7.1   Axial Perspective of the BART System, 1995. With the popularity of rail transit in the Bay Area, the 71-mi system of the 1990s is being augmented by over 20 mi of new lines as part of a $2.1-billion extension program.

7.2   PLEASANT HILL

BART's Pleasant Hill station has advanced the cause of transit village development more than any other station on the system. Its history is worth examining as it reveals much about the actions and political resolve needed for transit village implementation.

The impetus to transform Pleasant Hill into a transit village began in July 1981, when a newly formed steering committee for the Pleasant Hill BART station area first met. The committee was formed in response to the development that had *not* occurred around the Pleasant Hill station. Photo 7.1 shows the Pleasant Hill station area in 1971, which at the time was surrounded by open fields and scattered single-family homes. When BART services started, Pleasant Hill, as with other suburban BART stations, was expected, almost spontaneously, to spark high-rise commercial and residential development. Yet, over the first decade of BART service, nothing happened around the station. By 1981, the station area featured modest single-family homes, some on irregularly shaped parcels, and scattered fields—the remnants of a previously rural area.

The 1981 steering committee included representatives of Contra Costa County, the city of Walnut Creek, the city of Pleasant Hill, and BART. Chairing the committee was Contra Costa County Supervisor Sunne McPeak. McPeak, 32 at the time, was one of the rising political stars in the state. She was elected supervisor in 1978 and, already in 1981, was

Pleasant Hill Bart Station 1971

Photo 7.1 Pleasant Hill Station Area, February 1971, a Year Prior to the System Opening. The station area is surrounded by scattered single-family homes on former farmland.

being mentioned as a future candidate for governor. The Pleasant Hill BART station, which lies in an unincorporated part of the county, was within her district, and she lives nearby and frequently rides BART.

Prior to the committee meeting, McPeak met with Harvey Bragdon, the county's assistant director of planning, and Bill Gray, the director of public works. They described a planning opportunity to her that might gain state and national prominence: the transformation of the Pleasant Hill station area into a compact, modern complex of office buildings and affordable residences. The development, they counseled, would bring sorely needed revenues into Contra Costa County and also expand housing opportunities. It would do so in a way that minimized adverse traffic impacts on the increasingly congested freeways and local roads.

To achieve this vision, Bragdon and Gray urged that a specific plan be commissioned, a blueprint for targeting new development. Supervisor McPeak eagerly embraced the idea and proceeded to win support for funding a long-range planning endeavor. After receiving proposals from most of the large urban planning and design firms in the Bay Area, the committee at its July 1981 meeting chose San Francisco-based Sedway Cooke and Associates as the station area's master planner. The specific plan developed by Sedway Cooke over the next 13 months covered the waterfront of topics—land use, circulation, parking, areawide utilities, and urban design—set out by state law.[3] At its heart, the plan called out for concentrated office and residential development:

☐ High-intensity office uses were to be placed within a 700-ft walking distance of the station;

☐ Farther out, but within a one-third mile radius, multifamily housing was to be sited, tapering to single-family housing with greater distance; and

☐ Retail and public open spaces would be distributed throughout the 1-mi radius to create an active street life.

Over the next 12 years, parts of the Sedway Cooke plan were carried out, and a Pleasant Hill transit village began to rise in central Contra Costa. The station area, circa 1994, is shown in Photo 7.2. By October 1994, the quarter-mile radius around the station included over 1600 residential units, 1.5 million ft^2 of office space, and a 249-room Embassy Suites Hotel.

The Contra Costa County Redevelopment Agency emerged as a key player in bringing about this metamorphosis. Notably, it aggressively assembled irregular and small parcels into much larger developable parcels. It also paid for new public infrastructure and traffic improvements, using tax increment financing instruments. And it issued tax-exempt bonds to subsidize residential units and leverage private-sector financing.

7.2.1 Pleasant Hill's First Round of Development

The four major residential projects that have been built to date within a quarter mile of the Pleasant Hill BART station are listed in Table 7.1. The projects are similar in design, quality, and densities, and generally cater to a middle-income market. All are multistory wood-frame walk-ups. Bay Landing is three stories above parking. Park Regency features two- and three-story apartments. Treat Commons has two- and three-story apartments with carports. Though these projects are not high-rises, their densities are considerably above those of surrounding residential neighborhoods. Beyond the station area, residential densities average four to five dwelling units per acre. In contrast, Treat Commons and Bay Landing are both 43 units per acre, and Park Regency has 72 units per acre.

A brief review of experiences in developing these large-scale housing projects reveals the vital role played by the redevelopment agency, as well as the surprisingly strong market for transit-based housing in this region.

☐ *Bay Landing,* the first of Pleasant Hill's transit-based projects, was developed by Charles Oewel of Oxford Properties. Transit proximity was but one of several factors in Oewel's decision to purchase the site. At least as important were the strong market during the mid-

Pleasant Hill Bart Station

Photo 7.2   Emergence of a Transit Village: Pleasant Hill Station Area, 1994. The low-density land form in the county continues, with new development concentrated at the transit station.

1980s for housing in central Contra Costa, the proximity to Interstate 680, and the station-area infrastructure improvements funded by the redevelopment agency.

Bay Landing leased up far more rapidly than Oewel expected, and in the leasing, he discovered that transit proximity was a decisive factor. Bay Landing's tenants have been drawn heavily from persons working in San Francisco or Oakland, who want to live in the suburbs but avoid long, stressful auto commutes. Based on these positive experiences, Oewel began to actively seek out other transit-proximate sites in the region. Oewel followed Bay Landing 2 years later with the Verandas, a 360-unit project a block from the Union City BART station. Three years after the Verandas, he aggressively pursued and won the right to build 210 units of housing on the parking lot next to the El Cerrito del Norte BART station.

TABLE 7.1

Residential Elements of Pleasant Hill Transit Village, 1985–1992

Project	Year Built	Units	Density (Units/Acre)
Treat Commons	1987	510 (rental)	43
Bay Landing	1986–1988	282 (rental)	43
Wayside Plaza			
Phase 1	1985–1986	36 (ownership)	24
Phase 2	1986–1987	60 (ownership)	60
Phase 3	1987–1988	60 (rental)	60
Park Regency	1992	892 (rental)	72

☐ *Treat Commons* was built by the nationwide real estate giant Trammell Crow, which assembled the parcels for this 10.8-acre site. Like Oewel, the Trammell Crow developers were motivated by several factors, particularly the strong housing market in central Contra Costa. Also like Oewel, Trammel Crow grew increasingly interested in transit-based housing with the rapid absorption of leasable units at Treat Commons, and its Bay Area vice-presidents began searching out other transit sites. In evaluating the project's performance, Trammell Crow developer Bob Talbott concluded, "Treat Commons has been an extremely successful project for Trammell Crow Residential. Its proximity to BART and the Interstate-680 corridor have given it a significant location premium."[4]

☐ *Park Regency* was proposed in the late 1980s when GBW Properties out of Los Angeles won a competition to build on a 12.3-acre site assembled by the redevelopment agency. The 892-unit Park Regency complex was completed in fall 1992. It is an upscale mix of French chateau-style apartments, boasting swimming pools and spas, aerobics facilities, and recreation rooms. Contra Costa's redevelopment agency helped leverage the project by partially underwriting 15 percent of the units for low- and moderate-income households.

Park Regency began renting in January 1992; within 15 months, 875 of the 892 units (over 98 percent) were occupied. In 1994, a one-bedroom, one-bathroom unit rented for $715 to $785 per month, more than what "comparables" in the submarket went for. Park Regency's tenant mix is heavily weighted toward professionals and previous residents of San Francisco and Oakland, people who want to get away from the crime and hassle of city life, but still have an easy commute via BART. "The people I see coming to Park Regency want to keep a car, but they also want an alternative to commuting on freeways," explains the project's leasing agent, Ronni Weyerman. Park Regency's leasing director, George Ligoeros, characterized the project's lease-up as the fastest he has seen in the past decade and cites its proximity to BART as the main factor.[5]

As noted in Chapter 5, rail ridership among Pleasant Hill station-area residents is far higher than among the general public and even far higher than ridership among residents of the nearby city of Pleasant Hill. In 1993, we headed a study that examined the travel patterns of residents from two of Pleasant Hill's housing projects: Wayside Plaza and Park Regency.[6] For Wayside Plaza, nearly 55 percent of surveyed residents regularly commuted by BART. At Park Regency, 37 percent of the 124 surveyed residents commuted via BART on a regular basis. In contrast, just 16 percent of all residents in the city of Pleasant Hill routinely took rail transit to work in 1990.

The commercial projects that have over the years located near the Pleasant Hill BART station area are listed in Table 7.2. Pleasant Hill's commercial projects have similarly relied heavily on redevelopment agency initiatives, particularly the $30 million in redevelopment-financed infrastructure improvements. Converting a basically semirural and single-family area into a commercial center required new drainage and water systems. The redevelopment agency, through a combination of tax increment and assessment financing, installed these systems, as well as the undergrounding of utilities. Boulevards were also widened, and access to Interstate 680 was improved.

The agency's leadership in assembling multiple small parcels into developable sites was especially critical in luring large-scale commercial businesses. Three of the commercial structures—the ten-story PacTel Corporate Plaza, the six-story 3000 Oak building (Levi Strauss regional offices), and the eight-story Embassy Suites Hotel—were assembled by private developers. The sites for the two commercial buildings south of Treat Boulevard—the six-story Pacific Plaza and the five-story Urban West Business Park—were assembled by the redevelopment agency and later sold to private developers at market rates.

By late 1994, Pleasant Hill could lay claim to being BART's most intensely developed suburban station area. Yet, it still fell short of the targets set in the original Sedway Cooke

TABLE 7.2

Commercial Elements of Pleasant Hill Transit Village, 1985–1997

Project	Year Built	Ft²
Pacific Plaza	1987	250,000
PacTel Corporate Plaza	1991	205,000
Urban West Business Park	1986	125,000
Embassy Suites Hotel	1990	249 suites
3000 Oak	1991	102,000
Bank of West Headquarters	1985	120,000
Citicorp Headquarters	1985	80,000
Contra Costa Entertainment Village	1997	400,000

specific plan, most noticeably lacking a village atmosphere. Currently, development covers less than half the land area originally envisioned for the station area. Three large parcels near the station remain empty, and buildings are inward focused, unconnected to each other or to the station. Also, retail and public open space is conspicuous in its absence. Local planners and backers consider Pleasant Hill an unfinished design. Jim Kennedy, the redevelopment agency director who has helped coordinate Pleasant Hill's transformation from the very beginning, believes "the area still lacks a heart," owing largely to the absence of shops and a street life. Further, the pedestrian orientation has only been partly achieved. The station area is crossed by two busy thoroughfares. Eight-lane Treat Boulevard separates a quarter or so of the station-area development from the main sections, and although a pedestrian bridge has been proposed over Treat Boulevard, it has yet to be built. The two large parking lots on both sides of the BART station have created a vast "no man's land."

The Sedway Cooke plan hoped for a strong pedestrian orientation, as well as an inter-mixing of commercial development and public open space. But in the real world, a number of development proposals have been undermined repeatedly in recent years by tight bank lending policies, physical obstacles at the site, and community politics. To get anything built becomes a great accomplishment and means surviving a minefield of financing, traffic study, and neighborhood referenda. Chief among the impediments at Pleasant Hill have been:

- ☐ A nearby neighborhood association of single-family residents, the Walden Home-owners Association, fears that dense development will bring new automobile traffic to the area, and thus opposes station-area plans (or anything that threatens to increase densities).
- ☐ The nearby cities of Walnut Creek and Pleasant Hill have fought station-area development out of concern that new commercial uses will divert business away from their downtowns. Both cities have actively sought to lure merchants and office builders to their downtowns and have become increasingly reliant on local sales tax proceeds in the wake of Proposition 13 (which froze local property tax rates). Walnut Creek took legal action in the mid-1980s to halt a shopping center on Pleasant Hill's BART parking lots proposed by the Melvin Simon Company. The city of Pleasant Hill has periodically threatened legal action to halt any development that might compete with downtown Pleasant Hill's revitalization.
- ☐ The economic downturns of the late 1980s and the early 1990s either forestalled or killed several planned projects. The Homart Company, which owns the 7.3-acre property between the station parking lot and the freeway, won planning approvals in the mid-1980s to build two office buildings—one six stories, the other seven stories—and a 250-room hotel. As office vacancies soared in the East Bay, the plans were put on hold. Wallace-Olson Associates, which owns a 5-acre parcel behind the Embassy Suites Hotel, went through lengthy entitlement procedures for two 10-story twin towers, but was unable to obtain financing. Also on

hold are the 375,000-ft^2 Treat Towers, the 300,000-ft^2 Station Oaks, and the 211-unit fourth phase of Wayside Plaza. Developers of each project obtained planning approvals, but could not secure financing.

7.2.2 Future Rounds of Development

On a Wednesday morning in October 1994, seven men and a woman convened around a conference table on the first floor of the Urban West Business Park building. The men, all directors of the Contra Costa Centre Association (the marketing association for the area) and the woman, Lynette Tanner, executive director of the association, saw cause for alarm. They discussed Pleasant Hill's sluggish real estate market and, specifically, the difficulties of moving the transit village plan forward to full implementation. The weak market for office space, conservative lending practices by banks, and continuing in-fighting among local jurisdictions, they agreed, threatened to freeze Pleasant Hill's transit village program in its tracks.

On the surface, the station area seemed well positioned for a recovery. At the end of 1991, the office vacancy rate for the station area was 14.5 percent compared with 15.9 percent for all of Contra Costa County. By October 1994, the station-area vacancy rate dipped below 4 percent. However, none of the Contra Costa Centre Association directors were optimistic about a market turnaround. Two of the directors attending the meeting are consultants with Homart, the owner of a vacant 7.3-acre site near the station. They are the third wave of Homart developers to work on the project. All thoughts of one day building an office and hotel have been abandoned. Instead, they have been negotiating with a chain of health clubs to build a sports complex featuring a health club, gym, restaurant, and day-care center. However, the health club chain eventually withdrew its proposal after several focus groups and a feasibility study failed to show sufficient market demand.

Merle Gilliard, a developer with Wallace-Olson, has followed development in the Pleasant Hill station area since the mid-1970s and has seen building plans wash up against the rocks of office financing. On one hand, he is bullish on the station area's development future: "Being next to BART is an important factor in marketing and its influence is growing with Interstate-80 back-ups from the Bay Bridge to Hercules." Gilliard adds, "An emerging office market for the station area is companies that will keep a few executive offices in San Francisco, and move other personnel to lower-cost space on the BART line." At the same time, he is bearish on the difficulty of obtaining office financing, the unwillingness of banks to lend without a major tenant in hand, and the difficulty of competing with the suburban office parks, such as master planned Hacienda Business Park and Bishop Ranch along I 680 to the south. These office parks have acres of surface parking. "Our structured parking," he adds, "means an additional up-to-$32 per square foot over the surface parking."

Lynette Tanner, executive director of the Contra Costa Centre Association, has held the position since 1989, having previously worked in marketing for a cable television company. She sees the center's role in a very prodevelopment light: marketing the area to potential businesses and employers, as well as protecting the station-area plan against no-growth advocates, such as the Pleasant Hill city council majority. "We get visitors from throughout the United States, especially planners, who have heard of our development at a transit station," notes Tanner. "At the same time, we are struggling in the current economy, just like everybody else. Last week a real estate appraisal firm in the Urban West building went out of business, and we lost 200 employees in the area."

Yet, indicative of the turns in fortune in 1990s real estate, as dim as the prospects for station-area build out seemed in late 1994, by mid-1996 new commercial ventures were actively being planned. The centerpiece project is a 400,000-ft^2 Contra Costa Entertainment Village to be built on the BART surface parking lot adjacent to the station. Indeed, it has been the transit authority itself, BART, as opposed to local officials or other actors, that has resurrected Pleasant Hill's transit village plan and spearheaded this latest round of new private investment.

In early 1995, BART issued a Request for Proposals (RFP) for building on its 11.4 acres of surface parking lots. Six proposals were received. Chosen was an entertainment village proposed by a team of Millennium Partners, based in New York City, and the Bay Area's Western Development Group. Anchoring this village will be a 12-screen movie complex. Other key tenants will be a megabookstore, a high-tech music store, a health club, and a series of restaurants and shops. A computer-generated rendering of the planned complex, huddled around the Pleasant Hill station, is depicted in Photo 7.3. Millennium Partners is patterning the entertainment village after its New York City Lincoln Square, a mammoth $250-million, 47-story combination of rental apartments, condominiums, a seven-level health club, retail outlets, and the anchor tenant: the 13-screen Sony Theaters, complete with a 3-D IMAX theater featuring an eight-story-high screen.

For Millennium, Pleasant Hill offers not only attractive suburban demographics, but also two advantages over other suburban sites: (1) the commuter traffic generated by the BART station and (2) the presence of over 2000 parking spaces at the transit station, which can be shared by the entertainment village on nights and weekends. The entertainment village parking needs dovetail almost perfectly with BART's. Peak parking times for BART are on weekdays until 6:00 P.M., whereas the entertainment village's heaviest parking demands will be on weekends and evenings.

What distinguishes the entertainment village from most suburban transit nodes is that it will be a major destination point (i.e., versus a park-and-ride stepping off point). The movie complex is only one of the draws. The stores are meant to be places to spend time as well as to buy. The megabookstore will include a coffee shop for reading, and the music store will feature listening rooms. Thus, they are to work together in cross-promotions. After going to a movie, customers may stop at the cinema cafe-restaurant or megabookstore. The megabookstore plans to distribute coupons for the movie complex.

The entertainment village, according to its architect, Gary Hendel of New York, is built to be "in dialogue" with the station. The view lines will allow BART riders to see the entertainment village activity and elements, and from various points in the entertainment village, one will be able to look up and see BART trains going by.

Photo 7.3 Rendering of the Pleasant Hill Transit Village, with Entertainment-Cultural Complex in Predevelopment. The major gap in the emerging Pleasant Hill transit village has been the absence of a retail and cultural presence. In 1995, BART selected a developer for a 400,000-ft^2 retail-entertainment-cultural complex to replace the 8-acre surface parking lot, as shown here.

Beyond the entertainment village, two multifamily housing developments are presently moving forward in preconstruction. The first, a 211-unit project, is on the Wayside Plaza site, repurchased by the redevelopment agency in 1993. When the redevelopment agency issued an RFP in early 1995, it received nine proposals from multifamily builders in the area. The second, a 200-unit project, is on land adjacent to the existing Urban West Business Park building. The property owners had planned in the 1980s to build three office towers, but abandoned office space in favor of housing.

In the mid-1990s, Pleasant Hill shows promise of once again being on the move, building out, and more fully achieving its transit village ideals. Perhaps the person most pleased to see this turn of events is Sunne McPeak, who since 1981 has championed the transit village cause. While wearing her supervisor's hat, McPeak spent hundreds of hours at neighborhood meetings and public hearings going over the details of the station-area plan, playing peacemaker among transit village supporters and the cities of Pleasant Hill, Walnut Creek, and Concord, and prodding redevelopment officials to be proactive. "What is being done to move the projects forward?" she inquired almost daily. "Can the county assist in presentations to financing sources?" "Are there neighborhood presentations to be made?"

McPeak has not achieved the political success expected of her in the early 1980s. In 1988, restless to move up from supervisor, she challenged an incumbent Democratic state senator. She raised several hundred thousand dollars but lost in the primary. From then on, she seemed to have lost her political momentum and was no longer being talked about for higher office. Then in October 1993, she surprised other politicians by resigning her supervisor's position to take a job as the executive director of a regional economic development agency. In her resignation, she effectively declared her exit from elective politics. Yet, even after her resignation, McPeak has continued to follow Pleasant Hill development, which she calls "my life work." At a regional conference on the future of transportation in the Bay Area held in early 1994, she told the assembled Bay Area planners, including Contra Costa planners, "You thought you'd heard the last of me, but you haven't. I'm going to continue to prod you, scold you, and tell you what to do."

7.3 HAYWARD

The city of Hayward, located in southern Alameda County approximately 20 mi from downtown San Francisco, is one of many East Bay towns that grew up in the late 1800s along the path of the Southern Pacific Railroad. These early railroad towns were organized around an orthogonal grid of streets and sidewalks, with a public square at the center.

Up through the 1950s, Hayward had an active downtown, with numerous small businesses, people on the streets, and prominent civic buildings including the City Hall, Post Office, and Veterans Memorial Building. In 1952, First Street, which previously had served mainly local traffic, became Foothill Boulevard, a major north-south thoroughfare that brought heavy throughtraffic into the downtown area. Also undermining the walkable downtown was the emergence of large discount retailers in shopping plazas surrounded by free parking.

By the late 1980s, Hayward's aging downtown of single-room occupancy hotels, boardinghouses, and low-end retail shops was a shadow of its former self despite the presence of a nearby BART station. Hoping to return to the days of glory, Hayward's city council hired new urbanist architect Dan Solomon to develop a plan for revitalizing the downtown area. In January 1992, Solomon presented his plan, which centered on tying together the BART station and downtown by siting new multifamily housing, retail, and a civic plaza between them.

Photo 7.4 provides an overhead view of the Hayward BART station and its environs. The station is flanked by two large surface parking lots and several older industrial buildings that have been abandoned. Solomon's plan calls for 675 to 1345 new housing units, an additional 66,000 ft^2 of commercial-retail space, and mid-rise offices in "a clear and centered downtown Hayward with housing, shopping, restaurants, and well-formed

Hayward Bart Station

Photo 7.4 Hayward Station Area, 1994. The station is surrounded by two large surface parking lots and several older industrial buildings, a number of which have been abandoned.

public spaces for cultural and civic activities." The Solomon plan, illustrated in perspective in Figure 7.1, greatly increases density housing and office densities in the station area and reconfigures pathways to provide convenient pedestrian links from BART to downtown.

Construction on the first station-area housing, Atherton Place, started in 1995. When completed, Atherton Place will add 86 ownership units one block from the BART station. The land was assembled by the redevelopment agency and sold to the private developer, the Sares-Regis group. Two- and three-bedroom town homes are priced between $140,000 and $163,000, a very affordable range by Bay Area standards.

BART and the Hayward Redevelopment Agency jointly planned multifamily housing on a 7-acre site adjacent to the station (combining the BART surface parking lot and agency parcels). In 1993, they issued an RFP, and a developer was chosen to build over 200 units at a blended density of over 40 units per acre. This was followed, however, by local government indecision and political inertia. The city of Hayward decided it wanted to study the possibility of building a new City Hall on this jointly assembled site near BART. The study held the housing proposal in abeyance for nearly a year. Once the city decided not to

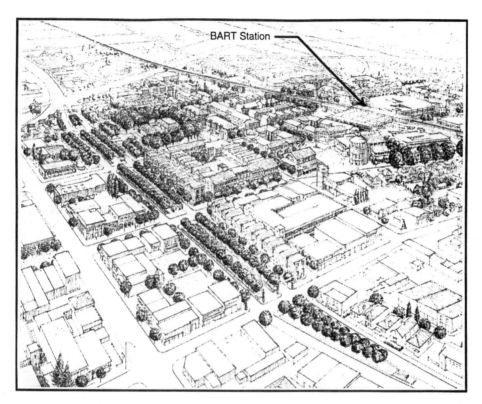

Figure 7.1 Illustrative Drawing of Solomon's Hayward Transit Village. A mix of housing, stores, cultural activities and public spaces flanks the station.

move forward on the City Hall proposal, the county of Alameda then requested that action be postponed for another year to study the feasibility of placing a new county administration building on the site.

By mid-1995, BART and Hayward's Redevelopment Agency finally issued a revised RFP that was a compromise, calling for two administration buildings as well as multifamily housing on land adjacent to the station currently occupied by parking and abandoned buildings. The winning station-area proposal by developer Sares-Regis and San Francisco architect Jeffrey Heller varies from the Solomon design (the civic buildings, plaza, and shops have been reconfigured), but it maintains a strong pedestrian orientation to BART. The illustrative site plan, shown in Figure 7.2, places both housing and civic offices near the station, with an assortment of retail services and amenities—a clock tower, pavilion, and water fountain—aligned opposite of and within the sight line of the BART station. By late 1995, the new design was moving through the preconstruction stages, with a ground breaking set for late 1996.

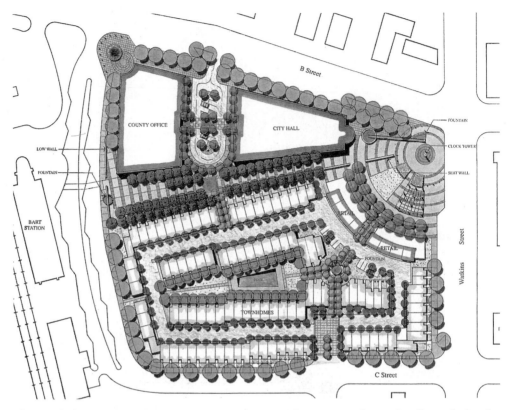

Figure 7.2 Hayward Transit Village Site Plan. This Hayward transit village design by architect Jeff Heller (building on the station-area specific plan of Don Solomon) intensifies the core area, with a new City Hall and County Office Building, and 100 new for-sale units.

7.4 EL CERRITO DEL NORTE

The El Cerrito del Norte station area, located 20 mi north of San Francisco on BART's Richmond line, is another emerging transit village that has undergone significant changes over the past decade. In 1988, the station was surrounded by rundown buildings along San Pablo Boulevard such as a cheap motel, an aging bowling alley, a tavern, and assorted small shops. Recognizing the potential benefits provided by BART's presence, the El Cerrito Redevelopment Agency prepared a plan to revitalize the area, beginning with the addition of new multifamily housing. The agency used tax-exempt financing to underwrite the cost of assembling parcels and building nearly $10 million of the $14 million in infrastructure improvements necessary to support intensive new development. These initiatives paid off. In mid-1992, the first housing project, Del Norte Place, was completed.

Del Norte Place, as shown in Photos 7.5 and 7.6, is a 135-unit apartment complex, 200 yd from the BART station, with three levels of rental housing above 19,000 ft^2 of ground-floor retail. The city worked closely with Del Norte Place's developer, John Stewart, to bring the project to completion. The redevelopment authority became an equity partner, leasing land to the developer for $1 per year and 15 to 20 percent of cash flows. Although the retail space has leased up slowly, residential units have leased quickly. By mid-1993, 97 percent of the apartments were occupied. Tenant records kept by the developers show tenants to be older "empty nesters," singles, or married couples without children, particularly individuals commuting to work in San Francisco and students at the nearby University of California, Berkeley.[7]

Of course, a single housing-retail project does not make a transit village. Getting a second large-scale project on line became essential in continuing the momentum toward a transit community. In 1993, a second transit-based housing project was prepared for a BART-owned surface parking lot, the 210-unit Grand Central Apartments. Grand Central, like Del Norte Place, is planned as three stories of residential above ground-floor retail. Following 2 years of project financing deals that fell through, the project finally took off in 1995 when the developer, Charles Oewel (who first got started building transit-based housing near Pleasant Hill's BART), was able to attract a movie complex—a 4000-seat

Photo 7.5 Del Norte Place, from San Pablo Avenue. The 138-unit Del Norte Place lies directly north of the El Cerrito del Norte station. It features two-story and three-story residential above ground-floor retail.

Photo 7.6 BART Train Arriving at the El Cerrito del Norte Station, Flanked by Del Norte Place.

AMC theater—to the adjacent parcel owned by the redevelopment agency. As with the Pleasant Hill station, the movie theater company is attracted by the unused parking available at the station on nights and weekends, as well as by the proximity of transit. And the movie complex provides the critical mass to support ground-floor retail at Grand Central Apartments. El Cerrito officials hope this complementarity of supportive land uses will form the building blocks of an eventual station-area metamorphosis that one day has the character and quality of a bona fide transit village.

7.5 ALMADEN

In the early 1990s, the board president of Santa Clara County's light rail system, Rod Diridon, launched a drive to build housing on the park-and-ride lots adjacent to station platforms. Diridon termed this station-area housing *trandominiums,* short for transit-oriented condominiums. The Almaden station, the southern terminus of the light rail line, was selected as the site of the first trandominium project. Planned for the existing park-and-ride lot is Almaden Lake Village, a 250-unit complex (of apartments, as it turns out, rather than condominiums). The illustrative site plan shown in Figure 7.3 includes two other proposed transit-based projects on city-owned land, the 84-unit for-sale Homes at Almaden

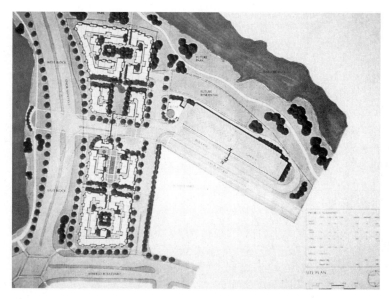

Figure 7.3 Almaden Lake Trandominiums. Almaden Lake Village, a 250-unit complex on the park-and-ride next to the Almaden station on Santa Clara's light rail, calls its "transit condominiums" *trandominiums*.

Lake and the adjacent 144-unit Apartments at Almaden Lake. As part of Santa Clara County's Housing Initiative Program, plans are underway to build some 1700 additional units of moderate-density housing near light rail stations over the next few years.

7.6 MOUNTAIN VIEW

Even stations along the Bay Area's commuter rail line, CalTrain, have attracted transit-based housing in recent times, most notably several large-scale owner-occupied projects catering to middle- and upper-middle-income households (Palo Alto Central at the Palo Alto station and San Mateo Central at the San Mateo station). The most recent addition to CalTrain's collection of rail-based housing is the Crossings, situated across from the soon to be built Mountain View station. The Crossings, shown in Photo 7.7, consists of 97 for-sale units built along narrow tree-lined streets and within easy walking distance to the planned station. The Crossings was designed by San Francisco architect Peter Calthorpe, one of the best known new urbanist architects who has also designed transit-oriented projects along light rail lines in Sacramento, Portland, and San Diego.

Photo 7.7 The Crossings in Mountain View. Designed by Peter Calthorpe, the 97 for-sale units built across from the station enjoy great transit accessibility.

7.7 NEW URBANISM AND TRANSIT VILLAGES IN THE BAY AREA

The new urbanists, a loose association of architects, planners, and urban designers from throughout the United States, are united in their critique of America's auto-oriented post-war suburbs. In the new urbanists' view, suburbia's galloping landscape, unless held in check, will only bring the kind of social isolation, traffic gridlock, and environmental degradation that characterize an automobile culture.[8] In this view, the new urbanists are not different than many other environmentalists who warn of the enormous social costs of rampant automobility. What new urbanists have added to this growing debate are designs of an alternative suburban community and a conviction to see that this alternative succeeds on the market. The designs, though varying widely, incorporate guidelines for walkable, compact, mixed-use communities, communities that recall the small towns and early railroad suburbs that arose in late 19th-century America. Among the trademarks of new urbanist designs are houses close together and close to the street, front porches (that draw residents to the neighborhood instead of their private and secluded backyards), and tree-lined streets. Among the broader community-design themes embraced by new urbanists are gridiron street patterns that make it easier to walk to any destination in a neighborhood; the elimination of cul-de-sacs in favor of streets connected to each other; the use of backlot alleys that eliminate driveways (thus reducing conflicts between pedestrians and

TRANSIT VILLAGE REDEVELOPMENT:
THE CASE OF OAKLAND'S FRUITVALE DISTRICT

New urbanists have mainly been concerned with the alternative suburban community. But the inner-city transit village can likewise incorporate new urbanist design principles. This has been the case at the Fruitvale BART station, the most advanced and arguably the most promising of the Bay Area's urban transit villages.

In the 1950s and even up through the 1960s, the Fruitvale district and especially its main street, East 14th Street, formed a vibrant commercial center. It was the opening of suburban shopping malls and big-box retail outlets that lured customers away and slowly sapped the vitality of the East 14th Street district and eventually the Fruitvale neighborhood itself. In the 1970s and 1980s, various urban renewal and antipoverty programs were devised to revitalize the area, with very little payoff. Clyde Brewer, a Fruitvale store owner for 18 years, commented at a 1993 symposium on Fruitvale revitalization, "You and I and 20 of our friends could retire on the money that has been spent studying this area."

In 1991, the Spanish-Speaking Unity Council (SSUC), a local community group headed by former HUD official Arabella Martinez, opted for a new approach, one using Fruitvale's biggest asset, the nearby BART station, as a spur to and center of new economic development. To jump start the process, a design symposium was held on a Saturday morning in May 1993. For this symposium, five prominent Bay Area architectural firms volunteered their time and energies, preparing and presenting different station-area design concepts. The small presentation room was filled with over 60 neighborhood residents, waiting in anxious anticipation to see if there were any brilliant ideas for turning their community around. The community stood united in the belief that the Fruitvale district needed more than cosmetic changes; rather, radical surgery was in order.

The challenges in transforming Fruitvale are immense, but in the course of the design competition, it was quickly recognized that what is often viewed as a liability—sterile surface parking lots, dilapidated buildings, vacant parcels—can over time be turned into an economic asset. Photo 7.8 portrays the nature of the design challenges facing Fruitvale's change agents. The station is flanked by two surface parking lots. The viewscape along 35th Avenue, which connects the BART station to East 14th Street's commercial strip, consists mainly of the backs of buildings. The nearest commercial establishments along East 14th Street are marginal businesses at best. There is little architectural consistency among the storefronts lining East 14th Street, and with the exception of a few taco stands and restaurants, there are few visual cues to remind people of the neighborhood's Hispanic culture and heritage. *(Continued)*

Photo 7.8   Fruitvale Station Area, 1994. A mix of parking lots and dilapidated buildings.

At the 1993 design charette, the volunteers presented a dazzling array of design concepts and approaches. Yet much remained unsettled. Should the housing be concentrated in one sector or spread throughout the area? Should parking be placed between BART and East 14th Street or be isolated to the side? How much attention should be given to rebuilding the business base of East 14th Street versus business in the immediate station area? Little consensus on plan details was reached at the charette, though the gathering served the very useful purpose of energizing the community and casting the political spotlight on the neighborhood.

Soon after the charette, the Spanish-Speaking Unity Council hired as the master site designer Ernesto Vasquez of the Costa Mesa-based firm of McLarand. In early 1995, Vasquez presented his plan, shown in Figure 7.4. Housing is prominent in the design, and it is spread throughout the area, primarily as second- and third-floor units above shops. This distribution, according to Vasquez, is intended to create an 18- to 24-h/day presence and to unify the community. The hope is to site enough permanent residents and other activities near the transit station to prevent its plazas and public spaces from becoming vacated after business hours and on weekends, which is the bane of many rail stations that are enveloped by surface parking.   *(Continued)*

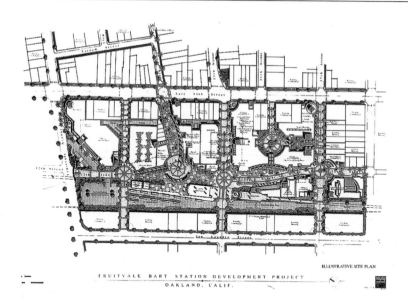

ILLUSTRATIVE SITE PLAN

FRUITVALE BART STATION DEVELOPMENT PROJECT
OAKLAND, CALIF.

Figure 7.4 Fruitvale Transit Village Design, 1995. The transit village design by architect Ernesto Vasquez features housing spread throughout the area, primarily as second- and third-floor housing above the shops, a public plaza directly in front of the station with a palm tree-lined walkway to East 14th Street, a mercado, child-care center, and a police substation.

The Vasquez plan sites a public plaza directly in front of the BART entrance, with a palm tree-lined walkway to East 14th Street. The structured parking lot is also placed near East 14th Street rather than adjacent to the station. Both of these design features are intended to promote foot traffic between BART and East 14th Street. Among the other notable features of the plan are an open-air mercado, a branch of the Mexican museum, and a Latin American library.

In reviewing the plan, neighborhood leaders, backed by the unity council, insisted that the first development phase concentrate on adding market-rate housing in addition to new commercial businesses. This, backers hoped, would cast the Fruitvale neighborhood in a more positive light, attracting other private investments. But Vasquez and others cautioned the unity council that no private interests would risk investing in Fruitvale unless a critical mass of new development is first achieved. This

(Continued)

being the case, the council's director, Arabella Martinez, set out to secure public funds to build first the upfront public infrastructure and subsidized senior housing that ideally would later lure in private investors.

Martinez took on the mission with a passion. Between 1993 and 1995, she raised a staggering sum of over $13 million, including more than $500,000 in predevelopment planning funds from the Federal Transit Administration as well as the Ford, Irvine, and Hewlett Foundations; $6.2 million for subsidized senior housing; $2.25 million for a senior center; and $780,000 for a pedestrian plaza. With the financial resources in hand, public improvements were made in earnest. By late 1995, construction on a senior housing project had begun, with plans to build a pedestrian plaza and bus transfer facility waiting in the wings. These seed monies appear to be having their intended effect. Recently, the unity council successfully negotiated with several private stores as well as a private operator to build an open-air mercado, an electronics store, and a full-service grocery outlet. Private investors seem particularly encouraged by the emphasis given to the public safety in the Fruitvale plan, notably the proposed placement of a police substation near BART and the presence of neighborhood foot traffic that keeps eyes on the street.

By 1996, Fruitvale had become the best known and one of the most promising of the emerging inner-city transit villages in America. To a large extent, this reflects Fruitvale's ability to raise more public money than any other area. However, it also reflects the scope of the Fruitvale effort—a commitment to rebuild the community, rather than to construct one or two new buildings. And it is also a testament to the savvy of local leaders to see to it that public safety and economic development incentives are aggressively pursued.

cars swinging into front-lot entrances); a variety of housing types; and most of all, intermixing of shops, stores, and housing.

Although new urbanists have attracted national press attention in the past few years, the number of new urbanist projects built in the United States through the mid-1990s has been limited: Seaside, a small resort community in the Florida panhandle; Kentlands, an upper income colonial style community outside of Washington, DC; and Harbor Town, Tennessee, an island development 5 min from downtown Memphis. The emerging transit villages in the San Francisco Bay Area represent one of the first attempts to implement new urbanist design ideas on a regional scale, and also the first links of new urbanism with rail transit. The Crossings complex in Mountain View is the purest example of a new urbanist community to date. Though the Solomon design proposed for Hayward has been altered, the downtown station area retains strong new urbanist characteristics, as does El Cerrito del

Norte. Pleasant Hill, although developing in fits and starts, is currently reconfiguring its street network and surface parking lots to become more like a new urbanist community.

For the transit village movement, the new urbanism provides organizing principles and useful design models. In turn, it is transit that gives relevance to the new urbanist designs. Without the transit connection, new urbanist communities can be isolated, even rarified land uses. But with the transit connection, new urbanist communities can become part of an integrated transit metropolis.

The intersection of station-area development and new urbanism in the San Francisco Bay Area has set the stage for a multitude of transit villages to take form during the 21st century. However, principles, designs, and good will alone will not be sufficient. Much of the success in attracting housing and office development in Pleasant Hill, and to a lesser extent Hayward, El Cerrito del Norte, and Almaden, can be credited to the roles of institutions and personalities. Among the keys to success in the Bay Area have been the creation of a market-realistic specific plan, supplemented by illustrative drawings that provide a common blueprint and frame of reference for guiding investments; the existence of a proactive local agency, typically a redevelopment authority, whose staff aggressively moves forward in implementing the plan by assembling irregular parcels into developable tracts, seeking out private coventures and investing in supportive public infrastructure; and having local elected officials who are willing to stake their political futures by becoming tireless advocates of the transit village cause. While not sufficient to guarantee success, experiences in the Bay Area suggest that these are often necessary precursors.

NOTES

1. Parsons, Brinckerhoff, Hall & McDonald, *Regional Rapid Transit* (San Francisco: Parsons, Brinckerhoff, Hall & McDonald, 1956).
2. Two pieces that discuss the expectations for BART to generate compact development at suburban stations are R. Johnston and S. Tracy, Suburban Resistance to Density Near Transit Stations in the San Francisco Bay Area, *The Social Constraints on Energy Policy Implementation,* N. Neiman and B. Burts, eds. (Lexington, MA: Heath and Company, 1983); L. Merewitz, Public Transportation: Wish Fulfillment and Reality in the San Francisco Bay Area, *Journal of the American Economic Association,* Vol. 62, No. 2, pp. 78–86, 1972.
3. Sedway Cooke, *Pleasant Hill BART Station Area Specific Plan* (San Francisco: Sedway Cooke, 1982).
4. M. Bernick and M. Carroll, *A Study of Housing Built Near Rail Transit Stations: Northern California* (Berkeley: Institute of Urban and Regional Development, University of California, Working Paper 546, 1991).

5. M. Bernick, The Bay Area's Emerging Transit-Based Housing, *Urban Land,* Vol. 52, No. 7, pp 38–41, 1993.

6. R. Cervero, *Ridership Impacts of Transit-Focused Development in California* (Berkeley: Institute of Urban and Regional Development, University of California, Monograph 45, 1993).

7. J. Stewart, *Resident Profile: Del Norte Place* (San Francisco: Sandy & Babcock Architects, 1993).

8. The most complete summary of new urbanist work is Peter Katz's *The New Urbanism* (New York: McGraw-Hill, 1994). See also D. Solomon, *Rebuilding* (Princeton, NJ: Princeton Architectural Press, 1992).

8

Washington, DC, Area: Postedge City

Emerging Transit Villages in Greater Washington, DC

Ballston

Rosslyn

Bethesda

Pentagon City

Grosvenor

Edge cities—the mammoth auto-oriented "suburban downtowns" that have sprouted over the past 20 to 30 years—are nowhere so prominent as in the greater Washington, DC, region. Joel Garreau, chronicler of the edge city, has identified 16 edge cities that orbit the nation's capital and cites one of them, Tysons Corner, as the archetype of this new form of suburban agglomeration.

With the slowing of office and commercial construction following the "go-go" building boom of the 1980s, suburban development in greater Washington, DC, has shifted in two new directions in recent years. Some growth has occurred beyond the first-generation edge cities in master planned communities like Fair Lakes and Reston, as well as in the greenfields where exurbia and countryside meet, such as Loudon County. Developers have been attracted by cheap land prices, low crime rates, and peaceful surroundings. The other center of new development activities has been suburban stations along Washington's Metrorail system. Ballston in Arlington County, Virginia, and Bethesda in Montgomery County, Maryland, are the most advanced of the new suburban transit villages, while Pentagon City and Grosvenor are in the beginning stages of a transit village transformation. Rosslyn, an auto-oriented edge city of the 1960s and 1970s, is also today being aggressively reconfigured to achieve a built form that more closely resembles the character of a transit village.

8.1 METROPOLITAN WASHINGTON'S POSTEDGE CITY MOVEMENT

In his celebrated 1991 book, *Edge City,* then *Washington Post* writer Joel Garreau set out to chronicle "the biggest change in a hundred years in how we build cities." From coast to coast, "every metropolis that is growing is doing so by sprouting strange new kinds of places," claims Garreau. He terms this new spatial phenomenon *edge cities*.[1]

America's edge cities are enormous suburban concentrations of office buildings, shopping complexes, convention hotels, garden apartments, performing arts centers, boutiques, and virtually everything else found in traditional urban centers. Many rival the downtowns of medium-sized cities in size and density. Growing so quickly that they often overwhelmed local infrastructure, edge cities have also given rise to a new phenomenon, suburban gridlock.[2] Today, edge cities are the downtowns of the information age, just as older core districts were downtowns of the industrial era. They also represent America's third wave of suburbanization, following the migration of households in search of single-family living and the later migration of retailers trying to locate closer to their customers, epitomized by the "malling" of America. This third wave has brought suburbia to maturity by balancing housing and retail plazas with job centers. With edge cities, it is possible to live, work, shop, and recreate without leaving the suburbs.

Garreau is by no means the first to recognize the office and commercial building explosions that occurred in suburbia over the past three decades. Others have written about these built forms using terms like *urban villages, technoburbs, megacenters, suburban activity centers,* and *perimeter cities*.[3] What Garreau does more successfully than other journalists and scholars is to give life to edge cities, to describe the movements and actions of developers, architects, builders, and occupants, and to place edge cities in the broader context of suburban America's culture, core values, and business ethos.

Being a resident of northern Virginia and having observed firsthand the radical changes going on around him, metropolitan Washington, DC, naturally became a focal point of Garreau's work. Perhaps more than anywhere, it was the incredible explosive growth of Tysons Corner, 12 mi east of downtown Washington during the early to mid-1980s that captured Garreau's fascination. Only a country crossroads with a general store and gas station in the 1950s, Tysons Corner has today become the biggest office-commercial complex in either Virginia or Maryland, boasting some 60,000 predominantly white-collar workers, 15 million-plus ft^2 of office space, two regional fashion malls, several luxury convention hotels, dozens of small retail plazas, and a few apartment and condominium complexes within its roughly 1700-acre boundaries. Tysons Corner is in many ways a nodal version of suburban strip development. By 1988, at the height of its growth, Tysons Corner had become an assemblage of independently designed and constructed buildings spaced at irregular intervals, enveloped by large surface parking lots and virtually absent of sidewalks or public spaces (see Photo 8.1). While structures were relatively close to each other by a crow's flight, the landscape of gated parcels, disconnected pathways, and uncoordinated building placements made walking from here to there akin to traversing an obstacle course (see Photo 8.2). Tysons Corner, and indeed most edge cities, had become, unapologetically, the land of the automobile. This proved to be Tysons Corner's undoing, for the nightmarish traffic jams that followed prompted a number of businesses to later pack up and move to greener pastures. In recent years, entire office buildings have

Photo 8.1 Tysons Corner, Fairfax County, Virginia, 1989. A sprawling concentration of offices, retail plazas, shopping malls, and hotels interspersed by surface parking and wide thoroughfares.

remained empty for the lack of a major tenant. Except for its two highly successful fashion malls, Tysons Corner's real estate market has fallen on hard times.

Tysons Corners developers, merchants, and residents were not lost on the fact that its heavy automobile orientation was quickly becoming a liability. Since 1988, four separate studies have investigated the feasibility of extending Metrorail to Tysons Corner and on to Dulles International Airport. One report, *The Future of Tysons Corner: A Vision,* issued by the Tysons Transportation Association in 1992, proposed a number of transportation improvements, including a possible rail link, both to tie together the spread-out buildings within Tysons Corner and to connect it to the region as a whole.[4] More recently, in early 1994, the Dulles Corridor Task Force issued a report that recommended constructing a rail line that would link Tysons Corner with the Falls Church Metro station and Dulles Airport.[5] Though none of these rail proposals have moved forward, the idea of retrofitting the built edge cities into more transit-oriented places is picking up force in a type of post-edge city movement.

Beyond the reconfiguration of highway-oriented edge cities, a movement is also afoot to enhance and embellish the built environments of edge cities clustered around rail transit stations. In contrast to the west coast transit villages, Washington's emerging transit-based communities are of greater size and scope, punctuated by high-rise office, retail, and residential towers. The continuing strength of metropolitan Washington's economy, anchored by the

Photo 8.2 Assemblage of Land Uses in Tysons Corner, 1988. The pell-mell layout of apartments (in the foreground), offices, and shopping centers discourages foot travel.

federal government's presence, makes the prospect for future transit-oriented development as promising in this part of the country as anywhere. More high-value commercial property has already been developed at more stations, with greater impact on the surrounding area, in metropolitan Washington than anywhere else in the nation during the postwar era.

Of course, the most valuable asset to the region's postedge city movement is the Metrorail system itself, the most extensive of the recent generation of rail systems in America. Operated by Washington Metropolitan Area Transportation Authority (WMATA), the system was built in the early 1970s and began operations in 1976. Extensions have been steadily added over the years to form the current 89-mi, 75-station system, shown in Map 8.1. Today, Metrorail carries about 520,000 passenger trips per weekday, up from 447,000 in 1987. The system extends outward from downtown Washington into the surrounding counties of Montgomery and Prince George's in Maryland, and Arlington and Fairfax in Virginia.

8.2 BALLSTON

Over the years, Arlington County has been the most aggressive of all jurisdictions in seeking to channel new growth in the vicinity of its Metrorail stations. By Virginia law, the

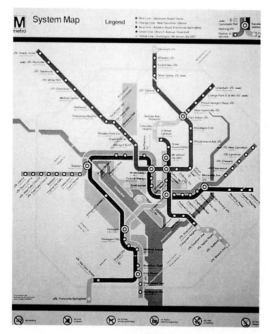

Map 8.1 The Washington Metrorail System. Opened in 1976, the system had grown to 89 mi and 75 stations by 1995.

county, rather than individual municipalities, possesses land-use powers. As early as 1968, when various Metrorail routes were being considered, the county launched an ambitious planning process that methodically evaluated proposed rail routes and their likely land-use impacts.[6] Over the ensuing three decades, Arlington County introduced a series of strategies—targeted infrastructure improvements, incentive zoning, development proffers—to entice private investment around its rail stations, particularly the five stations in the Rosslyn-Ballston corridor along the Orange Line. Of these five stations, the Ballston station has emerged as the county's showcase transit-oriented community.

8.2.1 Ballston, Spring 1979

In 1979, Metrorail's Orange Line was extended farther into Arlington County from the Rosslyn station to new stops at Court House, Clarendon, Virginia Square, and Ballston. Ballston, once a vibrant local village, by the 1970s had become an aging commercial district surrounded by surface parking lots, auto repair shops, fast-food outlets, older homes, and a handful of garden apartments (Photo 8.3).

Photo 8.3   Ballston, 1970. The Ballston area in April 1970 was a mix of strip commercial and sprawling residential development.

Ballston is one of Arlington's oldest communities. In the early 1800s, a scattering of residences was built near the current intersection of North Glebe Road and Wilson Boulevard. The intersection became known as Ball's Crossroads after a tavern was built at the crossing by the son of Moses Ball, one of the early landowners in Arlington. Ball's Crossroads was later renamed Ballston, and by the start of the 20th century, Ballston was one of several villages located along the main line of the Washington, Alexandria, and Falls Church Railroad.

The first subdivisions in Ballston were developed in the early 1920s, and by the middle of the decade, single-family homes with clapboard exteriors occupied much of the area. Garden apartments were built to complement single-family homes in the 1930s and 1940s. Ballston's commercial downtown prospered throughout the 1950s and 1960s, spurred by the construction of the Parkington Shopping Center in 1951, the area's first regional shopping mall. However, by the late 1960s, growth had shifted to the outer suburbs beyond the Capital Beltway. Ballston's population declined, as did its commercial district, including the

Parkington Shopping Mall. By the late 1970s, when the Metro system was about to arrive, downtown Ballston had been reduced to a series of one- and two-story commercial buildings and assorted transitional land uses. Once the Ballston station, located some 10 mi from Capitol Hill, opened in 1979, it functioned mainly as a bus turnaround and transfer point for several northern Virginia bus lines.

8.2.2   Ballston, Spring 1995

By spring 1995, the Ballston station area had been transformed, as shown in Photo 8.4, into a modern district of high-rise residential and commercial structures and was recognized as Arlington's premier urban center. Parkington Mall had been razed and replaced by a brightly lit, cheerfully new mall: Ballston Common. Directly above the transit station sits the 28-story Ballston Metro Center, a combination hotel, office, retail, and condominium complex. Since 1984, nearly 2500 residential units, 3.7 million ft^2 of commercial

Photo 8.4   Ballston, 1995. By 1995, 15 years after the Ballston rail station opens, residential and commercial development is concentrated, with nearly 2500 residential units and 3.7 million ft^2 of development within a short walking distance of the station.

space, and three luxury hotels have been built in the 79-block, 770-acre redevelopment area. Today, the area is the work address of over 20,000 people and home to around 6000.

What triggered this transformation? To a large extent, the same factors that induced change at the Pleasant Hill station in northern California can be found at Ballston: (1) a specific plan to orchestrate development, complemented by incentive zoning that promoted higher densities within a quarter mile of the station; (2) local government financial participation to jump start private investment; and (3) joint public-private development spearheaded by the regional transit authority. Added to this were fortuitous events beyond local control, namely, a healthy regional economy that created the conditions for station-area expansion and the extension of the Orange Line that freed up land around the station formerly used as a bus staging area.

8.2.2.1 Station-Area Planning and Zoning

When Metrorail came to Ballston in 1979, the neighborhood was at an all-time low and ripe for redevelopment. At the time, Arlington lacked a downtown in the traditional sense. Ballston was viewed as one of several possibilities, although a long shot. The Ballston Sector Plan, issued by the county in May 1980, looked at the area's unassuming mix of incompatible land uses and rather boldly entertained the possibility of transforming Ballston into a modern commercial center focused around the Metrorail station.[7] In contrast to Rosslyn (reviewed later in this chapter), though, the proposed district would mix its commercial development with an equal amount of housing within a quarter-mile sphere and would include other human-scale elements within this radius such as open space, neighborhood-serving retail, and pedestrian walkways to the station. "The Ballston Sector Plan represented a change in thought among County planners," explains Robert Klute, senior planner of Arlington County. "A reduced bulk of development, streetlife, walking link to the transit station—all were elements reflecting new thinking about what makes a liveable community."

Over the next 14 years, the Ballston station area largely followed the pathways set in the sector plan, becoming an impressive concentration of office towers, high-rise apartments, and the upscale Ballston Common Shopping Mall featuring nearly 100 shops. Besides providing a blueprint for development, the Ballston Sector Plan also laid out an aggressive approach to zoning, one that used density incentives to achieve a desired built form. A seven-block area around Ballston's Metro station was designated as a coordinated mixed-use development district. High-density development was permitted within the district: 3.5 floor area ratio (FAR, i.e., building area divided by lot size) for offices, 135 units per acre for apartments, and up to 210 units per acre for hotels. Street-level retail uses were also required for all commercial-office buildings within the district. Additionally, the permitted FAR of 3.5 for commercial buildings could be increased to 6 by devoting 50 percent or more of floorspace to residential units; projects that include 90 percent residential space were allowed an additional 0.5 FAR.

8.2.2.2 Local Government Financial Participation

Rezoning set the stage for the transit-oriented development, and the county jump started the process in 1982 when it agreed to cofinance, through issuing industrial development bonds, a 3200-car garage for Ballston Common (and also transit park-and-ride) three blocks from the Metrorail station. This was sufficient to give the project the green light in the developer's and lender's view, and within a year, Ballston Common was built on the site of former Parkington Mall. With its mix of upscale restaurants, coffee bars, and fashion shops, along with mall standards such as Walden Books and Foot Locker, Ballston Common quickly became the area's flagship development, providing an amenity base that appealed to many prospective builders. And attract projects it did. Buoyed by the area's robust real estate climate and Arlington's prime location, in addition to the lure of Ballston Common, nearly two dozen commercial projects were undertaken within one-third mile of the station during the mid- and late 1980s. In rapid succession, eight major office buildings came on line: Ballston One, 250,000 ft^2 of office space (completed 1986); Ballston Common Office Center, 176,000 ft^2 (1986); Arlington Square, 176,000 ft^2 (1988); Eclipse at Ballston, 183,000 ft^2 (1989); Ballston Station, 255,000 ft^2 (1990); One Stafford Place, 185,000 ft^2 (1990); Quincy Street Station, 165,000 ft^2 (1990); and Ballston Metro Center, 193,000 ft^2, along with a 209-room hotel, 277 condominiums, retail shops, and a health club, all located directly above the transit stop (1989–1990). Several established regional employers—Eastman Kodak, Environ, Sedgewick James, and Uslico—also moved to Ballston in the 1980s. Environ alone leased up 45,000 ft^2 of office space, moving its corporate offices from Georgetown. The proximity to Metrorail, along with office rents that were below those in Georgetown and downtown Washington, combined to make Ballston a particularly attractive location.

The federal government also had a hand in Ballston's renaissance, having established a policy in the early 1980s to site new government office buildings near Metrorail stops. For the same reasons private businesses liked a Ballston address, federal agencies found the area attractive, and in the 1980s, Ballston became home to the National Science Foundation, the National Pollution Fund Center, the U.S. Army Legal Services Agency, the Federal Deposit Insurance Corporation, and the Applied Research Planning Agency, along with the National Rural Electric Cooperative Association, which sited its national headquarters near the Metrorail station.

8.2.2.3 Joint Development

Over the years, WMATA has more aggressively pursued joint development (e.g., air-rights leasing, station-retail connections, shared use of heating-ventilation systems, etc.) than any transit authority in the country.[8] Rather than simply waiting and reacting to developer proposals, WMATA created an in-house real estate office and encouraged its staff to aggressively seek out mutually advantageous joint development opportunities. By 1994, WMATA had entered into 22 joint development ventures (mostly involving land leases) and was requesting proposals for development at several additional stations.

Ballston Metro Center, shown in Photo 8.5, is one of the best examples of a successful public-private partnership initiated by a transit agency. WMATA owned the 72,000-ft^2 site abutting the Ballston station, originally used as a bus staging area. When the Orange Line was extended to Vienna and bus transfer functions were relocated there as well in 1983, the site suddenly became available. WMATA hoped not only to secure lease revenues for the site, but also sought to attract a high-rise tenant that would generate sufficient ridership to help sustain Metrorail services. In 1982, WMATA issued an RFP for developing the site but received no proposals. Follow-up interviews with the area's developers revealed that most saw the site as being only marginally viable as a stand-alone parcel. Consequently, WMATA proceeded to assemble an adjacent parcel and altered its competitive proposal process to enter into a sole source agreement with the Ballston Metro Limited Partnership. Further, the transit agency, which previously had collected rent payments on land leases,

Photo 8.5 Ballston Metro Center, 1994. Built directly above the transit station, this 28-story structure combines condominiums, an office complex, and a hotel.

agreed to a percentage share of gross proceeds from the condominium sales after it became clear that condominium sales required a fee simple agreement.[9] This placed WMATA in the role of an equity partner rather than a landlord. In the early 1990s, WMATA was receiving around $200,000 in annual revenues from Ballston Metro Center. Arlington County further enticed the development of Ballston Metro Center by granting the project's developers density bonuses, partly in recognition of the project's housing component and public plaza, but also to affirm the project's importance as the visual focal point in the Ballston community.

8.2.3 Ballston's Maturation into a Postedge City

Community leaders recognized early on that the emergence of Ballston as a premier transit-oriented community depended on balancing commercial development with additional housing. Density bonuses were successfully used to leverage more housing construction. From 1985 to 1992, over 2500 condominiums and apartment units were built, with the largest projects being Randolph Towers, a 509-unit apartment building (1986); Summerwalk, 172 condominiums (1986); Quincy Street Station, 222 apartments (1989); Chase at Ballston, 344 apartments (1989–1990); Ballston Place, 232 apartments (1989–1991); and Lincoln Towers, 714 apartments (1992).

Lincoln Towers, twin towers of 22 stories each and 13,500 ft^2 of ground-floor retail, was fully leased up within 7 months of its 1992 opening. Jeff Franzen, a partner of the Lincoln Property Company who is in charge of the project, attributed the leasing speed to Metrorail's presence, noting that a similar property in size and quality more than a mile from the Metro took 2 years to lease up. According to Franzen, most renters are singles and couples without children who work either in downtown Washington, at other sites along the Metrorail corridors, or in Ballston. A smaller market consists of older couples and individuals who no longer want to live in larger suburban homes in Arlington and who see being near the rail line as an advantage. The apartments are aimed at more affluent renters, with a one-bedroom of 808 ft^2 leasing for $1025 and a two-bedroom of 1215 square ft^2 going for $1385.[10]

The best evidence on the value of Metrorail access comes from a 1989 survey of commuting habits of residents from the Randolph Towers complex, which lies 500 ft from the Ballston station portal.[11] The survey of several hundred Randolph Towers residents showed that 69 percent commuted to work by Metrorail. If they worked in Washington, the modal share was 88 percent. These modal splits are similar to those found for transit-based housing in the San Francisco Bay Area (see Chapter 5) and confirm the belief that many residents in transit-oriented communities consciously elect to live in these areas for the very purpose of economizing on commuting.

Tom Parker, chief planner of Arlington County, attributes the popularity of Ballston's housing stock not only to Metrorail but also to the presence of attractive and modern retail centers: "There is an opportunity for people to live and work there, and be part of a more vibrant community where the sidewalks aren't rolled up after five o'clock." Bill Condo, the executive director of the Ballston Partnership, an alliance of developers and businesses formed to market the area, adds that Ballston is "geared towards residents searching for a more urban lifestyle without the expense and danger of living in the city," but with the ability to get around the region. Jonathan Cox, development director for Trammel Crow, which developed The Chase at Ballston, estimates that the overwhelming majority of tenants are working either in Ballston, Washington, Vienna, or other locales easily accessible by Metrorail. "In a typical married couple, one may be a beltway bandit and the other may work downtown."

Despite the impressive building boom of the past decade and a half, Ballston today falls short of being a pedestrian-friendly transit village. Stuart Street, which runs in front of the Metro, and Fairfax Drive, perpendicular to Stuart, are major thoroughfares. As state highways, the mobility needs of motorists generally take precedence over those of pedestrians. Moreover, Ballston is largely devoid of active streetlife or street-level retail. High-rise structures dwarf pedestrians and cast shadows on open spaces.

At the same time, the Ballston area is less than 50 percent built out. Bill Condo, standing before a detailed miniature of the city set in the middle of the Ballston Partnership offices, acknowledges Ballston's current shortcomings. The partnership, he notes, is hoping to add new commercial and residential structures that will fill in the gaps, and also recreational opportunities and street-level activity that will increase the attractiveness of Ballston as a place to live. Only time will tell whether Ballston fully becomes a pedestrian-oriented, transit-based community; however, compared to its neighbor to the southwest, Tysons Corner, Ballston is well along in becoming a reconstituted, or postedge city. Its relative advantages—Metrorail access, compact development, integrated land uses—have already been translated into a rent premium of over $3 per square foot for office space relative to comparable projects in Tysons Corner.[12]

8.3 ROSSLYN

When taking the Orange Line from downtown Washington to Arlington, Rosslyn is the first station one reaches upon crossing the Potomac. Its growth predates Ballston's. Rosslyn blossomed as a major commercial center in the mid-1960s, and by the mid-1970s, it was packed with high-rise office towers. But with an auto-oriented built form, it was a far cry from being a transit-oriented center, much less a transit village. Rosslyn's 1960s building boom exposed the potential downside of rapid-pace, intensive development: mammoth buildings, absence of a pedestrian scale or streetlife, and a "sameness" about the built environment. In recent years, Arlington County has embarked on a concentrated effort to retrofit Rosslyn into a more balanced, mixed-use community focused around its Metrorail station.

In the early 1960s, the unincorporated 259 acres that made up Rosslyn were occupied by an odd mix of pawnshops, oil storage tanks, warehouses, service yards, and other marginal land uses, as shown in Photo 8.6. Being across the river from Georgetown and a relatively short distance from the White House, upon the announcement of a new Metrorail stop, many saw Rosslyn as being prime for redevelopment. In 1962, the county amended its General Land Use Plan and rezoned Rosslyn to encourage high-rise office and commercial development. This rezoning predated a rapid expansion in federal employment and the region's suburban office building boom. Between 1962 and 1970, 27

Future Metro Station

Photo 8.6 Rosslyn, 1962. The unincorporated 259 acres across the Potomac River from Washington is a mix of scattered, unrelated, and sometimes incompatible commercial and industrial land uses.

major commercial buildings were constructed. By 1994, as shown in Photo 8.7, Rosslyn boasted a towering skyline of high-rise offices, commercial structures, and condominiums linked by wide boulevards and a network of second-floor skywalks.

Rosslyn's physical form reflected the state of planning practice at the time: widely spaced, rectangularly shaped buildings situated off of plazas; a skywalk system to connect buildings and maintain the street level for automobiles; broad avenues, 70 to 80 ft wide, with narrow and sometimes discontinuous sidewalks. A report on Rosslyn's design in the late 1960s noted that "the pedestrian who crosses Rosslyn's streets will hazard more than his fatalistic companion who now attempts to cross the mixing bowl on Shirley Highway."[13] The Nash Street Building exemplifies the office high-rises that went up in Rosslyn in 1965. A 12-story structure with 150,000 ft^2 of office and 7100 ft^2 of retail, it is elevated above the street level, oriented to automobile movement, and allows access mainly through its parking garage. There are no nearby courtyards or attractively landscaped plazas that might serve as gathering spots for office workers during lunch hour or bring people together from surrounding buildings.

By the early 1970s, local residents' complaints about the scale, pace, and orientation of growth became increasingly vocal. In response, the Rosslyn-Ballston Corridor Committee,

Photo 8.7   Rosslyn, 1994. Over 6000 residences, 7 million ft^2 of office space, and 1654 hotel rooms lie within a 10-min walk of the station.

a citizens advisory group, issued a report in June 1975 urging that Rosslyn's growth not be repeated elsewhere in the corridor. The report also denounced Rosslyn for its lack of streetlife and balance between residential, commercial, and retail activities, a balance that would take advantage of Metrorail's presence. In the report, the committee wrote that it "is deeply concerned about the night-time 'ghost town' atmosphere in Rosslyn, which seems to result from the concentration of office space and the virtual exclusion of dwelling units and commercial retail space." The committee urged that greater attention be given to pedestrian access to transit, architectural quality, and amenities. Although the committee report never used terms like *transit village* or *transit-oriented development*, its criticisms of planning thought at the time anticipated the transit village movement.

In 1992, the Rosslyn Station Area Plan Addendum was adopted with the expressed goal of remaking Rosslyn into a transit village. The plan called for additional housing to complement office development, greater retail activity at all hours, and increased pedestrian access to and from the station.[14] The plan addendum noted the tremendous growth of Rosslyn since 1962: Thirty years later, 7 million ft^2 of office space had been added (and another 312,000 ft^2 approved), along with 1654 hotel rooms and over 6000 residences within a 10-min walk of the station. "Despite its attributes," the plan addendum admonishes, "the lack of integration between Rosslyn's various elements prevents it from being the premier office and residential area it can be. . . . The residential areas are not well connected physically or socially to the office core. . . . Many of Rosslyn's original buildings are undistinguished architecturally. . . . There is little continuity in the street-scale with large expanses of blank walls and office towers isolated from one another. . . . Retail establishments are scattered throughout the area and have little or no visibility from the street."

The plan addendum minced no words about what should be done. It proposed the renovation and expansion of existing aging buildings in the core area, the development of a Central Place within a 3-block radius of the station, and the addition of amenities and microdesigns to enhance the walking environment. Renovations began in 1994 with the Commonwealth Building. This obsolete office structure was gutted, expanded, and refaced. Three floors were added, and the building was redesigned at ground level to provide for street-level retail, a small outdoor patio eating area, and an upgraded streetscape. The building's additional height and floor area were development bonuses provided in return for the street-level improvements. As the building came on line in 1995, other property owners were awaiting the lease-up results.

Perhaps the area's highest hopes lie with the renovation of the Central Place block abutting the Metrorail station. Central Place aims to transform the transit node from a dimly lit, nondescript structure into one described by Arlington County planner Robert Klute as "a crossroads and principal transportation gateway to Rosslyn, surrounded by an active retail center, pedestrian plaza, and easy access to taxis and buses." Specific improvements that are planned include better lighting and public art within the station lobby, an upgrading of the Metrobus transfer facility adjacent to the station, and the planting of trees and greenery. Through this $1 million package of enhancements ($800,000 from the Federal Transit

Administration's Livable Communities Program and $200,000 in local funds), Arlington County hopes to leverage private investments that are transit-oriented in their designs.

8.4 BETHESDA

Bethesda has long been a suburban center in its own right; however, following Metrorail's opening, commercial development picked up considerably. In the late 1970s, downtown Bethesda claimed a few high-rise office and residential buildings, contrasted with the one- to two-story buildings located on or near Wisconsin Avenue, the community's major thoroughfare. However, its proximity to one of the highest income neighborhoods in the region, coupled with the close proximity of the National Institutes of Health and Bethesda Naval Hospital, prompted growing developer interest in the area.[15]

Similar to Ballston's experience, a proactive local government, combined with an entrepreneurial-minded transit authority, paved the way for a transit-oriented community to emerge in Bethesda. When Metrorail arrived in 1984, WMATA found a private sector ready to act and a powerful Montgomery County government interested in promoting station-area development. The county, which wields total control over land uses under Maryland law, helped leverage development through land assemblage and incentive zoning. First, it pulled together multiple parcels owned by different people into a consolidated and easily developable site at the Bethesda station. It then zoned the station area to allow for a doubling of densities (from 3 to 6 FAR) in exchange for developer contributions to open space and public amenities. Additionally, the county prepared transit-supportive design guidelines that laid the ground rules on how the station areas would be physically designed. The guidelines encouraged the siting of a few low-rise buildings adjacent to the main plazas and the construction of higher rise buildings with step-back, tapered designs to allow sunlight to enter.

These initiatives paid off handsomely, giving rise to one of the most pleasant, pedestrian-friendly suburban transit nodes in the country. In all, 7 million ft^2 of office space, 2.3 million ft^2 of retail shops and restaurants, a hotel-convention complex, 5000 housing units, and some 39,000 jobs are huddled in the two-thirds-mi^2 area that surrounds the Bethesda Metrorail station (Photo 8.8). Bethesda Place and Hampden Square, two towering mixed-use projects, flank the station, separated from each other by an attractively designed and landscaped plaza. Bethesda Place, situated almost directly above the station, features 370,000 ft^2 of office and retail space in a 17-story building, a 12-story, 380-room Hyatt Hotel, a 10-story residential tower with 100 rental units, and 38,000 ft^2 of retail space located in a food court off the plaza (Photo 8.9). The project yields $1.6 million in annual revenues to WMATA as part of a 99-year air-rights lease (by far, the most paid to a transit agency by a private developer in the country); the deal includes easement lease-backs to WMATA for the bus terminal, rail station access, storage facilities, and a passenger drop-off area. Nearby Hampden Square consists of a 12-story office tower and an

Photo 8.8 Central Bethesda, 1994. High-rise offices and commercial and residential buildings cluster along the linear axis established by the Metrorail Red Line and Wisconsin Avenue.

Photo 8.9   Bethesda Place. The mixed-use project, anchored by the architecturally distinct 12-story Hyatt Hotel, sits atop the Bethesda Metrorail station and fronts an attractive, contoured plaza.

adjacent 8-story residential tower (37 condominiums).[16] And at the heart of the Bethesda transit community is a 90,000-ft^2 open plaza that steps down to the street corner, embellished with a clock tower, water fountains, plentiful landscaping, and assorted sculptures.

Bethesda arguably has more of the "feel" of a transit village than any concentration of development in metropolitan Washington, DC. West and south of the station are hundreds of luxury condominiums and rental apartments. The office building boom of the 1980s has been followed by a restaurant and arts boom that continues to this day. Much of the community's success lies in the balance of complementary uses, which draw residents onto the streets on evenings and weekends, whether for a leisurely stroll or en route to a fine restaurant. Detractors, however, complain that the community has become too "high-end," designed mainly for well-off young professionals. Local officials seem aware of this and have sought to attract more affordable housing into the area. Creating a community that welcomes a wider range of the region's population poses a new planning challenge as central Bethesda matures.

8.5 BUDDING TRANSIT-BASED COMMUNITIES: PENTAGON CITY AND GROSVENOR

Ballston, Rosslyn, and Bethesda are the most advanced of greater Washington's emerging transit communities, but others—notably, Pentagon City in Arlington County and Grosvenor in Montgomery County, Maryland—are in the beginning stages. While Pentagon City is already a compact transit-oriented setting, as in Ballston and Rosslyn, local planners are seeking to diversify land uses and introduce various pedestrian amenities that will engender a stronger sense of community. Grosvenor is less intensively developed; however, if the visions of an ambitious, young developer materialize, this could soon change.

8.5.1 Pentagon City

Pentagon City is located in south Arlington County, where the Blue and Yellow Lines meet en route to National Airport. Between 1977, when the Blue Line opened, and 1990, the Pentagon City station area attracted over 2300 new residential units in seven high-rise developments, as well as two MCI office complexes and the Pentagon City Fashion Centre, an upscale shopping mall with a Nordstroms and a Ritz-Carlton hotel (Photo 8.10).

Station-area development in Pentagon City has been largely privately financed. The Pentagon City Fashion Centre was developed by Melvin Simon & Associates and The Rose Company, which purchased the property from a long-time local family owner in advance of Metrorail's opening. The transit station's proximity was a main factor in the developers' decision to build the mall, and in little time, the investment paid off hand-

Photo 8.10 Pentagon City, 1994. The Pentagon City Metrorail station is flanked by an upscale shopping mall, with a Nordstroms and Ritz-Carlton hotel, as well as over 2300 new residential units within a one-quarter-mile radius.

somely. Centre management estimates over 50 percent of its shoppers and customers arrive by Metrorail. Many are federal workers who come from the district (e.g., the Federal Triangle area) during lunch hour, a 5- to 10-min train ride away. Because of Metrorail's convenient connection, the Fashion Centre today commands a rent premium relative to other nearby retail space.

8.5.2 Grosvenor

Metrorail's Grosvenor station, located on the Red Line midway between Bethesda and Rockville, is surrounded by mid- and high-rise residential towers, most of which were built prior to the station's opening. These condominium and apartment complexes are set in a wooded area across Rockville Pike, a six-lane divided highway, requiring residents to walk through several passageways to reach the station. The Grosvenor station's identity has long been associated more with park-and-ride facilities than with transit-oriented development.

This could soon change, however. A new transit village, to be built on a 46-acre WMATA-owned site adjacent to the Grosvenor station, is moving through the advanced planning stages. The impetus for this change is a prominent Washington development family that sees transit-based housing as a promising niche market for the region's suburbs. Michael Gerwitz is the lead developer of the planned Residences at Grosvenor project, following in the footsteps of his grandfather and father. "My grandfather who started the company was of an earlier generation of developers, who were entrepreneurs, not corporate developers," explains Gerwitz. "My grandfather was an accountant who got into the field by bringing together other businessmen and taking a chance on a few small parcels of land. He graduated into small retail, and then during the 1950s began assembling land in the central business district." This latter strategy proved wildly successful. The Gerwitz family became one of the leading civic and philanthropic families of the area. Through the 1970s and 1980s, the Gerwitz development company actively built high-rise office structures and condominiums throughout the region.

Mike Gerwitz began working in the company part time in 1983 and came on full time after graduating from Georgetown Law School in 1990. He participated in several projects—an office building at 18th and L, a 50-unit townhouse project—but soon began looking at new markets for the company and himself. "I looked around and tried to figure out the best real estate opportunities for the future. It's tough driving now and only going to get worse. Being near the rail line will have real value."

In 1992, Gerwitz spent weeks driving around suburban Metrorail sites, conducting "windshield" surveys. Among all of the contenders, Grosvenor stood out due to the sizable amount of land owned by WMATA at the station, the absence of other buildable land in the area, and the "supportive" demographics (i.e., high incomes) of the surrounding residences. In early 1993, Gerwitz sent an unsolicited proposal to WMATA asking for the right to develop the transit agency's land next to the Grosvenor station. WMATA was reluctant to move forward. Its own marketing study, conducted by a corporate consulting firm, showed a questionable market demand for more high-density housing in the area. Nonetheless, after repeated letters from Gerwitz, the agency agreed to issue an RFP, and Gerwitz was awarded development rights.

The planned Residences at Grosvenor is slated as a phased residential development of 1403 units on 46 acres. A rendering of the project from the perspective of the Metrorail station exit is shown in Figure 8.1. The first phase will be on land farthest from the station, consisting of four-story walk-ups at 36 units per acre, totaling 150 to 300 units. A generous amount of land will go to open space and a day-care center. Phase Two will add 360 condominium units spread in four-story structures, with a community building and swimming pool. The next two phases of development will be on land closer to the station and will average higher densities. Phase Three will consist of two eight-story buildings housing 288 apartments, and Phase Four will complete the project with a 24-floor residential tower and 28,000 ft^2 of neighborhood-serving retail built adjacent to the station. In a narrative description of the residences, Gerwitz writes,

> This tower will give a strong overall identity to the development and reinforce the location to the Metro Station entrance. A main street promenade has been developed per-

pendicular to the station entrance and is framed by ground floor retail shops on both sides of the street. These shops help screen the Metro parking garage from the residences and the station and will bring a vitality to the area.[17]

The project is being marketed to three groups: (1) urban singles who like the city but want to live in a safer area; (2) double-income couples, childless or with one or two children; and (3) older couples in Montgomery County who want to stay in the area and decide to trade a home on an acre of land for a condominium with rail access. All are the most likely candidates for living in a suburban neighborhood with superior rail transit access complemented by public amenities and retail services around the rail stop.

Gerwitz hopes to obtain planning entitlements and to break ground on the project by 1997. He's not discouraged by the somber WMATA marketing study or the absence of other developers rushing to the site. "The corporate developers are cautious and rely on

VIEW FROM METRO STATION
THE RESIDENCES AT GROSVENOR STATION
FOR
POTOMAC INVESTMENT PROPERTIES

Figure 8.1 The Residences at Grosvenor. A four-phase project of 1403 moderate-to high-density housing units planned for the 46 acres adjacent to the Grosvenor station.

established products," he claims. "We went into downtown Washington D.C. when nobody thought you could make money. Transit development is the next niche market."

8.6 TOWARD THE POSTEDGE CITY METROPOLIS

In September 1994, Joe Garreau wrote a somewhat satirical yet perceptive piece for *The New Republic* about the coming reconfiguration of America's edge cities. By 1994, he had left his job as a reporter for *The Washington Post* and became president of the Edge City Group, lecturing, consulting, and maintaining a database on edge city growth. In the essay, Garreau notes that, because edge cities were shaped by market forces, they have been successful at delivering market goods—access to the airport, executive housing, worker housing. Being frontier boomtowns, only 20 or 30 years old, they lack "identity, community, civilization, soul." The next wave will see the retrofitting of edge cities. By such retrofitting, Garreau means mainly the replacement of surface parking lots with restaurants, bookstores, or "a place with soft music and candlelight."

The retrofitting of edge cities will occur gradually because the edge city built environment is designed around use of the automobile, not foot traffic. In the regional scheme of things, though, many of the Washington edge cities of the 1970s and 1980s are today being bypassed for greener pastures. More and more, developers are leapfrogging over these traffic-snarled, pedestrian-unfriendly environs to settle in areas where attractive new communities and workplaces can be created that avoid the sins of the 1980s edge cities. In northern Virginia, Herndon, outside of Dulles Airport, and Loudon County are more likely to be the sites of new corporate locations than Tysons Corner. However, all is not lost in edge cities. There is too much public infrastructure and private capital to abandon them. Nevertheless, what growth takes place is likely to end up in areas that have actively sought to rejuvenate themselves and that show promise as attractive walking environments and balanced mixed-use communities. In this regard, greater Washington's emerging transit-based communities—Ballston, Rosslyn, Bethesda, Pentagon City, and Grosvenor—have reason for optimism about the future.

NOTES

1. J. Garreau, *Edge City: Life on the New Frontier* (New York: Doubleday, 1991).
2. R. Cervero, *Suburban Gridlock* (New Brunswick, NJ: Center for Urban Policy Research, 1986).
3. See Ibid.; R. Cervero, *America's Suburban Centers: The Land Use-Transportation Link* (Boston: Unwin-Hyman, 1989); R. Fishman, *Bourgeois Utopias: The Rise and Fall of Suburbia* (New York: Basic Books, 1987); T. Hartshorn and P. Muller, *Suburban Business Centers* (Washington, DC: U.S. Department of Commerce, Economic Development

Administration, 1986); C. Leinberger and C. Lockwood, How Business Is Reshaping America, *Atlantic Monthly,* Vol. 258, No. 4, pp. 43–51, 1986; C. Orski, Suburban Mobility: The Coming Transportation Crisis, *Transportation Quarterly,* Vol. 91, pp. 457–476, 1985.

4. Tysons Transportation Association, *The Future of Tysons Corner* (Reston, VA: KRS Associates, 1992).

5. Fairfax County Dulles Corridor Task Force, *Alternative Land Use Concepts* (Fairfax County, VA: 1994).

6. M. Parris, *The Rosslyn-Ballston Corridor: Early Visions* (Arlington County, VA: 1989); Arlington County, *General Land Use Plan: Adopted 1961 with Amendments Through 1990* (Arlington, VA: 1990).

7. Arlington County Department of Community Affairs, *Ballston Sector Plan* (Arlington County, VA: 1980).

8. R. Cervero, J. Landis, and Peter Hall, *Transit Joint Development in the United States* (Berkeley: Institute of Urban and Regional Development, University of California, Monograph 42, 1992).

9. R. Miller, Joint Development at Ballston Metro Center, *Urban Land,* Vol. 52, No. 6, pp. 22–24, 1993.

10. E. Abrams, Multihousing Submarkets, *Units,* Vol. 17, No. 2, pp. 18–21, 1993; E. Abrams, Transit Villages: Cities on the Move, *Units,* Vol. 18, No. 2, pp. 42–49, 1994.

11. JHK and Associates, *Development-Related Survey II* (Washington, DC: Washington Metropolitan Area Transit Authority, 1989).

12. R. Cervero, Rail Transit and Joint Development: Land Market Impacts in Washington, D.C. and Atlanta, *Journal of the American Planning Association,* Vol. 60, No. 1, pp. 83–94, 1994.

13. R. Klute, Redevelopment in Rosslyn Since 1992 (Arlington County, VA: Department of Community Planning, Housing and Development, 1995).

14. Arlington County, *Rosslyn Station Area Plan Addendum* (Arlington County, VA: 1992); Arlington County, *The Rosslyn Metro Block* (Arlington County, VA: 1994).

15. Parsons, Brinckerhoff, Quade, and Douglass, Robert Cervero, Howard/Stein-Hudson Associates, Jeffrey Zupan, and Douglas Porter, Case Study, *Topic 2 Report: Station Area Development* (Washington, DC: Transit Cooperative Research Program, Project H-1, Transportation Research Board, 1995). Douglas Porter was the principal author of this case study.

16. Montgomery County Planning Department, *North Bethesda-Garrett Park Master Plan* (Silver Spring, MD: Montgomery County Planning Department, 1992.)

17. Potomac Investment Properties, The Residences at Grosvenor Station: Grosvenor Metrorail Site Joint Development Prospectus (Washington, DC: 1994).

9

Southern California:
Transit Villages in the Heartland
of the Automobile

Emerging Transit Villages in Southern California

Holly Street Village (Pasadena)

Little Tokyo-Arts District (Los Angeles)

La Mesa (San Diego)

Barrio Logan (San Diego)

Rio Vista West (San Diego)

Metropolitan Los Angeles and San Diego are among the most auto-oriented regions in the country. In 1990, over 70 percent of Los Angeles County commuters drove alone to work, and only 6.7 percent used public transit.[1] San Diego County had a similar percentage of solo commuters in 1990 and an even smaller share of employed residents (3.2 percent) who rode public transit to work.

Yet, both Los Angeles and San Diego are today aggressively building rail transit systems, hoping to relieve worsening traffic congestion and restructure their cityscapes so they are more conducive to transit riding. Planning officials in both areas have adopted policies and approved plans that seek to direct future growth to within a quarter- to one-half-mile radius of existing and future rail stations. Impressive progress has been made, with transit-based housing and commercial projects already on the ground or in advanced preconstruction, ranging from stand-alone projects, such as Holly Street Village and Pacific Court in Los Angeles County, to much larger master planned, transit-oriented communities, such as Rio Vista West in San Diego.

It is not only the suburban landscape, but the inner city as well, that is being targeted for a transit village transformation. The Little Tokyo-Arts District transit village is envisaged as a mixed-income community with cottage industries, small shops, and artist lofts in what is currently a run-down area on the edge of downtown Los Angeles. The Barrio Logan transit village, already partially built, is transforming a decaying industrial district south of downtown San Diego into a closely knit, working-class neighborhood with new housing, a retail center, and a civic complex.

237

9.1 THE TRANSIT VILLAGE MOVEMENT IN LOS ANGELES

In 1991, less than 30 years after the Pacific Electric Railway ended interurban passenger services in southern California, the first segment of a light rail system, the Blue Line, opened between downtown Long Beach and downtown Los Angeles. Two years later, subway services began on the initial 4.4-mi leg of the Red Line, from Pershing Square in downtown Los Angeles to Westlake-MacArthur Park to the west. Nearly 200 mi of commuter rail service stretching from downtown Los Angeles to Orange County, Riverside, Ventura, and San Bernardino were added between 1992 and 1995. Slowly but steadily, an expansive network of light, heavy, and commuter rail tracks are being laid that, if all goes according to plans, will more than match the spatial coverage of southern California's great rail network of yesteryear (Map 9.1).

The Metrorail system is being accompanied by an ambitious campaign to steer new development into neighborhoods surrounding rail stops. The rail network, slated to cover some 400 directional mi over the next 30 years, (although limited funds have forced officials to scale back their plans, at least for now) has sparked public discourse and a flurry of interest in the transit village idea:

- [ ] The regional mass transit operator-builder, the Los Angeles Metropolitan Transportation Authority (MTA), commissioned station-area concept plans for 12 of the rail stations to open in the 1990s, in the Vermont corridor, Hollywood, and the San Fernando Valley.[2] A six-person in-house staff was established at MTA to aggressively pursue joint development–station-area development opportunities.
- [ ] The City of Los Angeles Planning Department adopted a land-use–transportation policy that directs 75 percent of all new residential growth onto 5 percent of the city's land, primarily within a one-quarter- to one-half-mile radius of rail stations and major bus stops (creating "transit-oriented districts"). The policy—a break with previous Los Angeles growth-management strategies—was adopted by the city council in November 1993 and sent to the Planning Department for inclusion in the city's General Plan.[3]
- [ ] The regional planning agency, the Southern California Association of Governments (SCAG), even introduced the transit village concept to outlying San Bernardino and Ventura Counties, sponsoring a series of seminars on designing transit villages around new commuter rail stations. Both counties—Ventura, 60 to 70 mi north of Los Angeles, and San Bernardino, 80 to 90 mi to the east—are now connected to downtown Los Angeles via Metrolink commuter rail service. SCAG's board believes that even in the far outreaches of southern California, with enough forethought and conviction, commuter rail stations can also sprout new transit-oriented communities.
- [ ] On April 8, 1993, an overflow crowd of more than 300 architects, developers, planners, and city officials gathered in the downtown Los Angeles Hilton Hotel for a symposium on "Designing Transit-Based Housing." Several of the city's

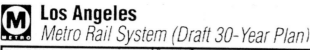

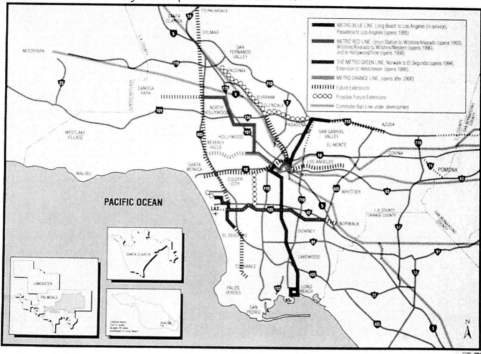

Map 9.1   Los Angeles Regional Rail Network. The Los Angeles regional rail network—heavy rail, light rail, and commuter rail—under construction is envisioned to reach over 400 mi by the year 2021.

leading design firms unveiled designs for new communities at the Vermont-Santa Monica, Willow Street, and El Monte rail transit stations. The *Los Angeles Times* and other local newspapers gave the event extensive coverage, and *Architecture* magazine followed up with a lengthy piece detailing each station design.[4]

In recent years, transit village concepts have moved from lofty discussions to actual implementation within Los Angeles County. Among the key projects that have moved forward are: two successful mixed housing-commercial developments, Pacific Court in downtown Long Beach and Holly Street Village in downtown Pasadena; Grand Central Market in downtown Los Angeles; and Union Station Gateway, a high-rise office-commercial complex at Metrorail's main transfer station (see Table 9.1). All are good examples of public-private partnerships. In each case, local governments assisted with financing.

TABLE 9.1

Transit-Based Developments: Los Angeles County, 1993–1995

Project	Station	Development	Year Completed
Pacific Court	Transit Mall (Long Beach)	142 apartments; 30,000 ft² retail; 16-screen theater	1992
Holly Street Village	Holly Street (Pasadena)	374 apartments; 11,000 ft² retail	1994
Grand Central Market	Pershing Square (Los Angeles)	121 apartments	1995
Union Station Gateway	Union Station (Los Angeles)	628,000-ft² MTA headquarters; bus plaza; rail depot	1995

9.1.1 Pacific Court

Pacific Court is as much a redevelopment-driven project as a transit-based housing project. Located one block from the Blue Line terminus in Long Beach, this $45 million complex features 142 upscale apartment units above two floors of retail (Photo 9.1). Connected to it is the Pine Court complex which includes a 16-screen AMC movie theater, additional shops, and a large food court (Photo 9.2).

The developer of Pacific Court-Pine Court, the Janss Company, has been active in the southern California real estate market since the early years of the century and, in more recent times, has begun specializing in mixed-use urban projects. The Janss Company was initially attracted to the downtown Long Beach site for two reasons: it is an urban site with potential market appeal to middle-class professionals seeking multifamily housing, and Long Beach's redevelopment agency was willing to provide significant public subsidies through writing down the cost of land acquisition and the issuance of tax-exempt financing. Pacific Court's residential component leased up quickly. This convinced Janss that there is a bonafide marketing advantage in locating near rail, even in southern California.

A recent survey revealed that Pacific Court's tenants indeed match the expected profile. In late 1994, 59 percent of the occupants worked in professional-managerial positions, 96 percent lived in one- or two-person households, and 60 percent of those households had either no car or one car available. Moreover, 42 percent worked in Long Beach and 13 percent in downtown Los Angeles. Ten percent commuted by public transit, a third more than the countywide average for employed residents.[5]

9.1.2 Holly Street Village

Encouraged by its success in Long Beach, Janss followed Pacific-Pine Court with Holly Street Village, a $56 million mixed-use project in downtown Pasadena containing 374

Photo 9.1   Pacific Court, Long Beach. An early transit-based project of 142 apartments on three stories of housing above ground-floor shops. The Blue Line train can be seen in the foreground.

Photo 9.2   Pine Court, Long Beach. Adjoining Pacific Court, the Pine Court complex features a multiplex cinema, assorted shops, and a popular food court.

apartments and 11,000 ft² of retail (Photo 9.3). The project is laced with an internal pathway network that ties housing to on-site retail and connects to the village square (Photo 9.4). Blended densities are approximately 55 units to the acre, a fairly compact housing project by southern California standards.

The Janss Corporation built Holly Street Village in close concert with both the Pasadena Redevelopment Agency and the MTA. The Blue Line extension from downtown Los Angeles to Pasadena is slated to be completed in the late 1990s, and Holly Street Village makes room for the future transit stop within the project itself. As shown in Photo 9.5, part of the project sits on top of the tracks reserved for the Blue Line extension.

Holly Street Village would not have been built without direct public subsidies. The Pasadena Redevelopment Agency contributed $6.9 million in low-interest loans, as well as $7.2 million in tax-exempt bonds through the formation of a Community Facilities District. The MTA provided $1.9 million in grants to fund the construction of the transit station. The downstream rewards to the city will be viable in-town housing and higher property tax receipts, and MTA can expect to benefit from the additional patronage produced by an integrated rail-housing project.

Photo 9.3   Main Entrance to Holly Street Village Pasadena. 374 apartments and 11,000 ft² of retail lie near the planned rail stop on the Pasadena extension. Holly Street Village was built in anticipation of the rail extension, expected to start operations in the late 1990s.

Photo 9.4 Interior Square in Holly Street Village.

9.1.3 Grand Central Square

Grand Central Square, across the street from the Pershing Square Red Line station in downtown Los Angeles, has similarly relied on assistance from the local redevelopment agency as well as MTA. Grand Central Square is composed of Grand Central Market, the Million Dollar Theater, and the Million Dollar Office Building.

When it opened in 1917, Grand Central Market was a fashionable marketplace for the wealthy living in nearby Bunker Hill, and a year later, the adjacent Million Dollar Theater opened as one of America's grand baroque movie palaces. The 12-story Million Dollar Building above the theater was a prestigious address, housing the powerful Metropolitan Water District.

Over the years, though, as wealthy residents moved out, the theater and market lost their luster, attracting lower income clientele and becoming a hangout for transients. After the

Photo 9.5 Holly Street Village: An Air-Rights Housing Project. The close physical integration of the project and the planned Blue Line extension guarantees that rail transit will be a prominent element of Holly Street Village for years to come.

Water District left in 1963, the office structure stayed largely vacant. By the 1980s, the neighborhood had become a mix of liquor stores, pawnshops, check-cashing outlets, and cheap hotels.

The developer of Grand Central Square, Ira Yellin, sees the neighborhood in a totally different light. To him, Grand Central Square is poised to become a bohemian residential district similar to New York's Greenwich Village or Denver's lower downtown: a lively, arts-oriented urban environment with a mix of incomes and cultures. "Broadway can become a real city walk," Yellin tells the *Los Angeles Times* as he unveiled a $64 million redevelopment project for the area consisting of 121 apartments, offices, loft space, retail shops, and a refurbished Grand Central Market.

One- and two-bedroom apartments are to occupy the upper floors of the six-story Homer Laughlin Building above Grand Central Market. In the 12-story Million Dollar Building next door, apartments will rise above ground-floor retail shops and the Million Dollar Theater. The adjacent Lyon Building on Hill Street will include 20,000 ft^2 of office space. Apartments will range from subsidized units for low- and moderate-income residents to market-rate units. Yellin tells the *Times* that the project will attract a range of tenants from downtown professionals to poor immigrants dependent on buses and subways to get around.

Despite Yellin's enthusiasm, he was unable to obtain financing for the project after leasing the land from the redevelopment agency in 1990. By 1990, the downtown office market had collapsed, and Yellin's meticulously restored Bradbury Building nearby was 60 percent unoccupied. It did not help matters that previous efforts to build market-rate housing on Bunker Hill in the 1970s and 1980s were largely unsuccessful.

Nevertheless, the redevelopment agency, determined to turn around this blighted part of downtown, stepped in to help with the financing, along with the MTA. The agency and MTA each agreed to guarantee half of the $13.5 million of taxable bonds and $26.5 million of tax-exempt bonds. The tax-exempt bonds primarily funded the construction of housing, whereas the taxable debt is being used to finance those portions deemed to be commercial or retail related. MTA also secured a $1.78 million federal grant to design and construct a walkway from the project to the nearby station portal. Edward Soja, former head of UCLA's urban planning school, has noted that proximity to transit may be the wild card that helps Grand Central Square succeed where other downtown residential projects have failed. But Soja cautions that the value of transit for a downtown Los Angeles residential complex may not be of significance until the system is completed some 30 years in the future.[6]

9.1.4 Union Station Gateway

The last of Los Angeles County's recently built transit-based projects, Union Station Gateway, lies several blocks east of Grand Central Market on the outskirts of downtown. Union Station is the downtown terminus of Metrolink commuter rail service. Trains from Orange County, Riverside, San Bernardino, and the other suburban counties converge on Union Station. The station is also a stop on the Red Line subway and Blue Line LRT.

Opened in 1939, Union Station is the last of the great train stations built in the United States. It is an imposing blend of architectural styles: mission, modern, art deco and Moorish. The surrounding area, though, is a hodgepodge of empty lots, surface parking, light manufacturing, and warehouses.

Union Station is *the* intermodal station for the Metrorail system. In the late 1980s, the MTA presented a plan for a refurbished and expanded Union Station, proposing a 50-acre pedestrian-oriented, mixed-use project that includes 7 million ft^2 of buildings. The project, to be phased over 25 years, extends from Union Station at the western edge of the site to a bus plaza on the east, featuring several office towers, including the new headquarters for MTA and a portal building that will serve as a gateway for the mass transit systems.

The transit improvements, collectively known as the Gateway Transit Center (shown in rendering in Figure 9.1), will include the Bus Plaza, a collector for buses coming off six nearby freeways; the East Portal Pavilion, a semicircular "mixing bowl" for commuters changing from bus-commuter rail to subway-light rail; and a park-and-ride facility, providing up to 2500 spaces adjacent to downtown freeways (encouraging commuters to park and use transit to circulate around downtown).

Figure 9.1 Union Station Gateway Center, Los Angeles. The historic Union Station in downtown Los Angeles is the site of the Gateway Center, a high-rise office and retail complex. Union Station is the terminus of each of the commuter rail lines, as well as a stop for the Red Line subway and Blue Line rail, and numerous bus routes.

In early 1996, the 628,000-ft^2 MTA headquarter building was nearing completion, as were two of the three Gateway Transit Center elements: the Bus Plaza and the East Portal Pavilion. The Department of Water & Power recently decided to move its headquarters to Union Station, and a new 540,000-ft^2 DWP building began construction in mid-1996.[7] Other plans are in the works for developing 16 of the 18 remaining sites in the project area, to be occupied by mid-rise housing, an entertainment complex, and additional commercial and retail space. However, financing has yet to be obtained for moving these additions forward.

9.2 TRANSIT VILLAGES AND COMMUNITY REDEVELOPMENT

In Los Angeles, the building of the new rail system has been seized by local planners as an opportunity for reversing the misfortunes of two depressed inner-city neighborhoods, Westlake-MacArthur Park and Little Tokyo-Arts District. Compact, mixed-use transit villages have been proposed in both neighborhoods, although their experiences provide contrasting lessons: Westlake-MacArthur Park reveals the difficulties of financing urban transit villages, short of huge public subsidies, and Little Tokyo-Arts District portrays the opportunities presented by some inner-city locations.

9.2.1 Westlake-MacArthur Park

Through the 1950s and early 1960s, the Westlake-MacArthur Park district of central Los Angeles was a popular recreational area and weekend destination, centered around its turquoise lake and colorful rowboats. By the late 1980s, though, the park and its surroundings had become a crowded, unattractive urban district noted for its population of poor immigrant households, run-down apartment buildings, formerly grand houses transformed into six-plexes, and a subculture of crime and drug dealing common to center-city areas.

The Westlake-MacArthur Park rail station, located directly across from the park and lake, was the first subway stop outside of downtown Los Angeles to open. Civic leaders held high hopes that the new station would be a catalyst to positive change. The MTA called upon several architectural firms, led by Kaplan McLaughlin Diaz (KMD), to design a mixed-use project for its property and the parcels adjacent to it. The subway station, community backers hoped, would spur the construction of new shops and theaters, a police substation, an open-air plaza, and good quality affordable housing, promoting both economic development and public safety in the process.

In a narrative accompanying its design, a KMD architect waxed poetic on the proposed transit village:

> Please step briefly into the year 2000 and share the experience of the village center at Westlake. From an apartment picture window above the village center at Westlake one sees the bustling activity below. Busy shoppers weave their way through the subway riders rising and descending through the portals in the Transit Plaza. Pushcart vendors and artisans barter with shoppers and attract gazers. The lines are starting to form at the cinema (among the five movies currently running, they're showing a vintage cut of "Blade Runner").[8]

The narrative goes on, even more enthusiastically:

> The village center at Westlake sits atop the Westlake/MacArthur Park Station of the Metro Red Line. It bustles with activity around the clock. It's a transportation hub and teems with a ceaseless stream of bus and subway riders descending into the Red Line Station, ascending from the Red Line Station making connections, waiting for buses, and being dropped at the Kiss-and-Ride curb. . . . The village center at Westlake is the energetic and vibrant 'heart' of the community. It hums with vendors, shops, and other commercial activity. The shops and services are arranged to overlook a series of plazas and paseos that are the neighborhood's major meeting places, offering neighborhood residents a community 'living room' where friends meet to exchange news over coffee and families come to see movies and shop in the market.

The MacArthur Park transit village received a boost in 1993 when a national development firm, Forest City Developers, committed to the project, which by then had grown to 220 housing units and 50,000 ft^2 of medical-commercial uses. Los Angeles-based McLarand Vasquez & Partners was hired as the project's master designers. Figure 9.2 depicts McLarand Vasquez's rendering of the project. The McLarand Vasquez plan was well received by MTA and the neighborhood.

In early 1995, however, Forest City abandoned the project, after several years' effort and with nothing built, in disagreement over the level of public support. Project financial consultants reported market conditions for retail, commercial, and residential construction in the immediate neighborhood to be very weak. Considerable public subsidies would be needed not only for the residential units but also for the costly up-front public infrastructure (e.g., the plaza, structured parking) and land assemblage (combining four privately owned parcels with the MTA land). With the subway system only minimally built, the presence of rail was not yet sufficient to dramatically increase station-area property values or market demand. Private investors wanted the public sector to absorb a far greater share of the upstream financial risks than public officials seemed willing to take on. Today, the future of the once promising Westlake-MacArthur Park redevelopment project remains uncertain.

9.2.2 Little Tokyo-Arts District

Although Westlake-MacArthur Park has stalled, Little Tokyo-Arts District is moving forward in what by all appearances is the most promising transit village opportunity in Los Angeles. Presently, the Little Tokyo-Arts District station area is thinly developed with a hodgepodge of light manufacturing, repair shops, warehouses, taverns, empty buildings, vacant lots, and a smattering of artist live-work quarters. The rail station is part of the Eastline subway extension from the current Union Station stop to Boyle Heights and East Los Angeles, scheduled to open in the year 2000.

Several factors combine to make this a promising site. First, ownership of the land within a quarter-mile station radius is concentrated among two landowners, MTA and Catellus Development Corporation, one of the nation's leading commercial developers and owner of an 11-acre site immediately adjacent to the station. Thus, there should be no land assemblage obstacles to project development. Second, neighborhood and community groups are united in wanting to densify the area, both to increase safety and bring in new business opportunities. Most of all, real estate brokers see the existing artists' community, and the potential for creating a lively and colorful urban neighborhood, as a promising niche market.

An initial transit village plan for the area has been drawn up by local architect Ted Tanaka. It envisions the station as a new bohemia: an "arts-oriented urban village," in Tanaka's terms, featuring a rich and finely grained mixture of artist-loft residential, commercial, and light industrial uses. In the *Urban Design* report for the Little Tokyo-Arts District project, Tanaka calls for an urban milieu sometime around the year 2000 that would

Figure 9.2 Westlake–MacArthur Park, Los Angeles. Transit Village rendering by architect Ernesto Vasquez, showing an open-air mercado leading to the village core.

have "a bevy of activity centered around newly restored historic structures and new development in a unique theme of L.A.'s celebration of the Arts."[9] His vision of the open plaza above the Little Tokyo-Arts District station, lined with flowering plum trees, is shown in Figure 9.3. The objective is to create a pedestrian environment that is just as pleasing and secure to commence and complete a journey as a pedestrian as it is for a train passenger.

The first stage of implementing the Little Tokyo-Arts District transit village is the consolidation of Catellus and MTA land into a single master planned development, which is currently being undertaken. This is to be followed by a site planning process and site design. Based on an assumed allowable increase in FAR of 3:1, the combined Catellus-MTA property could accommodate up to 7 million ft^2 of such mixed activities as art studios, retail shops, restaurants, entertainment centers, and residential-loft space.

Little Tokyo-Arts District is a departure from inner-city revitalization approaches in Los Angeles in its village scale and focus and in its mixes of income, home ownership, and public space. It is also a departure in its use of the transit station to stimulate commercial activities and enhance public safety, outcomes that have eluded previous inner-city redevelopment projects in Los Angeles.

The Little Tokyo-Arts District stands in particular contrast to the adjacent high-rise Little Tokyo redevelopment projects currently under way: the 2.7-million-ft^2 mixed-use Mangrove Development and the 1.9-million-ft^2 First Street South Development Project. Little

Figure 9.3 Proposed Pedestrian Plaza Outside the Little Tokyo-Arts District Station. The station-area design plan calls for an attractive pedestrian plaza linked with the streets and spaces leading from the station to workplaces, shops, and entertainment centers. One of the most effective features of the planned streetscape design is the proposed planting of flowering plum trees on both sides of the street connecting the station to the heart of Little Tokyo.

Tokyo-Arts District is redevelopment as focused community building rather than high-security, high-profile commercial enterprises that maximize returns to the private investors and city coffers. Little Tokyo-Arts District also stands in contrast to the expansive public housing projects in nearby east Los Angeles and south central Los Angeles, marginalized low-income communities that have been economically abandoned and that stand as monuments to the welfare statism of mid-20th-century liberalism in California.

9.3 SAN DIEGO'S TRANSIT VILLAGE MOVEMENT

The transit village experiences in San Diego have a longer history than those in Los Angeles, but they embody many of the same themes: the importance of a proactive local government and transit authority, an inner-city transit village that departs from traditional urban renewal-entitlement programs, and a master planned suburban transit village (Rio Vista West) that has gone through several design iterations in response to market shifts and local government concerns.

Since the late 1980s, the city of San Diego and the regional transit authority, the Metropolitan Transit Development Board (MTDB), have pursued an aggressive campaign to promote transit-oriented development. Conferences and community workshops have been held, design guidelines have been prepared, and specific station-area plans have been approved, all in hopes of strengthening the bond between rail transit and community development in the region.[10] The city of San Diego has formally adopted a policy endorsing "transit-oriented developments," the purpose of which is "to direct growth into compact neighborhood patterns of development, where living and working environments are within walkable distances. This development pattern is designed to support the substantial public investment in transit systems, and result in regional environmental and fiscal benefits over the long term."[11]

The 1981 opening of the San Diego Trolley marked the first light rail line built in the United States in over two decades. The inaugural 15.9-mi segment from downtown San Diego to the Mexican border was built quickly, cheaply, and without federal help. A decade later, the South Line was augmented by the 17.3-mi East Line to El Cajon and more recently a new Bayshore extension that skirts the waterfront west of downtown. Rail is highly popular among voters in the region, and the system continues to expand. Map 9.2 shows the trolley lines that existed in 1995 and those planned for coming years. By 1996, the East Line was extended by three stops to Santee's central district, a $114 million, 3.6-mi project. Also, a 3.2-mi North Line extension was completed that connected the central business district with San Diego's Old Town, one of the city's primary tourist destinations and the terminus of the commuter rail service, linking the city to the affluent suburbs of north San Diego County.

Ready to begin construction soon is the $240 million Mission Valley West Line. Mission Valley has grown rapidly in recent years, the recipient of two regional shopping malls, sev-

Regional Transit
Information:
233-3004

Mission Valley West Segment
"Opening By Late 1997"

Old Town Segment

See Centre City Inset

Santee

El Cajon

La Mesa

Lemon Grove

East Line

San Diego

Coronado

South Line

National City

Chula Vista

Imperial Beach

← **North Line**

C Street

Harbor Drive

Bayside

12th Avenue

Centre City

0   2.5   5 Miles
N   Approximate Scale

TIJUANA

San Diego Trolley *mts*

●━○ Trolley Stations
▬▬ Trolley Lines in Operation
■■■■ Trolley Lines Under Construction

Centre City
1 Imperial & 12th Transfer Station SP
2 Market & 12th
3 City College
4 Fifth Avenue
5 Civic Center
6 America Plaza Transfer Station SP
7 Seaport
8 Convention Center West
9 Gaslamp/Convention Center
10 Santa Fe Depot
11 County Ctr/Little Italy

South Line
S1 Barrio Logan   S12 San Ysidro/Int'l Border
S2 Harborside
S3 Pacific Fleet
S4 8th Street P
S5 24th Street P
S6 Bayfront/E St. P
S7 H Street P
S8 Palomar St. P
S9 Palm Avenue P
S10 Iris Avenue P
S11 Beyer Blvd. P

East Line
E1 25th & Commercial   E12 El Cajon Transit Center P
E2 32nd & Commercial   E13 Arnele P
E3 47th Street P   E14 Weld P
E4 Euclid Avenue P   E15 Santee Town Center P
E5 Encanto/62nd St. P
E6 Massachusetts Ave. P
E7 Lemon Grove Depot
E8 Spring Street P
E9 La Mesa Blvd.
E10 Grossmont Center P   SP = Pay Parking
E11 Amaya Drive P   P = Parking

Map 9.2   San Diego Trolley Network. The first of the 1980s light rail systems, San Diego regional rail started with 33.2 mi of track in 1981 and expanded to 33 mi by 1990. With the popularity of rail, the system was recently extended to Santee to the east (3.6 mi) and Old Town to the north (3.2 mi). The Mission Valley extension is currently under construction.

eral campus-style office parks, and San Diego's Jack Murphy Stadium. (The MTDB plans to open the line in time for the 1998 NFL Super Bowl.) Mission Valley is also slated for the region's most ambitious transit village initiative. To effectively serve transit-oriented development, the Mission Valley alignment crosses the San Diego River three times in order to site development on the flat valley floors and preserve the sensitive hillsides that define the valley. Whereas earlier trolley lines were aligned mainly along abandoned freight rail lines and freeway corridors to minimize land acquisition costs, San Diego officials have opted to align the Mission Valley corridor so as to maximize development potential, even if it means inflating the project's cost. The Mission Valley vision of transit village development appears well on its way to becoming a reality. Since 1982, when the Mission Valley extension was first proposed, the corridor has seen the addition of over 7,000 new housing units, 2,375 new hotel rooms, 1,585 million ft² of retail space, and some 5.9 million ft² of office inventory.[12] This is despite the fact that San Diego's economy has been hard hit by recession and military cutbacks since 1990.

The current inventory of transit-based developments in San Diego County is listed in Table 9.2. It spans three types of projects: transit-based housing along the La Mesa-El Cajon Line, commercial joint development in downtown San Diego, and initiatives to create transit-oriented communities, with Barrio Logan and Rio Vista West being the farthest along.

9.3.1 Transit-Based Housing

To date, the county's transit-based housing has been concentrated in the city of La Mesa. Two projects, Villages of La Mesa and La Mesa Village Plaza, were spearheaded by the La Mesa Redevelopment Agency in the interest of producing compact, transit-oriented housing units that were predominantly market rate. Another project, Creekside Villas in the city of San Diego, was similarly sponsored by a redevelopment authority, although all units there are priced below market rate.

Villages of La Mesa, which opened in 1989, is a 384-unit, two- and three-story apartment project on 19 acres adjacent to the La Mesa-Amaya station (see Photo 9.6). The La Mesa Redevelopment Agency assembled the land for the project and funded $2.75 million in local infrastructure costs using tax increment financing. Once Villages of La Mesa was designed, the MTDB relocated the station site and traded land with the developer to ensure better station access for residents and others walking to the station. Though a redevelopment-driven project, Villages of La Mesa has been targeted at young professionals and singles—80 percent of the apartments are market-rate units, and the project boasts a pool, tennis courts, and a recreational room. As shown in Table 9.3, the project has succeeded in attracting its intended market—43 percent of its tenants have professional-managerial jobs and the majority are 17 to 34 years of age. Over half of the households, moreover, earn more than $40,000 per year, approximately the median annual household income for the region.

TABLE 9.2

Transit-Based Developments: San Diego, 1988–1996

Project	Station	Development	Year Completed
Transit-Based Housing			
Villages of La Mesa	La Mesa-Amaya	384 apartments	1989
La Mesa Village Plaza	La Mesa Blvd.	99 condos/retail	1991
Creekside Villas	47th Street	144 apartments	1989
Commercial Joint Development			
American Plaza	American Plaza	34-story office structure; 272-room hotel; museum and retail	1991
MTDB Headquarters	Imperial & 12th	180,000-ft² office	1988
Transit-Oriented Communities			
Mercado	Barrio Logan	144 apartments 100,000-ft² commercial center	1992 1996–1997
Rio Vista West	Rio Vista	240 apartments (phase 1); 240 condominiums (phase 2); up to 1000 residential units	1996 1996–1997

La Mesa Village Plaza, a mid-rise project with 99 condominium units, ground-floor retail, and 20,000 ft² of office space adjacent to the Spring Street station, opened in 1991 (Photo 9.7). The complex is strongly oriented to the trolley stop; disembarking passengers exit onto a small plaza with shops, restaurants, and services on three sides (Photo 9.8). After assembling the 5.4-acre site, the La Mesa Redevelopment Agency issued several RFPs in the late 1980s soliciting compact, mixed-use projects. When several proposed developments fell through due to lack of financing, the agency significantly discounted the land costs. La Mesa Village Plaza is also a mix of 80 percent market-rate and 20 percent subsidized units. It has attracted a large cohort of empty nesters and retirees. Over half of its tenants are more than 65 years of age.

Within San Diego's city limits along the El Cajon-La Mesa corridor is Creekside Villas, a 144-unit garden-style apartment spread over 12 acres that opened in 1989. Also lever-aged as a redevelopment project, in contrast to the other two projects, Creekside Villas offers almost exclusively below-market-rate housing. This is reflected by its lower income

Photo 9.6 Villages of La Mesa, San Diego. There are 384 units on 19 acres adjacent to the La Mesa-Amaya station.

TABLE 9.3

Tenant and Ridership Characteristics of Transit-Based Housing, San Diego County, 1993–1994

	Average Household Size (Persons/HH)	Percent of Tenants			Percent of Households			Percent Trips by Trolley	
		Age (Years)		Professional-White-Collar Jobs[1]	No. of Cars		Income > $40,000 Per Year	Work Trips	All Trips
		17–34	>50		0	1			
Villages of La Mesa	2.1	60.6	20.4	67.9	2.7	52.0	50.7	12.4	10.8
La Mesa Village Plaza	1.7	8.6	87.9	77.8	0.0	47.1	40.8	7.1	7.7
Creekside Villas	3.5	46.2	7.7	38.5	33.3	55.6	11.1	36.4	35.5
Mercado	4.5	54.6	4.5	7.4	7.7	76.9	0.0	12.5	14.1

[1]White-collar employment includes positions as managers, administrators, professionals, clerical workers, secretaries, accountants, and information processing.

Source: V. Menotti and R. Cervero, *Transit-Based Housing in California: Profiles* (Berkeley, Institute of Urban and Regional Development, University of California, Working Paper 638, 1995).

Photo 9.7 La Mesa Village Plaza, San Diego. A mixed-use project, featuring 99 residential units and ground-level retail and office development, flanking the La Mesa Boulevard trolley station.

tenant composition. Nearly all of its tenants are African-Americans or Latinos, and most of its households have young children.

Table 9.3 shows that the three rail-based housing projects along the El Cajon-La Mesa corridor have succeeded in drawing residents to rail transit to varying degrees. Over a third of all trips by Creekside Villas residents are by light rail, partly reflecting the more transit-dependent demographics of the project. Rail modal shares at the other two transit-based projects, if modest by the standards of older east coast cities, are still five to six times higher than among the general population in San Diego—from the 1990 census, fewer than 1 percent of all work trips in San Diego County were by rail.

9.3.2 Commercial Joint Development

To date, most commercial-office development in the San Diego region has turned its back on the trolley, opting instead for campus-style office and business parks off freeways north of downtown. The alignment of the south and east trolley lines along least-cost right of ways, often using preexisting freight lines, has suppressed the system's commercial development potential.[13] While the 103-acre Grossmont Center shopping complex was opened in 1989 next to a trolley station in La Mesa, the center is unabashedly an auto-oriented mall whose only real connection to the trolley seems to be that some light rail

Photo 9.8   An Easy Connection from the Trolley to La Mesa Village Plaza. Technically, La Mesa Village Plaza is not a transit-oriented development (TOD) since its planning and program predate the planning of the extension of the San Diego Trolley by several years. But the site design and building orientations were subsequently altered to incorporate the transit stop into the project.

commuters use its massive parking lot to park-and-ride. In downtown San Diego, however, the trolley has a strong presence, and all agree it has been an important factor in revitalizing the city core and anchoring businesses that might otherwise have moved out (about 12 percent of downtown San Diego workers use rail transit during peak commuting hours.) It was without question the decisive factor behind the redevelopment of the Broadway-Kettner and Imperial-12th Street station areas.

Presently, downtown San Diego boasts two showcase transit-based commercial towers, America Plaza and the MTDB headquarters, both of which are distinguished by trolley stops built directly into their structures. America Plaza, located two blocks from San Diego's bustling waterfront, is particularly striking in its station design, sunlit trolley platform, and redevelopment role (Photo 9.9). As the Broadway-Kettner station's flagship project, the 912,000-ft^2 mixed-use high-rise features the 34-story America Plaza Tower, a 272-room hotel, the San Diego Museum of Contemporary Art, and ground-level specialty retail and restaurants. Architecturally integrated into the building, the Broadway-Kettner trolley station occupies center stage. Designed with an eye to the grand train stations of Europe, it features a crescent-shaped glass and steel canopy, banners, and public art (Photo

Photo 9.9 American Plaza. The main tower, consisting of a luxury hotel, is the city's tallest. Together, the mix of hotel space with ground-level shops, restaurants, and a museum has produced a "vertical" transit village of sorts in downtown San Diego.

9.10). Nearly four-fifths of the $5.2 million capital cost for the station was funded by the project's developer, Starboard Development Corporation.

American Plaza is one of the few integrated commercial developments in southern California that required no direct public assistance, riding on the inherent benefits of great transit access and quality design for its financial success. Prior to project construction, the land that America Plaza now sits on was a partially vacant city block, known as the Tower Bowl site, surrounded by a scattering of decaying two- and three-story commercial buildings. The project went through several iterations from 1986 to its completion in November 1991. In March 1987, Starboard Development unveiled its first plans, a 365-room hotel fronting on Broadway (downtown's main street) and only secondarily including a major office structure. By June of the next year, the project had been redesigned to accom-

Photo 9.10 The Trolley Station Lives Within American Plaza. The trolley line slices through the heart of the building. The brightly lit station platform makes for a pleasant setting to wait for a train.

modate Great American First Savings Bank as the lead tenant as well as a business center. Great American Savings subsequently collapsed in the early 1990s, but the project went forward. In November 1991, the 34-story American Plaza opened as the city's tallest building, complete with a four-story atrium entry and 40-ft-high waterfall.

Downtown San Diego's other significant commercial air-rights development is at the Imperial and 12th Street transfer station. Half of the first two floors of the 180,000-ft² 10-story office building houses the intermodal transfer station. The enclosed station opens onto the building's lobby, which contains several retail shops and eateries. Named in honor of James B. Mills, a former state representative who was a staunch supporter of local transit interests, the building serves as the headquarters for MTDB and its subsidiary, San Diego Trolley. Next to the office structure is an open plaza, a multideck parking structure, and a 16-story clock tower. The $43.6 million project was a coventure between Starboard Development Corporation and the MTDB. MTDB provided the land and transit infrastructure, and Starboard financed the building construction under a cost-sharing agreement. By siting the air-rights project on the fringe of downtown, MTDB hoped to accelerate the redevelopment of what historically has been a transition zone. The local recession has stalled redevelopment plans, though the Imperial-12th Street station has emerged as an active transit node, handling over 5000 passenger boardings and alightings per day.

9.3.3 Transit-Oriented Communities

Much larger transit-oriented developments have also recently broken ground in the San Diego region: an inner-city transit village, the Mercado at Barrio Logan, and a suburban transit village, Rio Vista West in Mission Valley. An even larger development, Otay Ranch—a 23,000-unit master planned community in the foothills of south San Diego County that is to have 12 "transit village centers"—is currently stalled, a victim of the local recession and a continuing disagreement over how the costs for extending the trolley will be apportioned.[14]

9.3.3.1 Mercado at Barrio Logan   The Barrio Logan transit station lies in a lower income, predominantly Mexican-American neighborhood just south of downtown San Diego on the line to Tijuana. Once the center of the Mexican-American community in San Diego, Barrio Logan was divided in the 1950s and 1960s by a combination of local planning policies and superhighways. Through its zoning policies, the city promoted industrial growth to take advantage of the area's proximity to the waterfront. In addition, Interstate 5 and the San Diego-Coronado Bridge, built during the late 1960s and early 1970s, severed the community.

Although the trolley stop opened in the early 1980s, nothing really happened until the Barrio Logan Redevelopment Project Area was designated in 1991. The redevelopment plan, drawn up by the San Diego Redevelopment Agency and MTDB, proposed a multiphased mixed-use project, only partially implemented at this time, that would involve significant up-front infrastructure investments. The project's first phase, completed in 1992, is the colorful Mercado Apartments with 144 units of "affordable housing," targeted at families earning between $14,000 and $25,000 annually (Photo 9.11). Mercado's low-income, transit-dependent tenant makeup is reflected in Table 9.3. In late 1994, around one in seven of all trips made by Mercado residents were by the San Diego Trolley, a remarkable capture rate given that over 90 percent of Mercado households have cars available.

A creative financing package was crafted to make the project work, involving both private lenders and local housing and economic development agencies: the San Diego Housing Trust Fund, the San Diego Housing Commission, the Centre City Development

Photo 9.11 Mercado Apartments, San Diego. The Mercado Apartments, 144 units, is the first stage of a transit village designed for this inner-city station.

Corporation, and the San Diego Redevelopment Agency. Forty percent of the $12.3 million project costs were absorbed through state and federal tax credits provided under the California Equity Municipal Bond Fund.

The second phase, which began construction in 1995, is the 100,000-ft² Mercado Commercial Center. When completed, the center will be anchored by a supermarket and supplemented by specialty retail and sidewalk vendors selling their wares in a public marketplace. In addition, a Mexican-American cultural museum and community college extension classrooms are planned.

Like the housing component, the Mercado Commercial Center will also depend on a considerable amount of up-front public investment. The redevelopment agency consolidated assorted small parcels for the project and wrote down the cost of the land. Federal community block grants, channeled through the city, are financing part of the predevelopment cost, and Economic Development Initiative funding is providing loans for small businesses.[15]

The Mercado Apartments and the Mercado Commercial Center are located within a block of each other, but some 330 yd from the transit station. The intervening property is largely vacant and weed strewn. MTDB plans to link the housing and commercial center to the station through a large public plaza and a built-up corridor lined with a community police office, a day-care center, a restaurant, and several two- and three-story office build-

CREATIVE FINANCING
OF A TRANSIT VILLAGE—BARRIO LOGAN

The $12.3 million project was financed through a combination of public and private sources. The deal was negotiated between six equity partners under a variety of terms. Key was the provision of tax credits in addition to public assistance with land assemblage, deferral of fee payments, subordination of loans, and the provision of up-front infrastructure improvements. Barrio Logan demonstrates that vested interests can get together and hammer out a cost-risk sharing arrangement with the prospects of ideally sharing in the downstream rewards. The financial package agreed upon by all parties that gave Barrio Logan the green light is itemized below.

Funding Source	Funding-Loan Amount	Share	Terms
Private Financing			
☐ American Savings Bank	$2,800,000	22.9%	30-year loan, 8.75%, fully amortizing
☐ Federal Home Loan	$800,000	6.5%	40-year loan, 3%, interest only, residual receipts
☐ Affordable Housing Program Tax Credits (Local Initiative Support Corporation, California Equity Fund)	$5,100,000	41.6%	Equity investment
Subtotal	$8,700,000	71.0%	
Public Financing			
☐ San Diego Housing Commission/Trust Fund	$1,425,000	11.6%	30-year loan, 6% residual receipts, forgivable on sale
☐ San Diego Redevelopment Agency/Centre City Development Corporation	$1,966,200	16.0%	Land write-down, subsidy
☐ City of San Diego	$161,000	1.4%	Development fee deferral
Subtotal	$3,552,200	29.0%	
Total	$12,252,200	100.0%	

ings. Day care is viewed as particularly vital in attracting parents to transit commuting by allowing them to consolidate day-care and work trips at a single stop. Presently, five child-care facilities lie within 500 ft of San Diego Trolley stops as a result of MTDB's active promotion.

9.3.3.2 Rio Vista West

In contrast to Barrio Logan, Rio Vista West is a very suburban transit village, an over 1000-unit residential community planned at one of the nine stations being built along the Mission Valley Line. The 95 acres surrounding the station are owned by a single developer, CalMat Properties. In 1992, encouraged by the city of San Diego to follow the newly adopted city TOD guidelines, CalMat hired Peter Calthorpe to assist in designing a suburban community of higher density housing, narrower tree-lined streets, and a central village area that leads directly to the rail station. The resulting master plan incorporates over $200 million in mixed-use development to be built over 7 to 10 years, including 1017 housing units, 325,000 ft^2 of retail uses, and 165,000 ft^2 of office space, all oriented around the future rail station.

In announcing the project in 1993, CalMat's press release stated: "The goal is to return to the basic qualities of older neighborhoods with more narrow, tree-lined streets organized in grid patterns to provide pleasant opportunities for people to comfortably walk or ride their bikes to public transit, shopping, entertainment and work destinations." However, reviewing the project in December 1994, *San Diego Union Tribune* architectural critic noted that, although the idea of walkable neighborhoods and houses may sound appealing, "it's the sprawling suburbs with their cul-de-sacs, single-family homes and gated entrances that have come to be viewed as the antidote for urban angst." Even CalMart's project director, Donald Cerone, admitted to the *Union Tribune* that he lived off of a traditional suburban cul-de-sac in San Diego County and loved it.[16] "The problem is that the suburban lifestyle is very popular and successful in Southern California," Doug Boyd, president of T&B Planning Consultants, told the *Union Tribune*. "People like to live on a cul-de-sac with a park across the street, and they've been willing to drive long distances in traffic to have that kind of lifestyle."

With southern California's economic downturn, Rio Vista West stalled in 1993. When it revved up again in 1995, it took on a decidedly different look, one with a conventional auto-oriented, suburban character. Rather than the small-scale shops and restaurants on cozy streets, the project's first phase was a big-box "category-killer" complex (anchored by Office Depot), engulfed in a 1038-space parking lot. This big-box phase provided immediate project income, seen by the development team as necessary to enable subsequent residential components to move forward.

Still, even if compromised, Rio Vista West retains transit village elements that differentiate it from the traditional suburban tract development and that abet transit use. A Spanish-style retail center surrounded by an open-air plaza is still planned for the trolley node itself (Figure 9.4). The first 240 homes, scheduled to come on line in 1996, are 600 to 700 ft from the station, in three-story structures, at blended densities of 33 units per acre—

Figure 9.4 Rio Vista West, San Diego. Rendering of the open-air plaza at the trolley stop, one of nine stations being built on the Mission Valley Line. The 1,000-plus unit residential community is to be transit-oriented in its design and character.

well above the surrounding suburban densities of 4 to 5 units per acre. A second residential phase of 240 condominium units is scheduled to break ground in quick sequence. Developer Cerone believes the housing will lease up and sell in a relatively short time and emphasizes that transit proximity is only one of several site advantages: "The site might well work without transit; with its proximity to the river and the other amenities of Mission Valley." In his view, the value of the transit link will appear mainly over time as the system expands and traffic congestion steadily worsens.

9.4 BUILDING TRANSIT VILLAGES IN THE LAND OF AUTOMOBILITY

In April 1995, a "Transit-Based Housing" symposium was held in San Diego, and as with the similar symposium in Los Angeles 2 years earlier, an overflow crowd of architects, planners, and developers gathered to discuss and debate the issues. In part, this crowd reflects the continued recession that has stubbornly hung on in southern California since 1990, sharply cutting into jobs among architectural, planning, and most of all, development firms, setting everyone in a scramble for work. With no significant office construction or retail (outside of big-box centers), the building and design professionals have turned to transit-based housing partly as a possible source of new work. Still, there was genuine excitement in the air about the prospects of creating new urban forms that draw people onto the streets and reduce the need to drive so much.

When people got into the details of building transit-oriented communities in specific neighborhoods, it became clear that the transit village movement must overcome a number of strong obstacles in the San Diego region. Foremost are residents' and developers' perceptions and biases about transit service, safety, and the desirability of transit customers. In a recent regional travel survey, a large number of respondents in the service area of the San Diego Trolley indicated threats to safety, and specifically the presence on the trolleys and around the stations of a high number of "undesirables," as primary among their reasons for not using transit. Indeed, the manager of La Mesa Village Plaza indicated that the mere presence of transit on-site raised operating costs of the project above those for similar-sized sites that were not located near transit. Many of these costs are associated with increased security (e.g., surveillance cameras, private patrols), as well as higher expenses for repairs and maintenance. The manager felt that these costs were not offset by any increases in property value that should accompany proximity to transit. At the 1993 annual meeting of the American Public Transportation Association held in San Diego, one local developer was even more strident about his concerns over safety and security. As a panelist in a session about transit-oriented development, the developer openly stated that he would not lease to a prospective retail tenant who expressly wanted to be near a trolley stop because he didn't want the "typical" transit rider hanging around his project.

There can be no question that some of the resistance to rail transit, and the villages designed around stations, is rooted in class and racial prejudices. Historically, transit's ridership has been drawn disproportionately from the inner-city poor. The prospect of extending rail services from central cities to the "tranquil" suburbs makes some middle-class homeowners edgy. Though potentially divisive, these matters cannot be casually set aside, and indeed must be taken on frontally if the transit village movement is to make much headway in suburbia. Stepping up security and surveillance is part, but certainly not all, of the answer. At least as important is creating functional transit-oriented communities that instill a sense of belonging, citizenship, and communalism. Also needed are tools for rebuilding and empowering inner-city communities. Transit villages like Barrio Logan are clearly steps in the right direction.

The San Diego symposium revealed at least one other significant obstacle to compact station-area development: liability suits. California law holds developers responsible for meeting minimum standards for building construction and workmanship for up to 10 years from the time of sale. Several litigious lawyers in the area have done well representing condominium owners whose units purportedly began falling apart sometime around the 8th or 9th year of ownership. The situation has gotten so bad that many San Diego area developers have stopped producing condominium units altogether.

In Los Angeles, the transit village movement is even more controversial and emotionally charged than in San Diego, a reflection of how divided the area is over building a mammoth, multibillion dollar rail network. Transportation scholars, bus proponents, and some elected officials argue that Los Angeles County is too spread out to benefit from rail, and even now want the rail extensions cut back. The transit village movement is dismissed by some as too minor to matter—at best, a boutique design approach and, at worst, a waste of taxpayer dollars.

The University of Southern California's School of Planning has led the charge against the Metrorail project. "They might as well flush all that money in to the Pacific Ocean," USC Professor Catherine Burke tells the *Los Angeles Times*. Her colleague, Peter Gordon, agrees, arguing that rail investments will only undermine the strength of the Metrobus system (presently the nation's largest), which can better serve the dispersed housing and commercial centers of southern California. Fewer than 7 percent of the region's workforce commutes to downtown Los Angeles, Monday through Friday, Gordon notes.[17]

Burke and Gordon recommend expanding MTA's bus network in the short term; in early 1995, the Blue Line, Metro Red Line, and Metrolink carried 75,000 passengers per day compared to 1.17 million daily trips on the buses. For the long term, Burke sees a futuristic parataxi service, in which riders punch in their destinations at curbside kiosks and motorists heading in the same direction are dispatched by an automated central computer to serve waiting passengers for a fee. A parataxi demonstration, in fact, is presently moving forward in the city of Ontario, on the eastern edge of Los Angeles County.

All Los Angeles transit officials concede that rail transit faces an uphill struggle in succeeding in the land of automobility, but many reach different conclusions about the future. Rail supporters argue that southern California's sprawling, auto-reliant settlement pattern must be altered for prosperity's sake. Finite fossil fuel supplies, deteriorating air quality, and the widening class and racial divisions that stem, in part, from people being confined to cars and sequestered neighborhoods, they maintain, leave no choice. The sustainable metropolis of the future, rail backers contend, will be the transit-oriented metropolis. Nick Patsouras has for years been one of the chief purveyors of this viewpoint. Patsouras, a member of the transit board since the late 1970s, spent much of the 1980s flying back and forth to Washington, DC, lobbying for funds to build Los Angeles's rail network. Once federal funding was secured, he turned his attention to heading Los Angeles's transit village movement. In 1993, he even ran for mayor of Los Angeles, primarily on a transit–land-use platform. "Linking land use and transportation decisions creates the opportunity to accommodate regional and local growth in transit station areas, where future development can be well-served by the regional transportation system, with minimal impact on existing residential neighborhoods," Patsouras wrote in *The Planning Report* in June 1993.[18]

The polarity of views on the appropriateness of an ambitious rail building program found expression at a meeting of the Los Angeles City Planning Commission in early March 1995, where a panel on transit-based housing was convened. The planning department staff has recommended the adoption of a land-use–transportation policy, one that would direct Los Angeles's future growth to within one-quarter to one-half mile of the rail stations and major bus stops. At the gathering, Peter Gordon of USC once again appeared to denounce the enterprise of rail transit in low-density Los Angeles. Undeterred, a transit official spoke glowingly in support of the policy, emphasizing its importance in generating rail ridership over the long run.

Also on the panel was Martin Wachs, then head of transportation studies at UCLA. Wachs opted for the middle ground, pointing out both the opportunities and difficulties facing the transit village movement in a spread-out metropolis. Wachs noted that "a city like Los Angeles should foster diversity in its urban form." The majority of Los Angeles residents may want to live in the dispersed single-family neighborhoods that constitute Los Angeles, but a niche market is likely to exist for compact, mixed-use neighborhoods around rail stations. Wachs added, though, that zoning and planning approaches alone are unlikely to lure developers away from building tract, single-family housing, which is their bread-and-butter business. "All of the forces pushing development to outlying areas over the past 40 years are still with us," he told the planning commission.

The transit village experiences in both Los Angeles and San Diego support Wachs's assessment of the limits of planning and zoning initiatives alone. The projects that have moved forward in both areas have required unusual efforts—primarily of local governments, redevelopment agencies, and transit operators—with assembling land and underwriting projects. In today's tough economic climate, there is no escaping the fact that governments must invest a considerable amount of money at the outset—money that goes to consolidating parcels, writing down land costs, and financing supportive infrastructure—and thereby absorb a significant share of the risks inherent in building transit-oriented communities in regions where the automobile still reigns supreme.

NOTES

1. The share of single-occupant commutes was even greater in outlying southern California counties in 1990: 76.8 percent in Orange County, 73.8 percent in Riverside County, and 75.2 percent in San Bernardino County. For the entire Los Angeles-Anaheim-Riverside Consolidated Metropolitan Statistical Area (CMSA), 87.8 percent of employed residents commuted by private automobile in 1990. See U.S. Bureau of the Census, *Summary Tape Files 3A* (Washington, D.C., U.S. Department of Commerce, Bureau of the Census, 1990); M. Rosetti and B. Eversole, *Journey to Work Trends in the United States and Its Major Metropolitan Areas, 1960–1990* (Cambridge, MA: John A. Volpe National Transportation System Center, 1993).

2. Halcyon Real Estate Advisors, *Los Angeles County Transportation Commission: System-Wide Assessment of Joint Development Potential: Phase I Final Report, Phase II Final Report* (Los Angeles: Los Angeles County Transportation Commission, 1992).

3. Los Angeles City Planning Department, *Los Angeles General Plan Framework Targeted Growth Areas Discussion Paper* (Los Angeles: Los Angeles City Planning Department, 1995).

4. J. Sheine, Los Angeles Builds on Transportation, *Architecture,* pp. 93–99, August 1993.

5. V. Menotti and R. Cervero, *Transit-Based Housing in California: Profiles* (Berkeley: Institute of Urban and Regional Development, University of California, Working Paper 638, 1995).

6. D. Walters, Two Los Angeles Agencies Will Join Forces to Boost Renovation, Encourage Mass Transit, *The Bond Buyer,* September 27, 1993, p. 23; M. Newman, Marrying Transit Stations with Housing, *The New York Times,* Sunday Real Estate section, p. 23, September 19, 1993.

7. G. Spivack, *Presentation on Union Station Gateway Intermodal Transit Center,* Transportation Research Board Conference, Washington DC, January 1995.

8. Kaplan, McLaughlin, Diaz, *Conceptual Master Plan for the Westlake/MacArthur Park Red Line Station Area* (Los Angeles: Southern California Rapid Transit District, 1992).

9. Tanaka/Tetra Design Architects, *Little Tokyo-Arts District Station/Community Linkages Program* (Los Angeles: Metropolitan Transportation Authority, Metro Red Line-Eastern Extension Project, Planning and Urban Design Strategies, 1994).

10. No fewer than four transit-supportive design manuals have been prepared in San Diego County to date: by MTDB, the city of San Diego, the county of San Diego Department of Planning and Land Use, and the North County Transit District. In addition to publishing a manual, *Design for Transit,* MTDB has produced a video, *Cities in the Balance: Creating the Transit-Friendly Environment,* which it provides free of charge to neighborhood groups, developers, and other interests as a way of marketing transit-supportive design principles.

11. The City Council of San Diego directed the planning department to update the city's general plan and zoning codes to reflect the transit-oriented development (TOD) policy of concentrating growth within a quarter-mile radius of transit stations. The TOD policy, #600–39 of August 1992, has been closely adhered to by the planning office.

12. Wilham Lorenz, *Designing Light Rail Transit Compatible with Urban Form* (San Diego: San Diego Metropolitan Transit Development Board, 1996).

13. R. Cervero, Light Rail Transit and Urban Development, *Journal of the American Planning Association,* Vol. 50, No. 2, pp. 133–147, 1984; San Diego Association of Governments, *San Diego Trolley: The First Three Years* (San Diego: San Diego Association of Governments, 1984).

14. The Otay Ranch project was originally submitted to the county of San Diego as a large-scale, mixed-use development with an on-site monorail, but no other transit provisions. In response to the proposal, the county formed an Otay Ranch Project Team. This team set up a citizens input process and sponsored a series of urban design charettes which led to a consensus that the project should become more transit oriented. One of the twelve planned villages is being designated as a regional

mixed-use node close to the trolley line with residential densities approaching 36 units to the acre, four to five times denser than the typical suburban San Diego community. Other neighborhoods will average lower densities, producing diversity in both housing products and neighborhood character. Plans call for a total of 27,000 dwelling units when the project is fully built out, some 30 to 50 years in the future.

15. City of San Diego Redevelopment Agency, *Barrio Logan: Project Summary for the FTA's Livable Communities Initiative* (San Diego: San Diego Redevelopment Agency, 1995).

16. L. Weisberg, A Test of Tradition, *San Diego Union-Tribune,* December 11, 1994, Section H, p. 1.

17. A. Curtiss, Experts Question Proposal to Link Growth and Transit, *Los Angeles Times,* March 3, 1995, Section B, p. 1.

18. M. Katches, Nightmare in Los Angeles, *California Journal,* pp. 41–43, June 1994; N. Patsouras, A Shared Vision for a New L.A.: Transportation as a Catalyst for Remaking Our City (Los Angeles: LACTC/RTD, 1995).

10

New York:
Commuter Town Revival

The New York region presents a far different transit village challenge than the west coast or the newer generation of heavy rail systems in Washington, DC, Miami, and Atlanta. It is not the challenge of building new suburban communities on land formerly rural or undeveloped. The New York rail lines have been in place since the early part of this century, and most station areas have been built up for years. The challenge is to revitalize and repair the fabric of these older suburban communities using the transit station as a spur to and center of development. Within New York City itself, some see subway nodes also as potential catalysts for community rebuilding and regeneration.

The transit village movement in New York up to now has been spearheaded by the Metro-North commuter railroad and the region's oldest planning organization, the Regional Plan Association. Metro-North has sought to revitalize several older suburban station areas, including Harrison, Port Chester, and Mamaroneck. The Regional Plan Association has advanced transit village designs for Yonkers, Wasaic, and Ossining. However, despite being one of the world's great transit metropolises, installing a "new generation" of transit villages has proven difficult in the New York area, proceeding at a glacial pace in many cases. Greater New York sheds a different light on the economics and politics of transit village development. It informs us that designing transit-oriented places in a mature, largely built-up metropolitan area can be an arduous enterprise indeed.

10.1 RECLAIMING COMMUTER RAILROAD TOWNS

Metro-North is a 338-mi commuter network radiating northward from Manhattan into the Hudson River Valley and southern Connecticut (Map 10.1). Metro-North was formed in 1983 through the consolidation of several rail lines that date back to the 19th century: the 71.8-mi Harlem Line, the 75.8-mi Hudson Line, the 119.4-mi New Haven Line, and the 71 mi west of the Hudson River on the Port Jervis and Pascack Lines. Daily ridership today stands at 216,000 passenger trips, with the largest number, 94,000 trips, on the line to New Haven.[1]

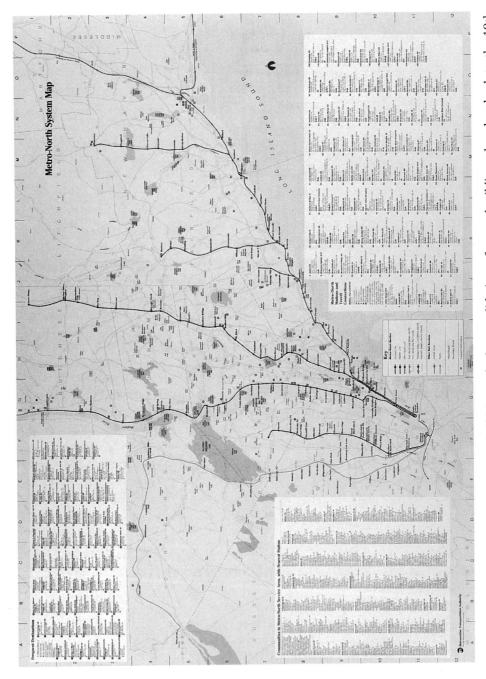

Map 10.1 Metro-North Commuter Rail Network. A consolidation of several rail lines that date back to the 19th century: the 71.8-mi Harlem Line, the 75.8-mi Hudson Line, and the 119.4-mi New Haven Line.

As discussed in Chapter 2, many suburban towns on the Metro-North Line date back to the late 19th century and owe their very existence to the siting of a train depot. A few, such as Scarsdale and Bronxville, have maintained the flavor of a transit village, boasting vibrant, walkable downtowns. Others, such as Port Chester and Yonkers, have seen their urban centers falter, victims of suburban exodus and disinvestment.

Beginning in the mid-1980s, the Metro-North planning staff launched a transit village initiative aimed both at reviving the cores of older commuter towns and stimulating ridership by encouraging housing construction near stations. The Metro-North planning director, Howard Permut, believed the high cost of flats and condos in New York City produced a ready-made market for moderate-income housing along the Metro-North corridor. It was just a matter of selling local communities and home builders on the idea.

In the fall of 1987, Metro-North and New York's other commuter rail system, the Long Island Rail Road, received grants from the U.S. Department of Transportation to explore joint development possibilities in the region. An initial evaluation of 25 stations identified three stations with the greatest commercial potential: Harrison, Port Chester, and Kew Gardens. Envisioned for all were mixed housing-retail complexes built on existing surface parking lots adjacent to stations with 40 residential units and 10,000 ft^2 of retail at Harrison and approximately 200 apartments-condos at Kew Gardens and Port Chester.[2]

Kew Gardens never got off the ground due to stiff neighborhood opposition. As a community of predominantly single-family homes, residents of Kew Gardens wanted no part of transit villages. The prospects for Port Chester, however, rose sharply when, in 1991, *The New York Times* announced that the Robert Martin Company was planning a massive downtown redevelopment project centered around the train depot. Only 26 mi from Grand Central Station and a comparable distance from New Haven, Port Chester was within a 45-min commuteshed of several million workers. The Robert Martin Company proposed redeveloping 17 acres near the station with 315,000 ft^2 of new retail and office space and 660 mixed-income residential units. After much fanfare, however, the project failed to obtain financing, and by 1995 was no longer active. Today, downtown Port Chester continues to struggle.

Station-area redevelopment in Harrison, however, is moving forward after several miscues. The township of Harrison lies 22 mi, or around 40 min, from Grand Central Station. The town's traditional main street, Halstead Avenue, is only a short walking distance to the station (Photo 10.1). As shown in Photo 10.2, parking lots and open tracts separate the train station from the main street.

In the late 1980s, township and Metro-North officials concluded that placing housing on the surface parking lot would help revive the local economy and reinvigorate main street. By marketing the housing to workers in New York City, they hoped to lure new residents to Harrison's core and thus infuse the retail district with new life.

Metro-North owns three large parcels, totaling 3.3 acres, that straddle the station and main street. In 1991, Metro-North issued an RFP to build housing on these parcels. No one responded. However, when a second RFP was issued in 1995, the real estate market

Photo 10.1   Village of Harrison Traditional Main Street. The village seeks station-area development in part to revive the once-vibrant Harrison main street, Halstead Avenue.

had rebounded, and developer interest was high. Six proposals were received. Into 1996, the proposals were still being evaluated by Metro-North staff. Though the proposals differ in design, all contained 120 or more residential units built as two- to three-story townhouses above ground-floor retail. This would reestablish the mix of housing and retail that characterized Harrison as a turn-of-the-century commuter rail town.

David Florio, real estate officer for Metro-North in charge of the project, notes the housing proposals call mainly for studio apartments and one-bedrooms aimed at empty-nesters and singles commuting to the city. "The Harrison RFP attracted some of the major development firms in the New York region, who see a residential market at our suburban train stations." The Harrison project, if small by transit village standards, is important to Metro-North as a precedent setter. Florio explains, "We need to see one project completed for our credibility; once developers and city officials are able to see a project on the ground, they will take us a lot more seriously."

Beyond Harrison, Metro-North has also pursued station-area development at Ossining on its Hudson Valley Line and at Mamaroneck on the New Haven Line. At Ossining, the mayor hosted a well-attended development symposium in December 1994 that explored ways of rebuilding the town's station area. A general consensus was reached that marginal industrial uses should be replaced by housing targeted at New York City commuters. At

Current station
area parking

Halstead Ave.
(traditional Main Street)

Harrison Station

Metro-North Rail Line

Photo 10.2 Aerial Shot of the Harrison Station Area. The Harrison station currently is surrounded by surface parking in front of the station and across from the rail tracks.

Mamaroneck, everything hinges on the future of the train station. A century ago, the Mamaroneck station was one of the busiest stops on the New Haven Line (Photo 10.3). Unfortunately, years of neglect and deferred maintenance took their toll, and today the once-colorful station, set in a rustic city park, is closed (Photo 10.4). The hope is to build upon Mamaroneck's greatest architectural asset, its charming train depot, by tying new commuter-based housing construction to the restoration of the station itself. Metro-North has entertained the thought of exchanging a portion of its surface parking lot in return for private restoration of the station.

10.2 COMMUTER STATIONS AS URBAN CENTERS

The Regional Plan Association (RPA) is the oldest regional planning organization in the country. Formed in 1922 to guide and manage growth in the region, RPA has long been

Photo 10.3 Mamaroneck Station, circa 1900. Before there was park-and-ride, there was horse-buggy-and-ride.

Photo 10.4 Mamaroneck Station, 1994. North of the station lies a wooded park with a stream and gently rolling terrain. Local officials hope the combination of a refurbished train depot surrounded by the sylvan parkscape will attract a home builder to the area.

recognized as an innovator at plan making. In 1929, RPA issued the first of its three seminal plans for the region, calling for massive transit and highway infrastructure investments that would channel growth from Manhattan to the outskirts. Over the next few years, it presided over the tremendous outburst of infrastructure—railroads, highways, bridges, tunnels, subways, and parks—under the stewardship of the great master builder Robert Moses.

Nearly 40 years passed before RPA released its second plan. The 1968 plan sought to limit infrastructure investments, particularly road improvements, as a way of containing growth and holding scattershot development in check. In its second plan, RPA endorsed an "urban centers" policy that called for redirecting growth to traditional centers like Newark, White Plains, and Yonkers. The plan also gave attention to the problems of inner-city poverty, neighborhood crime, and social dislocation. It recognized the city as not just a physical entity but as a social entity as well.

Greater New York's third regional plan was just released. It builds on the in-fill themes of the second plan, emphasizing rail transit locations as desired development sites. New York's phenomenal rate of employment decentralization in recent times has added great urgency to the plan.[3] One of the plan's principal authors, Tony Hiss, sees the area's early commuter rail towns as paragons for community building in the 21st century. "Transit villages," Hiss writes, "where people live within walking and biking distance from their neighbors and which are connected to the rest of a region by high-speed commuter rail lines, can do a lot to make the new urban regions work. We're going to have to make sure that all the people in these regions can stay in touch with each other easily; if we don't, they're going to drag down the economy and at the same time distort millions of people's lives."[4]

Robert Yaro, executive director of RPA, also believes the region should return to its roots. "The New York region grew up earlier this century as the nation's one great transit metropolis. It still is to a great extent, with over 80 percent of commuters into Manhattan using public transit. So our region's challenge is to build on the existing rail infrastructure, do a better job linking our suburban job and residential growth to rail, and rebuild our older and deteriorated commuter towns."

RPA has over the years led the charge in rebuilding station areas in Yonkers, Wasaic, and Patterson. These forgotten urban centers, regional planners hope, will become the building blocks for a constellation of transit-oriented communities that fan out from Manhattan. Nearly a century ago, the city of Yonkers, one of the first rail towns on the Hudson Valley Line, took great pride in its stately railroad station, shown in Photo 10.5, at that time the centerpiece of the community. Over the years, though, both the station and its surroundings fell into disrepair as businesses and jobs flocked to Westchester County's budding edge cities: Purchase-Rye, White Plains, and the Tarrytown area. By the early 1990s, the area around the station, shown in Photo 10.6 from overhead, had given over to surface parking lots, smokestacks, container yards, warehouses, and an underused marina.[5] The neighborhood immediately surrounding the Yonkers station is today largely devoid of streetlife and active businesses (Photo 10.7).

How should central Yonkers be rebuilt? When asked this question by the city leaders in 1994, RPA planners recommended strengthening the area's two greatest assets—the rail node and the waterfront—by linking them together. The design prepared by RPA called for a phased program of short-term (1 to 3 years) and longer term (4 years and more) improvements that would attract live-work households, commuter residents, and small businesses to the marina-station area.

The short-term strategies focused on improving the area's safety and aesthetics through infrastructure investments and landscaping. The train station is to be reestablished as an icon of the community and a functioning link to the waterfront. Metro-North plans to repair the clock and glazing in the entrance archway and upgrade underpass connections to the station. Further, Larkin Park, across from the train station, is to be beautified and reclaimed. One-half of the park area that has been taken over by surface parking will be restored to green space. On nearby Main Street, the sidewalks are to be widened, street trees will be planted and furniture installed, and building facades will be refurbished.

The hope is that modest public funding of immediate-impact improvements will help build the momentum for attracting private capital over time. A decade or so from now, civic backers hope a marina for recreational boating will be in place. At the Yonkers Transit-

Photo 10.5 Yonkers Stations, at its Height in the Early 1900s. One of the two Yonkers rail stations that were centers of downtown life a century ago.

Oriented Communities seminar in February 1994, Peter Abeles, a real estate consultant, noted that "a special advantage almost unique to Yonkers is that it can offer access to boating without the need for a car. For the seven million people who live just to the south in New York City, this is a very important factor. The fact that the Yonkers' waterfront is directly accessible by existing, effective, safe, and regular public transit gives the site an advantage over any other waterfront areas in the region." Still, most in attendance agreed that only so much could be achieved through physical redesign and that modest sights should be set for the transit village development. There are several reasons why. One, Yonkers' housing and commercial markets have been dormant for decades, creating a serious image problem that won't be easily overcome. Two, the city is cash strapped, with few

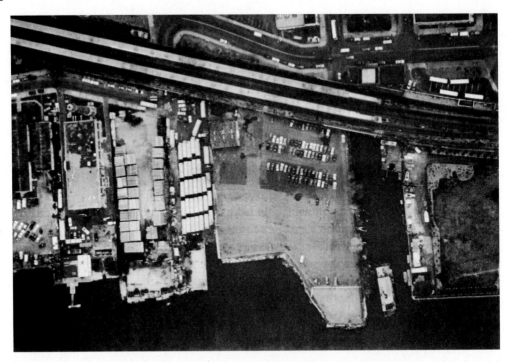

Photo 10.6 Yonkers Station-Marina Area, 1994. On the one hand, marginal industrial land uses create an eyesore, but on the other hand storage yards and industrial space provide large tracts of easily assembled and redevelopable land.

economic development resources to leverage private investments. And three, it is relatively expensive to tear down and rebuild a site. Developers can go to undeveloped sites farther out and build more cheaply.

Yet, even if limited in scope, revitalization of the Yonkers station is important both to the city and the region.[6] RPA is hoping Yonkers' transformation to a more transit-oriented community will give the "urban centers" concept a boost. Each successful transit village will increase the marketability of subsequent transit villages. Just as station-area development in Harrison is expected to spin off mixed-use projects around other stations on the New Haven Line, Yonkers' waterfront-rail redevelopment should pave the way for other communities along the Hudson River, like Ossining, to follow suit.

This is already occurring. In early 1995, at the Village of Ossining Community Center, Mayor John Pasquerella, Village Manager Genaro Faella, town planners, federal transit representatives, and three developers met to discuss redevelopment possibilities for the town's aging train station area, shown from the air in Photo 10.8. The station sits above the tracks near a small marina and is surrounded by decidedly nonwater-related uses: a large parking lot used by buses and oil storage trucks, the former Rand McNally building, and

Photo 10.7   Streets Around the Yonkers Station, 1994. The once-vibrant Yonkers station area is today better know for its conspicuous absence of streetlife.

oil storage tanks. Inland from the station is a dispiriting mix of the village public works compound and the near-empty though impressive three-story Brandreth Pill Factory (now used as a brake repair shop).

As in Yonkers, the village hopes that the synergy of an improved waterfront and enhanced station setting will spur housing and marine-related uses. Ossining is only 40 min by train to Grand Central Station. Town leaders believe attractive housing on the water-front will appeal to those craving a village lifestyle within a reasonable commute to the city. The village is presently negotiating with a microbrewery and an excursion boat operator to come to the waterfront as lead tenants.

At Ossining's transit village gathering, a variety of suggestions were offered on how to jump start redevelopment. "The Village needs to assemble parcels," one developer noted, since small projects are too costly to undertake. "A master plan for the area is needed," added another, to provide a blueprint and a clear direction for change. The third developer in attendance, who has built homes near the White Plains rail station, suggested that villagers design a process that breaks through public-sector inertia. Everyone agreed that the town needs to set a vision and be more proactive, although for many a full-blown transit village is decades away given current market conditions.

Certainly, as at Yonkers, redevelopment will not come easily because a built form exists that requires alteration, and considerable up-front public investment is needed. Whether central Ossining is transformed will hinge to a large degree on whether village leaders are

Older Ossining Village center Marina Metro-North
industrial uses Rail Station   Rail Line

Photo 10.8 Ossining Station Area, 1994. Land around the Ossining station, 40 miles from midtown Manhattan, is being primed for housing targetted at Manhattan workers who want economical housing in a village setting and an economical commute.

motivated enough to galvanize community support and nurture the often prickly redevelopment planning process over a period of years. The building of transit villages in smaller townships such as Ossining will be greatly aided by establishing a precedent in Yonkers or elsewhere in Westchester County.

10.3 ATLANTIC CENTER, BROOKLYN

Atlantic Center has been one of the few attempts to create a "new generation" transit village within New York City itself. It had a number of advantages, including two nationally known design firms—Calthorpe and Associates and Skidmore Owings & Merrill (SOM)—and political backing to write down land costs. Still it did not go forward, underscoring the many things that can go wrong in developing transit-oriented communities in established, built-up areas.

 The project has its roots in the mid-1980s, when New York City officials became alarmed over the number of back offices that were relocating to the suburbs of Long

Island, Westchester County, and New Jersey. Hoping to stem the loss of jobs and tax base, then-mayor Ed Koch introduced financial and development incentives aimed at keeping back offices within the city limits.

Downtown Brooklyn's Atlantic Center seemed a perfect candidate for back-office space. The master designers proposed an ultraurban transit village. Atlantic Center was to occupy a largely vacant 24-acre site, owned by the city, over a Long Island Rail Road commuter rail terminal. Nine subway lines and fourteen bus routes converge at the site.

Through an RFP process, the city hired Rose Associates, an established development company. Jonathan Rose, a member of the company and the lead developer, was attracted in good part by the site's superior subway connections. Rose in turn hired Calthorpe and Associates and SOM to design a "new town/in town" with multitenant office space, mixed housing, retail, and services all physically tied to the rail station.

Their community plan, shown in Figure 10.1, featured 2.7 million ft^2 of office space with half in two large office towers directly over the terminal and near the Williamsburg Bank Building. A skylit retail concourse with restaurants, shops, and a 10-screen cinema would occupy the center of the complex. Close by would be a 688-unit residential neigh-

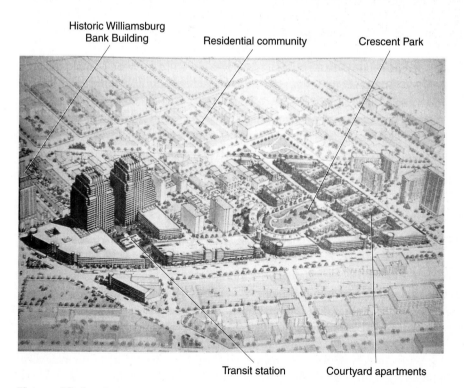

Figure 10.1 Atlantic Center Community Plan. A proposed mid-to-high rise transit village sited at a major intermodal station that met stiff neighborhood opposition.

borhood, Atlantic Commons, targeted at low- to medium-income households and a few ancillary shops.

In the site plan, neighborhood blocks were organized as four-story brownstone courtyard apartments that rimmed a crescent park, which according to the designers "reestablish the lost fabric of a neighborhood decimated by 1960s redevelopment." An office building along Atlantic Avenue would shield the residential neighborhood from the adjacent train tracks. Day-care and community centers would be situated at the base of a park, while neighborhood grocery stores and small retail shops would line the neighborhood's edge.

The project quickly won planning approval and was set to move into preconstruction in 1987. Then, a lawsuit was filed by a neighborhood group claiming that the project's densities were too high and that new units would trigger gentrification and the displacement of low-income households. The lawsuit was joined by the nationwide environmental group, the Natural Resources Defense Council.

A prolonged legal battle ensued that eventually doomed the project. The lawsuit wound its way through the courts for 3 years before being dismissed. The timing was unfortunate. By 1990, the market for office, including back office, had weakened, and the likely main tenant, the City Department of Community Development, had gone elsewhere.

Certainly, the lawsuit undermined the project's momentum. However, the city itself also bears some of the blame for the project's collapse. By 1990, no one in the city government or transit agency took on the role of the project's champion. Without a staunch public advocate, someone willing to shepherd the project through the everyday hurdles of implementation, the project's fate was sealed.

In the past few years, new development has come to the site, though it is anything but transit-oriented. Forest City took over for Rose Associates as the developer and set out to convert the site to a big-box retail project, complete with a large parking lot. It moved forward on housing, but in low-density, two-story townhouse configurations, amounting to fewer than 100 units.

10.4 NEW YORK'S TRANSIT VILLAGE DILEMMA

Despite being the nation's most transit-oriented city and having the good fortune of a visionary and vocal regional planning authority, there remains considerable skepticism about the prospects of creating new transit villages, either in the outskirts or within the city's five boroughs. A steady stream of businesses and households have been exiting Manhattan, Brooklyn, Queens, and the Bronx, in part to get away from transit-oriented environments. The notion of transplanting "slices" of New York City in the neighborhoods surrounding commuter rail nodes does not sit well with many suburbanites. For many, the lines are clearly drawn between the city and the suburbs, and the idea of transit-oriented communities threatens to blur these boundaries.

The advent of park-and-ride lots has diluted the importance of being near the region's commuter stations. Most suburbanites accept that they will be a number of miles from a train station when they buy a home. To them, the idea of living within walking distance of a suburban station is an anachronism. Some transit officials fear that converting surface parking spaces to transit-based housing will only chase park-and-riders away. If riding commuter rail becomes too inconvenient, suburbanites will find other ways to get to work, like the private commuter vans that in recent years have proliferated throughout the region. Not many transit officials seem willing to risk short-term ridership and fare receipts for the sake of potential long-term gains from having concentrations of residents near rail stops.

Although some of the obstacles to transit village development in greater New York are macroeconomic in nature (e.g., depressed real estate markets, conservative bank lending practices), others are more localized and political in nature. Faced with more pressing and potentially explosive urban problems, such as crime and poverty, transit villages are not high on the priority list of elected officials in the nation's biggest city. Proposals to densify housing in established, mature communities invariably spark community protests, ostensibly because of concerns over streets and schools becoming too crowded, though a desire to maintain suburbia's cultural hegemony and keep out those of a different race and class often underpins the opposition. Of course, these and other barriers have thwarted transit village initiatives in other areas. It is just that in the nation's largest, most transit-oriented metropolis they seem magnified all the more.

NOTES

1. The first rail network, the New York and Harlem Railroad, began as a horse-powered streetcar line in 1832, with the line extended and steam power locomotion introduced soon thereafter. The New York and New Haven Railroad Line was launched in 1848, and the Hudson River Railroad in 1849. Although the early railroads were noted for their freight and intercity passenger trains, commuter service began to gain importance in the late 19th century. A new and greatly enlarged Grand Central Station was built in 1898. The current Grand Central, covering 48 acres, was opened in 1913 following the electrification of the lines.

2. MTA Real Estate Department, *Feasibility Study of Joint/Multiple Use of Development of MTA Commuter Railroad Stations* (New York: New York Metropolitan Transportation Authority, 1989).

3. The New York metropolitan area experienced one of the fastest rates of suburban job growth in the country during the 1980s. Between 1980 and 1990, Manhattan added 54 million ft^2 of office space. The suburban ring, including Long Island, northeastern New Jersey, and Westchester County, added 173 million ft^2 (equal to the entire Chicago metropolitan office market). Thus, suburban counties captured two-thirds of

the region's office growth during the 1980s. Overall, Manhattan still accounted for 56 percent of all office space in the region in 1990, but its market share fell from 85 percent. See M. Hughes, Regional Economics and Edge Cities, *Edge City and ISTEA—Examining the Transportation Implications of Suburban Development Patterns,* Ben Chinitz, ed. (Washington, DC: Federal Highway Administration; 1992); R. Cervero, Changing Live-Work Spatial Relationships: Implications for Metropolitan Structure and Mobility, *Cities in Competition: Productive and Sustainable Cities for the 21st Century,* J. Brotchie, M. Batty, E. Blakeley, P. Hall, and P. Newton, eds. (Sydney: Longman Australia, 1995), pp. 330–358.

4. The quotes by Hiss and Yaro presented in this section were from early drafts of RPA's Third Regional Plan, provided to us by the authors. For the final plan, see Robert D. Yaro and Tony Hiss, *A Region at Risk: The Third Regional Plan for the New York-New Jersey-Connecticut Metropolitan Area* (Washington, DC: Island Press, 1996). For discussions on transit village proposals in the region, see pages 126–132 of this book.

5. Regional Plan Association, *Downtown Yonkers Station Area* (New York: Regional Plan Association, 1994); P. Abeles, *Economic, Land Use and Development Strategies for the Yonkers Waterfront and Larkin Square* (New York: Regional Plan Association, 1994).

6. Other studies by the Regional Plan Association on transit-based development include *Land Value and Transit Access: Modeling the Relationship in the New York Metropolitan Area* (Washington DC: Federal Transit Administration, 1993) and *Redesigning the Suburbs: Turning Sprawl into Centers* (New York: Regional Plan Association, 1994).

PART FOUR

Transit Villages Abroad

For inspiration, it is important that we look beyond America's borders for examples of transit-based communities. Anyone who has ever been to great transit metropolises like Stockholm, Tokyo, or Singapore quickly finds a built form that is supremely tailored to transit riding. Rail transit is the lifeline of these metropolises, serving as many as half of all intracity trips beyond several miles in distance. Nearly all suburban communities are physically oriented to train stops, leaving ample amounts of land for open space, ecological preserves, and farms. Particularly relevant to the United States is the fact that residents of these three metropolises—Stockholm, Tokyo, and Singapore—enjoy a high standard of living comparable to or above that of many U.S. cities. All three have managed to build transit-oriented communities and a sustainable built form without sacrificing quality of life. Part of their success has to do with culture and history, but an awful lot has to do with community planning and targeted public policies.

Stockholm tells us much about the value of regional planning in creating a transit-oriented metropolis. In Tokyo, we learn about the important role of entrepreneurship in coupling rail construction and new town development. And in Singapore, we get a glimpse of what is achievable when strong central planning is combined with aggressive programs that restrain automobile ownership and usage. Though lessons from abroad are never directly transferable, they open our eyes to different possibilities and portray transit villages on a much larger canvas.

11

Stockholm: The Sustainable Metropolis

Stockholm is arguably the best example anywhere of coordinated planning of rail transit and urban development. Stockholm, Sweden's capital and largest city, has some 750,000 inhabitants, around half of whom live in the central city. About half of the remaining residents live in planned satellite communities that orbit central Stockholm and are radially linked to the core by a regional rail system, Tunnelbana (Map 11.1). This star-shaped, multicentered built form is the direct outcome of a regional planning campaign that targeted overspill growth after World War II to these master planned, rail-served suburbs.

Nearly a century ago, Ebenezer Howard first advanced the idea of building satellite new towns separated by greenbelts and connected by intermunicipal railways.[1] As discussed in earlier chapters, Howard's vision was to build socially and economically self-sustaining communities that could relieve London from overcrowding and accommodate some of its poor, and at the same time apply value-capture principles to finance infrastructure and services.[2] The physical elements of Howard's plans featured mixed though physically separated land uses, naturalistic landscaping, and curvilinear, grade-separated passageways.

Many of Howard's followers borrowed from and extended the notion of building safe, peaceful satellite communities surrounded by greenbelts, such as the plans for Radburn, New Jersey, by Henry Wright and Clarence Stein, and Britain's early garden suburbs, Letchworth, Hampstead, and Welwyn, designed by Raymond Unwin and Barry Parker. Most of these places were designed on a superblock scale, with clustered housing grouped around communal greens and connected by pedestrianways. Unlike Howard's garden cities, however, they were not planned as self-contained towns; they were more like dormitory villages, with the source of employment for residents usually in nearby cities. Nor was transit a prominent feature of early British or American new towns. It was only when Stockholm began building, after World War II, what were to be self-contained satellite communities surrounded by protective, open spaces and served by rail transit that Howard's vision of "cities of tomorrow" began to take form.

289

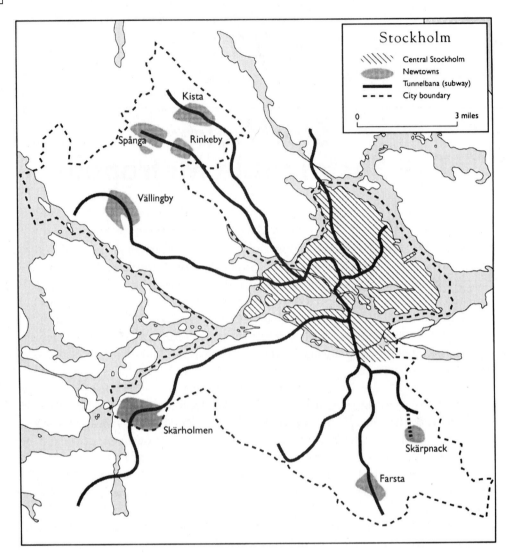

Map 11.1 Stockholm's Tunnelbana Rail Network and Its Major Satellite New Towns.

11.1 BUILDING A TRANSIT METROPOLIS

Over the past 50 years, Stockholm has been transformed from a prewar monocentric city to a postwar polycentric metropolis. The backbone of the multicentered Stockholm region is the Tunnelbana rail system. Over time, Stockholm's settlement pattern and rail network have become mutually dependent and, indeed, inseparable. They are also the product of perhaps the most comprehensive and ambitious regional planning efforts yet in the free industrialized world.

What makes the Stockholm story so remarkable is that the rapid transformation to a transit metropolis occurred in a well-to-do nation during a period of economic boom. Today, Sweden is one of the world's most affluent countries, with a 1990 GDP per capita of U.S. $17,900.[3] It also has one of the highest automobile ownership rates (420 cars per 1000 inhabitants) in Europe.[4] Much of the nation's wealth is concentrated in greater Stockholm. Among Sweden's 47 companies with more than 5000 employees, 37 have their main offices in the Stockholm region.

Because Sweden was among the last countries in Europe to industrialize, it grew at a rapid pace following World War II, particularly in urban areas. Given that Swedish cities sit in a large, flat, forested country, many could easily have followed a highway-oriented development pattern. Yet Europe's most prosperous country and its capital city took off on a radically different suburbanization path than did America and much of Europe. Why?

Stockholm's city council deserves much of the credit for orchestrating and coordinating land-use and transportation development over the postwar period. However, such planning would not have been possible were it not for two other factors. One, beginning in 1904, the Stockholm city council began purchasing land for future expansion decades in advance of need. By 1980, it owned 70 percent of the land within its boundaries and over 230 mi^2 of land beyond the city limits. Second, after 1934, Sweden was governed for 30 years by Social Democrats, committed to improving housing. During the postwar period of industrial expansion, Sweden suffered a serious housing shortfall and was unable to adequately house new immigrants and factory workers. Quarters were cramped with few kitchens and washing facilities. (At the end of World War II, 52 percent of Stockholm's housing stock consisted of no more than one room and a kitchen. Living space standards have increased markedly over the last two decades. Today, the region's dwellings have an average of almost three rooms plus kitchen, even though 40 percent are single households.) After World War II, the Swedish government began constructing multistory apartments on the outskirts of metropolises. Over 90 percent of the dwelling units built after 1946—virtually all built on the city's land—enjoyed some form of state subsidy. Most were built by municipally owned housing corporations and tenant-owned cooperatives.[5] Thus, two of the ingredients that have been crucial to transit village development in some U.S. areas—government ownership of land and public promotion of affordable housing—have been similarly vital to coordinated regional development in Stockholm.

The blueprint for building Stockholm's transit metropolis was Sven Markelius's General Plan of 1945–1952. Markelius, an architect by training, believed that, while suburbanization was inevitable and needed to be accommodated, Stockholm's vitality and preeminence as the region's commercial and cultural hub had to be preserved at all costs. This was to be accomplished by building satellite new towns connected to Stockholm by rail, that is, by putting Howard's garden city concepts into practice. Despite surveys that showed Swedes preferred low- to mid-rise suburban homes, Markelius set about building fairly dense satellite centers so that most residents could be within walking distance of a rail station. He hoped that, by doing so, many households would find it unnecessary to own or use a car to reach downtown Stockholm.

In designing Stockholm's first generation of new towns—Vällingby (1950–1954), Farsta (1953–1961), and Skärholmen (1961–1968)—city planners sought to avoid a "dormitory town environment." An overriding principle was to distribute industry and offices to satellites roughly in proportion to residential population (i.e., to achieve a jobs-housing balance). Public control of land allowed this. Tax incentives were used to lure industries to new towns and promote company-provided employee housing. New towns were also planned for a mix of housing types (single-family and multitenant residences) as well as land uses, with offices, civic buildings, and shops intermingled.

Markelius's plan did not intend to make them complete towns, however. Residents were still to think of themselves as Stockholmers. Accordingly, Markelius devised the rule of halves: Half the working inhabitants would commute out of new towns and half of the workforce was to be drawn in from elsewhere. Thus, in contrast to other postwar new towns, notably the Mark I new towns designed by Sir Patrick Abercrombie to handle London's overspill growth,[6] Stockholm's satellites were not meant to be fully "self-contained"; they were more like "half-contained," even though they were planned for a balance of jobs and housing units.

The regional rail system, Tunnelbana, became the principal device to achieve half-containment. Radial in form, the 64-mi Tunnelbana system focused on Stockholm's redeveloped core. Satellite subcenters would function as countermagnets to central Stockholm, leading to efficient bidirectional traffic flows. This meant building Tunnelbana in advance of demand and incurring huge operating deficits at the outset, with the expectation that the investment would begin to pay off as the new settlement pattern took form.

11.2 FIRST-GENERATION TRANSIT VILLAGE NEW TOWNS

During 1945–1957, the first three Tunnelbana lines were built, which allowed the first satellite towns to be built in parallel. Stockholm's first generation of new towns, called ABC towns (A = housing, B = jobs, and C = services), were designed using a common formula:

☐ Balanced communities of 80,000 to 100,000 people, with over 60 percent multi-family housing (at 30 to 80 people per acre);

☐ A hierarchy of centers with a main commercial and civic center near the rail station flanked by neighborhood centers with schools and community facilities (within 2000 ft of the main center);

☐ Tapering of densities: Residential densities were highest closest to the main center, high around neighborhood centers, and progressively lower away from these centers so as to make most destinations, including the rail station, easily accessible by foot; and

☐ Separation of pedestrian and bicycle paths from automobile traffic, including grade separation at intersections.

Although these new towns included the key elements of transit villages—mixed uses, mid-rise housing, and pedestrian amenities—they lacked a human scale, and thus have lacked the "feel" of a village. Rather, they were built more as monumental Le Corbusier-style communities, with buildings set on vast superblocks in the center of the community. Accordingly, they were roundly criticized by Swedish architects and sociologists as being too institutional and sterile. Still, surveys showed that residents of these towns were quite pleased with their surroundings, despite what experts thought.[7]

Vällingby, located 8 mi west of downtown, was Stockholm's first new town, completed in 1954. Vällingby is dotted by high-rise apartments near its core. Still, the community of 25,000 residents has a wide variety of building types, including detached single-family homes. The central elevated rail station is surrounded by a large open cobblestone plaza, reflecting pools, a civic complex, and a shopping center (Photo 11.1). Vällingby's road net-

Photo 11.1 Vällingby Station Area. Stockholm's first new town, Vällingby, has a pedestrian-friendly, car-free town center with entry to the rail station via the shopping center and surrounding civic space. High-density mixed land uses near the station taper off to lower densities farther away. (*Photo:* Jeff Kenworthy.)

work consists of loops encircling neighborhoods, with a secondary grade-separated pedestrian path system (Photo 11.2). The town is in a parklike setting surrounded by trees and rock outcroppings. Because Vällingby was conceived before widespread automobile ownership, it was planned with relatively little parking in its core. In most neighborhoods, cars are grouped into small clustered parking lots.

The second satellite community built, Farsta (current population 42,000), lies 14 mi from downtown Stockholm at the terminus of the southernmost Tunnelbana route. Because Farsta was mainly developed by private investors, industrialized building methods and prefabricated concrete materials were used to construct most apartments. Very high-rises surround Farsta's central open pedestrian mall, which has three times the car parking area built in Vällingby's core.[8] Residential neighborhoods are grouped into clusters of 5000 to 7000 dwelling units. Compared to other new towns, Farsta has a large number of light industries, most located on its periphery.

In the early 1960s, the third large new town, Skärholmen, was built 9 mi west of central Stockholm. Skärholmen was planned as a subregional center. It features the largest commercial core of all Swedish new towns, with an enclosed pedestrian mall and numerous commercial attractions. A vast multistory parking garage for 4100 cars was also built, the biggest in Scandinavia. Unlike its two predecessors, Skärholmen has no high-rises; most

Photo 11.2 Separation of Motorized and Nonmotorized Traffic. A gentle slope under the road from the Vällingby town center into the surrounding residential area encourages walking and bicycling. The popularity of bicycling is evident. (*Photo:* Jeff Kenworthy.)

apartments are two to four stories, though blended densities are high. Residential neighborhoods run east-west in parallel rows, descending down the hillside. Its civic square, fronting on the Tunnelbana station, contains two large pools and shade trees, providing an inviting place to sit on sunny days (Photo 11.3).

11.3 LATER GENERATIONS OF TRANSIT VILLAGE NEW TOWNS

Stockholm's later new towns—Spånga, Kista, and Skarpnäck—broke with tradition. Compared to their predecessors, each was designed or evolved as a more specialized community. Accordingly, recent new towns provide a contrast for studying relationships between planning styles, land-use patterns, and commuting (Table 11.1).

Built on former military grounds, Spånga has two primary cores, Tensta and Rinkeby. Spånga's development during the late 1960s coincided with the influx of many non-European immigrants to Sweden; thus, more out of timing than design, it attracted a large number of low-income industrial workers. Most apartments in Tensta and Rinkeby are three to six stories, and buildings are tightly huddled. Spånga intro-

Photo 11.3 Skärlholmen Central Square. The public square sits outside of the Tunnelbana station entrance (on the left side of the photo, with the (T) sign). Two large pools, shade trees, benches, and food stalls make it a popular gathering spot. One of Sweden's largest suburban indoor shopping complexes lies opposite the station.

TABLE 11.1

Population and Development Characteristics of Stockholm's Transit Villages

	New Towns					Central Stockholm
	First Generation[1]	Spånga[2]	Kista	Skarpnäck[3]	Täby	
Population						
1980	102,500	42,225	29,081	26,237	47,105	226,405
1990	96,124	44,105	36,415	25,785	56,714	240,098
Employment						
1980	56,298	21,260	15,185	13,516	24,916	114,433
1990	50,548	21,363	18,545	13,676	32,791	324,026
Density (Dwelling Units/ Gross Acre, 1991)	8.2	14.6	4.7	5.0	1.2	8.0
Percent D.U. Multifamily (1988)	86.1	99.5	91.4	90.8	48.3	99.9
Jobs-to-Housing Ratio (1990)	1.02	0.31	3.84	0.58	0.64	1.98
Median Household Disposable Income ($, 1988)	12,400	8,580	10,020	10,350	11,600	11,930
Percent Population Non-Swedish Origin (1988)	28.3	51.3	16.9	24.0	10.8	12.1

[1]These are statistics for Vällingby, Farsta, and Skärholmen combined.
[2]Consists of Tensta and Rinkeby.
[3]Statistics shown are for the Skarpnäck district. The planned new town is a small portion of this district and is to have up to 3000 dwelling units at build-out.
Source: Stockholms Läns Landsting.

duced Sweden's first residential parking structures, which allowed higher densities while preserving open space. Breaking from Markelius's half-containment formula, Spånga was planned as a residential community (1990 jobs-to-housing ratio of only 0.31). It also has the lowest median income of Swedish new towns and the highest crime rate (though still very low by U.S. standards). Its two Tunnelbana stations front onto bustling farmer's markets, where village residents both buy and sell fruits, vegetables, and wares (Photo 11.4).

Located 10 mi northwest of downtown Stockholm, Kista has emerged as Sweden's "Silicon Valley" (Photo 11.5). A few multinational electronics companies located there in the

Photo 11.4 Farmer's Market Outside the Tensta Station. A hallmark of many Tunnelbana stations is that passengers can pick up fruit, vegetables, and a fresh bunch of flowers when arriving home from work in the evening.

early 1980s, taking advantage of its proximity to Arlanda international airport (Europe's third busiest) and its location on the main auto route to the university town of Uppsala. Today, over 200 companies and more than 20,000 employees have moved to Kista. With a jobs-to-housing ratio of 3.84, Kista is hardly self-contained. Most companies are within walking distance of Tunnelbana, interconnected by a vast grade-separated pathway system. Kista's centerpiece is the Electrum Complex, an indoor shopping and business mall that includes training and conference facilities. Compared to earlier new towns, Kista has a variety of housing, including some high-rise apartments, terrace garden apartments, duplexes, and single-family detached (Photo 11.6).

The newest new town, Skarpnäck, is just 6 mi south of central Stockholm. Designed as a neotraditional community, Skarpnäck is radically different than its predecessors. Its designers, reacting to the massive scales and the institutional "feel" of earlier new towns, have sought to create an urban milieu that is human in scale with two- to three-story structures, a gridiron street pattern, a fine-grained integration of land uses, and ground-level retail stores and sidewalk cafes on the main street (Photo 11.7). Additionally, street crossings are at grade. A mix of housing is available. Apartments are concentrated in the center with row houses and some single-family structures farther away. Most residential and

Photo 11.5 The High-Tech Center of Kista. Compact development along the Tunnelbana Line in Kista station allows the preservation of large central green spaces. (*Photo:* Jeff Kenworthy.)

Photo 11.6 Mixed Housing in Kista. The pleasant and safe walking and cycling environment in neighborhoods surrounding the station encourages foot traffic.

Photo 11.7 Streetscape in the Neotraditional Town of Skarpnäck. A sidewalk cafe is surrounded by mid-rise apartments, in
striking contrast to Stockholm's earlier generation of "monumental" new towns.

office parking is in garages. While Skarpnäck is laid out on a grid, every other street ends
in a cul-de-sac to preserve enclosed courtyards. Everyone in the community is within a 10-
min walk of Skarpnäck's recently opened Tunnelbana station.

   In summary, the newest generation of Stockholm new towns stands out from its predecessors. Spånga is an ethnically mixed bedroom community, Kista is Sweden's technopolis, and Skarpnäck is evolving as a neotraditional community in the purest sense.

11.4 BALANCE AND SELF-CONTAINMENT

As noted, Stockholm's transit-oriented new towns were designed with a balance of land
uses in mind. This is one of their strongest transit village traits. Table 11.1 shows that the

new towns have varying degrees of jobs-housing balance. Spånga is largely a bedroom community, with three times as many houses as jobs. The newest planned community, Skarpnäck, is also predominantly residential, but in striking contrast to Spånga, it has a traditional urban design. Stockholm's first-generation new towns, Vällingby, Farsta, and Skärholmen, are today the most balanced, with roughly equal numbers of jobs and housing units. Kista, the region's technopolis, stands out as a corporate enclave, with nearly four workers for every dwelling unit.

Table 11.1 also presents data for a control suburban community, Täby, which lies roughly the same distance from downtown Stockholm as the new towns. Täby, however, is not a master planned community, but rather evolved as one of the region's first market-shaped suburbs, originally housing upper-income families in search of single-family living. Täby is a suitable comparison community because, besides lying a similar distance from Stockholm, it has comparable average household incomes. Its share of single-family dwellings is much higher than any of the new towns, however, producing a low average population density. Täby is also home to a much higher share of native Swedes. It is not on a Tunnelbana Line, although it is served by a passenger railroad line and, like most Swedish communities, has excellent bus service. (The Stockholm city council proposed extending a Tunnelbana Line to Täby; however, local officials refused the offer, purportedly because of concerns over other population classes riding transit to their community.) With a jobs-to-housing ratio of 0.64, Täby is predominantly a bedroom community. The other comparison area shown in Table 11.1, central Stockholm, has roughly two jobs for every dwelling unit.

Have the different jobs-housing balance formulas among Stockholm's new towns had any influence on how self-contained, or half-contained, they are? Figure 11.1 suggests not, regardless of how balanced a community is; small shares of workers live in Stockholm's new towns, and even smaller shares of residents work where they live. For all new towns, fewer than one of three workers live within the community, and in the case of Kista, the share falls below 15 percent. Far more workers live in Stockholm and reverse commute, and even more are imported from elsewhere in Stockholm County. The nonmaster planned comparison community, Täby, has a much larger share of locally residing workers, although part of this is explained by Täby's larger land area.

In all cases, fewer than one of five new town wage earners have local jobs. The overwhelming majority work in Stockholm. Even larger shares of new town residents commute to destinations outside of central Stockholm than within their own community. Thus, although the new towns are balanced, they are far from self-sufficient. Their businesses import the majority of workers, and they export most of their adult labor force to jobs elsewhere. The commuting pattern that emerges is a tremendous amount of cross-haul commuting throughout the Stockholm region each workday. Extensive cross-hauling means that Stockholm's satellites are closely tied to and economically dependent on the rest of the region for both labor and wages. They are far from being self-contained, or even half-contained, as Sven Markelius had hoped for.

Workers

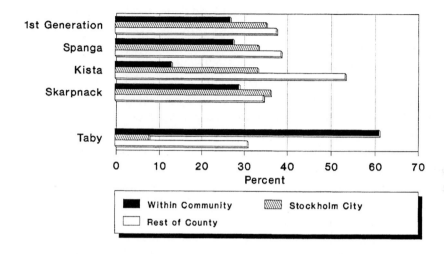

Residents

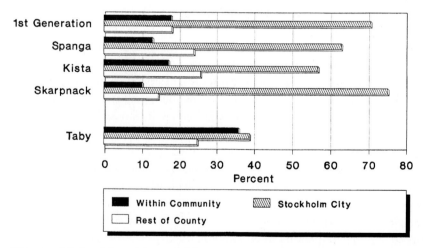

Figure 11.1 New Town Self-Containment. Percentage of workers residing in and percentage of employed residents working in Stockholm's rail-oriented new towns.

11.5 COMMUTING PATTERNS OF STOCKHOLM'S NEW TOWNS

With high levels of external commuting and large concentrations of housing and workplaces near rail stations, Stockholm's new towns provide a natural habitat for rail commuting. Figure 11.2 shows that for all new towns over half of all workers and more than a third of the residents commute via transit each day. These shares are considerably higher than those of the comparison suburb, Täby. Clearly, Stockholm's new towns have come far closer to achieving half transit commuting than half-containment. In combination, the built form of rail-fed suburbs and economic dependence on the hinterland have led to transit's extraordinary market share of journeys to work in greater Stockholm.

In the case of Kista, the region's technopolis, and Skarpnäck, the neotraditional town, more than twice as many of their workers take transit each day as drive. These shares are even higher than those for Stockholm city as a whole, which in 1992 averaged 325,000 workers commuting by public transit and roughly 290,000 driving their car to work each weekday.[9] Thus, in the Stockholm region, rail transit appears to be more heavily used for reverse commuting than for radial, downtown commuting. This is supported by the fact that in-commuters relied more heavily on rail to reach their jobs than residents who out-commuted. While over a third of new town residents took transit to work, with the exception of Skarpnäck, even larger shares commuted by car. Figure 11.2 shows that new town residents are more transit-dependent than residents of Täby, though far less than inner-city Stockholmers or other inhabitants of Stockholm County. The figure also reveals that among new towns, larger shares of residents got to work by foot in Skarpnäck, the human-scale neotraditional town devoid of grade-separated pathways, than in any of the older new towns.

An important determinant of how Stockholm area residents commute is where they are coming from and going to. Figure 11.3 shows that over half of new town residents with local jobs reach work on foot or bicycle. Moreover, nearly one out of four take bus transit to work. And if new town residents work in Stockholm, over three-quarters commute via transit. If, on the other hand, new town workers live in Stockholm, around 60 percent reverse commute on transit. These patterns hold for all sets of new towns. For those living and working within the same community, foot and bicycle commuting tends to be most popular. Over half of all work trips made by resident-workers of neotraditional Skarpnäck are by foot and bicycle. In Kista, the high-tech center, over a third of internal work trips are by bus.

Although having central rail facilities and good pedestrian and bus connections accounts for transit's popularity in Stockholm, other policy factors have made a contribution as well. Tunnelbana fares are comparatively low, around U.S. $1 to $1.50 depending on distance traveled, and multiuse passes lower the per trip cost considerably. Parking and taxi fares, on the other hand, are expensive in central Stockholm. Sweden also has among the highest value-added taxes on motor vehicles and vehicle registration fee structures anywhere.[10]

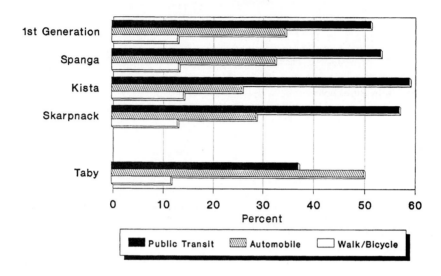

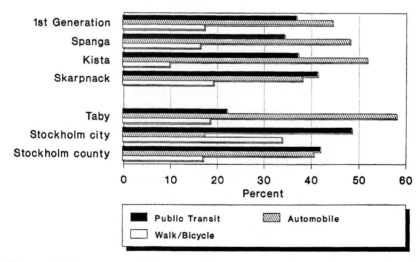

Figure 11.2 Work Trip Modal Splits. Share of commute trips by modes for workers (top) and employed residents (bottom) of Stockholm's rail-oriented new towns.

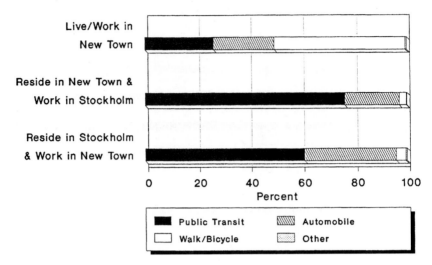

Figure 11.3 Work Trip Modes for Different Geographic Patterns of Commuting.

11.6 LESSONS FOR A SUSTAINABLE FUTURE

Stockholm's first generation of new towns was consciously planned to promote rail commuting into central Stockholm as well as to be somewhat self-contained. Commuting statistics reveal that new towns have certainly achieved the former objective but have been far off the mark of the second. Stockholm's new towns import large shares of their workforce and send off even larger shares of residents to jobs elsewhere. Commuting to and from new towns, however, is heavily oriented to transit, particularly for commutes into Stockholm. What internal commuting does take place tends to be by foot and bicycle. Thus, Stockholm's new towns are regional mobility "success stories" despite their lack of self-containment.

Overall, experiences in greater Stockholm reveal that transit villages are not isolated islands within the larger metropolis, but rather are dependent upon each other as well as major urban centers. Clearly, jobs-housing balance and self-containment are not prerequisites to reducing automobile dependence. In fact, when compared to British new towns, there appears to be an inverse relationship between self-containment and nonauto commuting. While British new towns are far more balanced and self-contained than their Swedish counterparts, they are also more auto-dependent. For instance, the overwhelming majority of working residents from Milton Keynes (a master planned new town around 50 mi north of London) have jobs there; however, around 75 percent drive their cars to work and only 7 percent commute by transit, resulting in one of the highest levels of vehicle miles traveled per capita in Europe.[11]

In closing, it is because of their economic linkages with the central city and the surrounding region, as well as their pedestrian-friendly designs and superb rail services, that Stockholm's new towns average such high levels of transit commuting. Stockholm's built form—a strong, preeminent regional core orbited by transit villages—largely accounts for low automobile dependence. From a mobility and environmental standpoint, this has more than compensated for the tendency of Stockholmers to live and work in separate communities. Thus, it has been the carefully planned codevelopment of new towns and rail transit that has put the Stockholm region on a sustainable path, rather than any kind of jobs-housing balance or self-containment.

For America, Stockholm's experiences underscore the long-term benefits of coordinated transit building and community building at a regional level. One or two successful transit villages in a landscape of sprawling development will not yield significant mobility or environmental benefits. Only when the atomistic planning of each transit village is coordinated so as to add up to a functional transit metropolis will long-term sustainability benefits accrue. In a free market, transit villages will likely always remain connected to the rest of the region, and if planned at a regional scale, rail transit will generally be the preferred mode of intervillage travel. It is because of the strong social and economic linkages among Stockholm's satellite communities, the core, and the surrounding region that so many transit village residents and workers in the region commute by train.

NOTES

1. E. Howard, *To-morrow: A Peaceful Path to Real Reform* (London: Swan Sonnenschein, 1898).

2. P. Hall, *Cities of Tomorrow: An Intellectual History of Urban Planning and Design in the Twentieth Century* (New York: Basil Blackwell, 1988).

3. P. Bovy, J. Orfeuil, and D. Zumkeller, Europe: A Heterogenous Single Market, *A Billion Trips a Day,* I. Salomon et al., eds. (Dordrecht, Netherlands: Kluwer, 1993).

4. K. Westin, Sweden: Moving Towards a Safer Environment, *A Billion Trips a Day,* I. Salomon et al., eds. (Dordrecht, Netherlands: Kluwer, 1993).

5. City of Stockholm, *The Development of Stockholm* (Stockholm: City of Stockholm 1991); Stockholm Stadsbyggandskontor, *Stockholm Urban Environment* (Uppsala, Sweden: Almquist and Wiksells, 1972).

6. A. Watson, New Towns in Perspective in England, *New Towns in Perspective: From Garden City to Urban Reconstruction,* P. Merlin and M. Sudarskis, eds. (Paris: International New Town Association Press, 1991); C. Ward, *New Town, Home Town* (London: Calouste Gulbenkian Foundation, 1993).

7. D. Popenoe, *The Suburban Environment: Sweden and the United States* (Chicago: University of Chicago Press, 1977).

8. While not initially planned for, Farsta's plan was modified to provide 2000 mostly surface parking spaces near the core. Parking was provided not only for visitors and workers, but also to attract large Swedish chain stores, something the private developers felt was essential if the development was to be financially successful.

9. AB Storstockholms Lokaltrafik, 'Stratgisk Utveckling Och Planering' (Stockholm: AB Storstockholm Lokaltrafik, 1993).

10. Bovy, Orfeuil, and Zumkeller, op. cit.; J. Pucher, Urban Travel Behavior as the Outcome of Public Policy: The Example of Modal-Split in Western Europe and North America, *Journal of the American Planning Association,* Vol. 54, No. 4, pp. 509–520, 1988.

11. J. Roberts and C. Wood, Land Use and Travel Demand, *Proceedings of Transport Research Council: Twentieth Annual Meeting* (London: Transport Research Council Education and Research Services, 1992); S. Potter, *Transport and New Towns* (Milton Keynes: The Open University, New Towns Study Unit, 1984).

12

Tokyo: Transit Villages and the Private Railway

A century ago, America's vast urban railway networks were built by entrepreneurs who packaged transit investments with real estate development. In Japan, and especially the Tokyo metropolitan area, this is still commonly practiced today. Nearly all suburban rail lines in greater Tokyo have been privately built, typically by large consortiums that link transit and new town development. In the United States, we have tried the model of publicly led transit and privately led land development over the past 50 years with disappointing results. This might be an area where we are well-advised to borrow from the past, encouraging developers to link transit and real estate projects just as they did a century ago, just as they currently do in Tokyo, and just as private tollway companies are attempting to do in northern Virginia and other parts of the United States.

12.1   RAIL DEVELOPMENT IN METROPOLITAN TOKYO

Tokyo is a huge metropolis with a dense and extensive rail transit network totaling over 1250 mi in length, with private lines making up 52 percent of metropolitan trackage in 1990. As a land-scarce country with a rapidly industrializing economy and urbanizing population, housing development has historically followed rail lines. New towns blossomed around the suburban rail stations because transit was virtually the only means for people to reach central Tokyo, which then and still today accounts for over a third of all regional employment.

While the suburbanization of Tokyo along railway lines began in the early 1900s, it was really during the post-World War II era of reconstruction and industrialization that new town building proliferated. Whereas publicly financed freeways paved the way for suburbanization in the United States, privately built rail lines became the channelways for suburbanization in greater Tokyo and other regions of Japan.

12.1.1   The Tokyo Region

Technically, there is no such entity as the city of Tokyo. The core area within a 12-mi radius of the historical center, Edo, is known as the Tokyo 23 Ward, home to 8.2 million residents. The entire Tokyo conurbation is called the Tokyo Metropolitan Region, an area measuring some 6000 mi^2 with a population exceeding 34 million that includes the surrounding prefectures of Saitama, Chiba, Kanagawa (which contains the city of Yokohama), and the southern part of Ibaraki (Map 12.1). The western part of the region, where much of the rail-oriented, new town activity has been concentrated, is known as the Tama District, a large district of hills. The region's two largest rail-oriented new towns, the pri-

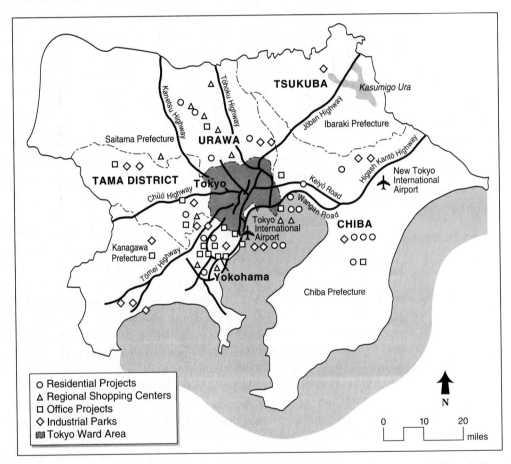

Map 12.1   Metropolitan Tokyo and Recent Regional Development. (*Adapted from:* Nomura Research Institute, *ULI Market Profiles: 1994,* Washington, DC: The Urban Land Institute, 1995.)

vately developed Tama Denin Toshi and the publicly sponsored Tama New Town, are in the Tama District, as suggested by their names.

Central Tokyo's primacy as an urban agglomeration is reflected in statistics. While the 23 Ward Area contains 10 percent of the nation's population (on 0.6 percent of its land), it boasts 58 percent of Japan's largest company headquarters, 47 percent of bank deposits, and 84 percent of foreign companies.[1] Along with primacy, however, has come overcrowding, enormously high land costs, jam-packed subways, chronic traffic congestion, pollution, and difficulties of supplying a huge metropolis with water, energy, and other necessities. In addition to providing affordable housing, the development of new towns on the periphery has been driven by the national policy of deconcentrating inner Tokyo. In recent times, land and roadway capacity constraints have undermined Tokyo's economic expansion.[2] Today, greater Tokyo averages 22,850 vehicle mi per day per square mi of land area, which is 1.9 times the vehicle traffic intensity of metropolitan Paris (Ile-de-France) and about 1.4 times that of the New York tristate region.

12.1.2 Regional Rail Network and Ridership

12.1.2.1 Rail System In 1990, a rail network of some 1300 directional mi of track served a commuteshed that expanded more than 30 mi from "ground zero"—the Tokyo station just east of the Imperial Palace and where the original Edo castle once stood (Map 12.2). Tokyo's rail network breaks down into the municipally operated subway, streetcars, monorail, and other modes serving mainly the core, the private suburban railways and subway, and the Japan Railway interurban system (Table 12.1). Since 1970, aging streetcar lines have been steadily replaced by subways.

Encircling Tokyo's core area is the Yamanote Line, with major terminals (and high-rise development) at Tokyo, Shibuya, Shinjuku, Ikebukuro, and Ueno. Within the Yamanote loop is a dense network of both public and private subways (Eidan and Toei) that crisscross central Tokyo and several lines of the now privatized Japan Railway (JR), formerly the publicly owned Japan National Railway (JNR).[3] Radiating outward from JR's Yamanote loop is a thicket of privately built rail lines, plus JR's interurban lines.

With over 4500 daily runs on the subway system alone, headways between trains in central Tokyo average 2 min and waits are usually under a minute. Most suburban railways average 6- to 8-min headways during peak hours. While headways are incredibly short by international standards, this has not hastened commuting. In 1990, the average one-way commute time within the region was 66 min. About 21 percent of commuters, or 1.85 million people, spent more than 90 min one way getting to work.[4]

12.1.2.2 Ridership Each morning, tens of thousands of neatly dressed Tokyo commuters pack into immaculately clean trains to begin their working day. In 1990, 3.5 million commuters took rail or some other form of public transportation to reach central Tokyo, 2.5 times as many as took transit into Manhattan or central Paris (despite Tokyo's subway

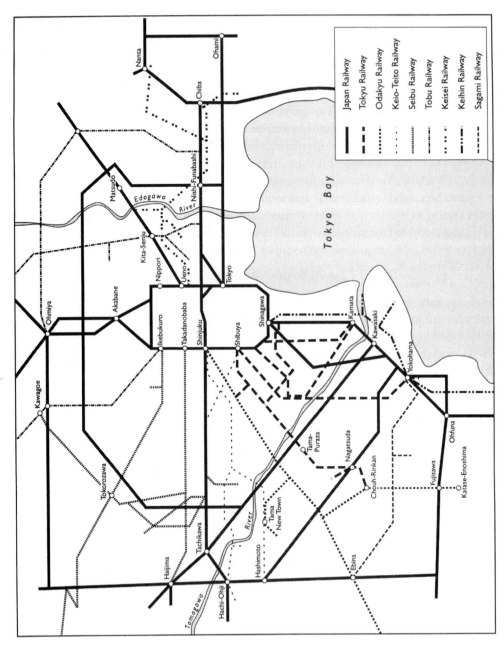

Map 12.2 Private Suburban Rail Lines and Japan Railway Lines in Metropolitan Tokyo.

TABLE 12.1

Length of Urban Railways in Tokyo Metropolitan Area, 1970–1990

System	1970		1990		Change 1970–1990	
	Directional Miles	Percent	Directional Miles	Percent	Miles	Percent[1]
Japan Railway	443.1	38.9	544.2	42.0	101.1	+3.1
Private suburban railway	500.3	43.9	560.7	43.3	60.4	−0.6
Subway[2]	81.6	7.2	149.7	11.5	68.1	+4.3
Streetcar-light rail	106.4	9.3	10.7	0.8	−95.7	−8.5
Monorail, peoplemover, other rail	8.1	0.7	30.9	2.4	22.8	+1.7
Total	1139.5	100.0	1269.2	100.0	156.7	—

[1] Percentage point change.

[2] Operated by the Teito Rapid Transit Authority (Eidan Lines) and the Municipal Subway Authority (Toei Lines).

Sources: Annual reports; K. Ohta, Transportation Problems and Policies of the Tokyo Metropolitan Region, *Contemporary Studies in Urban Planning and Environmental Management in Japan,* edited by the Department of Urban Engineering, The University of Tokyo (Tokyo: Kajima Institute Publishing, 1993).

network being less extensive than either city). Around half traveled during peak hours under extreme crowding, when loads on some lines exceed seating capacities by a 2.5 factor. Trains are so crammed that it is said sardinelike congestion is worse in winter months when passengers wear thicker clothing.

On a percentage basis, rail transit serves 25 percent of all nonwalk trips in greater Tokyo and 40 percent of those made within the central area. Rail is even more popular for commuting, handling 46 percent of all work trips in the region and 67 percent of commutes into central Tokyo. Overall, the Tokyo metropolitan area averages around 460 annual transit trips per capita, one of the highest rates in the world, higher than in Mexico City, Paris, London, and New York.[5]

12.1.3 Supportive Public Policies

Various policies enacted by national and local governments have paved the way for the Tokyo region's rail-oriented urban development. In light of the nation's land constraints (two-thirds of the country is mountainous) and total reliance on imported oil, Japan has historically imposed stiff controls on automobile ownership through various motor vehicle taxes such as a commodity tax on manufacturers and three taxes on purchasers: a vehicle acquisition (excise) tax, an annual automobile (registration) tax, and a surcharge based on vehicle weight. Japan's gasoline taxes, moreover, are three to four times higher than in the United States. In addition, all Japanese intra- and interurban expressways are tolled.

At least as important in constraining the motor vehicle population have been Japan's onerous garaging requirements. Anyone wishing to register a car must present evidence verifying the existence of an off-street parking space at their residence. Government's preference for small, space-conserving cars is reflected by the exemption of vehicles with engine capacities of 550 cc or less from registration and garaging requirements. In 1990, metropolitan Tokyo averaged 275 automobiles per 1000 inhabitants compared to a rate of 350 in greater London and over 600 in most U.S. cities.

Japan's central government further promotes transit riding through tax incentives. All Japanese workers receive a tax-free commuting allowance as high as $500 per month from their employers (which is fully deductible against corporate income taxes). While full transit commuting costs up to this ceiling are covered, automobile commuters only get 15 percent of this amount, based on distance traveled. This contrasts with U.S. policy, where historically workers have received the tax-free benefit of free parking, yet employer-paid allowances for transit riding have been treated as taxable income.

12.2 PRIVATE SUBURBAN RAILWAYS AND NEW TOWNS

West of central Tokyo, where many of the region's newest and most up-market suburbs are located, entire communities are today the domains of powerful conglomerates that are known best for their department store chains—Tokyu, Odakyu, Keio, and Seibu—but which first and foremost are in the business of railway and real estate development. All started as private railway companies in the early part of this century and over time branched into businesses closely related to the railway industry, including real estate, retailing, bus operations, and electrical power generation.[6] This was purely for financial reasons. Placing shopping malls, apartments, and entertainment complexes near stations generated rail traffic; in turn, railways brought customers to these establishments.

Government policies have had a direct hand in encouraging these side businesses. Because all rail fares in Japan are regulated by the Ministry of Transportation and kept at affordable levels, railway companies found it necessary to expand into other businesses in order to increase their profit margins. In greater Tokyo, moreover, private rail companies have over the years been granted exclusive franchises for specific territories. This has eliminated excessive competition and enhanced profitability. Within the same territory, buses are usually operated by the same company or its subsidiary. As a result, the subregional bus-rail network is coordinated both physically and institutionally.

12.2.1 Private Railway Operators

Presently, eight private railway companies own and operate suburban rail services in greater Tokyo (see Map 12.2). The Tobu Corporation operates the most extensive private network, with lines covering the northern part of the region (Table 12.2). From 1955 to 1993, private suburban railway patronage increased by over two and a half times.

Over the years, the Tokyu Corporation has been most successful at integrating rail and real estate development. Tokyu bought vast stretches of land in the early part of this century in advance of rail construction. Its first major project was Denin Chofu, one of the best known and most prestigious residential areas in Japan, built along Tokyu's rail line between the Shibuya station and Sakuragicho, the downtown of Yokohama. Tokyu anchored these two terminal stations with high-rise commercial centers (featuring Tokyu's own department stores) and attracted several prominent university campuses to intermediate stations. These commercial centers, along with the universities, have produced a steady bidirectional flow of passengers, ensuring efficient train operations.

Like the Tokyu Corporation, most private railway companies in Japan have pursued other commercial ventures, including bus operations and the construction and operation of hotels, department stores, sports stadia, amusement parks, and other ancillary businesses. Tokyo Disneyland, for example, was codeveloped by the Keisei Corporation, a rail-

TABLE 12.2
Service and Ridership Characteristics
of Private Suburban Railways in Greater Tokyo

Company	1993 Directional Rail Miles	Annual Passengers (in Millions)		% Increase in Ridership 1955–1993	1993 Passengers per Rail Mile
		1955	1993		
Tokyu	62.5	415.1	961.1	131.5	5,926,900
Odakyu	74.8	113.8	720.6	533.2	3,663,200
Keio-Teito	52.4	159.7	564.9	253.7	4,303,700
Seibu	109.0	149.5	667.3	346.4	2,359,700
Tobu	288.2	181.1	950.3	424.7	1,271,600
Keisei	56.9	97.7	281.4	188.0	1,907,400
Keihin	51.9	177.5	437.8	146.7	3,252,400
Sagami	21.7	26.9	247.9	821.6	4,399,500
Total	717.4	1321.3	4831.3	265.7	2,596,500

Sources: Japan Ministry of Transportation, *Tetsudo Yoran,* Tokyo, 1994; Japan Ministry of Transportation, *Mintetsu Toukei Nenpo,* Tokyo, 1994.

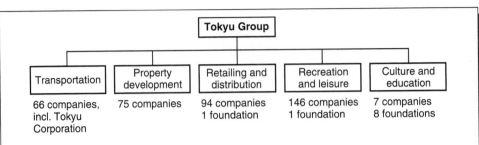

```
                        ┌─────────────────┐
                        │   Tokyu Group   │
                        └─────────────────┘
       ┌────────────┬────────────┼────────────┬────────────┐
┌──────────────┐┌──────────────┐┌──────────────┐┌──────────────┐┌──────────────┐
│Transportation││  Property    ││ Retailing and││  Recreation  ││ Culture and  │
│              ││ development   ││ distribution ││ and leisure  ││  education   │
└──────────────┘└──────────────┘└──────────────┘└──────────────┘└──────────────┘
 66 companies,   75 companies    94 companies    146 companies   7 companies
 incl. Tokyu                     1 foundation    1 foundation    8 foundations
 Corporation
```

The Tokyu Corporation is the nucleus of the Tokyu Group and the largest rail-based conglomerate in Japan. It operates seven main lines and one streetcar line, together totaling around 60 directional mi of track. In 1993, the Tokyu railway network served 961 million passengers, more than any private railway in Japan. Most lines are relatively short (the longest is less than 19 mi long). Consequently, rail trips tend to be relatively short, producing the highest patronage and farebox returns per mile of track of all private railways (see Table 12.2).

In all, the Tokyu Group owns 389 subsidiary businesses and 10 foundations divided into five major groups. In 1992, the Tokyu Group earned revenues exceeding $35 billion, owned capital assets worth more than $4 billion, and had a workforce of 113,000. The Tokyu Corporation itself claimed capital assets of over $1 billion, operating profits of $2.7 billion, and a work force of 5400.

Besides operating rail services, the Tokyu Corporation is also engaged in rail-related real estate development and in operating feeder bus services. In 1990, railway operations accounted for 35 percent of the corporation's revenues and real estate accounted for 26 percent; however, the company's real estate operations made up 59 percent of the firm's profits, compared to 47 percent generated by the railway enterprises (buses were money-losers, covering "only" 90 percent of costs).

way company. While real estate, retail, and tourism ventures have sought to create trip generators around rail stations, activities like construction, design, and engineering have sought to capitalize on and expand the domain of the railroad companies' labor forces.

12.2.2 The Economics of Japan's Private Railway Initiatives

Although rail operations have historically been the main business of railway consortia, these have hardly been the most profitable ventures. During 1980 to 1993, Tokyo's private railway sector averaged financial rates of return on railway businesses of 1.16 to 1.21 (Table 12.3). Profit margins increased slightly during the 1980s, but these were considered

TYPES OF BUSINESSES OPERATED BY RAILWAY CONSORTIA AND THEIR AFFILIATED COMPANIES

 The following represents the kinds of business activities typically pursued by large Japanese railway companies:

Business	Range of Activities
Transportation	Railway operations; bus services; taxi services; car rentals; trucking; aviation; shipping; freight forwarding; package delivery; manufacturing of rolling stock.
Real Estate	Construction, sale, and leasing of housing, office space, hotels; architectural and engineering services; landscaping.
Retailing	Construction and operation of department stores, supermarket chains, station kiosks, catering services, and specialty stores.
Leisure and Recreation	Construction and operation of resorts and spas, amusement parks, baseball stadia, multiplex movie theaters, fitness clubs, golf courses; operation of travel agencies.

modest returns during this period of rapid economic expansion. Still, every private railway made a profit, something which few passenger carriers worldwide can lay claim to. This is despite governmental regulation of what private railway companies can charge.

The major sideline business of most Japanese railway companies has been real estate. All companies earned at least a 30 percent return on real estate investments in 1993, though profits have fallen more recently following the crash in Tokyo's land markets in the early 1990s. Among all business sectors, Figure 12.1 shows the net profits in 1990 (prior to the real estate downturn) across four business sectors—rail, bus, real estate, and others— for the eight private railway companies. All except Keisei and Tobu earned more from real estate transactions than any business activity (excluding Keio-Teito, for which real estate financial data were unavailable). Interestingly, the two companies with the least successful real estate ventures, Keisei and Tobu, also have among the least intensively used suburban railway services, as reflected in the low annual patronage per track mile shown earlier in Table 12.2. This lends support to the proposition that integrated rail and property development are vital to attaining efficient rail passenger services.

TABLE 12.3

Financial Performance of Railway Businesses
Among Eight Private Railways, Greater Tokyo, 1980–1993

	Net Income (U.S. $, millions)[1]			Total Revenue/Total Costs			Net Profit per Passenger (U.S. cents)[1]		
	1980	1993	% Increase	1980	1993	% Change	1980	1993	% Increase
Tokyu	36.4	184.3	406.3	1.18	1.22	+ 3.4	4.9	19.2	291.8
Odakyu	32.6	154.7	374.5	1.19	1.22	+ 2.5	6.1	21.8	257.4
Keio-Teito	29.6	93.3	215.2	1.24	1.18	− 4.8	6.4	15.9	148.4
Seibu	11.8	153.3	1199.2	1.06	1.24	+17.0	2.1	23.0	995.2
Tobu	36.4	187.3	414.6	1.12	1.17	+ 4.5	4.9	19.7	302.0
Keisei	16.5	88.5	436.4	1.16	1.24	+ 6.9	7.0	31.5	350.0
Keihin	24.6	101.4	312.2	1.18	1.22	+ 3.4	6.5	23.2	256.9
Sagami	13.3	38.6	190.2	1.27	1.18	− 7.1	7.0	15.6	122.9
Total	201.2	1001.4	397.7	1.16	1.21	+ 4.3	6.3	23.9	279.4

[1] Actual (unadjusted for inflation) U.S. dollars; conversion from Japanese yen to U.S. dollars: 1980, U.S. $1 = 203 yen; 1993, U.S. $1 = 111 yen.

Source: Japan Ministry of Transportation, *Tetsudo Toukei Nenpo,* Tokyo, 1994.

Tokyo's railway companies clearly practice a form of internal cross-subsidization; they compensate for the low profitability of their railway and bus enterprises with profits from real estate development.[7] Because rail and bus fares are regulated, property development has become the chief means of increasing profit margins above those possible through rail operations. It has also increased the liquidity and creditworthiness of rail companies to the point that loans they need to finance rail expansion are usually available at very favorable terms (and often from within the consortia themselves, if necessary).

12.2.3 Approach to Property Development

The chief financial reason that Japanese railway companies have aggressively pursued real estate development has been to exploit *value capture* opportunities (i.e., the appreciation in land values that accrues from increasing the accessibility of properties near rail stations). Japanese railway companies have historically acquired low-priced agricultural land prior to rail construction. Because of Japan's economic prowess over the past half century and land constraints, land values have skyrocketed over the postwar era, enriching those fortunate enough to own vast suburban land holdings, including railway companies, with huge windfalls. A recent study revealed the tremendous premiums associated with being near

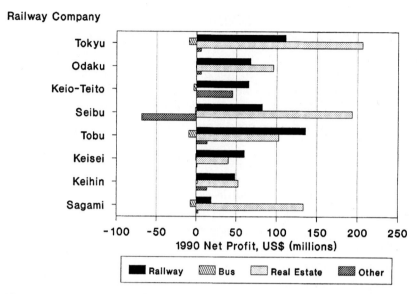

Figure 12.1   Net Profits Earned by Railway Corporations in Metropolitan Tokyo from Major Business Ventures, 1990, in Millions of U.S. Dollars.

suburban rail stations. The study showed that open parcels within 160 ft of stations on the Tokaido line (31 mi southwest of downtown Tokyo) were, on average, 57 percent more valuable than otherwise comparable parcels 1.25 mi away from the stations.[8] While the direct benefit of value capture has been to generate funds to retire capital bonds for rail investments, over the long run, a secondary benefit has been to generate ridership that helps sustain day-to-day rail operations.

The chief mechanism used by railway companies to assemble the land needed both to accommodate railways and to build real estate projects has been *land readjustment.* Under this approach, landowners form a cooperative that consolidates (often irregularly shaped) properties and returns smaller but fully serviced (and usually rectangular) parcels to landowners. Roads, drainage, sewerage, parks, and other infrastructure are funded through the sale of the "extra" reserved land contributed by cooperative members. Land readjustment has relieved railway companies of the tremendous up-front burden and cost of acquiring land and funding infrastructure.

12.3 THE TAMA DENIN TOSHI NEW TOWN

The growth spurred by the Denin Toshi Line in Tokyo's Tama area is the largest and widely viewed as the most successful land development initiative even undertaken by a pri-

COST-SHARING GUIDELINES
FOR JAPAN'S RAIL-ORIENTED NEW TOWNS

To promote integrated rail and land development, an administrative guidance regulation was promulgated in 1992 that sets guidelines for apportioning costs between rail builders-operators and real estate developers for situations where the two are not one and the same:

☐ the developer pays to the operator half of the construction costs of ground-level urban rail infrastructure;

☐ within the new town area, the developer sells the land for rail right of ways to the operator at market price, which reflects its undeveloped value;

☐ outside the new town, the developer pays the operator the difference in price for land at its historic undeveloped value and its actual value (which will have risen due to the proximity of the new town development); and

☐ on the basis of these contributions by the developer, central and local governments will each provide grant funding up to 18 percent of the construction cost of the rail system.

Construction of new rail lines to Chiba (northeast of central Tokyo) and in suburban Kobe have been constructed based on agreements similar to these.

Sources: P. Midgley, *Urban Transport in Asia: An Operational Agenda for the 1990s* (Washington, DC: The World Bank, Technical Paper Number 224, 1993); Padeco, Incorporated, *The Review of Integrated Urban Rail and Land Development in Japan* (Tokyo: Padeco, Inc., 1991).

vate railway company in Japan. From 1960 to 1984, the Tokyu Corporation's 14-mi rail line transformed a vast, hilly, and scarcely inhabited area into a planned community of 5000 ha and nearly a half million residents. Called Tama Denin Toshi (Tama Garden City), this amalgam of interconnected new towns stretches along a 10–20-mi band southwest of Tokyo that traverses four cities (Map 12.3).[9] Tama Denin Toshi proceeded from the initial master plan in 1956, to the commencement of land development in 1959, to opening the first rail segments in 1966, and to accelerated land and rail development in the 1970s and 1980s.

12.3.1 The Development Approach to Tama Denin Toshi

The concept for Tama Denin Toshi dates back to 1918 when Shibusawa Eiichi, one of the most successful entrepreneurs of the Meiji era (1868–1912), formed the Denin Toshi Cor-

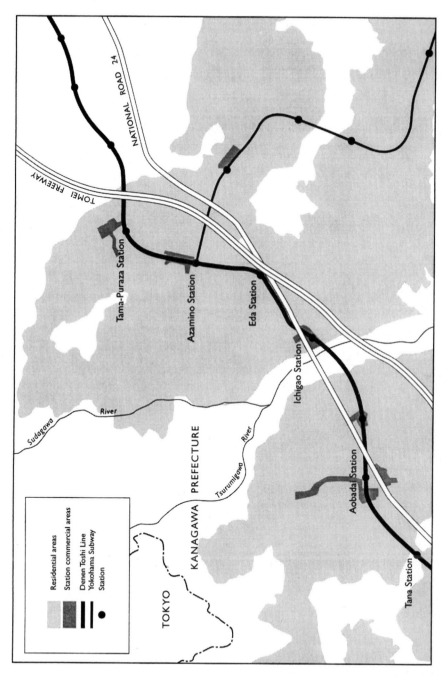

Map 12.3 Central Portions of Tama Denin Toshi. This map shows blocks 2 and 3, together which form 21,900 ha, or around 70 percent, of Tama Denin Toshi. The darker shaded areas reveal that commercial activities are concentrated around railway stations. In total, the Tokyu Corporation has built 17 shopping centers next to railway stations in Tama Denin Toshi.

poration (the Garden City Corporation in Japanese). As suggested by the company's name, Eiichi sought to relieve Tokyo of overcrowding by building communities in pastoral settings, borrowing heavily from the ideas of Ebenezer Howard. However, unlike Howard, who sought to create self-contained new towns that were physically and economically independent of London, Eiichi envisioned Japan's garden cities primarily as bedroom communities where commuters and their families would reside. While Eiichi managed to build several suburban housing enclaves, the most successful being Denin Chofu, which today remains one of greater Tokyo's most prestigious residential addresses, his dreams were largely sidetracked by World War II and the events that led up to it. It was through the vision and leadership of Eiichi's successor, Keita Gotoh, a former Minister of Transportation and highly successful entrepreneur in his own right, that Tama Denin Toshi began to take form.[10] A Japanese historian writes: "... the philanthropic garden city visions advocated by Shibusawa Eiichi had been transformed into a profiteering business venture by Keita Gotoh ... Gotoh had a conviction that the railway business was not about 'connecting points' but rather about the real estate opportunities that develop along a railway's corridor."[11]

As with other new towns, land readjustment was used to assemble land and finance infrastructure for Tama Denin Toshi. A total of 53 cooperatives were formed between 1953 and 1966 that allowed the consolidation of over 4900 ha of land. Most original landholders were farmers who placed trust in the Tokyu Corporation's ability to create high-quality communities because of the company's track record as a successful builder of garden cities (when known as the Garden City, or Denin Toshi, Corporation). Tokyu's roots as a town planning rather than a railway company gave the company an edge over its rivals in winning the support of landowners.[12] The cooperatives relinquished development rights and full control over project planning to the Tokyu Corporation. Among Japanese city planners, this unprecedented approach to new town development became known as the *Tokyu method*.

Under Tokyu's land readjustment system, landowners gave up 45 percent of their land in return for fully serviced parcels. Around half of the "land pool" went for public use and half was held in reserve and eventual sale to cover development costs. Reserve land sold for $1.40 per square foot during the first phase of development in 1953 to nearly $5 per square foot in the mid-1960s.[13] These were considered extremely expensive prices at the time; however, speculators willingly paid these amounts in anticipation of the high-quality community that would eventually get built. Tokyu's coordinated approach to land assemblage and project financing allowed a continuous urban area with uniform and high-quality roads, sewerage, drainage, and other urban infrastructure to take form.

12.3.2 Design of Tama Denin Toshi

Tama Denin Toshi was designed with town centers and housing estates sited around most of the 19 stations along Tokyu's Denin Toshi rail line. To jump start housing construction,

EXAMPLE OF LAND READJUSTMENT PROJECT IN TAMA DENIN TOSHI

The Akada Land Readjustment project is located between the Eda and Azamino stations (see Map 12.3). Developed between January 1985 and March 1992, the Akada project encompassed an area of 687.7 ha made up of 1078 original irregularly plotted lots. Of this total area, 175.2 ha (25.5 percent) was held in reserve and later sold for a total of $166 million (based on currency exchange rates from 1985 to 1992) to defray development costs. The city of Yokohama also contributed nearly a million U.S. dollars toward development. By 1992, the Akada neighborhood had the following land-use composition.

Land Activity	Area (Hectares)	Percent of Total Area	Population
Reserve Land:			
☐ Road development	134.7	19.7	
☐ Park development	35.5	5.2	
☐ Water courses, drainage, sanitation	5.9	0.9	
Land for Public Facilities (schools, shrines, etc.)	49.7	7.3	
Housing Development:			
☐ Detached housing (660 ft²/lot; 1488 lots)	297.7	43.3	5,952
☐ Farmsteads (980 ft²/lot; 250 lots)	75.0	10.9	1,000
☐ Low-rise group housing (280 ft²/lot; 267 lots)	22.7	3.3	668
☐ Mid-rise group housing (280 ft²/lot; 759 lots)	64.5	9.4	2,656
Total	685.7	100.0	10,276

Source: Tokyu Corporation, internal memorandum.

Tokyu sold land to public housing corporations, companies (for employee dormitories and corporate housing), and private homebuilders. The Tokyu Real Estate Company, a subsidiary of the Tokyu Corporation, also built homes. While proceeds from land readjustment defrayed the costs of basic infrastructure, Tokyu supplemented this by building swimming pools, tennis courts, museums, and sports facilities and by installing regional cable television services throughout Tama Denin Toshi. By providing high-quality neighborhood amenities, Tokyu was able to sell housing at premium prices.

Tokyu was particularly committed to attracting institutional land uses, including several universities and prestigious private schools, in addition to medical centers, post offices, libraries, fire and police stations, and government branch offices. Land was either donated or sold below market value to attract these uses. In 1975, Tokyu gave away 36 ha of land to Keio University to establish a campus south of the Tana station. Besides increasing the marketability of the Tama Denin Toshi project, universities and other institutional uses have generated much-welcomed off-peak and reverse-direction rail traffic.

The greatest concentration of commercial development has been around the Tama-Puraza and Aobada stations (Photos 12.1 and 12.2). Each station is flanked by a compact, mixed-use urban center featuring a shopping plaza anchored by a Tokyu department store, a large supermarket, mid-rise offices, hotels, banks, post offices, and recreational offerings, including sports clubs. Walkways radiate from the centers to nearby residential neighborhoods whose densities taper off with distance from the stations. Equally noticeable around most stations is the absence of park-and-ride lots. This, combined with good bus connections and landscaped pathways, has marginalized the automobile as a serious station access mode. In 1988, for example, only 6.1 percent of access trips to stations in Tama Denin Toshi were by automobile. By comparison, the share of access trips by bus was 24.7 percent and by walking-cycling was 67.8 percent.[14]

Photo 12.1 Tama-Puraza Station. Tama-Puraza, 14 mi southwest of the Tokyo station, was designed as the focal point of Tama Denin Toshi. *Puraza* means "plaza" in Japanese. The Tokyu Corporation, which owns 80 percent of the 118 ha of land comprising the Tama-Puraza community, introduced a Radburn style of neighborhood design, building internal pathways to separate pedestrians from automobiles, installing cul-de-sacs to create private residential enclaves, and planting street trees as a landscaping amenity. The Tama-Puraza station averaged around 65,000 daily passenger boardings in 1990.

Photo 12.2 Train on Denin Toshi Line Moving Between the Tokyu Department Store and the Aodaba Station. All stations along the Denin Toshi corridor are billed as "full service centers." Besides selling train and bus tickets, service centers list available housing units, make reservations and sell local theater and concert tickets, provide travel advice and booking services, and arrange document and package deliveries.

In 1988, 35 years after Tama Denin Toshi was first conceived, the Tokyu Corporation received awards from the Architectural Institute of Japan and from Japan's Minister of Construction in recognition of excellence in new town planning, the first-ever award given to a private railway developer. Tokyu is not content to rest on its laurels, however. The lack of employment opportunities and certain community facilities, notably hospitals, is widely viewed as a shortcoming of Tama Denin Toshi and other rail-oriented new towns. In response, the Tokyu Corporation has recently drawn plans to add a research and educational complex and several business-industrial parks, all laced with fiber optic cable and smart buildings. Over time, Tokyu hopes to transform Tama Denin Toshi from a predominantly bedroom community, albeit a transit-oriented one, into a diverse and dynamic city with an efficient and balanced flow of traffic and information.

12.4 RECENT PUBLICLY SPONSORED RAIL-ORIENTED NEW TOWNS

Borrowing a chapter from private industry, Japan's public sector has recently gotten into the business of building rail-oriented new towns. This is partly because of the near prohibitive cost of building new towns in contemporary Japan in the wake of meteoric increases in land values. Today, only a partnership of local and national authorities, in concert with private real estate developers, can muster the resources necessary to mount a venture of coordinated rail and new town development. In greater Tokyo, one of the largest publicly mounted efforts to create a new transit-oriented community has been the Tama New Town in western Tokyo. Other notable publicly sponsored new towns in the region include Tsukuba Science City (over 20,000 ha), Ryugasaki (671 ha), Chiba (1933 ha), and Kohoku (1317 ha).

Tama New Town is a joint venture of the Tokyo metropolitan government and the nation's Housing and Urban Development Corporation (recently formed under the national New Town Rail Construction Scheme Act). While master planned by the public sector, rail and property development has been a public-private coventure. The two major rail lines serving Tama New Town—Keio Sagamihara and Odakyu Tama—did not open until 1990. Both lines were built by a public railway corporation and later turned over to a private operator, with construction costs to be repaid over a 15-year period. The investment's 10 percent annual interest payments are being split between the private railway company and public-private property developers.

The physical development of Tama New Town has been divided geographically among public authorities (Table 12.4). Of the 21 residential areas, 8 in the western and northern sections of the New Town are being developed by Tokyo metropolitan government and 12 in the southern and eastern parts are being developed by the HUDC. One centrally located neighborhood is the development responsibility of the Tokyo Metropolitan Hous-

TABLE 12.4
Tama New Town Project Area and Target Populations, 1994

Development Responsibility	Development Area (Hectares)	Number of Residential Areas	Projected Target Population
Tokyo Metropolitan Government	738.4	7	96,500
Housing and Urban Development Corporation	1437.5	13	174,700
Tokyo Metropolitan Housing Supply Corporation	49.7	1	10,500
Privately developed or pending[1]	758.1	—	80,100
Total	2983.7	21	361,800

[1] Developed or sold by original landholders under land readjustment scheme or pending development approval.

Source: Tokyo Metropolitan Government, Housing and Urban Development Corporation, and Tokyo Metropolitan Housing Supply Corporation, *Tama New Town*, Tokyo, 1994.

ing Supply Corporation. As with other Japanese new towns, most up-front infrastructure in Tama New Town was financed through land readjustment schemes.

Today, Tama New Town boasts 170,000 inhabitants and 35,000 jobs within a 3000-ha area, with the target population and labor force set at 360,000 residents and 130,000 workers, respectively. Thus, unlike other new towns in greater Tokyo, Tama New Town is slated to be a balanced community. The Tokyo metropolitan government has aggressively recruited companies to locate in the new town, offering tax incentives and below market-rate land purchases. So far, a modest degree of self-containment has been achieved. A 1991 survey found that 20 percent of the employed residents had jobs within Tama New Town.[15] Of the remaining 80 percent leaving the New Town for jobs, two-thirds commuted to Tokyo 23 Ward and 70 percent commuted via rail transit.

Tama New Town is being physically designed along the lines of an American-style planned unit development (PUD), with the notable exception that rail stops anchor town centers and shopping plazas. The organizing principle of each planned enclave is a junior high school. All 21 residential areas contain a centrally located junior high school as well as two primary schools, are connected by distributor roads, and are interlaced by greenbelts. Tama New Town has won accolades for the variety of housing being offered, a novelty in urban Japan. Public housing built by local and national authorities consists of mid-rise and high-rise apartments sited near rail stops and targeted at low- and middle-income households. These are surrounded by privately built single-family detached units sold at market rate. By regional standards, Tama New Town's housing is considered spacious and attractive, and the wooded surroundings are highly prized by residents.

Four of Tama New Town's rail stations are flanked by urban centers featuring retail plazas, offices, banks, and institutional uses (Photos 12.3 and 12.4). The premier center is Tama Center in the heart of New Town (Photo 12.5). These urban centers are notable for their conspicuous absence of park-and-ride lots even though most Tama New Town households have a car and a garage. Tama's residents bus-and-ride, walk-and-ride, or bike-and-ride instead.

12.5 LESSONS FROM METROPOLITAN TOKYO

Tokyo's new towns clearly demonstrate the potential rewards of a more entrepreneurial approach to integrated rail and community development. Railway services have formed a strategic base from which a whole range of other business activities have been developed. While railway consortia have reaped huge profits from integrated rail and land development, often as protected franchises, the public at large has equally benefited from more sustainable patterns of regional growth, notably the emergence of well-designed suburban communities that allow for low-cost and efficient rail travel. The private sector's successes have spawned recent public-sector imitators, such as the Tama New Town coventure between the metropolitan and national government.

Photo 12.3 Minami-Osawa Station Area. Developed under the leadership of the Tokyo metropolitan government in the western district, this station contains a large retail-commercial center and the nearby Tokyo Metropolitan University which generates a steady stream of foot traffic between the campus and the station.

Photo 12.4 Horinouchi Station Area. Developed by the national Housing and Urban Development Corporation, a system of escalators and sloping shaft elevators connect residents living in apartments and condominiums on a nearby hillside to the station on the Neiko Sagamihara Line and the surrounding retail complex.

Photo 12.5 Tama Center. The premier center for Tama New Town, the Tama Center is punctuated by a wide pedestrian promenade that ties directly into the train station and is flanked by mid-rise office towers, government offices, and hotels.

It is interesting that currently in the United States private companies are building tollway systems in the suburbs and exurbs of several large metropolitan areas, partly to capitalize on the willingness of commuters to pay top dollar to avoid traffic congestion and partly to develop land parcels near tollway interchanges. The Dulles Greenway, a 14-mi tollway in the booming corridor between Leesburg and the Dulles International Airport in northern Virginia, was recently opened by a consortium of roadway builders, toll operators, and landholders. While the investors hope to reap profits from the $2-plus tolls motorists are paying to bypass traffic congestion, they also hope to profit from leasing and selling land around major interchanges. That is, they hope to capture the value added by transport investments, just as Japanese railway companies have done over the years and America's earlier generation of private-sector rail builders did a century or more ago. The prognosis only can be that integrated tollway-land development will lead to even greater auto-oriented suburban and exurban development in suburban Washington, DC, and other U.S. metropolises in years to come. America's transit industry might be well advised to borrow from the experiences of Japan's private rail builders and emulate the practices of contemporary U.S. tollway profiteers. Japan teaches us that the combination of profit-seeking entrepreneurs and community-minded government offers the best hope for creating the kinds of built environments that allow mass transportation to compete successfully with the private automobile in suburbia.

NOTES

1. R. Cybriwsky, Tokyo, *Cities,* Vol 10, No. 1, pp. 2–10, 1993.
2. In 1993, the 23 Ward Area averaged 20,712 persons per square mile. This exceeded the persons per square mile of New York City (1990: 14,149), Mexico City (1988: 11,080), and Los Angeles (1990: 4608). Sources: Tokyo Metropolitan Government, *Statistics of Large World Cities,* 1993; U.S. Bureau of the Census.
3. In 1987, Japan National Railway was broken into 12 private corporations after it had accumulated a debt totaling some $285 billion. Now called JR, or the Japanese Railway, the privatization initiative was undertaken in hopes of emulating the financial success of suburban rail companies.
4. K. Ohta, Transportation Problems and Policies of the Tokyo Metropolitan Region, *Contemporary Studies in Urban Planning and Environmental Management in Japan,* Department of Urban Engineering, ed. (Tokyo: Kajima Institute Publishing, 1993).
5. Excluding former and existing socialist and communist countries, only Singapore and Hong Kong average more transit trips per capita than metropolitan Tokyo. With 17.4 million annual passengers per mile of rail line, moreover, metropolitan Tokyo has one of the most intensively used systems anywhere (e.g., versus comparable statistics of 14.6 million in greater Mexico City, 9.6 million in greater Paris, 3.8 million in greater New York City, and 3.8 million in greater London). See Jane, Inc., *Jane's Urban Transport System, 1994–1995* (New York: Jane, Inc., 1994).
6. The first private railway was built in the Tokyo region in 1907. The majority of suburban rail lines were built between 1925 and 1940. See E. Aoki, *History and Culture of Private Railway Management* (Tokyo: Koin-Shoin, 1992).
7. Technically, businesses are not cross-subsidized in the sense that rail construction and operation costs are fully recovered through the farebox. Legally, income from property development cannot be earmarked to recover rail construction and operating costs. The purpose of this requirement is to prevent unfair fare increases that might occur if the accounts of rail and real estate businesses were commingled.
8. T. Yai, Institutions and Finance Systems for Urban Railway Construction. Paper presented at the Seminar on Urban Transportation in Indonesia, Jakarta, March 1991, Ministry of Construction, Government of Indonesia.
9. Tama Denin Toshi lies within the city limits of Yokohama, Kawasaki, Machida, and Yamato, all of which are within the Kanagawa Prefecture.
10. Keita Gotoh entered the railway business at an early age, in 1922 becoming director of Meguro-Kamata-Dentetsu, Inc., the branch company of the Denin Toshi Corporation that first built suburban railway lines in Tokyo's southwest suburbs. Because of the tremendous profitability of the railway business, Meguro-Kamata-Dentetsu eventually took over Denin Toshi Corporation and, through various hostile takeovers, several rival railway companies as well. In 1928, Gotoh became president of Meguro-Kamata-Dentetsu, which aggressively built rail-oriented projects during the 1930s and, through

various mergers, eventually became the Tokyu Dentetsu Railway Corporation. In 1944, Gotoh resigned his post as president to become Japan's Minister of Transportation, but soon after World War II, was part of a national purge of civil servants. When the purge was rescinded in 1951, Gotoh returned to become president of Tokyu Corporation. The life and history of Keita Gotoh as a great railway builder and power broker are chronicled in a book *The Myth of Land* by Naoki Inose (Tokyo: Shogakukan, 1988).

11. Inose, op. cit., pp. 154, 162.
12. To coordinate the activities of the many cooperatives, the Tokyu Railway Corporation formed various development committees comprised of company employees, local residents, and municipal officials. Six of the thirteen members of development committees consisted of Tokyu Corporation employees.
13. Tokyu Corporation, *35 Year History of Tama Denin-Toshi* (Tokyo: Tokyu Railway Corporation, 1989).
14. Tokyo Metropolitan Government, *Person Trip Survey for Tokyo Metropolis, 1988* (Tokyo: Tokyo Metropolitan Government 1990).
15. Tokyo Metropolitan Government, *Tama New Town: Commuting by Residents* (Tokyo: Tokyo Metropolitan Government 1992).

13

Singapore: The Master Planned Metropolis

During the past 25 years, the city-state of Singapore has progressed from relative poverty to become one of Asia's most dynamic newly industrialized economies (NIE). With little land or natural resources, Singapore has relied on its strategic location, low-cost labor, infrastructure investments, and an unprecedented level of physical master planning to catapult itself into the ranks of a modern, industrialized country, with living standards that now match those of Japan and western Europe. Key to Singapore's economic transformation has been the creation of a comprehensive and efficient transportation system. Today, Singapore boasts the world's busiest containerized port, a major international airport, a top-ranked airline, a sizable national shipping line, a network of superhighways, and a new, modern mass rapid transit system (MRT). This massive buildup of transportation infrastructure occurred within the framework of a highly centralized physical and economic planning system which has carefully guided the country's development over the past few decades. Another outcome has been the emergence of some 20 satellite new towns that are linked by the new MRT, like pearls on a necklace. All have the land-use makeup and amenities of a transit village, though with a distinct high-rise profile. Complementing this integration of rail and new towns has been a series of draconian measures taken to restrain automobile ownership and usage, diverting the majority of motorized trips into trains and buses.

A review of Singapore's experiences shows what is achievable under extremes: near complete centralized control over urban development and community design, punitive pricing of the automobile, and a socially minded, protransit government. Singapore can today claim one of the most efficient transit–land-use connections anywhere, though some might say at the expense of excessive government interventions and limitations on lifestyle choices. Still, most Singaporeans strongly back their government, viewing a degree of authoritarianism as a small price to pay for living in a modern, prosperous metropolis with public amenities and services, including a world-class rail system, that are matched by few.

13.1   FROM RICKSHAW TO RAPID TRANSIT

Situated just north of the equator, Singapore consists of several small islands, the largest of which is the diamond-shaped main island of Singapore (26 mi from east to west and 14 mi from north to south) (Map 13.1). The entire island-nation is 398 mi^2 in size and is home to some 3 million residents. Seventy-eight percent of Singaporeans are of Chinese descent.

Following a century and a half of mainly British rule, in 1965 Singapore became an independent republic with a single-tier parliamentary system of government. Lee Kuan Yew was elected the country's first prime minister, a post he held until his resignation in 1990. It was under Yew's stewardship and firm control that Singapore's dramatic economic and physical transformation into a modern industrial state took place.

In the early part of this century, Singapore was a poor island-outpost, with a modest port ringed by slums and squalor, though teeming with streetlife. Most residents relied on either primitive means of transportation, notably rickshaws and horsecarts, or the several hundred tiny Chinese-run buses, known as "mosquitos," to get around. As Singapore prospered, the conflict between human- and horse-drawn modes, mosquito buses, and other motorized traffic prompted authorities to consolidate bus services and all but ban most slow-moving modes.[1] By the mid-1970s, the eleven Chinese-owned bus companies that had long served the island were, under government directive, merged into three and eventually into a single state-controlled enterprise.[2] And by 1990, many cross-island bus routes had been replaced by a sleek, modern metrorail system. Today, the MRT is complemented by feeder and mainline bus services, a downtown shuttle system, and one of the world's largest taxi fleets. Although long gone from most quarters, one can still find rickshaws in older parts of town and plying the tourist trade near Singapore's renowned shopping district, Orchard Road. In ways, the transformation from rickshaw to rapid transit stands as a metaphor of Singapore's transformation from a remote, backward port town to a modern, prosperous metropolis.[3]

13.2   MASTER PLANNING IN SINGAPORE

Singapore's physical transformation has first and foremost been driven by national economic development policies. Recognizing that Singapore's primary asset was its abundant and cheap labor, soon after independence, the country's leadership embarked on an industrial development strategy that emphasized export manufacturing and multinational investments. Tax concessions attracted foreign capital, and industrial towns were built using prefabricated infrastructure, allowing foreign manufacturers to quickly start up low-cost branch plants. The mix of public-sector involvement in commerce and industry under a free-enterprise system gave rise to what today remains Singapore's peculiar brand of social capitalism.

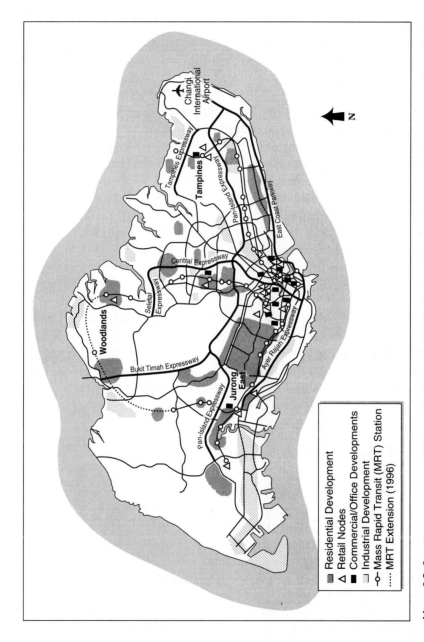

Map 13.1 Development of Singapore Island, 1995. (Adapted from Richard Ellis [Singapore] Pte., Ltd., *ULI Market Profiles*, Washington, DC: The Urban Land Institute, 1995.)

Legend:
- ▨ Residential Development
- △ Retail Nodes
- ■ Commercial/Office Developments
- ▨ Industrial Development
- ⊸o⊸ Mass Rapid Transit (MRT) Station
- ⋯⋯ MRT Extension (1996)

Singapore's one-party rule provided the political unity and stability necessary for a highly centralized strategic planning process to emerge. And its land and natural resource constraints meant that the newly independent government could justify to its citizens that a strong guiding hand was needed to launch Singapore onto a path of sustained economic growth. One of the first steps taken to gain popular support for centralized planning was the relocation of most residents from crowded, poorly serviced slum housing and semirural compounds into modern high-rise housing units. Retail, cultural, and service facilities were over the years gradually added to high-rise residential nodes, and a network of feeder roads and expressways was laid to connect residents to the urban core and newly built industrial estates. From 1970 to 1990, while Singapore's population increased by nearly a half (2.07 to 3.01 million), the number of dwelling units almost quadrupled (180,600 to 735,900), and commercial and industrial space increased more than 7.5 times (2.33 to 18.45 million ft²). During the same period, Singapore's urbanized area went from covering 32 to 51 percent of the island. Average densities, on the other hand, fell from 17,600 to 14,100 persons per square mile.[4]

Singapore's development during the 1960s was guided in large part by town planning principles carried over from British colonialism. Rapid growth, however, underscored the need for a more comprehensive regional planning campaign. This led to the approval of a Concept Plan in 1971 that provided a blueprint for the country's physical development for the next 20 years. Known as the Ring Plan, it called for configuring high-density housing, industrial sites, and urban centers in a ring around the urban core, linked together by a high-capacity and efficient transportation network. This plan formed the basis for the construction of new towns and the MRT that would interconnect them. The restructuring of the island's star-shaped transport network into a series of rings would allow cross-island traffic to bypass the crowded city center.

13.3 IMPLEMENTING THE PLAN

In Singapore, like Stockholm and Tokyo, one finds one of the most efficient connections between transport technology and settlement pattern anywhere. As with all good planning, land-use visions guided eventual transport investments. Specifically, it was the Ring Plan's vision of a multinodal settlement pattern, featuring satellite new towns, that gave rise to Singapore's highly acclaimed fixed-guideway rail network and supporting bus system.

Certainly an important part of plan implementation in Singapore has been uninterrupted, top-down decision making. Singaporeans are generally highly respectful and compliant of government. There is no discernible outcry over the lack of grass-roots input into urban development decisions. This has greatly streamlined and expedited plan implementation.

13.3.1 New Town Design

A hierarchical pattern of development was chosen for Singapore's satellite new towns, exemplified by the layout of Ang Mo Kio, shown in Map 13.2. While designed according

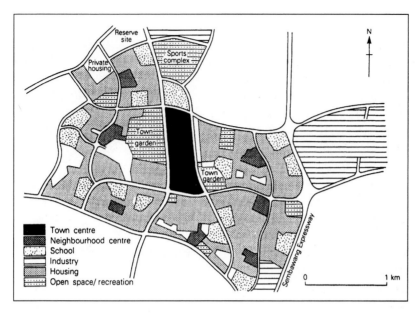

Map 13.2   Settlement Pattern and Land Uses in Ang Mo Kio New Town, 1985. (*Source:* L. Wang, Residential New Town Development in Singapore: Background, Planning, and Design, *New Towns in East and South-east Asia: Planning and Development,* D. Phillips and A. Yeh, eds. Hong Kong: Oxford University Press, 1987.)

to the principles of a transit village, most new towns predated the MRT, though rail transit's eventual arrival was anticipated and planned for.

Each of Singapore's new towns is made up of five to seven interlocking residential neighborhoods that orbit a higher order town center (Photo 13.1). Most span around 40 ha in size, contain some 4000 to 6000 dwelling units, and have a small neighborhood center within 5 min of all units featuring retail shops, schools, and recreational facilities. With Ang Mo Kio and other more recent new towns, neighborhood precincts have also been introduced wherein some 600 to 1000 dwelling units surround a landscaped village square containing playgrounds, a few small shops, and one or two eateries.[5] A system of walkways links precincts with neighborhood centers, which in turn are tied to the town center. Major pedestrian streams are separated from busy roads by gently sloped under- and overpasses.

New town centers were Singapore's first real attempt to create commercial districts outside of downtown. This involved a unique blend of American-style shopping malls and traditional shop-houses found throughout Southeast Asia. Besides retail shops, town centers provide a full array of community services, including theaters, banks, medical clinics, and telecommunications centers. What is missing from most, however, are offices and other major employment sites. Thus, while the 1971 Ring Plan called for some degree of

Photo 13.1 Town Center at Ang Mo Kio Station. A village green opens onto the MRT station from the town center. Ang Mo Kio, 7.5 mi north of downtown Singapore, was developed in the mid-1970s as a predominantly residential new town. In 1990, 69.6 percent of employed residents of Ang Mo Kio commuted via MRT or bus transit.

self-containment, few satellite new towns can claim this. In 1990, 79.3 percent of employed residents worked outside of their new town of residence.[6] Thus, like Stockholm and Tokyo, a considerable amount of cross-haul commuting occurs between new towns and the urban core as well as amongst the new towns themselves.

13.3.2 New Town Housing

The prototype building chosen for Singapore's new towns was a high-rise slab structure, ranging from 10 to 20 stories in height and averaging 200 units per hectare (Photo 13.2). The standardization of housing substantially reduced the time and cost of construction, though at the expense of creating a somewhat monotonous built environment. Still, in light of earlier slum conditions and the nation's land constraints, Singaporeans quickly adapted to high-rise living, and surveys suggest that they have a high degree of satisfaction with it.[7]

By 1995, Singapore's chief home builder, the Housing and Development Board (HDB), had housed 87 percent of the population in some 700,000 flats, all located in the island's 20 new towns. Ownership of publicly built flats increased from 25.4 percent in 1970 to 84

Photo 13.2   Prototypical Publicly Built but Privately Owned Housing Aligned Along the MRT, Midway Between the Ang Mo Kio and Yio Chu Kang Stations.

percent in 1995. Including private housing, Singapore's home ownership rate today stands at 86 percent of all households, significantly higher than in most developed countries. This has been achieved both through government subsidies and the provision of a basic housing shell which keeps prices low and allows residents to embellish their homes as they choose.

Singapore's housing planners hope to diversify the island's housing stock by promoting more low-rise, private home construction. From 1991 to 1995, HDB released over 200 ha of land for private housing development. Some parcels are near MRT stations, like Bishan (Photo 13.3), Simei, and Yishun, in hopes of giving some stations a spacious, open character.

13.4   URBAN TRANSPORT IN SINGAPORE

By Southeast Asian standards, Singapore boasts an impressive roadway system with some 1800 mi of paved roads and 68 mi of grade-separated expressways. The city-state averages three times as much road space per capita as Bangkok, Jakarta, and Manila.[8] Consequently, its roads are relatively congestion free, with peak hour travel speeds in the central area averaging approximately 20 mi per hour.[9]

Photo 13.3   Low-Density Housing Near the Bishan Station. An MRT train, right side of the photo, arrives at the Bishan station, which is flanked to the west by mainly single-family detached housing in the Marymount district. East of the station is the Bishan town center and high-rise public housing. In all, 14 percent of Bishan's 23,425 housing units are low-density, and the remaining are mid- and high-rise.

Photo 13.4   Tampines Town Center. Privately built shopping complex lies east of the MRT station.

TAMPINES

 From its humble beginnings as a wasteland, in the past two decades Tampines has emerged as Singapore's principal regional hub for the eastern side of the island (Photo 13.4). The centrally located town center contains an MRT station, bus interchange, and the DBS (Development Bank of Singapore) Tampines Center and Pavilion Cineplex, both built through the tried and trusted government land sale program. Surrounding the town center are eight neighborhoods, each with between 5000 and 6000 mid- and high-rise flats. Each neighborhood has its own center featuring retail shops, restaurants, and services like dry cleaners and salons. All flats are within a 10-min walk of neighborhood centers, while schools, parks, and recreational centers are within a short bus ride. Tampines was also the first Singapore new town to feature green connectors, a series of interlinked walkways and open spaces through the housing precincts that bring play areas and landscaped green strips almost to residents' doorsteps. In recognition of its exemplary built form and strong transit orientation, the Tampines new town received the coveted World Habitat award in 1992.

It is Singapore's public transportation, however, that is the workhorse of the urban transportation system, serving two-thirds of motorized trips. The combination of MRT trunkline services and motor bus feeders, all privately operated, has produced one of the most efficient and integrated transit networks anywhere.

13.4.1 Singapore's Transit Services

Singapore's 1971 Concept Plan called upon a new mass rapid transit system to serve as the island nation's lifeline, linking residents of new housing estates to jobs, shopping centers, and recreational offerings throughout the island. MRT construction began in late 1983, with the main east-west line opening in 1987 followed by the opening of two north-south spurs in 1990, forming a 41.6-mi, 42-station system that was completed 2 years ahead of schedule and under budget (U.S. $2.2 billion). An additional 10 mi and 6 stations were added in 1996, linking the two north-south lines via a new northern loop. The timing of the MRT investment was fortuitous, for it occurred when Singapore's pace of urban development was probably the fastest in the world. This meant the MRT was in an unusually good position to steer and reinforce where and when growth occurred.

The MRT's performance is impressive by any standard. Trains average speeds of 25 mi/h, 25 percent faster than the average car moves. Peak-hour headways are just 3 to 4 min, while off-peak headways are about twice as long. Trains arrive within a minute of schedule over 99.7 percent of the time. And the MRT goes where its customers are; approximately half of Singapore's population resides within 0.60 mi of a rail station.

Complementing the MRT are privately owned, profit-making bus services under license to the Singapore government. The largest company is the Singapore Bus Service (SBS), which provides feeder runs to MRT stations and cross-town links that both parallel and operate in areas unserved by MRT. Buses on SBS's 200 routes operate on 3- to 5-min peak headways. In 1983, the Transit-Island Bus Services (TIBS) was formed and given 10 percent of islandwide bus services, mainly in northern districts, to promote greater competition in the local bus sector. Also, there are five shuttle bus routes that connect peripheral parking lots to urban centers operated by the Singapore Shuttle Bus Company.

13.4.2 Transit Ridership

Ridership on the MRT has increased steadily since its opening, rising from around 370,000 average weekday riders in 1990, to 676,000 in 1992, and to over 800,000 in 1994. However, buses continue to capture the lion's share of transit patrons, carrying over 2.9 million passengers a day in 1994.

In 1994, the typical Singapore resident made 427 transit trips. Only Hong Kong could claim as many transit trips per capita. A combination of factors—efficient services, high-density development (over 16,000 persons per square mile), socioeconomics, and auto-restraint policies—account for transit's phenomenal popularity among Singaporeans. The strong correlation between transit ridership and housing density is revealed by census journey-to-work statistics. In 1990, two-thirds of Singapore's workers commuted via mass transit with 12 percent riding the MRT and 54.4 percent using bus transit.[10] Among those living in high-rise public housing, 72.3 percent commuted via public transit. By comparison, only around 37 percent of those living in lower density private homes commuted by rail or bus; over half traveled by car. These modal split differences reflect a combination of land-use and income effects: Those living in public housing typically are closer to and better served by transit, and also are less able to afford automobile travel.

Modal split differences along socioeconomic lines are further revealed by cross-tabulating commuting statistics by occupation. Over 75 percent of clerical and sales workers commuted via mass transit versus over 50 percent of professionals and production workers and just 20 percent of administrators and managers. The relatively high share of rail commuting among professionals and clerical-sales workers reflects the fact that many work downtown and in urban centers well served by the MRT. Transit is the preferred mode of commuting even to satellite job centers. At Jurong, Singapore's showcase industrial estate, 67.9 percent of the 157,600 workers reached their jobs via MRT or bus in 1990.

It is noteworthy that Hong Kong is more than three times as dense as Singapore (and has fairly comparable income and transit service levels), but the two city-states' transit ridership levels per capita are nearly identical. Singapore's far-reaching set of government strictures that restrain automobile travel largely explains why.

13.5   RESTRAINING THE CAR

Vital to the mission of creating a transit-oriented metropolis have been government initiatives that limit automobile ownership and usage. Since 1972, Singapore officials have increasingly tightened the noose on the island's car population through a steady stream of automobile surtaxes, road-use surcharges, and even a vehicle quota system designed to avoid the traffic gridlock that plagues many world cities, especially those in Southeast Asia.

13.5.1   Vehicle Ownership Restraints

Since its introduction in 1948, an annual road tax has been collected that reaches as high as U.S. $3,500 for vehicles with large engines. In the late 1960s, Singapore instituted a surtax on automobile imports (all cars are imported), which over the years has risen to 45 percent of a car's market value. In 1980, a one-time registration fee of around U.S. $670 (in 1996 currency) was tacked on. But as disposable incomes steadily rose, these surtaxes failed to dampen car ownership. Thus, an additional registration fee was introduced, reaching 175 percent of a car's open market value during the 1980s and standing at 150 percent today, with hefty penalties for registration of vehicles more than 10 years old (to keep older, more polluting vehicles off the road). Together, these surcharges have made new car purchases in Singapore as expensive as anywhere. Despite having one of the highest per capita incomes in Asia, fewer than 30 percent of Singaporean households own cars.[11]

In addition to fiscal restraints on car ownership, Singapore also regulates the vehicle population as a means of keeping roads free flowing. In mid-1990, the Vehicle Quota System (VQS) was introduced which requires all new vehicles to have a Certificate of Entitlement (COE), which is obtained through monthly sealed-bid tenders and is valid for 10 years. Transportation planners set the maximum allowable vehicle stock each month based on prevailing traffic conditions, with new certificates apportioned among eight vehicle categories based primarily on engine size. Singaporeans bid on a COE for each category. Since the introduction of the quota system, prices of COEs have increased geometrically. In mid-1990, the premium for luxury cars (engine capacities of 2000 cc and above) was U.S. $330. Two years later, the premium had jumped to U.S. $11,400. By late 1994, it had surpassed U.S. $70,000. Besides moderating automobile ownership, the COE has been a cash boon, generating U.S. $890 million in 1993, up from around U.S. $100 million in 1991.[12]

13.5.2   Vehicle Usage Restraints

Import surtaxes, registration fees, and vehicle quotas act as subscription fees, that is, an initial "buy-in" charge motorists must pay for the luxury of owning a car and to cover part of the fixed costs of transport infrastructure. In an effort to further refine automobile pricing, Singapore officials have also introduced a series of use-related charges, beginning with the introduction of the world's first area licensing scheme (ALS) in 1975. That year, government officials designated a 3.75-mi^2 core area as a "restricted zone," which required a special license displayed prominently on one's car windshield for entry from 7:30 to 10:15 A.M. at a cost of U.S. $2.00 per day. Motorists without special licenses face stiff fines if caught by patrol officers stationed at zone entrances (Photo 13.5). Within the ALS's first year, there was a 76 percent reduction in cars operating within the zone during peak hours; 9 percent of motorists formerly driving through the zone had switched over to bus travel.[13] In early 1994, the ALS was extended to a full day, resulting in an immediate 9 percent drop in traffic entering and leaving the restricted zone.

After more than 20 years of only minor changes, Singapore plans to replace the ALS with a full electronic road pricing system in 1997. Under this scheme, a fee will be automatically deducted from a stored-value card (inserted into an in-vehicle reader unit) when a vehicle crosses a sensor installed at the entrance to potentially congested zones. The amount debited will vary by time and place according to congestion level. Cameras mounted on gantries will snap pictures of violating vehicles to enforce the scheme. Although long touted by transportation economists as the only fail-proof means of eliminating traffic congestion, road pricing proposals have always been stonewalled by political opposition. If all goes according to plans, the Singapore electronic pricing scheme will be the world's first true attempt to pass on real-time congestion charges to motorists.

In addition to road pricing, Singapore motorists face other use-related charges. Fuel taxes are set at 50 percent of pump prices, comparable to most European countries. An

Photo 13.5   An Entry Point to Singapore's Restricted Zone.

additional per liter surcharge is levied on leaded fuels. Moreover, regulations require all Singapore vehicles leaving the country to have at least a three-quarters tank of gasoline to deter cross-border fuel purchases in nearby Malaysia (where fuel taxes are much lower). Also, while there are private parking garages in Singapore, most off-street parking is government owned and costly. Currently, a surcharge of U.S. $40 per month is charged for downtown-area parking.

Despite this punitive pricing, Singapore's automobile population continues to grow— from 162,000 in 1980 to 301,100 in 1993, or from a car per 15.8 persons to one per 9.8 persons. Even in Singapore, officials are resigned to the reality that as disposable incomes continue to rise, increased motorization is inevitable. Singaporeans have over the years shown themselves to be extremely resilient to rising motoring charges, in part because of their high savings rates and comparatively modest outlays for housing. (In 1991, a four-room public flat cost 2.29 years of an average Singaporean's income; a Toyota Corona would have cost 3.65 years of income.[14]) While future plans call for more freeways and lower density residential construction, the tight controls over vehicle supplies and motoring charges, combined with the island's efficient transit–land-use nexus, almost guarantee that traffic congestion will never get out of hand.

13.6 LOOKING TO THE FUTURE: THE CONSTELLATION PLAN

Having succeeded in building a healthy and prosperous export-oriented manufacturing economy, as it looks to the future, Singapore has now set its sights on becoming the Switzerland of Asia, exporting not only goods but also information and services. Through continued infrastructure investments, a highly educated work force, and high-quality business and financial services, Singapore hopes to attract the regional headquarters of large multinational corporations and to globalize its service industries, providing everything from banking to construction services for other industrializing countries in the region. Singapore appears well on its way to becoming a global information-age city; in 1993, three times as many people worked in the financial and business services sector as in 1970.[15]

To meet the demands of an affluent populace in what the government has called the "next lap" of national development, the physical planning component of Singapore's new national development strategy is set forth in the revised 1991 Concept Plan. The plan is structured in three stages: to the Year 2000, to the Year 2010, and to the Year X (some 50 to 70 years in the future when the island is expected to reach its ultimate population of around 4 million and enlarge in area by another 17 percent). Most notably, it replaces the "ring" concept with a "constellation" scheme. A tidy hierarchical pattern of urban centers, interconnected by the MRT, is called for. The central area will remain the island's premier commercial and financial hub. A new world-class downtown and the addition of in-town housing will ensure the core continues to be the focal point of the island's economy and culture. Inner-city housing is viewed as particularly important in creating a 24-h downtown streetlife. Orbiting the core will be four regional centers—Jurong East, Tampines, Woodlands, and Seletar—each with around 800,000 residents, interspersed by smaller centers. The Constellation Plan also calls for the eventual build-out of some 50 new towns of various sizes. Overall, the plan hopes to orchestrate an orderly pattern of "concentrated decentralization"—decentralized to relieve the core of overcrowding, but concentrated into dense, mixed-use nodes to allow for efficient rail services.

The Constellation Plan also distinguishes itself from the previous Ring Plan by calling for a more equal distribution of jobs and housing throughout the island. By creating more self-sufficient communities, the plan seeks to contain transisland commuting. It also places a great deal of emphasis on more varied housing (calling for more single-family and midrise structures), open space, and public access to shorelines, all necessary amenities for attracting the high-paid executives and professionals who will staff a global service-oriented economy. Moreover, the plan confirms and strengthens the role of the MRT in future transisland movement. New MRT extensions will link the island's primary residential and employment centers, radiating from the core area along three primary axes and providing circumferential connections between outlying centers. The "half-cobweb" rail network envisaged for the future is shown in Map 13.3. Buses and new light rail lines will link MRT stations with nearby residences, jobs, shops, and districts unserved by MRT.

13.6.1 Singapore's Future Centers

Subcentering will continue to be the primary means of sustaining Singapore as a transit-oriented metropolis. Under the Constellation Plan, the four regional centers will function as minidowntowns, taking Singapore's commerce and industry to the already decentralized workforce. Each regional center will have up to 5.0 million ft^2 of commercial floorspace and will head a new hierarchy of commercial centers, including five smaller subregional centers to be created around MRT stations and seven even smaller fringe centers formed around the edge of the core area (and also served by MRT). Plans call for centers to have varying degrees of self-sufficiency so that jobs and amenities are distributed as closely to homes as possible (Table 13.1).

Each regional center is to have its own industrial and economic base and a distinct identity. Woodlands, close to Johore, Malaysia, will be the golden triangle business hub (for the trinational area of Singapore, south Malaysia, and the Riau Islands of Indonesia). Tampines, close to Changi International Airport, will become a corporate headquarters with an information technology park. Jurong East, already at the heart of manufacturing activities, will add a business park. And Seletar, already a regional airport and not slated for MRT services until the year 2010, will house an aviation business park to serve the aerospace and oil-related industries. Presently, Singapore's four regional centers are surrounded by vast expanses of open fields. Singapore officials hope to capitalize on this by practicing Japanese-style value capture to help finance public investments, including MRT extensions.

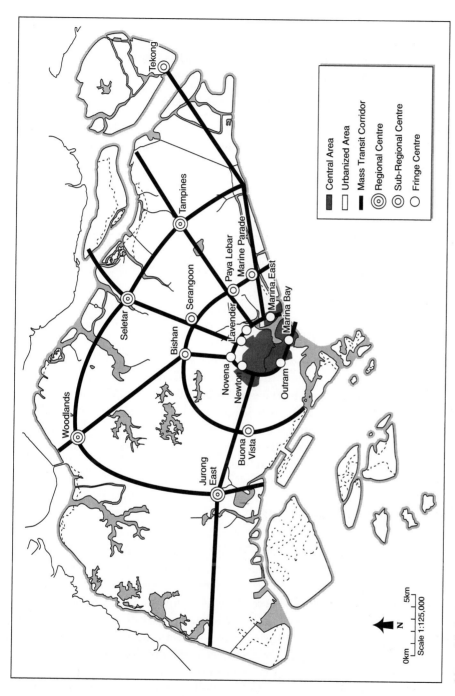

Map 13.3 Long-Range Rail Transit Plan. The Constellation Plan envisages five long radial MRT lines ultimately radiating from the central area, together with three circumferential routes: a core area circle line, a middle semicircle, and an outer, sweeping semicircle. The current 48 MRT stations will increase to around 130 stations.

TABLE 13.1

Nonresidential Land Development Among the Constellation Plan's Hierarchy of Urban Centers

	Nonresidential Area (ft²)	Share of Nonresidential Floorspace			Average Distance to Downtown (mi)
		Office	Retail & Eating	Hotels & Entertainment	
Regional Centers	4.9 million	50%	35%	15%	8.0
Subregional Centers	1.6 million	40%	40%	20%	4.0
Fringe Centers	0.7 million	35%	45%	20%	1.5
Town Centers	0.3 million	40%	60%	0%	—[1]

[1]Depends on location of new town.

Source: Singapore Urban Redevelopment Authority, *Living the Next Lap: Towards a Tropical City of Excellence,* 1991.

13.6.2   Development Phasing

The Constellation Plan is to unfold over three distinct stages. The Year 2000 stage calls for the accelerated development of new towns (e.g., Woodlands, Sembawang, Simpang) along the new MRT northern loop. By the year 2010, a new light rail line is to link the Yishun new town with Tampines via the new Seletar regional center. By this stage, all four new regional centers should be substantially developed. In the build-up to Year X, development will shift to new landfills along the southern and eastern shores. By then, one of the world's great transit metropolises should become even greater.

13.7   LESSONS FROM SINGAPORE

Farsighted and judicious planning has transformed Singapore into a multicentered metropolis supported by a world-class transit system. Like Stockholm and Tokyo, Singapore's standard of living is high, as is its per capita transit usage. Also like these places, everyone enjoys high and equal levels of accessibility—young and old, rich and poor, and the physically abled and disabled alike can conveniently and inexpensively travel from anywhere to everywhere. Singapore's impressive transit–land-use nexus is the outcome of deliberate and carefully thought-out government decisions, decisions to restrain ownership and usage of the car, to build compact, transit-oriented communities, and to ensure equality of access to housing, education, and medical care, in addition to travel destinations. It is important to recognize that what is called centralized planning in Singapore is spatially comparable to the regional planning jurisdictions of medium-sized U.S.

metropolises such as Indianapolis or Denver. Of course, Singapore's government wields considerably more power than any regional planning venture in the United States. And the absence of multiple levels of government, made possible by Singapore being a tiny island-state, has allowed for efficient and streamlined decision making. Also unlike other places, authorities in Singapore are widely respected and rarely challenged. Part of the reason is that they deliver on their promises. Another is that they are careful to delineate the responsibilities of the public sector from those of private businesses. Still another reason is government's vast talent pool. In Singapore, each year some of the best and brightest high school students are recruited into the ranks of civil servants, are sent to top Ivy League and British universities, and upon their return are given compensation packages pegged to the best-paying private-sector jobs.

Singapore's transformation into a great transit metropolis, of course, cannot be easily repeated elsewhere. And it has not been costless. Residents have had to make do with less housing, fairly compact living conditions, and a semiautocratic government whose presence creeps into virtually all facets of everyday life. The real value of Singapore's experiences is that they show the kinds of efficient and sustainable patterns of urban development that can be achieved in a prosperous economy as well as the kinds of lifestyle sacrifices that people must make to achieve these results.

NOTES

1. A. Spencer, Modernisation and Incorporation: The Development of Singapore's Bus Services, 1945–1974, *Environment and Planning A,* Vol. 20, pp. 1027–1046, 1988; R. Cervero, Paratransit in Southeast Asia: A Market Response to Poor Roads? *Review of Urban and Regional Development Studies,* Vol. 3, pp. 31–39, 1991.
2. P. Rimmer and H. Dick, Improving Urban Public Transport in Southeast Asian Cities: Some Reflections on the Conventional and Unconventional Wisdom, *Transport Policy and Decision-Making,* Vol. 1, pp. 97–120, 1980.
3. For an in-depth account of Singapore's political economy and modernized transportation system, see P. Rimmer, *Rikisha to Rapid Transit* (Sydney: Pergamon Press, 1986).
4. Richard Ellis (Singapore) Pte., Ltd., "Republic of Singapore, *ULI Market Profiles* (Washington, DC: The Urban Land Institute, 1995).
5. L. Wang, Land Use Policy in a City-State: The Singapore Case, *Land Use Policy,* Vol. 3, pp. 180–192, 1986.
6. Statistics measure the percentage of employed residents working outside of their Development Guide Plan (DGP) area, a designated subarea within the five planning regions of Singapore that corresponds closely to new town boundaries. Singapore has 55 DGPs with 11 in the core area and 44 in the outlying areas. Source of statistics: Singapore Census of Population Office, Department of Statistics, *Singapore Census of*

Population, 1990: Transport and Geographic Distribution (Singapore: Singapore National Press, Pte. Ltd., 1994).

7. L. Wang, Residential New Town Development in Singapore: Background, Planning, and Design, *New Towns in East and South-east Asia: Planning and Development,* D. Phillips and A. Yeh, eds. (Hong Kong: Oxford University Press, 1987).

8. Cervero, op. cit.

9. J. Kenworthy, P. Barter, P. Newman, and C. Poboon, Resisting Automobile Dependence in Booming Economies: A Case Study of Singapore, Tokyo and Hong Kong Within a Global Sample of Cities, Paper presented at the Asian Studies Association of Australia Biennial Conference, Perth, Australia, July 1994, Murdoch University.

10. Source: Singapore Census of Population Office, op. cit.

11. Ibid.

12. N. Chia and S. Phang, Motor Vehicle Taxes: Their Role in the Singapore Revenue System and Implications for the Environment, Paper presented at the Third Biannual Workshop of the Economy and Environment Program for Southeast Asia, November 1994, National University of Singapore.

13. C. Seah, Mass Mobility and Accessibility: Transport Planning and Traffic Management in Singapore, *Transport Policy and Decision-Making,* Vol. 1, pp. 55–71, 1980; A. Spencer and C. Sien, National Policy Toward Cars: Singapore, *Transport Reviews,* Vol. 5., No. 4, pp. 301–324, 1985.

14. S. Phang, Singapore's Motor Vehicle Policy: Review of Recent Changes and a Suggested Alternative, *Transportation Research,* Vol. 27A, No. 4, pp. 329–336, 1993.

15. Ellis, op. cit.

PART FIVE

Into the Future

Moving transit villages from idea to implementation remains a significant challenge in contemporary urban America. Recent experiences from both the United States and abroad provide signposts that can facilitate the journey. Successful experiences share certain things in common: political leadership, a shared vision, a willingness to experiment and take risks, and, of course, a supportive economic and political climate.

This concluding part of the book advances principles that, we believe, are crucial for moving transit villages from theory to practice in contemporary urban America. In Chapter 14, we draw from our recent experiences as consultants in planning for transit-oriented growth in San Juan and San Diego. These experiences have helped us crystallize our thinking on the precursors to successful transit village development. The book closes with the reminder that, ultimately, what transit villages are all about is people—people who seed the idea, people who move things forward, and people who live, work, and recreate within the community.

Building Transit Villages in the Real World

14.1 PRINCIPLES FOR TRANSIT VILLAGE IMPLEMENTATION

In recent years, we have been asked to help with transit village planning efforts in different parts of the country: on the rail extensions under consideration in St. Louis, Santa Clara County, and San Diego; the Pasadena and Eastside Lines nearing construction in southern California; and San Juan, Puerto Rico's new rail system, to name a few. We found working in the trenches to be both a refreshing change from thinking in the ivory towers and a real awakening to the trials and tribulations of building a transit village.

In all of these budding rail cities, the bottom line is implementation. Most everyone we worked with seemed to have bought into the idea that transit villages are desirable. What they wanted to know more about was how to actually build them. How do we finance rail-oriented development? When should we move forward? How do we select the most viable sites? How much risk should the transit agency or local government assume?

In Puerto Rico, for example, the rail network, Tren Urbano, is nearing construction. And not too soon. The city of San Juan suffers some of the worst traffic congestion in the Americas. San Juan today averages three times more motor vehicles per lane-mile of road than any city on the U.S. mainland.[1] The first segment of Tren Urbano will extend 11.8 mi, from Santurce (San Juan's major business district) through the "miracle mile" office corridor of Hato Rey and terminate at the town center of Bayamon, a large suburb southwest of the city. The line will traverse a wide array of activity centers including a university, a medical complex, a sports arena, and a judicial center, in addition to the commercial centers of Santurce, Hato Rey, and Bayamon. It will also penetrate a number of open fields. On the surface, the opportunities for redeveloping existing sites and developing new ones into transit-oriented communities seem tremendous.

The Puerto Rico Highway and Transportation Authority, the project sponsor, posed various questions to us: What development is most likely to occur following the introduction of Tren Urbano and where? At what point after the opening of Tren Urbano should the transit agency become involved in transit village implementation? What incentives are available to spur station-area development along the Tren Urbano corridor? In the absence of detailed market assessments about the development potential of each and every station, we were left to draw upon our experiences from other places and to make generalizations.

Table 14.1 sets out a number of general principles for transit village implementation, prepared for Tren Urbano, but relevant to rail projects elsewhere. Point 5, the need for the transit agency and local government to assume a proactive role, is perhaps most crucial. Without government leadership, nothing will happen. Building transit-based housing in most cases will be far more difficult than conventional housing, which is a more familiar commodity to mortgage lenders, or even low-income housing that is often almost fully subsidized. To move a transit village proposal forward from theory to implementation, some form of public-sector financial participation—in the form of infrastructure investment, land assembly, or direct equity participation—is absolutely essential.

To be sure, some of the major transit-based projects we have reviewed in this book have been built without active transit agency or local government financial participation. Development around the Bethesda and Pentagon City stations in Washington, DC, and Rio Vista West in San Diego took off soon after zoning changes allowed higher density and mixed-use construction. However, in most cases, especially in inner-city and older suburban districts, whether development occurs or not hinges crucially on whether local entities are willing to share some of the financial risks in return for possible downstream benefits, such as neighborhood regeneration and increased property tax receipts.

14.2 TOOLS FOR IMPLEMENTATION

Table 14.2 lists planning and financing tools that, experiences show, are vital to transit village implementation. Not all are applicable to each and every transit village initiative. The challenge is to pick and choose among these tools in light of local circumstances and exigencies.

1. *A market-based site and phasing plan:* First and foremost, the transit village plan must be realistic from a market perspective. Any graduate student in architecture can put forward an attractive and illustrative transit village design. The challenge is to ground visual representations in market and neighborhood realities. At a minimum, every transit village plan should be accompanied by financial pro formas that demonstrate a project's market viability and a staging program that details how various elements of the transit village will be sequenced.

In addition to being sensitive to market forces, the transit village plan must also be tempered by what neighborhood groups and major stakeholders want and expect. Architect

TABLE 14.1

General Principles for Transit Village Implementation

1. *New Rail Investments, by Themselves, Do Not Automatically Translate into Significant Land-Use Changes:* Among metropolitan areas in the United States, the introduction of a regional rail network has not by itself significantly affected urban form and property values. This is in good part because rail has been added during an era of high automobile accessibility and freeway development. Many localized factors can affect land-use outcomes. Among these are a healthy local real estate environment, community support, an attractive physical and social environment, and pro-development public policies.

2. *Transit-Oriented Development as Long-Term Commitment:* The most successful examples of rail influencing urban form and guiding growth have been direct products of careful strategic planning. Cities like Stockholm, Singapore, and Tokyo offer the best examples of this. In these places, an overall vision of the future settlement pattern of the region was first established. Through selective and judicious station-area planning, these regions have successfully guided urban growth while creating world-class transit networks. Importantly, a stronger emphasis was placed on long-term development objectives as opposed to short-term financial ones. Many rail cities have limited their joint development activities to making leasing and cost-sharing deals that have often yielded minimal financial benefits. Successful systems, on the other hand, have created station-area plans, formed joint development offices, banked land, and strategically introduced development incentives. In effect, they have controlled station-area development. Their payoffs have been over the long term in the form of high ridership and farebox returns associated with station-area development.

3. *Critical Mass in Suburban–Inner-City Community Building:* Suburban stations, especially ones at which the transit agency or other public entities own most of the land within a one-quarter to one-half mile radius of the station, offer opportunities for building new suburban communities that are oriented toward rail versus cars and highways. These communities might feature a civic and commercial core flanked by housing with varying densities and prices, interlaced by sidewalks and parks. Mixed land uses are critical to ensuring balanced, bidirectional flows on a rail system, with comparable on and off counts at stations each morning. This has been an important part of the financial success of rail systems in Stockholm, Singapore, and Tokyo.

   For inner-city stations, new community building also is possible through a critical mass of good quality and attractive development and redevelopment within a quarter-mile radius of a station. Successful inner-city community rebuilding emphasizes private businesses and co-investment (versus only public-led development and entitlements); home ownership (rather than predominantly subsidized rental housing); empowerment through such actions as establishing community-based business enterprises and neighborhood associations; and the establishment of a visible public safety presence.

4. *Concentration of Resources in Achieving the First Built Projects:* Contemporary rail systems usually feature a diversity of station settings, each with varying levels of development promise. Planning efforts should be devoted initially to developing or redeveloping a handful of station areas at most. This allows resources to be effectively targeted. Demonstrating that positive land-use changes are possible in conjunction with a rail investment is important for producing good "models" that the larger development community can emulate, as well as convincing banks and lenders that investing in station-area projects can be financially remunerative. Still, planning should be flexible, allowing for contingencies, to respond appropriately to shifting market conditions.

5. *Proactive Role of the Transit Agency and Local Government; Assumption of Risk by the Public Sector:* Rail investments can be important agents of economic growth, creating new forms of suburban development, enhancing commercial districts that lack weekend or evening activities, revitalizing otherwise stagnant urban districts, and even regenerating depressed, inner-city neighborhoods. Such changes, however, require a proactive public sector, one which takes the lead in preparing specific plans that win the consent of neighborhood and community groups, land banking and assembling of land into developable parcels, writing down the cost of land in return for participation in the project revenue, providing the infrastructure necessary for new development either through direct investment or through tax-increment financing, creating development incentives such as density bonuses, and underwriting early phases of housing or retail development to generate private-sector interest in later phases. A key player is the rail transit agency; the rail agency sometimes owns much of the land around stations and perhaps has the most to gain from good quality development. Other public-sector participants are also needed—the housing agency, the redevelopment agency, the regional planning agency—but none is in the position to spearhead positive change as much as the transit agency. The private sector needs to be brought into the development process early, along with neighborhood groups. At times, the transit agency or local government must be prepared to assume some degree of financial risk for a project to move forward.

TABLE 14.2

Implementation Tools for Transit Villages

- ☐ A market-based site and phasing plan
- ☐ Land assembly
- ☐ Infrastructure investment (directly or through tax-increment financing)
- ☐ Shared parking
- ☐ Expedited permits and reviews
- ☐ Write-down of land costs (in return for project revenue participation)
- ☐ Direct financial participation (issuance of tax-exempt bonds, low-interest loans, loan guarantees, equity participation).

Jeff Heller of Heller & Manus, the lead designer for the Hayward (California) transit village, notes, "The design process is an equilibrium process, balancing the desires of elected officials and community activists with what is market-realistic."

2. *Land assembly:* Around some rail stations, such as Little Tokyo in Los Angeles, available land is owned by one or two major landowners. At most station areas, though, land is divided among multiple owners. Enough land needs to be assembled to allow a development of sufficient size to be economically viable. If developers face the prospect of negotiating individual land purchases among multiple property owners, any one of whom can renege and doom a project, little is likely to happen. The risks and uncertainties are just too great.

Because of their ability to acquire land through eminent domain powers, local governments and redevelopment authorities must often become partners of a transit village initiative. Villages of La Mesa, La Mesa Village Plaza, Barrio Logan's Mercado (San Diego), Del Norte Place (San Francisco Bay Area), and Ryland Mews (Santa Clara County) are all California examples of transit-based housing achieved only after the local redevelopment agency assembled multiple parcels into a site of sufficient size to support a large-scale project. The quid pro quo, of course, is that localities will eventually cover their up-front expenses, possibly many times over, through higher downstream property tax receipts and more viable, self-sustaining neighborhoods.

The transit agency also can assemble parcels, as in the case of the Ballston Metro Center. After the transit agency, WMATA, discovered that no developers were interested in the former bus staging area of 72,000 ft^2, it proceeded to assemble adjacent parcels. The consolidated parcels produced a site large enough to attract a developer who eventually paid WMATA lease rights to build the 28-story office-condominium-hotel Metro Center complex. Indeed, one of the greatest assets of transit agencies is land devoted to surface park-and-ride lots and bus transfer points, which might eventually be converted to mixed-use projects if and when market conditions permit. In America, holding on to parking lots as an "interim land use" is one of the best opportunities for successful land banking. Without public ownership of land, nowhere near the amount of transit-oriented development would exist in the suburbs of Stockholm and Singapore as is found today. In the absence of government's far more limited ability to bank land in the United States, strategic initiatives to convert surface parking lots and bus staging areas into housing and commercial projects, such as in Ballston Metro's case, are among the next best things.

3. *Infrastructure investment (directly or through tax-increment financing):* Before private capital will come to depressed urban districts, substantial infrastructure improvements are often necessary not only to improve a neighborhood's appearance and enhance development potential but also to demonstrate a bona fide public commitment to turning the area around.

In Oakland's Fruitvale neighborhood, the first stage of the planned transit village transformation includes three types of new public infrastructure: a police substation, a pedestrian plaza, and a bus turnaround. At Rosslyn, the changeover of the Metrorail station from a dimly lit, nondescript structure to a "crossroads and principal transportation gateway to Rosslyn" is now under way. Among the public improvements have been better lighting, public art in the station lobby, and an upgrading of the adjacent Metrobus transfer point. At Pleasant Hill, a semirural area when BART first arrived more than two decades ago, the redevelopment agency installed new drainage and water systems and placed utilities underground to jump start private-sector investment.

4. *Shared parking:* Plentiful parking at many suburban transit stations can be used to lower the parking costs of nearby commercial developments. The sharing of parking spaces by rail stations and nearby entertainment centers is the most obvious example. Entertainment complexes such as cinemas and concert halls need parking on nights and weekends, precisely the times when park-and-ride lots are usually empty. Through a shared parking agreement, not only can the entertainment center reduce its outlays for new parking construction, but the transit agency can obtain potential lease revenues as well. Moreover, since surface parking consumes, on average, 350 ft^2 per stall (including aisles and entrances), shared parking conserves land and thereby promotes more compact, pedestrian-friendly development.

At El Cerrito del Norte in the San Francisco Bay Area, for example, a theater-entertainment complex is presently being built adjacent to the BART station. Investors were attracted to the site, in part, because of the ability to reduce parking costs, along with the ability of some customers to ride BART to venues.

5. *Expedited permits and reviews:* The development process of the 1990s has become an obstacle course of obtaining development permits from local planning authorities, allaying the fears of neighborhood groups at public meetings, and adhering to a long list of environmental requirements. A policy of fast-tracking the review and approval of transit

village proposals can be a strong attraction to developers who have experienced firsthand the entanglement of red tape.

In the case of the 86-unit Atherton Place project near the Hayward BART station, the local redevelopment agency expedited the project through the city bureaucracy. Mark Kroll, the lead developer of Atherton Place, remarked, "In this building environment, we look at how cooperative an agency is, and in particular how much an agency is willing to push the project through local permits and reviews."

6. *Write-down of land costs:* In some cases, a transit agency or redevelopment authority will need to commit to even more financial resources and assume even greater risks if a transit village is ever to break ground. The most common form of public-sector risk sharing is the underwriting of land costs in return for project participation.

For the Ballston Metro Center, the regional transit authority, WMATA, waived the collection of fair market rent (for the portion of the land leased to the developer) and instead accepted a percentage share of gross proceeds from condominium sales. For the 135-unit Del Norte Place, the redevelopment agency leased the land to the developer for $1 per year and 15 to 20 percent of the cash flow. Villages of La Mesa and Mercado del Barrio in San Diego and the Strobridge Apartments in the San Francisco Bay Area are other transit-based projects where the transit agency or redevelopment agency accepted below-market rents in return for a percentage of revenues.

7. *Direct financial participation (issuance of tax-exempt bonds, low-interest loans, loan guarantees, equity participation):* Issuance of tax-exempt bonds, low-interest loans, and loan guarantees are other shared-risk approaches adopted by public entities to jump start transit village implementation. For the 121-unit Grand Central Market in Los Angeles, for example, the redevelopment agency agreed to guarantee half of the $13.5 million of taxable bonds and $26.5 million of tax-exempt bonds issued for the project. The transit agency, LACMTA, agreed to finance the other half.

Table 14.3 summarizes the various public-sector approaches used in California in recent years to leverage transit-based residential projects. As is evident, no one approach is applicable to every project, and some projects, such as Grand Central Market and Del Norte Place, required multiple inducements. Among the menu of options, assistance with land assembly and below market-rate lending have been relied on most often to induce transit-oriented investments in California.

To illustrate the applicability of various approaches to leveraging transit village investments, we turn to the case of the Market and 12th station near downtown San Diego. In early 1995, we were asked by the Centre City Development Corporation (CCDC) in San Diego and the regional transit authority (MTDB) to evaluate opportunities for transit village development in this station area.

At first glance, the development opportunities around the Market and 12th Street trolley stop seemed nil. The surrounding neighborhood is home to a deteriorating housing

TABLE 14.3

Financing Sources and Government Roles for Transit-Based Residential and Mixed-Use Projects in California

Development	Grand Central Market	Villages of La Mesa	Apartments at Almaden Lake	Homes at Almaden Lake	Atherton Place	Ohlone Court	Strobridge Apartments	Del Norte Place	Grand Central Apartments	La Mesa Village Plaza	Holly Street Village	Mercado Apartments
Transit Station	Pershing Square	Amaya	Almaden	Almaden	Hayward	Ohlone-Chynoweth	Castro Valley	El Cerrito del Norte	El Cerrito del Norte	La Mesa	Pasadena	Barrio Logan
Transit System	LA Red Line	San Diego Trolley	Santa Clara Light Rail	Santa Clara Light Rail	BART	Santa Clara Light Rail	BART	BART	BART	San Diego Trolley	LA Blue Line	San Diego Trolley
Governmental Role												
Assembled multiple parcels into single ownership	■	■			■		■	■		■		■
Accepted reduced land costs in return for project participation								■	■			
Accepted reduced rent payments in return for project participation							■	■				
Served as a guarantor on project loans	■											
Issued tax-exempt bonds to reduce financing costs	■							■			■	
Provided below-market rate loans			■	■	■	■	■				■	■
Improved infrastructure through tax increment financing		■						■				
Enhanced transit station-area plaza through site improvements	■	■					■		■	■		
Reduced parking costs through shared parking									■			
Expedited local permits and reviews					■							■

stock as well as several drug and alcohol treatment centers, homeless shelters, and short-term residential occupancy (SRO) hotels. Because some of the meal centers close down after food has been served, indigents loiter around until their next meal. For most San Diegans, this is an area to be avoided.

Yet, the area has strengths. It is within a short walk of downtown and is close to Balboa Park, home to San Diego's world-renowned zoo. The neighborhood also has good freeway access, and as the San Diego Trolley continues to expand, it will become even more accessible to the region at large. Furthermore, the station area has the infrastructure capacity—water and sewer trunklines and underutilized roadways and sidewalks—to accommodate millions of square feet of new growth, something that not all development sites can claim. Also, the neighborhood has a well-defined streetwall of storefronts and a fine stock of sturdy, older Victorian residences. Equally important, land is fairly cheap, and many buildings can be easily assembled because they are empty.

The challenge of redeveloping an area like Market and 12th is to add enough development incentives so that, in the minds of prospective developers, the many assets are enough to offset the many liabilities. Table 14.4 presents guidelines we prepared for transit village development at Market and 12th Street. They speak specifically to the necessary steps for redeveloping depressed inner-city neighborhoods into transit-oriented communities, what we have called the "urban" transit village. And they build on the experiences of other reasonably successful inner-city transit village efforts: Fruitvale in Oakland, Barrio Logan in San Diego, and Lloyd Center in Portland, Oregon.

Here we briefly summarize each of these points.

1. *Interagency coordination and participation:* The urban transit village requires the polling of resources among the transit agency, the redevelopment agency, and the city. At the emerging Fruitvale transit village, the city of Oakland, BART, and the Oakland Redevelopment Agency have combined land and resources in a quest to bring the project to fruition. No one of the agencies alone is able to achieve the scope of development needed for the 12th and Market area. Strength will lie in numbers.

2. *Critical mass:* One or two new developments at 12th and Market will not be sufficient to revitalize the area or even to survive economically themselves. The critical mass of development in other inner-city transit village plans is in the range of 500 to 1000 new housing units, at least 40,000 ft^2 of retail, and a regional draw, like an entertainment-cultural center.

3. *Essential transit village elements:* Housing is the glue of an urban transit village because it means personal commitments to a neighborhood and a near 24-h presence of human activity. However, housing is by no means sufficient. It must be complemented by neighborhood services, sources of employment, public gathering spots, and community amenities like libraries and playgrounds.

For Market and 12th, the most likely housing will be tax-credit supported, subsidized senior or family housing. A niche market of young professionals and middle-class retirees,

TABLE 14.4

Guidelines for San Diego's Market and 12th Urban Transit Village Development

☐ The active participation of the CCDC, MTDB, and city of San Diego will be necessary, as the first stages of development will require significant public investment before any private investment will be forthcoming.

☐ The transit village will be more than a handful of structures; a critical mass of development will be needed to form a revitalized community.

☐ Housing should be the main component of any transit village plan, though the plan needs to include other elements as well: mixes of uses, civic spaces, and both physical and symbolic connections to the surrounding community.

☐ The second major step should be the preparation of an illustrative site plan that sets out a vision for the quarter-mile radius around the station and that defines a phasing plan. The site plan should be prepared in conjunction with neighborhood and community groups and private developers.

☐ As a third step, potential sponsors from the public sector and private foundations should be approached and their participation sought as an appeal to bettering the community. Important in approaching outside sponsors is clarity in how the transit village differs from previous inner-city revitalization approaches.

☐ At the same time that project financial support is being lined up, market interest should be tested through an RFP process that seeks a master developer or a developer of one or more phases.

☐ Public safety elements are always a critical component of transit village success. This is all the more so in depressed inner-city areas.

---

found in California's suburban transit villages, is unlikely for Market and 12th any time soon. Possible retail and civic uses should be identified during the site planning process and through a careful market assessment. The kinds of inducements needed to leverage ancillary investments, like land write-downs and tax credits, need to be spelled out in financial pro formas.

4. *A site plan, illustrative designs, and phasing strategy:* The site plan is needed from the start to guide the design and implementation process. It must be embellished by illustrative drawings and building proposals for individual parcels to give the plan some concreteness. When specific improvements will be phased in also needs to be articulated.

Experiences with the Fruitvale transit village in Oakland are illustrative in this regard. There, a design charette was held in May 1993 that brought nearly 50 local residents into the development process. The design charette is important for it allows ideas to be put on paper. In Fruitvale, it served to energize the community and bring focus to the process. Over the next 2 years, Ernesto Vasquez, the architect hired to transform the Fruitvale neighborhood, sought to balance neighborhood goals against market realities. This was instrumental in winning the financial support of the Federal Transit Administration through its Livable Communities program.

Housing is the main component of Vasquez's design, and it is liberally spread throughout the Fruitvale district, primarily as second- and third-floor units above shops. This distribution, according to Vasquez, is intended to create a 24-h a day presence, absolutely indispensable for unifying the neighborhood. Housing above shops also provides opportunities for families to start small business below their residences. Other key elements of the Fruitvale design are an open-air mercado, a branch of the Mexican museum, and a Latin American library.

5. *Public-private partnerships:* The first phases of the urban transit village—housing, civic plaza, physical infrastructure—normally require public-sector subsidies. As with the Fruitvale transit village, funding sources must come from public agencies or private foundations. In Fruitvale, the Spanish Speaking Unity Council was fortunate to receive support from both—grants from federal housing and transit agencies as well as support from the Irvine, Ford, and Hewlett Foundations.

In inner-city areas, the transit village is a departure from urban renewal initiatives of the 1960s and 1970s in several important ways: in its village scale (in contrast to the high-rise public housing or redeveloped office buildings), in its mixes of demographics and income levels, in its allowance for home ownership, and in the physical blending of new residential projects and commercial ventures. It is essential that these differences be clearly spelled out.

6. *RFP for private sector partner:* At Fruitvale, the Spanish Speaking Unity Council decided to follow the site plan with a feasibility analysis conducted by a leading real estate planning firm. This proved to be a mistake, since it only concluded what was obvious to everyone: that the present market was an extremely weak one for privately built market-rate housing. Rather than ending the project, though, the Spanish Speaking Unity Council decided to move forward by getting the city of Oakland, the redevelopment authority, and BART to offer various financial incentives and absorb some of the up-front development risks. With the Market and 12th project, consideration should be given to issuing an RFP in parallel with efforts to secure public-sector and private-foundation support to "test the waters" as well as to bring the experiences and creative thinking of private developers into the process. The RFP should be viewed as an iterative process of securing eventual private-sector participation in return for the right mix of development incentives.

7. *Public safety:* No issue is more important to attracting people to live and work in the urban transit village than public safety. Residents must regard the transit village as a secure,

enjoyable place to live, work, and relax. This is especially the case given the run-down character of the Market and 12th Street neighborhood. A police substation can help create a sense of security in an urban transit village. Equally important is the presence of permanent residents and merchants who help to create an active streetlife and provide the "eyes" of the community.

There is an additional element of transit village implementation that is not included in the list, but is at least as important as any one factor. This is the presence of a "champion," someone who takes up the project and advances it, step by step, through the thicket of almost daily obstacles and bureaucratic inertia that stand in the way of implementation. The emergence of someone who tirelessly advocates the cause of a transit village is perhaps the single most important factor that distinguishes projects that have moved forward from those that have not. In the closing chapter, we address more closely the role and meaning of championing a transit village proposal.

So far, we have focused on what needs to be done at the neighborhood and local levels to move a transit village idea forward. Often, this must be buttressed by initiatives taken at higher levels of government, notably regional and state authorities, to create a political and economic environment that is conducive to transit village implementation. We conclude this chapter with a discussion of more macrolevel policy reforms that need to be introduced.

14.3 REGIONAL POLICIES

Experiences in Stockholm, Tokyo, and Singapore teach us that creating successful transit villages hinges to a large degree on the kinds of supplementary regional policies that are introduced—those which, on the one hand, target tremendous public resources at creating high-quality station-area living environments throughout a region and those which, on the other hand, eliminate hidden subsidies to motorists. Any effective linkage of transportation and urban development is inherently a regional enterprise. As a consequence of how we design and build places, transportation knows no boundaries. A decision to open a big-box retail outlet in one jurisdiction, for example, will invariably have mobility repercussions on neighboring jurisdictions. It is therefore essential that the planning of transportation services and urban growth occur across multiple political boundaries. This includes the planning of transit villages. One or two locally developed transit villages within a region of almost exclusively automobile-oriented growth will not only add up to very little but the villages themselves might be unsustainable.

Regional policies for promoting transit villages should work on both the land-use and the transportation side of the equation. On the land-use side, zoning is the traditional tool for governing how land is used, although zoning is inherently a local (not a regional) prerogative. In the competition for tax base, jurisdictions across the United States have increasingly used zoning as a tool for fiscal gain. In California, where Proposition 13 has prompted intense competition for tax base, better-off communities often zone-in high tax-yielding land uses, like offices and retail stores, and zone-out high services-demanding activities, notably low- and moderate-income housing. This "antiaffordable housing" bias clearly works against the goal of transit village development. One policy response is tax-base sharing, wherein job-surplus cities share their local tax receipts with communities that end up housing their workers. In theory, this would remove the incentive to zone-out apartments and higher density housing. In the Minneapolis-St. Paul region, as much as a third of local property tax proceeds are pooled among municipalities and redistributed according to population. The state of Oregon recently signed into law a local property tax abatement bill that seeks to "stimulate the construction of multiple-unit housing in the core areas of Oregon's urban centers to improve the balance between the residential and commercial nature of those areas, and to ensure full-time use of the areas as places where citizens of the community have an opportunity to live as well as to work." Initiatives like extraterritorial tax sharing and tax abatements require the passage of state enabling legislation, something which few states, other than Minnesota and Oregon, seem willing to do. Other options for encouraging greater land-use diversity like fair-share housing programs (attempted in New Jersey with moderate success) and regional control of land uses are apt to receive even less political support.

So far, the greatest inroads in creating a regional forum for linking transportation and land-use decisions in the United States have been in Portland, Oregon. Portland has a long history of progressive land-use and environmental initiatives going back to the urban growth limit boundaries set in the 1970s. In 1992, voters of the Portland metropolitan area approved the Metro Charter giving the Portland area a directly elected regional government that serves more than 1.2 million residents in three counties and 24 cities. Metro is responsible for growth management, transportation, land-use planning, and open space preservation. It is governed by an elected seven-member council and an executive officer, who is also elected at large. One of its first actions was the adoption of the *Region 2040 Growth Concept,* a blueprint for guiding the next half century of regional development. Besides calling for a continuation of the urban growth boundary, the policy plan proposes six to eight regional growth centers that would absorb nondowntown commercial growth and would be interlinked by an expansion of Portland's already successful light rail (MAX) system. If a regional network of transit villages is ever to evolve somewhere in the United States during the 21st century, it most likely will be in metropolitan Portland.

14.4   STATE INITIATIVES

Besides passing enabling legislation that promotes land-use diversity, jobs-housing balance, and regional planning, states can also directly promote transit-oriented development. This has occurred with a moderate degree of success in California. In October 1993, Governor Pete Wilson signed the Transit Village Act, Assembly Bill 3152, which encourages California cities and counties to build higher density housing and compact communities around the state's rail stops. The act stipulates that no public works projects, tentative sub-division maps, or parcel maps may be approved, nor zoning ordinances adopted or amended, within an area covered by a transit village plan unless the map, project, or ordinance is consistent with the adopted transit village plan. This was a small but important step toward bringing the transit village idea to fruition. The bill, as originally drafted, would have allowed municipalities to designate a "transit village district," similar to a redevelopment district, with special land assemblage and tax-increment financing privileges. The original bill also stipulated that developers building within the district be granted density bonuses of at least 50 percent. Because of stiff opposition from fiscal conservatives, most of these provisions were later stripped from the bill. Regardless, the act gave new-found legitimacy to California's transit village movement.

As passed, AB 3152 is a voluntary statue encouraging cities and counties to plan more intensive development around rail stations, though it provides few fiscal powers and little special authority to do so. Sponsors hope the bill will be expanded in coming years to provide more financial incentives, perhaps granting transit village districts priority access to discretionary state funds, such as from the national transportation act (ISTEA) and fuel price rebate programs. California's transit village movement suffered a setback, however, when Governor Wilson vetoed an assembly bill (AB 1338) in the spring of 1995 that would have established local revolving funds (from state and federal transportation planning monies) and provided loans to cities and counties to enable them to prepare specific transit village plans. The veto, most observers agree, had more to do with the generally conservative fiscal mood of the times than with opposition to the principle of transit-oriented development. Still, the veto underscores the reality that transit-oriented development does not head the priority lists of many politicians and that transit villages must still win over a lot of political converts in states like California.

14.5   TRANSPORTATION INITIATIVES

So far, we have focused on regional and state land-use initiatives for promoting transit villages. On the transportation front, regional and state policies are needed that correct the mispricing that continues to plague America's urban transportation sector. Foremost is the removal of as many of the hidden subsidies to motorists as possible. Faced with higher motoring costs, Americans would be more inclined to live closer to major transit nodes to economize on travel, just as in Stockholm, Tokyo, and Singapore. Road pricing and other initiatives have historically been politically stonewalled because those who wield the most political clout (i.e., professionals, businesspeople, developers, industrialists) receive the most benefit from underpricing automobile travel. True market-rate pricing of the automobile is probably unattainable in a pluralistic, openly democratic society like the United States. Martin Wachs, as chair of a Transportation Research Board Committee on Congestion Pricing, concluded that "except for professors of transportation economics and planning—who hardly constitute a potent political force—I can think of few interest groups that would willingly and vigorously fight for the concept in what will surely become a pitched battle, if ever the idea is seriously proposed."[2]

The best near-term hope to correct price distortions is the elimination of free parking, something which over 80 percent of American workers presently receive. One promising approach is cashing out free parking. The Clinton administration's parking cash out program, included as part of the 1993 Climate Change Action Plan, proposed giving federal workers the option of a free parking space or cash allowance, and exempting up to $75 in employer-provided monthly transit passes and vouchers from taxable income. The initiative sought to promote transit by helping to level the urban mobility playing field. Recently, however, Congress has been backing off of its get-tough-with-free-parking stand. In 1995, a congressional plan to charge federal employees commercial rates was abandoned in the face of strong opposition from employee unions.

Lastly, transit itself needs to be continually enhanced to make transit villages viable. This does not necessarily mean expanding conventional bus and rail services. More attention needs to be given to private paratransit options (e.g., jitneys, shuttle vans, and minibuses) that could provide "niche market" services such as providing feeder runs into rail nodes. In Mexico City, well over half of all access trips to rail stops are by privately owned vans (peseros) and minibuses (coletivos). One doesn't have to look farther than New York City, however, to find a thriving private paratransit sector in place. There, an estimated 15,000 vans provide daily feeder runs into subway stations in Brooklyn, Queens, and the Bronx, making a profit while public bus operators struggle to return 30 cents on the dollar. The marriage of advanced technologies, like satellite-based vehicle tracking systems, could create a form of "smart paratransit" that might one day begin to match the on-call, minimum-wait service features of the private car. Smart paratransit needs to be pursued if for no other reason than billions of dollars are now being invested in making transit's chief competitor, the private automobile, much smarter. To the extent transit fails to keep pace with the increasingly intelligent auto-highway system, it is inevitable that more and more Americans will rely on their cars to get around, even in spite of the very best efforts to create more liveable transit-oriented communities.

NOTES

1. Puerto Rico Department of Transportation and Public Works, Highway and Transportation Authority, *Draft Environmental Impact Statement, Tren Urbano* (San Juan, Puerto Rico: Puerto Rico Department of Transportation and Public Works, 1995).
2. M. Wachs, Will Congestion Pricing Ever Be Adopted? *Access,* University of California Transportation Center, UC, Berkeley, No. 4, pp. 15–19, 1994.

15

Building Villages
in the 21st Century

15.1 CHAMPIONING THE CAUSE

All transit village success stories to date have been marked by political resolve and inspired leadership. Overseas, there was Sven Markelius's stewardship of Stockholm's regional plan, Keita Gotoh's entrepreneurial drive to couple rail and new town investments in suburban Tokyo, and Lee Kuan Yew's commitment to enriching Singapore by luring multinational corporations into efficient, transit-served industrial estates. In California, we are reminded of Sunne McPeak's perseverance in transforming Pleasant Hill from a bedroom community into a transit village, Rod Diridon's vision of the Silicon Valley and surroundings being populated by trandominiums, and Nick Patsaouras staking his political future by relentlessly pursuing transit-oriented development in the land of automobility, Los Angeles.

To gain a richer perspective into the role and importance of visionaries and believers, we need to step back and look at the personalities behind the village-building enterprises from earlier this century. Here we must start with Ebenezer Howard, someone whose name has surfaced at different junctures throughout this book.[1] Howard, an obscure shop owner and a self-taught architect-planner, inspired and indeed led the charge in building an entirely new kind of British settlement, the garden city. Howard's vision of the garden city was not particularly distinguishable or original. It drew heavily from popular writings on social cooperation, political economy, and town planning. What distinguished Howard from the many other amateur theorists and urban designers in the intellectual hothouse of Victorian England was his persistence in getting his ideas published in book form and, more importantly, in translating these ideas into two early 20th-century garden cities: Letchworth and Welwyn.

Howard was born in London in 1850. He left school at 14, taught himself shorthand, and set up his own stenography business, achieving reputable, if unspectacular, business success. Howard, though, was not content just to run a successful company. Like Dr.

Lydgate of *Middlemarch,* his real passion was discovery and change. Howard wanted to create entirely new kinds of settlements that would transform society and bring an end to the wretched poverty that had inflicted 18th- and 19th-century urban England.

Victorian England gave rise to numerous associations devoted to constructive social change and overcoming the harshness of contemporary capitalism: Owenites, Fabian Socialists, Georgists, and Anarchists; Liberals favoring incremental, market-oriented reforms, Radicals favoring big-government socialism, and Libertarians favoring the outright dissolution of formal government, to be replaced by locally based cooperatives. Howard gravitated to the radical thought that favored peaceful change from Victorian capitalism to an economy and society based on cooperation and decentralization of power and industry. Rather than businesses divided by owners of capital versus labor, industrial enterprises would be cooperatively run. In place of crowded cities would be smaller urban villages surrounded by greenbelts and inhabited by people from different social classes. In place of urban tenements would be semidetached homes, each with a garden.

During the 1880s, Howard formulated these ideas, giving birth to his now-celebrated book and the garden city movement. These became the forums for advancing his ideas about land reform, communalism, and social justice, which he borrowed heavily from the writings of Edward Bellamy on social cooperation and Peter Kropotkin on the decentralization of industry through railroad investments. Howard first presented his vision of the garden city at a meeting of the Ballamite Nationalisation of Labour Society in 1893. In his mind's eye, garden cities would blossom throughout the English countryside. Over time, the overcrowded cities of London, Manchester, and Birmingham would empty out as Englanders moved to the more balanced and bucolic garden cities.

Each garden city was to be sited on roughly 1000 acres and surrounded by a permanent greenbelt of around 5000 acres that included farms, open space, and institutions like reformatories and convalescent homes that could benefit from a more rural location. The garden city would be home to approximately 32,000 persons, including some 2000 engaged in farming. Other garden city residents would pursue craft and industrial ventures, with local smaller scale factories replacing the cavernous factories of London.

The garden city would be self-contained and self-sufficient. Local farms and industry would serve the everyday consumption needs of residents. (Local wares would be displayed at a central market, what Howard christened the Crystal Palace.) All land would be owned by those residing in the garden city. It would be purchased from a philanthropic, limited-dividend company that had acquired the land earlier. The company would capture the value-added by garden city and rail investments, returning some of the profits to the community and placing the remaining proceeds in a reserve account for future land purchases.

Howard compiled his ideas in a text he titled *The Master Key* and began submitting the manuscript to publishers in 1893. His repeated submissions proved unsuccessful. In 1896, he submitted a shorter version, entitled "A Garden City or One Solution to Many Problems," to the *Contemporary Review,* which was rejected. Undaunted, in 1898, he used his own money to publish the manuscript under the title *To-morrow: A Peaceful Path to Real Reform* (published in 1902 under its better known title, *Garden Cities of Tomorrow*).

The book met with only a mild reception and seemed destined to go the way of the numerous utopian tracts published at the time. However, Howard continued to market his ideas and push them toward implementation. He lectured throughout England at churches, civic associations, and Radical and Liberal political gatherings, to anyone who would listen. By 1899, Howard had gained a large enough following to form the Garden City Association.

After winning over converts and the endorsement of the Land Nationalisation Society (attracted by the back-to-the-land component of the garden city), Howard's major step forward came in 1901 when a prominent Liberal attorney, Ralph Neville, signed on as chairman of the Garden City Association and devoted himself to its implementation. Neville regarded the cooperative aspects of the garden city as hopelessly unrealistic, even silly. However, he saw in the garden city a means of saving capitalism by expanding industrial and land ownership and by defusing the revolutionary potential of large cities.

Neville, who had many contacts in the business community, succeeded in attracting two wealthy entrepreneurs, George Cadbury (of the Cadbury chocolate fame) and W. H. Lever (of the Lever soap company), who in 1901 sponsored a Garden City conference, attended by over 1500 officials and invitees. By July 1902, the Garden City Pioneer Company had raised 20,000 pounds to purchase some 3800 acres in Hertfordshire, 195 mi northeast of London.

Over the next 7 years, the city of Letchworth was constructed. As the city took form, it departed from Howard's original vision in several ways. Howard wanted everyone, even unskilled workers, to live in semidetached housing, but the economics simply did not work out, and most of Letchworth's unskilled laborers ended up living in small apartments in surrounding towns. Howard also envisaged people from different economic classes living amongst each other, yet Letchworth was populated mainly by middle-class households of independent means (and their servants) and skilled artisans who had built the new town. Howard had also hoped that hundreds of garden cities would dot the English countryside, but two decades into the 20th century, Letchworth stood alone.

Whatever Letchworth's limitations, it succeeded in attracting industry and residents. By 1907, it was a fully functioning and reasonably self-sustained community. A second garden city, Welwyn, also in Hertfordshire, was built in the early 1920s. Howard, in fact, spent his last years living in a cottage in Welwyn until his death in 1928.

The story of Ebenezer Howard's garden cities highlights important elements of seeing an urban vision through to implementation. One was a strong desire to break the mold of conventional urban settlements and advance a new alternative. Another was a considered and detailed plan that became the blueprint for building the garden city of Letchworth. Still another was Howard's uncanny ability to market his idea, recruit supporters, and forge a consensus among followers and potential stakeholders. Yet another was Howard's willingness to alter his plan in the face of market realities. Most of all, however, Howard's story reveals the undeniable importance of a champion, someone with a vision who is doggedly persistent in advancing his view of the world.

Nearly a century later, as we approach a new millennium, the challenges facing America's burgeoning transit village movement are not terribly different from those that Howard faced. Today, the mold that needs breaking is the entrenched belief that low-density, auto-oriented development is the only viable and acceptable pattern of suburban living. To this, supporters must reply, transit villages are not a replacement, only an alternative—a different form of urbanism. Some of the other contemporary challenges—crafting detailed site plans rooted in market realities, taking and sharing risks, building consensus, and adapting to market shifts—have been met with varying degrees of success by transit village campaigns in different parts of the United States, as discussed in the previous chapter. The most elusive item in the list, the one which only happens through fate and circumstances, of course, is inspired leadership: the emergence of someone who, against the odds, is willing to make the kinds of sacrifices necessary to see a transit village proposal through to implementation. People cannot be recruited into such roles. They must seek them out themselves. In them must be the passion, the commitment, and determination to see that transit-oriented communities get built. In recent years, political champions of the transit village movement have surfaced across the United States, and many of the inroads so far are indebted to their leadership. Whether the transit village movement continues to gain momentum will depend greatly on whether others follow in their footsteps.

15.2 TRANSIT VILLAGES IN THE NEW MILLENNIUM

In this book, many reasons have been given for why we should be designing transit villages in the 21st century, such as to create alternative living environments, to increase supplies of affordable housing, to reduce automobile dependence, and so on. As we look to the future, we think there is at least one other compelling reason transit villages deserve serious consideration. This has to do with both the opportunities and liabilities posed by the onslaught of the information age. Advances in telecommunications and changes in the way people live and work could very well give rise to the kinds of self-sufficient villages that Ebenezer Howard and his contemporaries dreamed of. The number of contract workers, self-employed entrepreneurs, and cottage industries is on the rise, and computers, multimedia devices, and satellite communications are increasingly within the reach of average consumers. These developments will foster rapid growth in home-based enterprises in coming years.[2]

Distributed workplaces of the future will take the form of neighborhood telecenters, equipped with videoconferencing, on-line data-search capabilities, and facsimile transmission and voice mail, allowing more Americans to work at home at least a few days a week.

In Orange County and Sacramento, California, several developers have included home offices and neighborhood telecenters in new mixed-use developments. Oberlin, Kansas, and Steamboat Springs, Colorado, have added telecommunications posts in their town centers and marketed themselves as live-work communities. Neighborhood coffee shops and corner cafes have sprouted in these places, becoming watering holes where home-based workers socialize and network. Today's cyberkids, reared on the Internet and interactive media, are apt to be even more receptive to the idea of working at home and living in a reasonably self-contained village when they reach adulthood.

New-age technologies, along with a growing preference for small-town living, could spawn a constellation of self-contained urban villages across North America. There are tremendous opportunities, we believe, for making these villages more transit oriented in their designs. Many of their residents will have escaped car-clogged cities and will likely welcome alternative means of travel, whether by bicycle, electric vehicles, or clean forms of transit. Some information-age villages will likely locate along rail corridors and perhaps rely on high-speed trains for intercity travel. Sometime during the 21st century, we believe, the nation's first "high-speed rail" transit village will have surfaced.

As mentioned, advanced technologies also pose liabilities to transit villages. Foremost is the prospect of automobiles becoming vastly more intelligent. Detroit's Big Three automakers and the U.S. Department of Transportation have joined ranks and already spent billions of dollars on developing the nation's Intelligent Transportation System. Plans call for equipping future cars with on-board navigational aids, fed by satellite tracking, that will allow motorists to bypass traffic congestion. Computerized control and guidance devices embedded underneath heavily trafficked corridors, designers hope, will one day allow appropriately equipped cars and trucks to race along freeways almost bumper to bumper. While the goals of making cars more comfortable and safer are unimpeachable, the inevitable outcomes of making cars more fleet-footed and far smarter than their competitors, especially mass transit, are not. New-age technologies could very well spell a future of even greater automobile reliance and perhaps the demise of many mass transportation systems.

Transit villages, we believe, can not only invigorate the transit industry in the face of stiffer competition from smarter automobiles, but can also provide an alternative built form that helps reduce the need for automobility in the first place. Transit villages are consonant with the growing interest in smart "telecommunities" where Americans live and work at home or close by most of the time. They are also consonant with the growing preference for small townlike atmospheres where people can walk or bicycle to a nearby video store or delicatessen.

As we look toward the future, transit villages have an important role to play in the coming information age. While an alternative to automobile-oriented living, transit villages can also be an integral part of a new kind of community, one where people spend more of their time living, working, and socializing within their neighborhoods.

15.3 BUILDING MOMENTUM

As we close, we are reminded of the tremendous progress that has been made in promoting transit villages in recent years and the sheer momentum behind today's transit village movement. In the past decade, transit-oriented projects have broken ground in low-income neighborhoods like San Diego's Barrio Logan, in middle-income areas like Pleasant Hill, and even in more well-to-do settings like Bethesda, Maryland, and Palo Alto, California. In St. Clair County, Illinois, across the Mississippi River from St. Louis, current plans for a light rail extension have brought together station-area citizens groups who meet biweekly in hopes of guiding this county of farmsteads and suburban homes along a pathway of more transit-oriented development. In Oregon and California, recently enacted state legislation promotes more balanced, transit-oriented development, which in Oregon's case involves state tax abatements. In New York City, Los Angeles, and other U.S. rail cities, recent symposia on transit villages have sparked spirited debates among planners, architects, developers, politicians, and local activists, capturing the imagination of some and drawing skepticism from others. Regardless of whether people agree or not, what is important is the themes embodied in transit villages development have become part of the contemporary debate over what to do about the plight of our cities and suburbs. There is now some momentum that we hope and believe will build and gain a force of its own as we enter the next century.

We find cause for optimism in the many grass-roots initiatives to promote transit villages, and it is on this point that we conclude with an anecdote from southern California. In June 1994, over 100 planners, civic leaders, community activists, and regional representatives gathered in San Bernardino, 90 mi inland from Los Angeles, to debate and seek consensus on the desirability of creating transit villages in a region where the automobile reigns supreme. The meeting was held in San Bernardino's central train depot, an ornate structure of tiled walls, colorful murals, and an impressive dome built in 1921 by the Southern Pacific Railway. At the time, San Bernardino was an eastern terminus of southern California's great interurban rail system and the regional headquarters for Southern Pacific.

After years of inactivity, the depot is today a stop on southern California's Metrolink commuter rail system. The assembled group was assigned the task of transforming the neighborhood surrounding the depot into a residential transit village. This was a tall order indeed given that surface parking lots, dirt fields, and a few aging stores surrounded the depot. After a morning of presentations and group discussions, the afternoon involved participants moving the housing and retail "pieces" of a scale model around, not unlike a game of chess, under the watchful eye of Los Angeles-based urban designer Mark Futterman. Various configurations of housing (with densities varying from 12 to 40 units per acre) and retail space were proposed and debated. Should the housing be concentrated around the depot, away from the depot, or scattered throughout the area? How should the village be tied to downtown San Bernardino, three-quarters of a mile away? What amenities and community services would be needed to attract both developers and residents?

By the day's end, the general consensus was that a transit village is not likely to surface around San Bernardino's train depot any time soon. Commuter trains come by too infrequently today. There is little development around other Metrolink stations east of Los Angeles to form convenient destinations. Single-family homes in San Bernardino remain too cheap to attract much interest in more compact living arrangements. Yet, in the years ahead, the Metrolink system will add more trains and increase service frequency. Other stations along the Metrolink Line will attract businesses and housing. And as San Bernardino continues to grow, over time a niche market will evolve of individuals who are attracted to well-designed transit villages, whether for reasons of price, convenience, or amenities.

Perhaps the gathering's most noteworthy achievement was engaging over 100 people in a day-long debate over transit village designs, in summer heat, in a once-grand train depot 90 mi east of Los Angeles. This is how transit villages get started.

NOTES

1. For detailed accounts of Ebenezer Howard and the garden city movement, see P. Hall, *Cities of Tomorrow* (London: Basil Blackwell, 1988), pp. 88–108; J. Simonds, *Garden Cities 21: Creating a Livable Urban Environment* (New York, McGraw-Hill, 1994), pp. 207–212.
2. R. Cervero, Why Go Anywhere? *Scientific American,* Vol. 273, No. 3, pp. 118–120.

Selected Bibliography

Altshuler, Alan. *The Urban Transportation System: Politics and Policy Innovation* (Cambridge, MA: MIT Press, 1980).

Black, Alan, *Urban Mass Transportation Planning* (New York: McGraw-Hill, 1995).

Blumenfeld, Hans, *The Modern Metropolis: Its Origins, Growth, Characteristics, and Planning.* (Cambridge, MA: MIT Press, 1968).

Calthorpe, Peter, *The Next American Metropolis: Ecology, Community, and the American Dream* (Princeton NJ: Princeton Architectural Press, 1994).

Cervero, Robert, *Suburban Gridlock* (New Brunswick, NJ: Center for Urban Policy Research, 1986).

Downs, Anthony, *New Visions for Metropolitan America* (Washington, DC: The Brookings Institution and Lincoln Institute of Land Policy, 1994).

Fishman, Robert. *Bourgeois Utopias: The Rise and Fall of Suburbia* (New York: Basic Books, 1987).

Flink, James, *The Automobile Age* (Cambridge, MA: MIT Press, 1988).

Fogelson, Robert. *The Fragmented Metropolis: 1850-1930* (Cambridge, MA: Harvard University Press, 1967).

Garreau, Joel, *Edge City: Life on the New Frontier* (New York: Doubleday, 1991).

Gordon, Deborah, *Steering a New Course: Transportation, Energy, and the Environment* (Washington, DC: Island Press, 1991).

Hall, Peter, *Cities of Tomorrow: An Intellectual History of Urban Planning and Design in the Twentieth Century* (New York: Basil Blackwell, 1988).

Jackson, Kenneth, *Crabgrass Frontier: The Suburbanization of the United States* (New York: Oxford University Press, 1985).

Jacobs, Jane. *The Death and Life of Great American Cities* (New York: Vintage Books, 1961).

Jones, David, Jr., *Urban Transit Policy: An Economic and Political History* (Englewood Cliffs, NJ: Prentice-Hall, 1985).

Katz, Peter, *The New Urbanism* (New York: McGraw-Hill, 1994).

Mumford, Lewis. *The City in History: Its Origins, Its Transformations, and Its Prospects* (New York: Harcourt, Brace & World, 1961).

Newman, Peter and Jeffrey Kenworthy, *Cities and Automobile Dependence: A Sourcebook* (Brookfield, VT: Gower, 1989).

Pushkarev, Boris and Jeffrey Zupan, *Public Transit and Land-Use Policy* (Bloomington: Indiana University Press, 1977).

Rusk, David, *Cities without Suburbs* (Washington, D.C.: Woodrow Wilson Center Press, 1993).

Simonds, J., *Garden Cities 21: Creating a Livable Urban Environment* (New York: McGraw-Hill, 1994).

Solomon, Daniel, *Rebuilding* (New Jersey: Princeton Architectural Press, 1992).

Stern, Robert A., *The Anglo American Suburb* (London: Architectural Design, 1981).

Untermann, Richard. *Accommodating the Pedestrian: Adapting Towns and Neighborhoods for Walking and Bicycling* (New York: Van Nostrand Reinhold, 1984).

Warner, Sam Bass. *Streetcar Suburbs* (Cambridge, MA: Harvard University Press, 1962).

Yaro, Robert and Tony Hiss, *A Region at Risk: The Third Regional Plan for the New York-New Jersey-Connecticut Metropolitan Area* (Washington, DC: Island Press, 1996).

Index

About the Authors

MICHAEL BERNICK, an attorney and Co-Director of the U.C. Berkeley National Transit Access Center, specializes in the law and implementation of transit-based development. Since 1988, Mr. Bernick also has been a Director of the San Francisco Bay Area Rapid Transit District (BART), and has served as President of the BART board.

ROBERT CERVERO is a professor in the Department of City and Regional Planning at U.C. Berkeley and Co-Director of the U.C. Berkeley National Transit Access Center. Mr. Cervero is the author of several books and numerous articles on transportation and urban development, and has advised governments abroad on these topics.